Children's Literature Review

Guide to Gale Literary Criticism Series

For criticism on	Consult these Gale series
Authors now living or who died after December 31, 1999	*CONTEMPORARY LITERARY CRITICISM (CLC)*
Authors who died between 1900 and 1999	*TWENTIETH-CENTURY LITERARY CRITICISM (TCLC)*
Authors who died between 1800 and 1899	*NINETEENTH-CENTURY LITERATURE CRITICISM (NCLC)*
Authors who died between 1400 and 1799	*LITERATURE CRITICISM FROM 1400 TO 1800 (LC)* *SHAKESPEAREAN CRITICISM (SC)*
Authors who died before 1400	*CLASSICAL AND MEDIEVAL LITERATURE CRITICISM (CMLC)*
Authors of books for children and young adults	*CHILDREN'S LITERATURE REVIEW (CLR)*
Dramatists	*DRAMA CRITICISM (DC)*
Poets	*POETRY CRITICISM (PC)*
Short story writers	*SHORT STORY CRITICISM (SSC)*
Black writers of the past two hundred years	*BLACK LITERATURE CRITICISM (BLC)* *BLACK LITERATURE CRITICISM SUPPLEMENT (BLCS)*
Hispanic writers of the late nineteenth and twentieth centuries	*HISPANIC LITERATURE CRITICISM (HLC)* *HISPANIC LITERATURE CRITICISM SUPPLEMENT (HLCS)*
Native North American writers and orators of the eighteenth, nineteenth, and twentieth centuries	*NATIVE NORTH AMERICAN LITERATURE (NNAL)*
Major authors from the Renaissance to the present	*WORLD LITERATURE CRITICISM, 1500 TO THE PRESENT (WLC)* *WORLD LITERATURE CRITICISM SUPPLEMENT (WLCS)*

ISSN 0362-4145

volume 72

Children's Literature Review

Excerpts from Reviews,
Criticism, and Commentary
on Books for Children
and Young People

Rebecca J. Blanchard
Editor

Tom Burns
Assistant Editor

GALE GROUP

THOMSON LEARNING

Detroit • New York • San Diego • San Francisco
Boston • New Haven, Conn. • Waterville, Maine
London • Munich

STAFF

Scot Peacock, *Managing Editor, Literature Product*
Kathy D. Darrow, Ellen McGeagh, *Product Liaisons*
Rebecca J. Blanchard, *Editor*
Mark W. Scott, *Publisher, Literature Product*

Tom Burns, *Assistant Editor*
Jenny Cromie, Mary Ruby, *Technical Training Specialists*
Deborah J. Morad, Joyce Nakamura, Kathleen Lopez Nolan, *Managing Editors*
Susan M. Trosky, *Director, Literature Content*

Maria L. Franklin, *Permissions Manager*
Julie Juengling, *Permissions Associate*

Victoria B. Cariappa, *Research Manager*
Sarah Genik, *Project Coordinator*
Ron Morelli, Tamara C. Nott, Tracie A. Richardson, *Research Associates*
Nicodemus Ford, *Research Assistant*

Dorothy Maki, *Manufacturing Manager*
Stacy L. Melson, *Buyer*

Mary Beth Trimper, *Manager, Composition and Electronic Prepress*
Carolyn Roney, *Composition Specialist*

Michael Logusz, *Graphic Artist*
Randy Bassett, *Imaging Supervisor*
Robert Duncan, Dan Newell, Luke Rademacher, *Imaging Specialists*
Pamela A. Reed, *Imaging Coordinator*
Kelly A. Quin, *Editor, Image and Multimedia Content*

Library of Congress Catalog Card Number 76-643301
ISBN 0-7876-4578-8
ISSN 0362-4145
Printed in the United States of America

10 9 8 7 6 5 4 3 2 1

Contents

Preface vii

Acknowledgments xi

Literary Criticism Series Advisory Board xiii

Preface

Literature for children and young adults has evolved into both a respected branch of creative writing and a successful industry. Currently, books for young readers are considered among the most popular segments of publishing. Criticism of juvenile literature is instrumental in recording the literary or artistic development of the creators of children's books as well as the trends and controversies that result from changing values or attitudes about young people and their literature. Designed to provide a permanent, accessible record of this ongoing scholarship, *Children's Literature Review* (*CLR*) presents parents, teachers, and librarians—those responsible for bringing children and books together—with the opportunity to make informed choices when selecting reading materials for the young. In addition, *CLR* provides researchers of children's literature with easy access to a wide variety of critical information from English-language sources in the field. Users will find balanced overviews of the careers of the authors and illustrators of the books that children and young adults are reading; these entries, which contain excerpts from published criticism in books and periodicals, assist users by sparking ideas for papers and assignments and suggesting supplementary and classroom reading. Ann L. Kalkhoff, president and editor of *Children's Book Review Service Inc.,* writes that "*CLR* has filled a gap in the field of children's books, and it is one series that will never lose its validity or importance."

Scope of the Series

Each volume of *CLR* profiles the careers of a selection of authors and illustrators of books for children and young adults from preschool through high school. Author lists in each volume reflect:

- an international scope

- representation of authors of all eras

- the variety of genres covered by children's and/or YA literature: picture books, fiction, nonfiction, poetry, folklore, and drama

Although the focus of the series is on authors new to *CLR,* entries will be updated as the need arises.

Organization of the Book

A *CLR* entry consists of the following elements:

- The **Author Heading** consists of the author's name followed by birth and death dates. The portion of the name outside the parentheses denotes the form under which the author is most frequently published. If the author wrote consistently under a pseudonym, the pseudonym will be listed in the author heading and the author's actual name given in parentheses on the first line of the biographical and critical information. Also located here are any name variations under which an author wrote, including transliterated forms for authors whose native languages use non-roman alphabets. Uncertain birth or death dates are indicated by question marks.

- A **Portrait of the Author** is included when available.

- The **Author Introduction** contains information designed to introduce an author to *CLR* users by presenting an overview of the author's themes and styles, biographical facts that relate to the author's literary career or critical responses to the author's works, and information about major awards and prizes the author has received. The introduction begins by identifying the nationality of the author and by listing genres in which s/he has written for children and young adults. Introductions also list a group of representative titles for which the author or illustrator being profiled is best known; this section, which begins with the words "major works include," follows the genre line of the introduction. For seminal figures, a listing of major works about the author follows when appropriate, high-lighting important biographies about the author or illustrator that are not excerpted in the entry. The centered heading "Introduction" announces the body of the text.

- **Criticism** is located in three sections: **Author Commentary** (when available) **General Commentary** (when available), and **Title Commentary** (commentary on specific titles).

  The **Author Commentary** presents background material written by the author or by an interviewer. This commentary may cover a specific work or several works. Author commentary on more than one work appears after the author introduction, while commentary on an individual book follows the title entry heading.

  The **General Commentary** consists of critical excerpts that consider more than one work by the author or illustrator being profiled. General commentary is preceded by the critic's name in boldface type or, in the case of unsigned criticism, by the title of the journal. *CLR* also features entries that emphasize general criticism on the oeuvre of an author or illustrator. When appropriate, a selection of reviews is included to supplement the general commentary.

  The **Title Commentary** begins with the title entry headings, which precede the criticism on a title and cite publication information on the work being reviewed. Title headings list the title of the work as it appeared in its first English-language edition. The first English-language publication date of each work (unless otherwise noted) is listed in parentheses following the title. Differing U.S. and British titles follow the publication date within parentheses. When a work is written by an individual other than the one being profiled, as is the case when illustrators are featured, the parenthetical material following the title cites the author of the work before listing its publication date.

Entries in each title commentary section consist of critical excerpts on the author's individual works, arranged chronologically by publication date. The entries generally contain two to seven reviews per title, depending on the stature of the book and the amount of criticism it has generated. The editors select titles that reflect the entire scope of the author's literary contribution, covering each genre and subject. An effort is made to reprint criticism that represents the full range of each title's reception, from the year of its initial publication to current assessments. Thus, the reader is provided with a record of the author's critical history. Publication information (such as publisher names and book prices) and parenthetical numerical references (such as footnotes or page and line references to specific editions of works) have been deleted at the discretion of the editors to provide smoother reading of the text.

- A complete **Bibliographical Citation** of the original essay or book precedes each piece of criticism.

- Selected excerpts are preceded by brief **Annotations,** which provide information on the critic or work of criticism to enhance the reader's understanding of the excerpt.

- Numerous **Illustrations** are featured in *CLR*. For entries on illustrators, an effort has been made to include illustrations that reflect the characteristics discussed in the criticism. Entries on authors who do not illustrate their own works my include photographs and other illustrative material pertinent to their careers.

Special Features: Entries on Illustrators

Entries on authors who are also illustrators will occasionally feature commentary on selected works illustrated but not written by the author being profiled. These works are strongly associated with the illustrator and have received critical acclaim for their art. By including critical comment on works of this type, the editors wish to provide a more complete representation of the artist's career. Criticism on these works has been chosen to stress artistic, rather than literary, contributions. Title entry headings for works illustrated by the author being profiled are arranged chronologically within the entry by date of publication and include notes identifying the author of the illustrated work. In order to provide easier access for users, all titles illustrated by the subject of the entry are boldfaced.

CLR also includes entries on prominent illustrators who have contributed to the field of children's literature. These entries are designed to represent the development of the illustrator as an artist rather than as a literary stylist. The illustrator's section is organized like that of an author, with two exceptions: the introduction presents an overview of the illustrator's styles and techniques rather than outlining his or her literary background, and the commentary written by the illustrator on his or her works is called "Illustrator's Commentary" rather than "Author's Commentary." All titles of books containing illustrations by the artist being profiled are highlighted in boldface type.

Indexes

A **Cumulative Author Index** lists all of the authors who have appeared in *CLR* with cross-references to the biographical, autobiographical, and literary criticism series published by the Gale Group. A complete list of these sources is found facing the first page of the Author Index. The index also includes birth and death dates and cross-references between pseudonyms and actual names.

A **Cumulative Nationality Index** lists all authors featured in *CLR* by nationality, followed by the number of the *CLR* volume in which their entry appears.

A **Cumulative Title Index** lists all author titles covered in *CLR*. Each title is followed by the author's name and corresponding volume and page numbers where commentary on the work is located.

Citing *Children's Literature Review*

When writing papers, students who quote directly from any volume in the Literary Criticism Series may use the following general format to footnote reprinted criticism. The first example pertains to material drawn from periodicals, the second to material reprinted from books.

Cynthia Zarin, "It's Easy Being Green," *The New York Times Book Review* (November 14, 1993): 48; excerpted and reprinted in *Children's Literature Review,* vol. 58, ed. Deborah J. Morad (Farmington Hills, Mich: The Gale Group, 2000), 57.

Paul Walker, *Speaking of Science Fiction: The Paul Walker Interviews,* (Luna Publications, 1978), 108-20; excerpted and reprinted in *Children's Literature Review,* vol. 58, ed. Deborah J. Morad (Farmington Hills, Mich: The Gale Group, 2000), 3-8.

Suggestions are Welcome

In response to various suggestions, several features have been added to *CLR* since the beginning of the series, including author entries on retellers of traditional literature as well as those who have been the first to record oral tales and other folklore; entries on prominent illustrators featuring commentary on their styles and techniques; entries on authors whose works are considered controversial; occasional entries devoted to criticism on a single work or a series of works; sections in author introductions that list major works by and about the author or illustrator being profiled; explanatory notes that provide information on the critic or work of criticism to enhance the usefulness of the excerpt; more extensive illustrative material, such as holographs of manuscript pages and photographs of people and places pertinent to the careers of the authors and artists; a cumulative nationality index for easy access to authors by nationality; and occasional guest essays written specifically for *CLR* by prominent critics on subjects of their choice.

Readers who wish to suggest new features, topics, or authors to appear in future volumes, or who have other suggestions or comments are cordially invited to call, write, or fax the Managing Editor:

Managing Editor, Literary Criticism Series
The Gale Group
27500 Drake Road
Farmington Hills, MI 48331-3535
1-800-347-4253 (GALE)
Fax: 248-699-8054

Acknowledgments

The editors wish to thank the copyright holders of the excerpted criticism included in this volume and the permissions managers of many book and magazine publishing companies for assisting us in securing reproduction rights. We are also grateful to the staffs of the Detroit Public Library, the Library of Congress, the University of Detroit Mercy Library, Wayne State University Purdy/Kresge Library Complex, and the University of Michigan Libraries for making their resources available to us. Following is a list of the copyright holders who have granted us permission to reproduce material in this volume of *CLR*. Every effort has been made to trace copyright, but if omissions have been made, please let us know.

Literary Criticism Series Advisory Board

Betsy Byars
1928-

American author of books for elementary students and pre-teens.

Major works include *Summer of the Swans* (1970), *The Pinballs* (1977), *The Night Swimmers*(1980), *Cracker Jackson* (1985), *The Burning Questions of Bingo Brown* (1988).

For further information on Byars's life and works, see *CLR,* Volumes 1 and 16.

INTRODUCTION

The author of more than thirty books for children, Betsy Byars has been hailed by Nancy Chambers, editor of the British journal *Signal,* as "one of the ten best writers for children in the world." Her works are noted for their sensitive portrayals of troubled adolescents who suffer from feelings of isolation and loneliness, and she has been commended for her ability to express crucial incidents of trial and change in simple language. Byars' well-developed comic sense is considered refreshing. When writing about children under stress, it is the humor she finds in a situation that enables her to approach issues usually considered too painful for young readers. Critics enjoy her energy and her ability to create resilient characters and believable situations that are both intense and accessible. This endows her books with a fundamental hopefulness despite alienated protagonists beset by disturbing problems, such as abuse and neglect, or common ones, such as coming to terms with their own sexuality. The humor Byars depicts comes from a sense of the absurdity of the human condition and serves to enhance her adolescent and preadolescent characters. She understands how ordinary upsets and minor crises can impact a child, and presents the inner life and outward behavior of her characters as they grow into adulthood.

BIOGRAPHICAL INFORMATION

Byars had a happy childhood in and around Charlotte, North Carolina. Reading was an important part of her parents' lives, and they passed their passion to

Byars. She learned to read before she went to school, although she never read children's books, and still rarely reads them. She thought the idea of being a writer was boring and entered Furman University as a math major, but soon switched her major to English. In 1950 she married an engineering student, now a professor; they have two daughters and a son. While her husband was in graduate school, she began to write in her free time. Her first sale was a short article for the *Saturday Evening Post*. She began her first children's book in 1960, and since then has written over thirty books. Some of her stories are original and some she bases on family and friends. A summer job tutoring retarded children gave her the inspiration for *Summer of the Swans*. Byars has said, "Living with my own teenagers has taught me that not only must I not write down to my readers, I must write up to them. Boys and girls are very sharp today, and when I visit classrooms and talk with students I am always impressed to find how many of them are writing stories and how knowledgeable they are about writing."

MAJOR WORKS

Summer of the Swans, Byars' Newbery winner, is about a day in the life of fourteen-year-old Sarah, told from the point of view of her mentally handicapped brother Charlie. Sarah's mother is dead, her father travels and rarely visits, and she and her siblings are cared for by their aunt. Sarah is moody and worried about her changing body. She sometimes takes Charlie to see the swans, and he loves to watch them glide on the water. When Charlie disappears one night, Sarah is sure he has gone to find the swans. Because he cannot speak, he is helpless, and Sarah spends the next day frantically searching for him. By concentrating on another's needs instead of her own, Sarah learns important lessons about adulthood.

In *Cracker Jackson,* Byars takes on the serious theme of abuse, interweaving it in a story containing hilarious moments. When Alma, eleven-year-old Cracker's babysitter, confides in him about her abusive husband, Cracker feels responsible for her and decides to take her and her baby to a shelter for abused women. Unlicensed and inexperienced, guided by his clueless friend Goat, Cracker drives the car to get her there. Mixing humor with pathos, Byars paints a very funny picture of the car ride. Although he has done his best, Cracker is too young to adequately protect Alma. Fortunately, his parents relieve him of this burden, acknowledging his courage in attempting to help, and Cracker is able to comfort Alma when he visits her in the hospital.

Retta is the oldest of three children in *The Night Swimmers.* Their mother is dead, and their father, a country western singer, leaves them alone for long periods of time while he goes away to perform. It is up to Retta to feed, clothe, and entertain her two young brothers. Longing for a life of affluence, she discovers that a neighbor with a swimming pool goes to bed early, allowing the children the opportunity to sneak into his yard at night to swim and pretend they are living like rich people. A crisis occurs when her brothers begin to get out of control and one of them nearly drowns. This incident brings the family back together, with the father finally acknowledging his responsibilities toward his children. Critics especially liked Byars' depiction of family frustrations and affections.

The Pinballs are a trio of foster children living in the same group home. Carlie has been abused by her father; Harvey, suffering from depression, had his legs broken when his father ran over him in a car during an argument; Thomas J. was abandoned to be raised by his silent and unaffectionate elderly twin aunts until Child Welfare took him away. Each of them feels like a pinball—out of control, without rights, and pushed around by others. Led by Carlie, they discover together that they have choices and can make things better for themselves and each other.

In the three Bingo Brown books—*The Burning Questions of Bingo Brown, Bingo Brown and the Language of Love,* and *Bingo Brown, Gypsy Lover*—Bingo Brown explores his budding sexuality. In the first of these, Bingo, who wants to be a writer, has many questions, such as "Has there ever been a successful writer with freckles? Why did no one notice my mousse? Am I ready for mixed-sex conversation?" While he is trying to sort all this out, one of his teachers becomes suicidal, presenting even more serious issues for Bingo to face. In the end, Bingo realizes that some questions do not have answers.

AWARDS AND HONORS

Byars has been the recipient of many awards including the coveted Newbery Medal which was awarded to *Summer of the Swans* in 1971. The Child Study Association named many of Byars' books as America's Book of the Year selections. They were *The Midnight Fox* in 1968 (it also won the Lewis Carroll Shelf Award in 1970), *Trouble River* in 1969, *Summer of the Swans* in 1970, *The House of Wings* in 1972, *The Winged Colt of Casa Mia* and *The 18th Emergency* in 1973, *After the Goat Man* in 1974, *The Lace Snail* in 1975, *The TV Kid* in 1976, and *The Night Swimmers* in 1980. *The School Library Journal* named *Go and Hush the Baby* as a Best Books for Spring selection in 1971, *House of Wings* to its Book List in 1972 (also named a National Book Award finalist in 1973) and *After the Goat Man* in 1974; they also named *The Night Swimmers* Best Book of the Year in 1980 (it also won the 1981 American Book Award for Children's Fiction).

Named the *New York Times* Outstanding Book of the Year were *The Winged Colt of Casa Mia* and *The 18th Emergency* in 1973 (*The 18th Emergency* also won the Dorothy Canfield Fisher Memorial Book Award from the Vermont Congress of Parents and Teachers in 1975), *Goodbye Chicken Little* in 1979, and *The Two-Thousand-Pound Goldfish* in 1982.

Several of Byars' books have won multiple awards.

The Pinballs won the Woodward Park School Annual Book Award and the Child Study Children's Book Award from the Child Study Children's Book Committee at Bank Street College of Education, both in 1977. It was named to the Hans Christian Andersen Honor List for Promoting Concern for the Disadvantaged and Handicapped and won the Georgia Children's Book Award in 1979. In 1980 it won the Charlie Mae Simon Book Award from the Arkansas Elementary School Council, the Surrey School Book of the Year Award from the Surrey School Librarians of Surrey, British Columbia, the Mark Twain Award from the Missouri Association of School Librarians, the William Allen White Children's Book Award from Emporia State University, and the Young Reader Medal from the California Reading Association. It was a runner up for the Nene Award in 1981 and 1983 and won the Golden Archer Award from the Department of Library Science of the University of Wisconsin in Oshkosh in 1982.

The Cybil War was named a Notable Children's Book by the *School Library Journal* in 1981 and Children's Choice by the International Reading Association in 1982. It also won the 1983 Tennessee Children's Choice Book Award from the Tennessee Library Association in 1983 and the Sequoyah Children's Book Award in 1984.

In 1982, *The Animal, the Vegetable, and John D. Jones* won the Parent's Choice Award for Children's Literature from the Parents' Choice Foundation and was named Best Children's Book by the *School Library Journal*. In 1983 it received the CRABbery Award from the Oxon Hill Branch of Prince George's County Library, and in 1985 it won the Mark Twain Award.

The Computer Nut won the Charlie Mae Simon Award in 1987, and in 1988 *Cracker Jackson* won the South Carolina Children's Book Award and the Maryland Children's Book Award.

In 1987, Byars won the Regina Medal from the Catholic Library Association for her contributions to children's literature.

AUTHOR COMMENTARY

Betsy Byars

SOURCE: "Taking Humor Seriously," in *The Zena Sutherland Lectures, 1983-1992,* edited by Betsy Hearne, Clarion Books, 1993, pp. 210-27.

I equate Zena Sutherland with humor. In the times—too few actually—we have been together, she has never once failed to make me laugh. Because of that, I chose my topic, and tonight I place this very classy lady in the company of some very classy gentlemen who have also made me laugh.

When my daughter was in second grade, she took me to school one day for "Show and Tell." This was the teacher's suggestion. She felt it would be beneficial for the kids to see what a real live author looked like. I went on, as I recall it, between some guppies and an interesting piece of fungus. And I hope you won't think I'm being immodest when I say I was the best.

I took a manuscript with me that day. I had just gotten it back, complete with editor's notes in the margin, and I showed the kids some of the editor's comments, one of which was "MAKE THIS FUNNY!" There was a great deal of interest in this demand, and the general consensus was that the editor meant for me to put some jokes in. If only it were so simple, for the truth is that there are far too many jokes in the world and far too little humor.

I once read that there are three ways to learn to write. They are to write, to write, and to write. This is true, but I would add—certainly if the goal is to write humor—to read. I have always been drawn to humorous writing simply because I like to laugh and be amused. For years as I was growing up, the only thing I read in *The Saturday Evening Post* was the "Post Scripts" page. And while I was reading, by osmosis, I was absorbing certain facts about what is funny and why.

In Max Eastman's "Ten Commandments of the Comic Art," Commandment Three is "Be effortless." I especially like that, although there's a lot to be said for commandments five through eight—"Be plausible, Be sudden, Be neat, and Be right with your timing." But being effortless is almost my sole commandment, my goal in writing. I work on something until it looks as if I haven't worked on it at all, and if it looks as if I've worked on it, I go back and work some more. But it's especially important in humor. Humor demands naturalness and simplicity. To appear spontaneous may require a week of work. It's not like a James Thurber drawing that turned out funnier the faster he drew. More than any other type of writing, humor has got to resemble play.

Perhaps because they resembled play, humorous books attracted me as I was growing up. The titles of Leo Edwards's books drew me like a magnet—*Poppy*

Ott and the Prancing Pancake; *Jerry Todd and the Purring Egg*. The books themselves rarely lived up to their titles, but they did make me realize that by manipulating language, you could be funny; by using an unusual adjective or adverb or description, you could intrigue a reader. *Jerry Todd and the Buffalo Bill Bathtub*; *Poppy Ott and the Stuttering Parrot*; *Jerry Todd and the Flying Flagdoodle*.

My uncle read the Cosmo Topper books, and I progressed to these. I must have read dozens of Thorne Smith's books during summer vacations when I was in high school. The Topper books, which have been ill-served by both the movies and TV with their emphasis on effects—cocktail shakers shaking in midair, tires changing themselves—are as fresh today as they were fifty years ago. They are very funny books, and Cosmo is a very funny man. The more familiar you become with him, the funnier he is, which may be the measurement of a truly humorous character.

One of the reasons the Topper books are so funny is that Cosmo takes himself seriously, just as Bingo Brown does in my books. They are earnest and straightforward. If Bingo and Cosmo thought they were funny, they wouldn't be. In my all-time favorite comic scene, Cosmo and the invisible Marion are sitting in a park. Cosmo reveals to Marion that as a boy he wanted to become an actor, and that the only encouragement he got was from a drunken uncle who gave him a book with photographs that showed you how to do Hate and Fear and Modesty and Surprise and practically all the other emotions. Unconsciously, Cosmo presses his hands to his cheeks and does Surprise for the invisible Marion, and he looks up to see a small group of bystanders, all of whom are registering the most eloquent surprise themselves, so that "Mr. Topper appeared to be leading a class in dramatic elocution."

I read a lot of Wodehouse too, and his young men also took themselves seriously. When love goes wrong, one of Wodehouse's characters plays "The Rosary" with one finger on the piano for hours. One can hardly be more serious than that.

I knew I owed a debt to both Thorne Smith and Wodehouse for the character of Bingo Brown, but I didn't realize the depth of my debt until I was re-reading some of Wodehouse's books in preparing this talk. In my mind, Bingo had sprung into my head like a feat of magic. I had been working on a manuscript, and I needed a name for a character, and the name Bingo popped into mind. I liked it, but this was a minor character, and I didn't want to waste such an original name.

I tried to continue writing, but the character was beginning to form himself. Suddenly, I knew how he had gotten the name Bingo. When he was born, the doctor said, "Bingo!" I knew that later Bingo would say to his mom, "Mom, he wasn't naming me, he said that every time a baby was born." And pretty soon, I had to put aside the book I was working on and start writing about Bingo.

A name, a character wholly out of my imagination, I thought, and then I came across a Wodehouse short story called "No Wedding Bells for Bingo." Bingo Little is a minor comic character who appears frequently in Wodehouse stories. He is always becoming infatuated, and after seven ill-fated and very funny courtships, he falls in love with and marries the novelist Rosie M. Banks.

It doesn't always happen that I can trace a character or an incident directly to its source, but I know that while I was reading Wodehouse as a girl, Bingo Little entered my mind and emerged, as if from a cocoon, forty years later as Bingo Brown.

I am drawn to humor, but I am not a humorist: My own books are serious, with comic episodes. However, the humor is not what Mark Twain called "only a fragrance, a decoration." The humor in my books serves a dual purpose. It balances out the serious things. The more difficult the theme, the more humor is needed—for my own relief as well as the reader's. It also humanizes things that are so dreadful, they are in danger of dehumanizing us—wife abuse and child neglect, for example. The ability to laugh is the ability to put a distance between us, to give us the feeling that we're still in control.

The humorous parts of my books are my favorite parts. When I get one of my books and hold it in my hands for the first time, I open it immediately to the page with the Library of Congress summary. "A boy is puzzled by the comic and confusing questions of youth." This is helpful to me. Now when someone asks me what my new book is about, I am ready. "It's about a boy puzzled by the comic and confusing questions of youth."

After that, I leaf through the book, pausing at the parts I considered funny when I wrote them, to see if they have survived and are still funny in print.

Humor comes naturally to children. Max Eastman says that to children, "Every untoward, unprepared for, unmanageable, inauspicious, ugly, disgusting, puzzling, startling, deceiving, shaking, blinding, bolting, deafening, banging, bumping or otherwise shocking and disturbing thing, unless it be calamitous enough to force them out of the mood of play," is funny. He doesn't give the list for adults, but he does mention that it's a lot shorter.

The gap between what adults think is funny and what kids think is funny is considerable. Even Thurber says of children's humor, "There have been a great many times when I haven't the vaguest idea of what the hell they were laughing about." I know that there is a theory that we must never write *for* kids, not even humor, and if we even become aware that we are writing for kids, we've already lost the game, and after all, we're all just big kids, but I don't believe this. I refuse to think of myself as a large wrinkled child.

So, I'm always looking for things that are funny to kids. One of my daughters had some friends over one day, and one of the boys who was always comical noticed there were two cobwebs hanging from the ceiling. He got up on the piano bench and pretended to be Tarzan, attempting to swing from one to the other. It was very funny.

And so, in **The 18th Emergency,** when Mouse Fawley looks up on his ceiling and sees a cobweb, he doesn't try to swing on it, but he has previously written UNSAFE FOR PUBLIC SWINGING and drawn an arrow to it. This opened up a whole facet of Mouse's personality. When he sees a crack in the wall, he writes, TO OPEN BUILDING TEAR ALONG THIS LINE, and I would never have thought of that on my own.

My son had a friend who did whale imitations. I was never privileged to see them, because Phil never did his imitations on request but only when moved to do so. When this happened, the word would spread and kids would appear from blocks around to watch and roll on the floor, helpless with laughter. "What are the imitations like?" I asked my son. "They're like—whales," was his explanation. I sometimes found myself looking at Phil, the comic imitator of whales, wondering, but he looked back with his face in neutral, as all my son's friends did, and I could never imagine the imitations for myself. Years later, writing **Cracker Jackson,** with Jackson's friend Percy doing whale imitations, I did get a glimmer, and I can tell you the imitations were like—whales.

The forbidden is always funny, and usually the first kind of humor that kids discover is bathroom humor, and all too often, the appetite for this kind of humor

is lifelong. At first, certain words are just plain hilarious, and the appeal of reducing one's friends to helpless laughter and, at the same time, shocking adults is considerable.

The funniest word in the vocabulary of a second-grader is *underwear.* When I speak to second-graders, I always read the opening sentence of **The Night Swimmers.** "When the swimming pool lights were turned out and Colonel and Mrs. Roberts had gone to bed, the Anderson kids came out of the bushes in their underwear." It is such a successful sentence with second-graders that I often have to repeat it. I have even been asked if I had any other funny sentences.

The difficulty with using bathroom humor, of course, is that it's hard to be tasteful. One of the ways is that you simply describe the joke rather than tell it. In **Cracker Jackson,** Goat had interrupted assembly by telling a joke during the Pledge of Allegiance. The principal calls Goat up and asks him to share "what was so funny" with the assembly.

I limit myself to: "The trouble was that the joke was about a man who had taken an overdose of laxative, and the principal couldn't shut Goat up before he gave the punch line, which consisted of a sound effect." That is too tasteful. Kids don't think that's funny.

I reached my peak as a bathroom humorist in **The 2000-Pound Goldfish.** The goldfish has been flushed down the toilet, into the sewer, where it comes to weigh two thousand pounds and has slurped five or six people to death. The soldiers are marching into the sewer to kill Bubbles, and Warren gets the idea that if everyone in the city flushed their toilets at, say, ten o'clock, the floodgates would open and Bubbles would be swept out to sea "where she could live the rest of her life in peace and harmony." This is the section I read aloud to kids, and at this point, some intellectual type raises his hand and says, "Mrs. Byars, goldfish can't live in salt water." I say, "Listen, I'm the boss of this book, and if I want Bubbles to live in salt water, Bubbles will live in salt water."

There follows a seven-page countdown in which the announcer is entreating listeners to flush their toilets. "It's five minutes to ten. If you have more than one bathroom, get a neighbor to come flush with you." "It's four minutes to ten, open your windows, yell, 'Flush!' to the people in the streets below." It takes two pages to get everyone in their bathrooms, and the final countdown is "Five-four-three-two-one-

FLUSH!" and if I read this correctly, I never have to actually say the word *flush,* because the entire school will make the sound of a toilet flushing. It may not sound thrilling to you to hear two hundred kids flushing like toilets, but it has never failed to move me.

Bad grammar is more amusing to kids than good grammar although, increasingly these days, it seems no one knows the difference. The humor of bad grammar arose from the "bohunk" type of humor popular in early America. It was rural humor and the appeal was twofold—a feeling of superiority or gratified vanity that we ourselves knew better, and the enjoyment of irreverence and rebellion against the despised grammar book of youth. Even Mark Twain used it for humorous effect, and Artemus Ward made up a name for it, "ingrammaticisms," the thought being that as soon as you have learned that some grammatic form is "wrong," you are prepared to have fun with it.

My particular weakness has always been for the double negative. I am drawn to it. I am not sure I would have read and enjoyed H. Allen Smith's *How to Write Without Knowing Nothing* if the title had been, say, *How to Write Without a Great Deal of Education.*

Sometimes I use the double negative not to be funny, but to make the character's speech more authentic. In *Trouble River,* the grandmother says, "We ain't got no chance . . ." and "I didn't come no one thousand miles . . ." This was not meant to be funny, and it actually turned out to be unfunny, because I got letters from English teachers chastising me for reinforcing the unfortunate speech patterns which they were trying to change.

I've never quite come up to Robert J. Burdette, who, in "Romance of the Carpet," gained immortality with the quadruple negative, but then nobody has:

> And he turned away with a heart full sore,
> And he never was seen, not none no more.

Used properly, the double negative is funny. In *The 18th Emergency,* Mouse Fawley remembers when the boys decided, during a recess lull, to put the girls in the school trash cans. There's a long screaming charge, which ends with Mouse having Viola Angotti pinned against the garbage cans. He realizes he's not going to be able to get Viola in the garbage can without a great deal of help, but no help is forthcoming. Actually, the rest of the boys are being marched into the front door by the principal.

He called again, "Come on, you guys, get the lid off this garbage can, will you?"

And then, when he said that, Viola Angotti had taken two steps forward. She said, "Nobody's putting me in no garbage can."

He cried, "Hey, you guys!" It was a plea. "Where are you?"

And then Viola Angotti had taken one more step, and with a faint sigh she had socked him in the stomach so hard that he had doubled over and lost his lunch.

As she walked past his body she said again, "Nobody's putting me in no garbage can." It had sounded like one of the world's basic truths. The sun will rise. The tides will flow. Nobody's putting Viola Angotti in no garbage can.[1]

Mark Twain said, "Repetition is a mighty power in the domain of humor," and James Thurber said that if "you keep on doing a thing, the audience will laugh," so it must be true. Repetition for fun is born early in a child's life, and who of us has not taken pleasure in the question, "Fuzzy Wuzzy wasn't fuzzy, was he?" Even in adulthood there's a certain pleasure in the fact that there was—and may still be—a newspaper called *The Walla-Walla Wahoo,* Walla-Walla, Wash.

I use mostly repetition of event. In *The Blossoms Meet the Vulture Lady,* it's funny when Junior is trapped in the coyote cage. It's funnier when Mud is trapped in the same coyote cage. If I could have trapped two or three more Blossoms in the coyote cage, I would have, and it would have been funnier each time.

When I was in school, the simile and the metaphor were things I encountered on English worksheets. "Find two similes and one metaphor in the second chapter of *Moby Dick.*" The rules for using similes to comic effect in children's books are, I think, the same as the rules for using metaphors: (1) Stick to the familiar and (2) Don't use them at all unless you absolutely can't stop yourself.

A simile in a children's book must be within the child's reach. The Bingo Brown books lend themselves to the simile, because the reader accepts that these are Bingo's comparisons, rather than mine. When Bingo has a mixed-sex conversation with Melissa, it's "like the Olympics of mixed-sex conversations." When he lies down on his Smurf sheets, he's "as uncomfortable as if he were lying on real Smurfs." When he takes off half his eyebrow during his first shave, the remaining eyebrow has "a suggestive snarl, like the curl of Elvis Presley's lip."

Even the best writer gets carried away by past experience. When Mark Twain has Huck describe a piece of meat as no better than "a hunk of old cold cannibal in the morning," surely he was swayed by his own travels in the Sandwich Islands, rather than by Huck's experience. I had a book as a child in which the sky of the North Pole had a gargoylelike face that blew down on the world. Because of the lingering effect of this picture—I can still see it sixty years later—I wrote a line in *The Cybil War* describing a teacher who, in her displeasure with Simon, speaks, and "It was as if the North Pole had spoken." That was not a good simile; it was self-indulgence.

We also tend to repeat our similes, possibly because we're afraid the reader might have missed one. Time and again one of Wodehouse's characters makes a noise like a dying duck. I could never imagine it—other than a sort of feeble quack—and then I read somewhere in a footnote that these rubber ducks used to be popular, and when the air went out of them, the last sound was quite comical, similar to a whoopee cushion. Certainly, it amused Wodehouse everytime he thought of it. Occasionally, he varies this with a noise "like the gasp of a dying zebra," but his heart never seems to be in it.

Wodehouse was a master at building up to a simile or metaphor. In *The Butler Did It*, he describes Roscoe Bunyan: "His face was red, the back of his neck overflowed his collar, and there had recently been published a second edition of his chin." He also invented the three-part simile, in which something is compared to three other items, the first two of which are normal, the third, exaggerated. He describes a friendship as compared to those read about in literature—"Damon and Pythias, David and Jonathan, Abercrombie and Fitch." Here's my attempt. Bingo Brown has just been grabbed around the neck by CiCi Boles, which made "Bingo feel he was the helpless victim of a force of nature, a tornado or an earthquake or one of those baboons that kill their mates by twisting off their heads."

Max Eastman compares punning to the "bodily joy of being tossed through the air toward the arms of a nice plump mother and failing to arrive." There was even a book printed in Swift's time with seventy-six rules for punning, such as "Any person may pun upon another man's puns about half an hour after he has made them."

The pun is not for all of us. To be funny, a pun must be terrible. Groucho Marx made one of the worst—therefore best—puns in *Animal Crackers*. He found when he was hunting elephants in Africa that the tusks were hard to dig out, but that "in Alabama, the Tuscaloosa."

In almost forty books, I have only one pun, and I was so pleased that I wrote a whole book to go with it. I recall the exact moment I got this pun. I had just finished reading Alison Lurie's *War Between the Tates,* and I was wishing I could think of a clever title like that, and almost immediately. *The Cybil War* popped into my mind. I don't know if all writers get such intense pleasure out of their puns, but I typed up the title page and sat there smiling at it for some time.

Understatement is one of the funniest forms of humor, but easily lost on kids. The knack of producing humor by using understatement is to finish a sentence with a word or phrase that is milder than the listener expected, anticlimatic. Kids have an innate ability for this kind of humor and do it without even trying: "Dear Betsy, Everyone has to write a real live author and I hope you're alive or I have to write a poem."

My favorite letter was written, not to me, but to Laura Ingalls Wilder, but I used it in *The Burning Questions of Bingo Brown.* "Dear Laura Ingalls Wilder, I know that you are dead, but please write if you can and let me know where you get your ideas."

The master of finishing sentences with something incongruous, something the reader did not expect, was Kin Hubbard, who wrote the shortest newspaper column in journalistic history. Kin Hubbard could express all he wanted to say in so few words, that each of his columns consisted of one sentence. One of my favorites was, "Miss Linnet Spry was confined to her home with a swollen dresser drawer."

Supposedly, once you start defining humor, you lose it, but I don't think it would hurt to look at the origin of the word. In Latin, *humor* meant wetness, as in today's *humidity.* Then, in Hippocrates' day, it came to mean the liquid currents that flowed through the body. So a man was "out of humor" and the physician's job was to keep him in "good humor." Later, the word branched out, and one meaning—from which came our modern word—was "odd or incongruous."

This meaning is the basis for the humorous character in literature, and by "humorous character" I mean the individual in whom some particular quality is developed beyond those of his fellow man, such as Mr.

Pickwick's self-forgetfulness or Don Quixote's knightly dedication. Humorous characters seem to walk off the pages and directly into our lives—Sancho, Falstaff, the Vicar of Wakefield, Jeeves, The Ruggles of Red Gap, Huckleberry Finn.

The true humorous character does not clash with reality. There has to be the element of plausibility, or the result is a comic character, which is different. I consider Mad Mary a humorous character because not only is she plausible, she is based on a real woman. But she is in no way comic.

The humor of situation arises out of confusion, mix-ups, blunders, and misadventures. Plato pointed out that we laugh at the misfortunes of others for joy that we do not share them. That may be part of it. But the humor of confusion depends more on the characters involved than the action itself. The Blossom characters came first, and the confusions befell the most vulnerable of them—Pap, Mad Mary, Ralphie, Junior, and Mud. Although confusion is a part of all the Blossoms' daily existence, it's somehow most humorous when it happens to these five.

Children need parody, just as adults do, because it is a form of humorous protest. The essential point in the use of parody, I think, is to prick a balloon, to show how ridiculous or even how painful some element of our daily lives is.

My favorite target, of course, is the *National Enquirer.* Among the headlines Bingo Brown fears to appear in are BOY LOVES TWO GIRLS FOR INFINITY, SETS WORLD RECORD; but in *The Midnight Fox,* long before I was aware of the *Enquirer,* I parodied headlines. Petie Burkis writes of a personal humiliation at a park—BOY FALLS DOWN BANK WHILE GIRL ONLOOKERS CHEER—and then goes on to write a story that sounds like it had come from a real newspaper.

TV lends itself particularly well to parody, which is one of the reasons I enjoyed writing *The TV Kid.* I relished the creation of "Give It a Spin," the game show where YOU pick your prizes and WE see that you take them, and the commercial for "Friend," the lifesize doll that allows you always to have someone to talk to. My favorite was a commercial that Lennie imagines for Fail-Ease, the tablet that eases failure and makes you less afraid to fail the next time. "Yes, for the nagging relief from failure take Fail-Ease, the failure reliever that requires no prescription." Don't we wish.

Actually, it is not I who think up these parodies. It is a character in the book, in the same way that while I could never write a country-western song, I can create a character who can write "My Angel Went to Heaven in a DC-3." I cannot write poetry, but I can create a character who, without batting an eye, can turn out complicated rhymes: "I love the roof and that's the troof."

There's a whole area of what I would call negative humor—insults, sarcasm, ridicule—hostile humor. Children, in real life, dread ridicule so much, they guard against it. If they are afraid they won't get an invitation, they say, "I wouldn't go to the party if I was invited." If scorned for sloppiness, they become twice as sloppy to show they couldn't care less.

They like insults as long as someone else is the target. Milton Berle, who should know, says the insult is popular because it boosts an audience's feeling of superiority over the object of the gag. When I needed insults in *The Burning Questions of Bingo Brown,* I got a book of insults, just as Billy Wentworth did, and I dealt them out with the same ruthlessness as he did.

"Mamie Lou, you are a perfect ten. Your face is a two, your body is a two, your legs are a two—" Mamie Lou wisely didn't wait around to hear what her other twos were.

"Harriet, you may not have invented ugliness, but you sure are the local distributor."

"Miss Fanucci is so ugly that when she goes to the zoo she has to buy two tickets—one to get in and one to get out."

Since Miss Fanucci overhears her insult, that puts a blessed end to the insults. Speaking of insults, Sinclair Lewis pointed out there are two insults that no human will endure—that he has never known trouble and that he has no sense of humor.

Nonsense is comical, and it's comical in essentially the same way to grown-ups and to children. That is not true of all humor. Nonsense has a disarming lack of pretense, and yet it requires a keen, logical mind to write nonsense which will endure. I have never—intentionally—said anything nonsensical, but one of my first loves was Uncle Wiggily. I looked forward particularly to those nonsense endings—"If the dogwood tree doesn't bark at the pussy willow and make its tail fluff up, I'll tell you about Uncle Wiggily and Nurse Fuzzywuzzy."

My father read me these books at bedtime, and when I reread them today, I still seem to hear my father's voice quicken as he got to the nonsense at the end of the chapter. It may well have been relief that he could get back to his easy chair and newspaper and Camel cigarettes, but I thought it was pleasure. And even the least of the endings is dear to me. "And if the ice cream cone doesn't jump up and down on the table-cloth, and poke holes in the loaf of bread . . ."

And my father would audibly close the book and give a three-note, down-the-scale, "Ha, ha, ha" that Pavarotti would have envied. No one could wrap up a chapter in a more satisfying way than Howard Garis and my father.

I have come across a lot of comments about humor that I like: Fred Allen's "All I know about humor is that I don't know anything about it." I thought about that as I was writing this paper, as well as the disquieting, "With notable exception, humor is written about by people who haven't any." I like Thurber's "Humor is emotional chaos remembered in tranquility."

But Stephen Leacock seemed to sum it up best.

> Humor goes on its way, moving from lower to higher forms, from cruelty to horseplay, from horseplay to wit, from wit to the higher humor of character and beyond that to its highest stage as the humor of life itself. Here, tears and laughter are joined, and our little life, incongruous and vain, is rounded with a smile.[2]

"And now if my typewriter doesn't go in swimming and get its hair ribbon all wet, so it's as crinkly as a corkscrew . . ."—I'll see you next time.

Notes

1. Betsy Byars, *The 18th Emergency* (New York: Viking Press, 1973).

2. Stephen Leacock, *Humor and Humanity* (New York: Holt, Rinehart & Winston, 1938).

Betsy Byars with Ilene Cooper

SOURCE: An interview in *Booklist,* Vol. 89, No. 10, January 15, 1993, pp. 906-07.

Some writers are acclaimed for their literary talents, and some are popular with kids. Betsy Byars is one of that select circle who is both. A children's author for 30 years, Byars has such distinguished titles to her credit as *The Midnight Fox, The Summer of the Swans,* and *The Pinballs* as well as popular series

like those featuring the Blossom family and Bingo Brown. In a telephone interview, Byars looked back over her career and talked about some of her more recent works.

BKL: *Everyone knows you for your fiction, but recently you did something a little different, a memoir,* **The Moon and I.** *How did that come about?*

BYARS: I had been working on a piece of biographical writing, but I'd decided it wasn't publishable and put it aside. Then, when a publisher [Julian Messner] called me, and said they wanted me to write a memoir, "in your own words," it really gave me the feeling I could do it any way I wanted to. I told them, "Well, I've started this thing about snakes." I only had the first three chapters, but I sent those, and Messner was very enthusiastic.

BKL: *For those who haven't had a chance to read* **The Moon and I,** *it's about a snake that moves into your house, but it's also about your life.*

BYARS: What I tried to do was give the flavor of my childhood, rather than actual facts about it. My sister has read the book, and she feels I portrayed our life the way it was. The childhood episodes almost wrote themselves.

BKL: *Because you remembered them so well?*

BYARS: Yes, I remember things. The difficult part about this book was getting the three separate elements of the book—the childhood, the present, and the writing—to mix together.

BKL: *What kind of books did you like to read when you were a child?*

BYARS: I started reading very early. I think my sisters taught me to read, and I read everything from Uncle Wiggley to *National Geographic.* And I was very fond of something called the Poppy Ott series.

BKL: *When you write now, how much of your material do you draw from your own childhood? I interviewed Beverly Cleary, and although she has children, she said that almost everything she writes about really comes from her own childhood. How much do you pick up from yours?*

BYARS: Very, very little. I had no interest in writing when I was growing up, so I wasn't keeping journals or writing things down. Just a very few incidents that stuck in my mind have I put in my books. I do draw a great deal from my children's childhoods. They were very communicative kids and would come home and say, "Guess what happened to me?" or "A funny thing happened at school," and I used all of those things.

BKL: *How did they feel about that?*

BYARS: All right as long as I disguised them. They were always saying, "Don't put anything about me in your books." From age 8 or 9, they began realizing these books would be in their library, and that kids they knew would read them. Now they enjoy the books because they can read about their own lives.

BKL: *How was it for them having their mom be a famous author?*

BYARS: I'm not sure they ever thought of my career like that. My daughter thought it was something I did to keep from being bored. Now she's writing herself, and she realizes what little time I had to write while raising four children.

BKL: *You've been writing for 30 years now. How do you think children's publishing has changed?*

BYARS: I think there's been a great evolution. When I first started writing, children's books had to be nice. I can remember some editor writing in the margin, "Don't have him lie" or something like that. And now you're very free. You don't feel any pressure, you don't find yourself thinking things like, "I can't say this" or "This will be too tough a subject for kids."

BKL: *What about your audience? You must get many letters from children. Has what they write about changed over the years?*

BYARS: I don't think so. I save the letters that touch me, but I don't see a great deal of difference.

BKL: *So what do they write to you about?*

BYARS: The majority of my mail is school oriented. For instance, one child wrote, "They said I had to write to an author. I picked you. And the teacher said, 'Is she alive?' Are you alive? I guess if you're reading this, you must be."

BKL: *Do they write about personal things?*

BYARS: Oh yes. And sometimes it's very difficult to write back because you realize the parents might read it, and you cannot reveal anything that this child has said that might upset the parents.

BKL: *In* **The Moon and I,** *you talk about your love of flying, but you also mention the book about flying you were working on at the same time and the problems you were having with it. Last fall you published* **Coast to Coast,** *about a girl who takes a cross-country airplane trip with her grandfather, so you obviously untangled the knots. Sometimes it's difficult to write about a passion because you're so eager to communicate that love to the reader. Was that the hard part? Or was it just thinking up a plot?*

BYARS: The plot was the hardest part for me. What was going to happen on this trip? Most people think a flying book has to have a crash to be any good, and I wasn't going to have that. I started this book in 1987. The plots came and went; editors came and went; and I was still working on it. Finally, I was told that I needed to put a new chapter in the front and take two off the back. I ranted and raved, and then I finally put a chapter in the front and took two off the back. And it worked, because if you start with a new chapter it frames the story. There was always a reason why the grandfather had to go across the country. That's what I had to figure out.

BKL: *How did you get into flying?*

BYARS: My husband was a flyer. We courted in a 1931 Stinson airplane. And now that he's retired, he's restoring antique airplanes because that's always been a big part of his life. We've always flown instead of driving somewhere. I've never had a fear of flying.

BKL: *You fly yourself now, don't you?*

BYARS: Yes, I took my first lesson on April Fool's Day, 1983. I thought flying would be easier than everyone said. I was wrong. Like writing, it's harder.

BKL: *Do you write everyday?*

BYARS: I used to write everyday, but now I write in a more concentrated fashion. If I've got something going I will write maybe for an hour and a half, and then I'm through for the day. And sometimes, for two or three months I don't write at all. Then I'll go through another period when I write at a very rapid rate.

BKL: *What makes you come back to some of your characters like Blossom and Bingo Brown?*

BYARS: Because they're enormous fun. Blossom was the first one that I came back to. Those books always start with Junior making something. Almost against my will, I'll think of something that Junior would want to make, and suddenly a book will have started in my mind. The good part about any series is getting to know the people. You never have to think, "What are they thinking? What would they do now?" because it's just ingrained in you. You really know those people better than you know people you are actually living with.

BKL: *And what about Bingo? What fascination does he hold for you?*

BYARS: Well, Bingo is also fun to write about because he really just took off on his own. But I'm not going to do another Bingo. I feel that I've taken him as high as I can. I wish I'd started him a year earlier, but it's too late now.

BKL: *Which of your books holds up the best for you? I know you like to reread* **The Midnight Fox.** *Do you have favorites?*

BYARS: Well, the ones that seem to hold up well for me were all written in the same period—***The Midnight Fox, The Eighteenth Emergency,*** and ***The House of Wings.*** Sometimes I read them and I think, "I wish I could still write like that."

BKL: *How about* **Summer of the Swans**?

BYARS: That's not one of my favorites.

BKL: *Really? That was the one that won the Newbery. Have awards affected your life?*

BYARS: Oh, certainly that one did. In those days, the author was present at the announcement. When I arrived, the first thing someone said to me was, "It's so refreshing to have someone win that nobody has ever heard of." That was true. I was someone that no one had ever heard of. Astounding. I had gotten almost no mail prior to that time. And now we had to get a bigger mail box. It made an incredible amount of difference in my life.

BKL: *Have you ever done picture books?*

BYARS: I did a few. I did one called ***The Lace Snail,*** which is out of print now. And I did one called ***Go and Hush the Baby.*** And then one of the first books I did was a little picture book.

BKL: *But it wasn't your niche?*

BYARS: No, but in some ways I wish it had been. It's just a wonderful feeling to see all these bright pictures and realize that, in a sense, your words created them.

BKL: *And yet I've had authors tell me just the opposite. They've written a story that someone else has illustrated, and when they finally see the pictures at the very end, their response is, "Oh, dear. That's not quite the way I imagined it."*

BYARS: Yes, I've heard that, too. Fortunately, it never happened to me.

BKL: *From things I've read, I get the impression that you sometimes seem surprised you wound up a writer.*

BYARS: I never had a teacher who suggested I become a writer, and until I won the Newbery Medal I was very insecure about my writing. Now I can say nothing has given me more pleasure. And I'm still thrilled when I receive the finished copy of my latest book.

Betsy Byars

SOURCE: "Ladders and Authority: Creating the Gift," in *Journal of Youth Services in Libraries,* Vol. 7, No. 2, Winter, 1994, pp. 141-46.

Dear Betsy, Everyone in our class has to write to a real, live author, and I hope you're alive—otherwise I have to write a poem.

Dear Betsy, Our class was trying to figure out how old you are and we put down 1991 and under that 1928 and it came out that you were 3919.

Dear Betsy, I was reading ***The Burning Questions of Bingo Brown,*** and I came across the word *brassieres* and I didn't know what that was, and I raised my hand and asked the teacher. You could have saved me a lot of embarrassment if you had just said bras.

Forty years ago when I wrote my first children's book, I had no idea that I would spend my golden years answering letters like those. I had no intention of becoming a writer when I was in school. In all my years of public school and college, not one person said to me, "Perhaps you should consider becoming a writer." I read creatively, and by that I mean that I went through books as if they were coloring books, mentally coloring the scenes to suit my personal tastes. When I said, back then, as I frequently did, "This is the best book I ever read in my life," what I meant was, "This book had the pictures that I particularly like to color."

If I thought of writers at all, I thought of them as supercreative people whose minds conceived stories that literally had to be told. In *Gulliver's Travels,* which was only a so-so coloring book, Gulliver comes across a thinking machine. It was a square frame with handles on the outside and by turning these handles "even the most ignorant person with little bodily labor may write books in philosophy, poetry, theology without the least assistance from genius." That was the kind of machine I would have needed to write a book.

After graduation I married, became a mother, and then when I was twenty-eight my husband decided to go to Illinois to graduate school. We moved with our daughters into a barracks apartment. The decorative highlight of the apartment was an ax on the wall with a sign saying, "In case of fire, chop hole in wall and exit." I didn't want to wait for a fire. I wanted to exit then and there.

But I did what I always do in times of personal turmoil—I read and I read and I read, and then one day, and I genuinely believe this is why more people start writing than any other, I thought, "This doesn't look that hard. I can do this." Now, I did not think this while I was reading *Moby Dick* or *Wuthering Heights.* I thought it while reading a two-hundred-word article on the Posts Scripts page of the *Saturday Evening Post.* So that's where I got my start. They bought the first piece I sent them, and with the seventy-five dollars they paid me, I bought the oldest car in the state of Illinois. I now had wheels and a career and my personal turmoil began to ease.

Although my style and interests have changed enormously since those early days, my working habits are pretty much the same. I wrote on the typewriter as fast as possible, because until I had something down on paper, I didn't have anything to work with. I took the typewritten pages and sat down somewhere else to edit what I had written. Then I went back and retyped it. I went through this process again and again, and although I use the word processor now, I still go through the same procedure. I write until it looks as if I haven't worked on it at all, until it's absolutely simple. If it looks as if I've worked on it, then I go back and work on it some more.

I relied back then, as I do now, on instinct. If my instinct tells me the story is not moving fast enough, I speed it up. If my instinct tells me I've told this too quickly, I divide the chapter and add some description. And the main difference between someone who's just starting and someone who's been writing for forty years, is the amount of trust you have in your instinct. I now follow my instinct without question—even if it's costly.

I had my most costly last-minute, instinct-driven change in *A Blossom Promise.* There were only going to be three Blossom books, but as my editors and I were having supper one night, one of them said, "Why don't you do one more?" I said, "No, these people are very vulnerable and one of them might die." Everybody at the table said, "Pap." Pap was the grandfather. I said, "Yes, and I do not want that on my conscience." Then my editor said, "But if you do one more, we can put them in a box."

So I did the fourth book and, of course, Pap died. And not only that, his dog, Mud, who is my alltime favorite character, died too. Mud had a misery hole under the porch, and every time something happened to make him miserable, he would go under the porch and get in this hole. Now, after Pap died, he went in there and I couldn't get him out.

I sent the manuscript in, I got the advance, I spent the advance, and then in the spring, I got the galley proof sheets for the book. My editor, Olga, said to get the galleys back on Monday, and this was Friday. I went through the manuscript, and there were only two or three little things in question. But as I put the manuscript in an envelope, this terrible feeling came over me. My husband came in and I said, "Ed, I've done something terrible." He said, "What?" I said, "I killed Pap and Mud." He said, "I thought you did that six months ago." I said, "I did, but I'm just now realizing what I've done." Plus, I was beginning to get letters from readers saying, "We can't wait to see what happens to the Blossoms next," and it was like, what happens next is everybody dies.

Then I said, "I think I can bring them back to life." Ed said, "Call Olga." Olga had left for the weekend. George had left for the weekend. And I said, "If I'm going to bring these characters back to life by Monday, I've got to get started." So I went to the word processor and I rewrote the whole last half of the book. I worked from Friday noon to Friday midnight, got up Saturday and wrote till midnight, got up at dawn on Sunday and wrote till six o'clock, and I was finished. My husband and I went to a picnic that night, and someone asked me how my writing was going, and I said, "I'm exhausted. I've spent the whole weekend bringing characters back to life." She said, "Oh, that sounds just like 'Dallas.'"

One of the difficult things about writing is that there are no rules. You can't say a book must have sixty pages, because it can have three hundred or twenty-four. You can't say a book must have three characters—a book can have one or two or five hundred. So what you have to do, as a writer, is to make your own rules. By rules I mean, what works for you. Many times, this is a costly procedure because you sometimes have to do it the wrong way to find out that won't work.

It works for me to have a book take place in a very short period of time—one or two days. A couple of my books have taken place in twenty-four hours. It just gives me an immediacy that I don't get when I have to start a chapter with "Three months later, he still had not . . . "

It works for me to get rid of the parents. I'm not the first writer to make this discovery, but I don't know any writer who has done it with more verve than I. I've sent parents to Ohio to work, to Detroit to seek work, to Europe on holiday, to Hunter City to give birth. I favored occupations like truck driving, turquoise mining, and country and western singing, and I fell back on pneumonia, plane crashes, and coal mine disasters. In *The Pinballs,* I got rid of six parents in two and a half pages, which may be a record—certainly something for other writers to shoot for.

It works for me to have either one character or three characters. If I can pick how many characters I'm going to have, I always pick three—two girls and a boy or two boys and a girl. These are my favorite kinds of books to write because I can jump from one character to another. The Blossom books started out as three-character books, but then I decided to take the point of view of Mud and Ralphie and the vulture lady and anybody else that came along. These books got so complicated that I had to physically lay them out. I have a twenty-four-chapter kitchen table, and when I'd reach a certain point in the books, I'd go in the kitchen and lay them out, chapter by chapter. And I'd say, "Oh, I've got too much about this character—I'll move this part back here—and I don't have enough about Ralphie, I'll put something in about right here."

In the one-character book there will be other characters, of course—but I never take their point of view. These are straightforward. I take my main character and throw him or her into some sort of crisis. I know where I'm going because I have to solve the crisis.

Coast to Coast is a one-character book, although it didn't start out with a crisis as my other one-character books, such as *Cracker Jackson* and *The 18th Emergency,* did. It started in my living room. I had wanted to write a book about flying ever since I started to write, but the only plot I could think of was a plane having engine trouble and crashing, and that didn't appeal to me. So one night I had the glimmer of a plot—a grandfather and his granddaughter have to fly across country in an old airplane. I mentioned it to my husband, and within minutes maps were stretched out on the living room floor and it was, "When do you want to leave?" I didn't want to do it, but I finally said, "All right, you be the old grandfather and I'll be the attractive young girl."

We left on the trip in March. We had our choice of taking luggage or our dog since it's a small plane. We opted for the dog. We both knew there would be times when we wouldn't be speaking to each other and we'd need the dog to talk to. Well, I crossed the U.S. with a note pad in my lap, taking down everything we saw and did, and when I got home, I started writing. I wrote for two or three years. Editors came and went, and I still couldn't get the book right. The last editor read the manuscript and said, "What you need to do is put a new chapter on the front and take off the last two chapters." I thought, "What an idiot. The book starts slow and what good will it do to put another chapter there? And the last two chapters are my best." I fumed for a week, and then I put a new chapter on the front and took off the last two chapters. I don't know why, but it worked.

I have to have the names right or the characters won't evolve. The name Bingo came to me in the middle of a Blossom book. I was looking for a name for a minor character, and I liked the name Bingo too much to waste it. I went back to my book, and then it came to me how he got the name Bingo. When he was born the doctor said, "Bingo!" It came to me that later Bingo would say to his mom, "Mom, he wasn't naming me, he probably said that every time a baby popped into the world." Later he would write in his diary, "Who knows what kind of person I might have become if the doctor had said, 'Richard.'"

One of the things that interests me about young people is what they're reading. When I was writing *Bingo's Guide to Romance,* I asked a girl who was about Bingo's age, what they were reading in school. She said,"*The Red Badge of Courage,*" and I immediately got a copy. I had read the book years before, but this time I read it through Bingo's eyes, and it was a completely different experience. I had been at the point where I could think like Bingo and talk like Bingo, but this was the ultimate—I could read like Bingo.

I have, by now, probably used every single thing that has happened to me or my husband or our kids. One time when my daughter was in second grade, she called home. Now, when my children went to school, I went to the typewriter, and it wouldn't have occurred to me to stop writing to answer the phone. So the family had a secret ring when there was trouble. They would let the phone ring twice, hang up, dial again. So anytime I heard two rings, silence, then more rings, I answered the phone. Everybody in the world has the same secret ring.

The ring came one morning. I picked up the phone and my daughter was crying so hard she could barely speak. "Mom, the principal wants to see you." I said, "Oh, what's happened?" "Just come." Bang. I clicked off the Smith Corona and went to the principal's office, where I was no stranger. My daughter was on one side of the desk, weeping. Her best friend was on the other side, also weeping, and on the principal's desk was a drill that I recognized as coming from my husband's workshop. I had noticed that morning that her bookbag was heavy but I hadn't thought to say, "You don't have a drill in there, do you?" What had happened was that Nan and her best friend had always been in the same room, but this year they were in side-by-side rooms. It had occurred to them that it would be a good idea to drill a hole in the school wall so they could pass secret notes to each other. At the time I didn't think, "Oh, this is funny—I'll use it in a book one day." It was an interruption to my writing, rather than an asset.

The first piece of advice I got about writing was in third grade. Miss Stroup told us, "Write about what you know." I thought that was the stupidest piece of advice I had ever heard. It might be fine to write about what you know if you're Lindbergh, but if you were a girl growing up in rural North Carolina by a cotton mill, you'd better make up some stuff—which I did.

What nobody told me back then is why you write about what you know, and I finally figured it out for myself. The greatest asset that an author has is authority. The two words go together—author and authority. When you write about what you know, you write with authority. One of the greatest gifts an author can give to a reader is the feeling, "This author knows what she's talking about," which is really what authority is.

A couple of years ago I went to Keene, New Hampshire, to a conference, and when I got there I discovered that Robert McCloskey might come and get a special award. That was all I could think about. I mean, you think of the person you would want to meet more than anybody, and that's how I felt about Robert McCloskey.

Well, he came, and I sat in the audience and listened to him read *Make Way for Ducklings*. As I listened, I could remember sitting in that barracks apartment reading that book to my daughters, in a time when there was no hope I could ever meet this man, there was no hope that I could publish a book. And now here I was on the same program with him. It seemed a monument to what hanging in there can do for you.

After he read, he took questions from the audience, and someone said, "How do you see your books in the grand scheme of children's literature?" He answered with great charm and modesty, "Oh, my books were just ladders to lead children to other books." And that stayed in my mind and stayed in my mind and finally I realized the reason it stayed in my mind was because that's what our books are. Sometimes kids write and ask for a sequel to a book, and even if I started writing that minute, by the time I finished the book, the child would be on up the ladder and out of reach. I had a letter from a teacher that meant a lot to me, and she told me of a boy who hadn't been much of a reader, but he liked my books. "Now," she said, "he's gone on to Roald Dahl." She said he'd even read Donald Trump—which made me think my ladder was up against the wrong building that day.

At any rate, I've come to be very fond of the idea of myself as a ladder maker, and I hope that you, who are in the same business, will become fond of yourselves as ladder makers too.

GENERAL COMMENTARY

Betsy Hearne

SOURCE: Introduction to *Betsy Byars,* in *The Zena Sutherland Lectures, 1983-1992,* edited by Betsy Hearne, Clarion Books, 1993, pp. 206-09.

Betsy Byars's 1992 Autobiography, *The Moon and I,* is the best possible introduction to her work. She can no more resist telling a good story, even on herself, than fly. Actually, she flies, too, with the full credential of a pilot's license. Perhaps lifting over those clouds has contributed to a perspective that makes her one of the finest serio-comic writers in children's literature. Beginning with the Newbery Award for *The Summer of the Swans* in 1971, Betsy Byars has won enough awards, both critical and children's choice, to fill up columns of small print in several authors' biography series. Her fiction, book after book, has been included on the notable lists of major review journals and professional organizations, as well as on the programming of after-school television specials.

There's a clue to this success in one of Byars's recollections: "When I was young, I was mainly interested in having as much fun as possible." Somehow, she's kept that in mind for the children who comprise her audience. Byars's novels seem to reconcile that old polarity between the great literary works children won't read and the popular-appeal books so many of them cherish; here's a good writer whom children love to read.

Who among us, child or child-at-heart, could fail to identify with the likes of Mouse Farley in *The 18th Emergency,* the victim who must ultimately go forth alone and face his fate at a bully's hands? Marv Hammerman, the biggest boy in the sixth grade, is out to get Mouse for labeling him "Neanderthal Man," and we feel Mouse's agonizing suspense as he waits for vengeance to pounce. Comedy is tricky: too light, and it lacks substance; too dark, and it lacks balance. Try *The 18th Emergency* for substantial balance.

Byars is well known for her ability to render sad situations from a good-humored protagonist's perspective. *The Burning Questions of Bingo Brown* is a poignantly funny book about the first love between two classmates whose teacher is so smitten with an aerobics instructor that he attempts suicide after being rejected. Through classroom conversations and dynamics, which Bingo observes during his perpetual journeys to the pencil sharpener, readers gradually learn that it is the adult, rather than the pre-adolescent, who is losing control. Yet, neither is stereotyped, despite a prototypical middle-schooler "who had been in love three times in one day and had already had four mixed-sex conversations!" There's even a modicum of irony here, which is rare in humor for children. Bingo's nickname, applied because of the doctor's pronouncement upon delivering him, strikes Bingo as being more ludicrous than lucky. When a classroom drawing comes up, "Bingo

knew his name would not be picked. He had never been chosen for anything in his life." In this event, he's proven wrong.

Byars has described her childhood as "uneventful." Reading one of her own accounts might even convince you to call her life "ordinary." Then you'll find yourself smiling at her extraordinary descriptions of an early hobby or perhaps, later, an obsession with boys. Here's an example of the hobby: "I was making my own clothes by the second grade, although I have a vague recollection of not being allowed to wear them out of the yard. I could make a gathered skirt in fifteen minutes. I sewed fast, without patterns, and with great hope and determination, and that is approximately the same way that I write." What she does in her writing is turn the ordinary inside out so that we see the inside seams—the quirks of what appear to be "average" people.

The first title in her Blossom series, *The Not-Just-Anybody Family,* could describe the distinctive characters in many of the thirty-four Byars books now in print, characters realized with such special effect that any reader who identifies with them feels suddenly a lot less like "just anybody." All this is rendered without a breath of didacticism; plot and dialogue do all the talking, from the beginning-to-read Golly sisters series through a versatile range of fiction including popular series books which can bridge that yawning gap between Francine Pascal and Rosemary Sutcliff. Whether she's handling contemporary metaphor with flair in *The Cartoonist* and *The TV Kid,* or dealing with problems of abuse and neglect in *The Pinballs* and *Cracker Jackson,* or juggling points of view among Blossom family members and their dog Mud, each narrative rings with a personal voice. Even in her series, more of the same is never quite the same.

For in vivid details lies Byars's greatest strength. Who else has described the writing process with such fresh perception as she does in her new autobiography? I myself have been sustained through several midnight deadlines by Betsy Byars's description of writing a book: "Walk to refrigerator . . . 11 seconds. Take miniature Snickers from freezer . . . 3 seconds. Warm Snicker in microwave . . . 16 seconds. Return eating Snicker . . . 11 seconds. Total elapsed time . . . 41 seconds."

My personal favorite of all Betsy Byars's books is *The Midnight Fox.* Lest I be charged with nostalgia, for it came out in 1968 and was one of the first books I reviewed during my first year as a professional reviewer, I reread it this week, twenty-four years later, and found myself moved once more both to laughter and to tears. I laughed at Tom's imagining himself, on an unwelcome visit to a farm, stampeded by two hundred chickens, "flattened on the ground while the lead hen snatches the egg from my crushed hand and returns in triumph to the coop." I cried as Tom deals tragedy a sleight of hand by uncaging a doomed fox. Experiencing those extreme emotions in such close proximity is a sure sign that a reader is in Betsy Byars country, roaming around in an imagination populated with ordinary people whose individualistic traits and hardearned bits of wisdom make us see things in a different way. Welcome tonight to Betsy Byars country.

TITLE COMMENTARY

BEANS ON THE ROOF (1988)

Kirkus Reviews

SOURCE: A review of *Beans on the Roof,* in *Kirkus Reviews,* Vol. 56, No. 1, September 1, 1988, p. 1320.

In a novel [**Beans on the Roof**] that is hardly more difficult than an easy reader (though longer), the Beans are a typical Byars family: Papa sells fruits and vegetables; they live in an apartment house from which they wave at neighbors across the street; and they are distinguished by their common-sense and love for one another rather than by their cleverness.

Sensibly, no one is allowed on the roof, which is reserved for a neighbor's rabbits and the laundry; but today Anna Bean is up there—with permission—writing a poem to be included in a book being complied at school. Soon the other Bean children join her—they too will write poems. George wants to write "the best poem in the world," but has trouble with writer's block; Little Jenny's brief poem comes more easily. Even Mrs. Bean produces a poem—not great, she says, "but it is a true one." Anna is proud of her own effort, but it is not picked for the book after all; still, as her father points out, the important thing is that she was the first Bean to write a poem; if she goes on writing, one may yet be in a book.

The way Byars can explore a loving family—and the act of creation—through such a simple device is little short of miraculous. She holds attention; she makes

every word count; she devises believable, childlike verse—and does it all with a clear eye, a gently amused voice, and disarming affection. Young readers should be delighted.

Nancy Vasilakis

SOURCE: A review of *Beans on the Roof,* in *Horn Book Magazine,* Vol. 65, No. 1, January-February, 1989, pp. 63-4.

Without the slightest hint of condescension Betsy Byars lowers herself to the eye level of her exuberant young characters in this winning book [**Beans on the Roof**] that could easily sit on the reading shelf of any second-grade classroom. When elder sister Anna Bean is allowed the previously forbidden pleasure of visiting the roof of their apartment building for the express purpose of composing a poem, all the younger Beans suddenly find themselves infused with the poetic spirit. The youngest, Jenny, is the first to be struck by inspiration. "I love the roof, / And that's the truth," she recites to the caged rabbits and pigeons who live there. Even Father Bean, home from work, ventures a song. Tension is maintained by brother George's difficulties in finding his own muse—he fears he'll be the only Bean without a roof poem—and by Anna's tearful reaction when her poem isn't among those chosen for school publication. Her family quickly gathers around, and their solicitous support gives her the moral courage to persist in her dreams of becoming a poet someday. Assiduously devoid of ethnic labeling, the story nevertheless adroitly reiterates the immigrant American dream. Although the Beans' grandfather never learned to write his name, their mother never finished school, and their father is a humble purveyor of fruits and vegetables, education is revered, and the children all aspire to a better life.

BINGO BROWN AND THE LANGUAGE OF LOVE (1989)

Carolyn K. Jenks

SOURCE: A review of *Bingo Brown and the Language of Love,* in *Horn Book Magazine,* Vol. 65, No. 5, September-October, 1989, p. 619.

Bingo Brown continues his poignantly funny journey through puberty, earnestly immersed in the awesome task of understanding himself, other people, and life as soon as possible. He has tried to stop asking the questions that filled his journal during sixth grade in *The Burning Questions of Bingo Brown*; the following summer the journal is still there, but it has changed to a score-keeping device: "Trials of Today" and "Triumphs of Today." Life is swarming with the former. His first love has moved to Bixby, Oklahoma, and when his mother discovers an item on the telephone bill for $54.29, he may no longer call her. Cici, a "big blonde" who is older than he, comes into his life, and Bingo is bewildered to discover that his outwardly macho friend Billy would like to have her come into *his* life instead. Bingo finds himself in the amazing position of counseling Billy on the subject. While all this is going on, Bingo's mother, who has finally gotten a job that she loves, discovers that she's pregnant; this state is one she would have been happy about ten years earlier, but it is now a traumatic event that shakes up the family structure for a time. Bingo gradually realizes that "the language of love" is not only about the way to talk to a girl but also about understanding the love language of others, which sometimes needs to be translated. He sees that this mysterious language is a many-splendored thing and that no one of any age knows how to do it right all the time. Bingo may someday learn to lighten up; meanwhile, Byars's sense of humor makes us laugh without ever ridiculing his sensitive, emerging personality.

Language Arts

SOURCE: A review of *Bingo Brown and the Language of Love,* in *Language Arts,* Vol. 67, No. 3, March, 1990, p. 300.

In this sequel [*Bingo Brown and the Language of Love*] to *The Burning Questions of Bingo Brown,* almost-twelve-year-old Bingo falls out of love and back in love with Melissa, a classmate who has moved to Oklahoma. He agrees to cook supper for his parents for thirty-six nights to pay off his long distance phone bill ($54.29) for calls to Oklahoma. He survives the unwanted attentions of Melissa's friend, Cici, "much too big and too blond . . . more like a high school girl—no, make that a college girl." And he weathers the shock of hearing that his mother is pregnant ("He had assumed that he would be child enough for any family.") All in all, as Bingo muses at the end, "he had learned to dog-paddle in the mainstream of life."

The author uses humor to soften the preadolescent angst she has created for Bingo. There's a mock maturity in his inner monologue that provides distance on his problems and allows for nonstop one-liners. Byars typically brings remarkable insight to her characterizations of pre-teen boys, and Bingo is no exception. A two-parent household, however, is something of a departure. This one is offbeat and thoroughly engaging.

BINGO BROWN, GYPSY LOVER (1990)

Nancy Vasilakis

SOURCE: A review of *Bingo Brown, Gypsy Lover,* in *Horn Book Magazine,* Vol. 66, No. 4, July-August, 1990, p. 453.

Bingo Brown's problems with the opposite sex continue to fester in this latest leg [*Bingo Brown, Gypsy Lover*] of the sensitive youth's disaster-prone journey through early adolescence. When his long-distance girlfriend, Melissa, informs him of his resemblance to the hero of the romance novel she is reading, the news sends him rushing to a bookstore for a copy of *Gypsy Lover.* There he encounters another girl, Boots. "It could not be pleasant to be named for footwear," Bingo thinks sympathetically. Boots complicates his life by taking an avid interest in his reading matter and engaging him in excruciating telephone conversations that leave him exhausted and speechless. Meanwhile, his mother informs him that the baby she is expecting will be a boy, to be named James. Bingo is distressed that his new sibling will be honored with the dignified name that has eluded him. Most of the same characters that populated *Bingo Brown and the Language of Love* (Viking) return to continue their humorous assaults on Bingo's tender psyche. While the nostalgic self-parody of the humor may hold more appeal for adults, middle-graders who enjoyed the previous volumes will no doubt nod in appreciative recognition over Bingo's predicaments. The tenuous plot revolves around Bingo's search for the perfect Christmas present for Melissa—something as good as the handsewn notebook holder she has given him. The only tense sequence concerns the premature birth of his baby brother, though there is never any question that all will end well, or that Bingo will continue to wrestle in amusing fashion with myriad self-doubts before it does.

HURRAY FOR THE GOLLY SISTERS (1990)

Carolyn K. Jenks

SOURCE: A review of *Hurray for the Golly Sisters!,* in *Horn Book Magazine,* Vol. 67, No. 1, January-February, 1991, p. 63.

The wacky actresses of the frontier, May-May and Rose, participate in five action-packed adventures in this sequel to *The Golly Sisters Go West* [*Hurray for the Golly Sisters*]. In one town on their traveling road show itinerary, May-May decides to use pigs instead of rabbits in her magic act; when she makes them "disappear," she realizes that pigs are not nearly as quiet as rabbits. "'Well, May-May, at least we know one thing. We know why magicians use rabbits.' 'Yes,' said May-May, 'rabbits don't go *Weeeeee.*'" These resilient sisters brave wide rivers and mysterious swamps, making sure that the show will not only go on but will be filled with innovative bits and fine style. Sue Truesdell's ink-and-watercolor illustrations are dashing and full of humor. As May-May and Rose are discussing the importance of getting genuine cheers at the end of their show, the accompanying pictures reveal them to be having tea, complete with china and tablecloth on a trunk near their covered wagon, while their horse eats May-May's red flowered hat. A funny, solid book for early readers.

THE SEVEN TREASURE HUNTS (1991)

Elizabeth S. Watson

SOURCE: A review of *The Seven Treasure Hunts*, in *Horn Book Magazine*, Vol. 67, No. 1, July, 1991, pp. 151-52.

That rare commodity—a chapter book for second grade—is as much sought after as any of the treasures of the title. This book [*The Seven Treasure Hunts*] is a good example of the form: it is accessible, of suitable length, and built around a theme familiar to the reader. Byars's unerring ear for dialogue is evident throughout, and the treasures themselves speak to her understanding of her audience. A Matchbox car with one wheel missing, two bird feathers, and a balloon from the dentist's office that says "I was a good patient" are three of those possessions. Each chapter deals with a different aspect of the game, but the whole adventure is played out in one day with high good humor as Jackson and his friend Goat make up a series of treasure hunts for each other, complete with clues and "tricky" maps. Although illustrations bridge the gap for the inexperienced reader from the heavily illustrated easy reader to the novel, the ones in this book rely a bit heavily on Charles Schulz's famous characters for inspiration. While the book would otherwise be a sure recommendation, there is one problem that is worrisome.

Reference is made in both text and illustrations to the unsupervised use of matches by a child. While not an important part of the plot, this detail may be cause for concern.

Bulletin of the Center for Children's Books

SOURCE: A review of *The Seven Treasure Hunts*, in *The Bulletin of the Center for Children's Books*, Vol. 44, No. 8, April, 1991, pp. 185-86.

Jackson and his friend Goat spend seven chapters [in *The Seven Treasure Hunts*] looking for secret treasures that they hide from each other—in fact, making maps and clues is most of the fun. Their game involves escapades that kids will enjoy; in one, Jackson sneaks out of piano practice, runs to Goat's house for a chocolate popsicle, and slips back in time for a successful piano lesson. In another episode, both boys sort through a huge pile of garbage for something Goat's sister has actually hidden in the freezer. The plot seems more repetitive than spontaneous, but this may prove an advantage for struggling readers, who appreciate light fare with a familiar flavor.

WANTED ... MUD BLOSSOM (1991)

Kevin Kenny

SOURCE: A review of *Wanted . . . Mud Blossom*, in *Voice of Youth Advocates*, Vol. 14, No. 3, August, 1991, p. 168.

Even for a family which is admittedly not ". . . a normal, everyday family," this week-end is bizarre by Blossom standards. A cave-dwelling friend of the Blossom's, Mad Mary, is missing, her abandoned cloth bag (containing one dead possum) and cane portend evil doings. Scooty, the class hamster entrusted to Junior for the weekend is missing and presumed consumed by Pap's dog Mud, a crime for which, in the finest Blossom tradition, he will have to stand trial. Vern is convinced that someone's out to get him, mother Vickie Blossom's new beau has stood her up because of his horse detective dealings, and the burgeoning romance between Maggie and Ralphie wavers between rapture and rupture.

Byars's fifth Blossom offering, *Wanted . . . Mud Blossom* is every bit as charming as its predecessors. Once again the undercurrent of love is evident beneath the sibling bickering, teasing, and posturing. Once again the inherent dignity of the Blossoms is showcased against a backdrop of relative familial mayhem. It is, in short, a much needed celebration of individuality, the unique, and even the eccentric. God bless the few remaining Blossoms of the world.

Like *A Blossom Promise* and the others which preceded it, *Wanted . . . Mud Blossom* is ably illustrated by Jacqueline Rogers. Accessible to most readers, fans of the series and novices alike won't be disappointed. I, however, will be disappointed if the budding romance between Ralphie and Maggie and the intriguing relationship between Pap and Mad Mary are not addressed at some hopefully not-too-distant date.

Margaret M. Burns

SOURCE: A review of *Wanted . . . Mud Blossom,* in *Horn Book Magazine,* Vol. 67, No. 5, September, 1991, p. 595.

Undaunted by earlier mishaps, that indefatigable inventor, Junior Blossom, continues his search for the absolutely perfect creation [in *Wanted . . . Mud Blossom*]. For a short time, he believes that he has discovered it: a tunnel for exercising Scooty the school hamster, who is entrusted to his care for the weekend. Unfortunately, Junior doesn't anticipate that Pap's dog Mud, with his natural canine curiosity, will demolish the structure once he catches Scooty's irresistible scent. When Junior discovers that the hamster has disappeared, he jumps to the obvious conclusion: Mud is a murderer. Mud, interested in self-preservation, seeks refuge under the porch. Meanwhile, Junior's problems are eclipsed by the suspicious disappearance of Mad Mary, cave-dwelling senior citizen and Pap's friend; Vern Blossom's secretive conversations with his friend Michael, which seem to hint that they may know more about Mad Mary than they want to admit; the budding romance between feisty Maggie Blossom and her love-struck Romeo, Ralphie; and mother Vicki Blossom's efforts to make her family appear normal when her new beau comes to call. The hilarious extravaganza reaches its climax when Mud is put on trial—in absentia, as he is still cowering under the porch—in what is surely one of the great comic sequences in recent fiction for children. Betsy Byars has a sure hand for dealing with the absurdities of human follies, deftly plotting her narrative in short chapters, each ending in a cliffhanger that leaves her audience pleading for more. Her characters in this particular series are genuine originals. As Maggie proudly states, "'We Blossoms have never been just anybody.'" And for that we can all be grateful.

THE MOON AND I (1991)

Kirkus Reviews

SOURCE: A review of *The Moon and I,* in *Kirkus Reviews,* Vol. 50, No. 7, April 1, 1992, p. 462.

An adroit blend of telling experiences from Byars's life and ingenuous confidences about her writing, linked by her friendship with a huge blacksnake ("Moon") that she first observed coiled on a porch beam at the log cabin where she writes—all recounted in the inimitably forthright, witty voice that has endeared her to readers of her 36 children's books.

Flashing back to childhood encounters with snakes and to escapades like riding "the first skateboard in the history of the world" ("Bee told me to . . . Fortunately . . . we didn't know you were supposed to stand up . . . Otherwise I wouldn't be alive today"), Byars interpolates glimpses of herself as writer (in order of importance: characters, plot, setting, "good scraps"; "Most of the other things—like theme and mood—I don't think about"). There are nifty anecdotes (emboldened by curiosity, she picks up a dead snake on the road, then panics when the bag it's in crackles), slyly revealing how her mind works while also entertaining readers with hilarious conversations, outrageous details, and pithy lists (e.g., good scraps that later turned up in books: "a woman who made varmint stew"; "puce tennis shoes").

This ebullient self-portrait is so delightfully informal that it may seem artless; actually, the dovetailing of the several elements is extraordinarily skillful, the comments on writing as sage as they are succinct. A must.

Maurice Saxby

SOURCE: A review of *The Moon and Me,* in *Magpies,* Vol. 8, No. 4, September, 1993, p. 37.

When Betsy Byars spoke in Australia in 1987, she held audiences, both young and old, spellbound. Her energy, her sheer hard work, her sense of humour, and, above all, her integrity, impressed all who met her. Since that visit Betsy Byars has written some seventeen or so novels for upper-primary readers, all of them successful.

While *The Moon and Me* is self-revelatory, especially with regard to her writing technique, this is not a conventional autobiography. It is chatty—even low key—yet robust but also strangely self-effacing and never promotional. In the context of a simple, amusing yet moving tale about the writer's love affair with Moon, a large black snake, Byars drops clues and some very direct statements about her method of writing: not just the nitty-gritty of word processing but the creativity that makes her work unique. She tells how certain characters were named—including the now-famous story of the real Marv Mammerman; how she goes about researching for a novel; and the simple truth about writing from experience. "The words *author* and *authority* go hand in hand. If an author is writing about what she knows, she is writing with authority". Better than any "writing" guide for would-be authors this is a door, left invitingly open, to the heart and mind of a woman who is a splendid writer and whom to know is a privilege.

COAST TO COAST (1992)

Judy Fink

SOURCE: A review of *Coast to Coast*, in *Voice of Youth Advocates*, Vol. 15, No. 5, December, 1992, p. 275.

Imagine flying cross-country in a small plane with your grandfather. Thirteen year old Birch never considered it until the night she finds her grandfather pouring over maps at the kitchen table, just days before the sale of his plane is to be finalized. He's already sold his house and will be moving into a retirement community. Birch coaxes her grandfather into seeking his dream of flying to California, but it's harder to get him to agree to take her along. Once convinced, they sneak off while Birch's mother is immersed in a garage sale of the grandfather's belongings. During the preparations for the sale, Birch finds a box of poems written by her grandmother, and she takes it along, hoping to get her grandfather to discuss one particularly troubling poem, written on the day of Birch's birth. During their exhilarating trip, Birch and her grandfather stop at many small airports, all the while talking about their family and about the joys of flying. Eventually Birch learns the meaning of the poem and begins to come to terms with it.

The details about flying [in *Coast to Coast*] will draw readers in, as will the loving story of friendship over the generations. As in Byars's "Blossom family" books, grandparents play a key role in the grandchild's life. . . . The integration of the poetry into the story subtly shows it as a vehicle for concise expression of complex emotions.

Lois Ringquist

SOURCE: A review of *Coast to Coast,* in *The Five Owls,* Vol. 9, No. 1, September, 1994, p. 2.

Exploration of a new territory is only one reason to take to the road. In Betsy Byars's **Coast to Coast**, it is a dream that motivates her characters to travel. Birch's grandfather has always planned to fly his old Piper Cub from his South Carolina home to California. Now he's getting old, selling his home and the plane, and it's costing him his will to live. After Birch talks Pop into a short, spur-of-the-moment flight over the beach, he decides to risk his dream—and Birch insists on going along. At first the trip seems a series of short hops over rivers and mesas, stopping often to refuel the Piper Cub, but in the end it is the trip as a whole that is important. It gives Birch perspective, makes Pop a new, happy person, and best of all, cements their special relationship.

McMUMMY (1993)

Bulletin of the Center for Children's Books

SOURCE: A review of *McMummy,* in *The Bulletin of the Center for Children's Books,* Vol. 47, No. 2, October, 1993, p. 41.

The quirky characters here—elfin-faced Mozie Mozer, his friend Batty Batson, a small-time beauty contestant named Valvoline, and a plant mutant that seems to have human and perhaps dangerous propensities—are signature Byars, though the plot seems more of a spoof than a successor to her characteristically fine-tuned seriocomic fiction. Mozie has been put in charge of a greenhouse full of travelling Professor Orloff's experimental "vegetables," one of which compels Mozie's presence with a magnetic attraction that terrifies him. The plant, in turn, seems attracted to Valvoline, who inadvertently gives it a hug during one of Mozie's visits to turn on the sprinkler system. A classic storm destroys the greenhouse; the bean pod escapes, disrupts the beauty pageant to bring Valvoline her lost lucky mustard-seed necklace, and then disintegrates into luminous scraps of green, leaving Mozie with a chance to grieve over his father's death for the first time and with two seed pods from the plant, just like Jack and the Beanstalk. There are lots of story elements here, including Mozie's friendship with Batty, his budding crush on Valvoline, his difficulties with a boy for whom he babysits, his anxiety to please Professor Orloff, his affection for a cat that fell out of an airplane into his yard, his loneliness for his father, and his rapport with his mother. Unfortunately, the fantasy creates an overload and the novel [*McMummy*] becomes fragmented, though kids will love the individual scenes, which are goodnatured and goofy to the point of slapstick. *Little Shop of Horrors* gets an allusion; *The BFG's* "human beans" do not.

Books for Keeps

SOURCE: A review of *McMummy,* in *Books for Keeps,* No. 97, March, 1996, p. 9.

I've never trusted plants, especially those that grow taller than me. This book [*McMummy*] suggests my mistrust is soundly based. A weird shaped seed pod which seems to have a beating heart (but then who wouldn't when cuddled by the local beauty queen?) keeps on growing, especially when the beauty's lost necklace turns up. Apart from a rather wobbly ending this makes growing runner beans in the classroom seem a hazardous pursuit.

THE DARK STAIRS (1994)

Kirkus Reviews

SOURCE: A review of *The Dark Stairs: A Herculeah Jones Mystery,* in *Kirkus Reviews,* Vol. 62, No. 16, August 15, 1994, p. 1122.

A versatile standby (1971 Newbery) brings her usual brisk aplomb to a projected series about a self-reliant early teen whose first adventure [*The Dark Stairs*] is closer in spirit, despite her name, to the Nancy Drews recalled by its jacket than to the exploits of Indiana Jones. Neither of Herculeah Jones's divorced parents—Dad's a cop, Mom's a PI—welcomes her participation in discovering the role played by the hulking "Moloch" in an apparent death ten years ago in the empty old mansion known as Dead Oaks. Still, the girl and her sidekick, Meat, explore the house, where someone traps Herculeah; fortunately, she's able to burst open the nailed-shut door. Finding out that the Moloch is Mrs. Jones's client, they eavesdrop on a tape of an interview between the two and learn his identity. In the end, Herculeah not only deduces what happened years ago but locates a missing body by inadvertently tumbling down a secret stairway. For sophisticated readers, it might have been more fun if Byars had chosen to parody the

genre; instead, she plays it almost straight, although there are occasional touches of wit in the pert dialogue and descriptions. Meanwhile, she establishes characters with a sure touch and provides enough spooky atmosphere to bring readers back for more.

A promising start for a series that could easily become a popular alternative to mass-market mysteries.

Beverly Youree

SOURCE: A review of *The Dark Stairs,* in *Voice of Youth Advocates,* Vol. 17, No. 6, February, 1995, p. 336.

Here is a new female detective for younger teen readers. Herculeah Jones comes by her sleuthing naturally, with her father a police detective and her mother a private investigator. Even though her parents are divorced, she still solicits help from both. With her reluctant, and sometime comical, sidekick Meat, she pursues the mystery of what happened to Mr. Crewell who has been missing for years. Even though several years ago the police received an anonymous tip that Mr. Crewell had been murdered, they could not find a body. Now, with the mysterious "Moloch" in town and Herculeah's hair starting to frizzle—a sure sign that something is about to happen—she searches for who the "Moloch" is and what really happened at the Dead Oak's estate. Full of suspense, this [*The Dark Stairs*] contains all the elements of this genre. Herculeah proves to be a remakable sleuth by listening in on her mother's tape recorder where she recorded her interview with the Moloch, getting her father to do some of her leg work, and talking Meat into standing guard—even though he falls asleep on the job—while she slips into the deserted mansion and is nearly caught. Truly a light-hearted suspense story for mystery fans.

ANT PLAYS BEAR (1997)

Hazel Rochman

SOURCE: A review of *Ant Plays Bear,* in *Booklist,* September 1, 1997, p. 116.

With the same tenderness and comedy found in *My Brother, Ant* (1996), this easy-to-read chapter book [*Ant Plays Bear*] includes four more episodes about a boy and his younger brother, Ant. As they are about to go to sleep, Ant makes his exasperated, scowling brother check on that "something" at the window. Another time, Ant pesters his brother to play bear and then gets scared of his own game. One small episode captures a whole range of emotions: when his friend comes over to play, the older boy starts off by being embarrassed by Ant's silliness but then ends up protecting Ant when the visitor acts mean. The first-person narrative, the perfectly tuned dialogue ("Are you being a dog again? . . . Well, stop it. My new friend is coming over. I don't want him to think my brother is a dog"), and [Marc] Simont's small, haunting pictures in line and watercolor capture the exasperation in the sibling scenarios, and the love. In the tradition of the award-winning easy readers by Sendak, Lobel, and others, Byars and Simont continue to make simplicity a delight.

Additional coverage of Byars' life and career is contained in the following sources published by the Gale Group: *Authors and Artists for Young Adults,* Vol. 19; *Dictionary of Literary Biography,* Vol. 52; *Major Authors and Illustrators for Children and Young Adults; Major 20th-Century Writers,* Vol. 1; *Something about the Author,* Vols. 4, 46, 80; *Something about the Author Autobiography Series,* Vol. 1.

Eleanor Frances Cameron
1912-1996

American pioneer of children's literature criticism, author of children's, young adult, and adult books, and librarian.

Major works include *The Wonderful Flight to the Mushroom Planet* (1954), *The Green and Burning Tree: On the Writing and Enjoyment of Children's Books* (1969), *A Room Made of Windows* (1971), *The Court of the Stone Children* (1973), *To The Green Mountains* (1975), *The Seed and the Vision: On the Writing and Appreciation of Children's Books* (1993).

Major works about Cameron: "WLB Biography: Eleanor Cameron" (S.V. Keenan, *Wilson Library Bulletin,* 37, October 1962), "The Depths of All She Is: Eleanor Cameron" (Perry Nodelman, *Children's Literature Association Quarterly,* Winter 1980), *The Fantasy Tradition in American Literature* (Brian Attebery, 1980), "Beyond Explanation, and Beyond Inexplicability," in *Beyond Silence* (Perry Nodelman, *Children's Literature* 12, 1980).

For further information on Cameron's life and works, see *CLR,* Volume 1.

INTRODUCTION

Eleanor Cameron's writing for children demonstrates outstanding creativity and versatility, and is especially noteworthy for its richness of characterization and setting. Her works spanned the creation of other worlds, including those of the fast-paced, action-filled *Mushroom Planet* books and the more sophisticated worlds of the past and present in her "Julia Redfern" books. Cameron's commentary on children's literature shows her to have been an expert critic, well read in critical theory and able to handle competently many styles of literary interpretation.

BIOGRAPHICAL INFORMATION

Cameron was born in Winnipeg, Manitoba, Canada, on March 23, 1912, the only child of English-born parents, Henry and Florence Butler. In 1915, the family moved to South Charleston, Ohio, and in 1918, to

Berkeley, California. "I have been preoccupied with the craft of writing since the age of eleven, and since my teens with the question of what makes a book memorable," the author once commented. She spent much time at the Carnegie Library in Berkeley, and decided as early as twelve to become a professional writer and to work as a librarian until her writing could support her. When Cameron was sixteen, she moved to Los Angeles where she finished high school, then attended UCLA for two years and the Los Angeles Art Center School for one. During this period, she also worked as a clerk in the literature department of the Los Angeles Public Library. In 1934 she married printer and publisher Ian Stuart Cameron. From 1936 to 1942 Cameron worked at the Los Angeles City School Library helping teachers choose books for classroom use, then worked as a research librarian in advertising until the birth of her son, David, in 1945. In 1956, she returned to this career until she became a full-time writer. She often contributed both commentary and criticism for *Horn Book, Wilson Library Bulletin,* and *Childen's Literature Association Quarterly*, and spoke frequently at children's literature conferences. Cameron died on October 11, 1996, in Monterey, California.

MAJOR WORKS

In Cameron's only novel for adults, *Unheard Music* (1950), her career as a librarian provided both setting and characters. This novel was, in the author's words, "a critical success if not a financial one." She turned to writing for children when her son David asked her to write him a story "about himself and his best friend and how they would build a spaceship and go off and find a planet just their size, just big enough to explore in a day or two." The answer to his request was *The Wonderful Flight to the Mushroom Planet* (1954), followed by *The Stowaway to the Mushroom Planet* (1956), *Mr. Bass's Planetoid* (1958), *A Mystery for Mr. Bass* (1960) and *Time and Mr. Bass* (1967). Before Cameron finished writing the "Mushroom Planet" books, she had also published four other tales: *The Terrible Churnadryne* (1959), a combination of mystery and fantasy set in the California coastal town of Redwood Cove, a sequel called *The*

Mysterious Christmas Shell (1961), an original fairy tale called *The Beast with the Magical Horn* (1963), and a mystery called *A Spell is Cast* (1964). In 1969 Cameron published *The Green and Burning Tree: On the Writing and Enjoyment of Children's Books.* This collection of critical essays marked a turning point in Cameron's career as a writer. The author said that the book "has seemed to divide my work into two so decidedly that some have told me they were surprised to find it was the same Cameron who wrote the earlier books as the late. What has happened is that I have now been basing (but only basing) them on childhood experience, using an actual situation as the takeoff into events that never happened in real life, whereas the earlier books are wholly imaginative."

The new direction of Cameron's writing led to the "Julia Redfern" books, the first of which, *A Room Made of Windows*, was published in 1971. Set in Berkeley, where Cameron herself lived as a child, it is the story of a young girl's growth in understanding and awareness of her family and of others around her. Both Julia Redfern's desire to be a writer and the changes in her family are reminiscent of events in Cameron's own early life. In Zena Sutherland's review of *A Room Made of Windows,* (*Saturday Review*) she commented: "The writing makes no concession to a young audience, but is intricate, thoughtful, and mature." More "Julia Redfern" books would follow, but meanwhile, Cameron produced two other books: *The Court of the Stone Children* (1973), called by critic Brian Attebery ". . . [one of the two] most satisfying American time fantasies to date" and 1974 winner of the National Book Award; and *To The Green Mountains* (1975), a complex treatment of the adolescent's need to face what *is* rather than delude themselves. *To The Green Mountains,*first written as a one-act play in 1947, also deals with the necessity of human beings not trying to possess one another. Cameron then went on with the second "Julia Redfern" book, publishing *Julia and the Hand of God* in 1977. Since this second book deals with Julia as a younger character than does *A Room Made of Windows*, there are fewer subplots, resulting in a tighter, even more unified novel. In 1980, a second time fantasy, *Beyond Silence,* was published. The intricacies of Cameron's understanding of time are most evident in *Beyond Silence* and *The Court of the Stone Children.* Perry Nodelman, in his essay "Beyond Explanation, and Beyond Inexplicability, in *Beyond Silence*" said, "Both *The Court of the Stone Children* and *Beyond Silence* begin with a set of three quotations, one about how the past still exists, one about how the future is happening now, and one about

limitations of our conceptions of reality. The idea that the ordinary perception of time's passage ignores a larger reality underlies and gives order to all of Cameron's work." Cameron herself says of time fantasies, "Time is not a thread at all, but a globe." *Beyond Silence* has proven unsettling to some readers and has occasioned more unfavorable criticism than Cameron's other books. The last two "Julia Redfern" books appeared next, *That Julia Redfern* (1982) and *Julia's Magic* (1984), and are about Julia's younger years. Like the first two "Julia" books, they are richly textured stories. A reviewer for the *Bulletin of the Center for Children's Books* said of *That Julia Redfern*: "This has more substance than most of the many stage-of-childhood books for children, since it has depth and consistency of characterization, strong dialogue and exposition, and a credible change and growth in the protagonist." *The Seed and the Vision: On the Writing and Appreciation of Children's Books,* a collection of eleven critical essays exploring aspects of the writing, appreciation, and analysis of fiction for children, was published in 1993. Cameron, knowing that J. D. Stahl had differing opinions on some theories of literary criticism from her own, still asked his opinion of her book, for which he eventually wrote the foreword. He commented on how typical this action was of her, saying that Cameron had a "questing, courageous mind."

CRITICAL RECEPTION

Cameron's first book for children, *The Wonderful Flight to the Mushroom Planet,* in which the author skillfully combines fantasy and scientific fact, was well received by reviewers. Alice Brook McGuire (*Saturday Review*) compared Cameron's skill at characterization favorably with Ellen MacGregor's, writing, "A new favorite has come to challenge the popularity of the eccentric and amusing 'Miss Pickerell!'" The second book of the series, *The Stowaway to the Mushroom Planet,* has proved to be especially popular, so much so that in 1979, twenty-three years after it first appeared, it was one of the 100 best sellers on the Scholastic Booklist. The five books in the "Mushroom Planet" series are light and entertaining, and according to the author, were written "with a twinkle of the eye in the tone." The series is both fantasy and science fiction, but manages to incorporate the true scientific wonders of the universe in a way that has appealed to young readers for more than one generation.

Reviewers frequently point out Cameron's strengths in characterization and in the description of setting. Many of her books feature the California countryside which she knew as a child. "Place does not give theme," Cameron said, ". . . but without the power of place, without that discovery of a special country of the mind right for this tale, the story could not have been told at all. . . . And yet, it seems to me that in instance after instance it is place that releases whatever feeling is absolutely essential to the writer to enable him to carry out his work of creation. And very often, one discovers, this place lies in childhood or is somehow, perhaps most obscurely, related to childhood."

In *Beyond Silence,* Cameron was accused by some of being "woodenly predictable" and of "hackneyed writing", but not all critics shared this opinion. Perry Nodelman credited *Beyond Silence* with the unstated motive of presenting a psychologically convincing statement about the limitations of psychology. *The Seed and the Vision* met with mixed reviews. It has been called both "an impressive book, scholarly but not pedantic. . . . a book both thoughtful and provocative," and "What she's written is not really a critical book at all. It is more like a 'commonplace book': a collection of interesting observations and passages recorded in a journal."

Overall, Cameron is recognized as an author with tremendous strengths, both in the technical aspects of writing as well as in her comprehension of the world of children and young adults. Her abilities allowed her to create unusually satisfying stories which convey the somber moments in a child's life and provoke serious thought, while at the same time providing humor and enjoyment for young readers.

AWARDS AND HONORS

Eleanor Cameron was honored with the Kerlan Award from the University of Minnesota in 1985 for her body of work. Her reputation as an accomplished children's author and astute critic of children's literature led to her selection to deliver the annual Whittall Lecture at the Library of Congress in 1977. Other honors include: membership on editorial boards of *Cricket: The Magazine for Children* and *Children's Literature in Education*; member, advisory board for the Study of Children's Literature at Simmons College (Boston); judge, 1980 National Book Awards; Boston Globe-Horn Book Award, 1971, for *A Room Made of Windows*; National Book Award, 1974, for *The Court of the Stone Children*; finalist, National Book Award, 1976, for *To the Green Mountains*; the previous three books were named ALA Notable

Books as was *Julia and the Hand of God*, 1977; Junior Literary Guild selections: *The Wonderful Flight to the Mushroom Planet* (1954), *The Stowaway to the Mushroom Planet* (1956), *Mr. Bass's Planetoid* (1958), *The Terrible Churnadryne* (1959), *The Mysterious Christmas Shell* (1961), *A Spell is Cast* (1964), *The Court of the Stone Children* (1973) and *Julia and the Hand of God* (1977); Commonwealth Club of California's Silver Medal Award, 1964, for *A Spell is Cast,* and 1969, for *The Green and Burning Tree;* 1965 Annual Award for Distinguished Contributions to the Field of Children's Literature.

AUTHOR COMMENTARY

Eleanor Cameron

SOURCE: "Writing From Experience," in *The Five Owls,* Vol. V, No. 3, January-February, 1991, pp. 45-7.

Once upon a time my mother and my son David and I went back to Berkeley in search of that brown-shingled bungalow with the white roof where my mother and I lived when I was eleven and twelve. It had been next to the big barn-red house on the corner of Berkeley Way and Grove Street, the big house where I was compelled to have Rhiannon Moore live, Julia's mentor in *A Room Made of Windows,* the fourth novel in the sequence of books I have written about Julia Redfern.

We drove along Grove Street, just a block or so over from University Avenue—and there it still was, the brown bungalow, looking smaller somehow, lower than I remembered. And it was on this first return after so many years, to a neighborhood I hadn't seen since I was twelve, that I found Addie's house along Berkeley Way. Addie it was who had the frightening father who lay in wait for me at the top of the dark stairs, and who, in *Room,* got drunk and overturned the dining room table all set for dinner. How much of this was swimming in my head at the time, beginning to coalesce ready for writing, I can't recall, because *A Room Made of Windows* took nine or ten years to get itself ready for the first chapter.

At that time David and my mother and I went scouting to find what was Gramma's house in *Julia and the Hand of God,* but was in reality the first house my mother and father ever owned. I should say that my mother owned it, for it was she who had worked for it and owned it as far as money was concerned.

My father, that father in *To the Green Mountains,* was always away on his failing little farm with the idea of "putting us on Easy Street," as he invariably said. But where *was* Easy Street, exactly? I always wanted to know. What did it look like?

As for that stucco box on Parker Street where we lived when I was nine, it was here that something precognitive happened. My father was not killed in the First World War when I was small, as Julia Redfern's father is, but died many years later not far from where I live now. And in view of his complete lack of feeling for me (as I thought), here is an anomaly, the most ironic I've ever experienced. For he, who had never shown me the slightest sign of affection, made me a desk, something that was to symbolize the central absorption of my life. I wonder if it would have meant anything to him at all to have known this and what has happened to me as a writer. I have put the desk into *That Julia Redfern,* when Daddy makes it for her just before he goes off to camp to begin training as a fighter pilot.

It is the desk I have in *A Room Made of Windows,* for in real life we have moved out of the stucco box and my mother and I have found the little two-story apartment in the brown bungalow with the white roof described in *Julia and the Hand of God.* It was a snug arrangement of small living room and smaller kitchen downstairs, and upstairs an airy bedroom for my mother, and my very small "room made of windows" about nine by nine feet, though it might have been smaller. I've tried to measure it off from memory.

When Julia and Mama go upstairs to investigate, "they came out into a burst of light. For there was a well that had been built up from the hall below that became a glass well as it ascended through 'Julia's room' to the roof, where it was covered by a frosted pane. There was glass in the door opening into the big bedroom, as well as in the door opening onto the balcony. There was a skylight in the sloping roof 'right over the place where I'll have my camp cot,' Julia decided at once, 'so that I can look up at the sky.' And the two big windows along the garden side, to the right of the balcony door, were each made of four large panes and opened outward." She would have her desk under the big windows, she decided in a kind of bliss, and between the balcony door and her mother's door there was just space for a small bookcase. As for the view, it was of Rhiannon's house with all its trees and the tall old windmill that didn't work anymore but that creaked madly in

storms in the midst of all those trees thrashing their branches around.

It was here that I began writing, sending in my stories and poems to the Berkeley *Daily Gazette* and seeing myself in print for the first time. I *would* be like Louisa May Alcott, I said. I *would* be a writer; there was no least doubt in my mind. Though I went to art school much later in my early twenties, it was with the idea of illustrating my own books.

A strange thing happens when real life is wound into one's novels. If one's characters are all vividly alive in the writing, even though many of them are created out of the unconscious, then later one becomes confused. (I say the unconscious because this is the only source I can figure for that eerie, slow gathering of qualities, expressions, habits, ways of walking, of speaking, reactions to certain moments, tones of voice that make up the people of one's novels.)

No, I remind myself, there never really was a Rhiannon Moore, whom I met in that waking dream when I was lying sleepily trying to read and finally let the book fall on my chest. I then (and who can ever in this world explain why?) saw the back door of the barn-red house next door open and a woman come out and walk over to the fence between her own house and the brown bungalow. She was an older woman with fine features and long hair, very dark and streaked with white, which she had caught back with a ribbon. She had a housecoat on, still, though it was now mid-afternoon, so that she must simply have had breakfast and gone right upstairs again to the music room where she had been working at the piano until now. She came over to the fence, smiling at Julia, and Julia went to her at once, and they fell into that kind of long, intimate, immediately comfortable and revealing sort of conversation that people have who are going to be lifelong friends. Julia loved Rhiannon from that time on, and was destined to have long confidential conversations with her throughout *A Room Made of Windows* and *The Private Worlds of Julia Redfern,* the kind that one doesn't always or even rarely have with one's parents, much as one might love them. For there is no defensive wall made up of what one is expected to do, of what one hasn't done and should have, or may, regretfully, do. In other words, she was like a grandmother to Julia, as indeed Julia looked upon her.

There never was an Uncle Hugh nor an Aunt Alex, and this is something that I myself sometimes cannot believe. Nor were there ever, in real life, a Professor and Mrs. Penhallow up in their house in the hills. (A friend sees the name Penhallow as a symbolic choice on my part concerning the importance of writing to both Mrs. Penhallow and Julia.) There *was* a professor, but his wife didn't actually edit the children's page of the *Gazette,* called then the Sunnyside Club for budding young Berkeley writers.

I have been back to Berkeley several times since and can report that the bungalow that Julia and Greg and Daddy and Mama lived in, not the one with the white roof but the one with the hot golden berry garden and the gringling in it that I wrote about in *Julia's Magic* and *That Julia Redfern* now has an apartment house built right up against it so that there is no longer a garden.

Meanwhile, the brown bungalow with the white roof and the room made of windows has been torn down, and all the trees and the old creaking windmill and Rhiannon's house. First of all there was, by the time I saw it, a big dirty gas station there. By the time of my next visit, that too had gone, and now there is a business building painted a kind of lavatory green. So much for all that—I shall never return; my past there is gone forever, vanished, as so many of our physical pasts have vanished.

But Berkeley seems more full of trees each time I see it, and the hills have long since recovered from the terrible fire that almost devoured it back in 1923. After a day and a night of cinder-laden winds from the burning Oakland hills and smoke-filled air that turned the shrunken sun copper, we stood in the street toward late afternoon watching our own Berkeley hills burn, saw the flames advancing down Berkeley Way, and knew that we must pack and leave at once. But just then the wind changed, blowing back over its own charred and smoking path scattered with desolate chimneys, a path that Daddy Jefferson (Daddy Chandler in *Room*) said afterwards looked like the remains of Sherman's march to the sea in the Civil War. I have put the fire earlier than this in the Julia novels, ending *Julia and the Hand of God* with it and centering *Room* around my mother finding someone with whom she was to find a long, loving companionship at last.

Now, there are writers who would never use personal experience, and perhaps never could, and others who can use specific events out of their own lives, specific people, as I have here and there, as catalytic centers around which imagined events and characters coalesce into a pattern in a way in which I, for one,

cannot explain. It all seems an act of pure magic to me. I know only this, that childhood is the enchanted cauldron out of which so much arises that there is far more than can be used, and I don't mean simply the raw material, simply happenings, but apprehensions, perceptions, intuitions, moods, longings. But of course the results of adult experience imbue books for children. They would not be worthy of being published otherwise, for books that are confined purely within the perceptions of childhood cannot bring more to the child than it already knows. They would bring no illuminations, woven through the story in such a way that only an adult's craft and knowledge of later life could make possible. But an intense recovery, intense reliving (so that I don't mean simply recollection) of the experiences of childhood must be there in the depths if a book children can enjoy, and perhaps even treasure, is to speak to them at all.

GENERAL COMMENTARY

Perry Nodelman

SOURCE: "Beyond Explanation and Beyond Inexplicability, in *Beyond Silence*," in *Children's Literature,* Vol. 12, 1984, pp. 122-33.

A first reading of Eleanor Cameron's *Beyond Silence* confused me. The novel somehow both satisfied what Frank Kermode calls "our deep need for intelligible ends"[1] and did not satisfy it, so that as I finished the novel, I both felt and did not feel that delight in problems solved and suspense fulfilled that I expect from good stories, and that I had felt at the end of her earlier and deceptively similar novel, *The Court of the Stone Children.*

Of these two feelings, the sense of satisfaction the two novels share is easier to explore. Both *The Court of the Stone Children* and *Beyond Silence* begin with a set of three quotations, one about how the past still exists, one about how the future is happening now, and one about the limitations of our conceptions of reality. The idea that the ordinary perception of time's passage ignores a larger reality underlies and gives order to all of Cameron's work. Gil in *The Court of the Stone Children* says, "All time—past, present, and future—is one Time."[2] Dr. Fairlie in *Beyond Silence* agrees: "It's quite possible that all is coexistent."[3] In her discussion of time fantasies in

The Green and Burning Tree, Cameron herself says, "Time is not a thread at all, but a globe."[4] Furthermore, she praises the English time fantasists for expressing the same idea: "The past and creative magic! Is it the inextricable mingling of these two, the taken for granted presence in their lives of a past thick with myth and legend and fairy tale, that gives the English fantasists, and especially the time fantasists, their depth and their peculiar power of evocation?"[5]

Both *The Court of the Stone Children* and *Beyond Silence* pay homage to that English tradition and its immersion in a living past. But as an American, Cameron cannot take the tradition for granted. In fact, she seems to value it for its distance from contemporary American life, which she finds disorderly and dismisses as incomplete. Of course, life in the past was just as disorderly, just as incomplete; but it was so in a different way, and the difference gives it glamor for Cameron and for us, a glamor that it did not have for those who were stuck with it.

In English fantasies like Boston's Green Knowe series or Uttley's *A Traveler in Time,* the past comes alive in an old house; in *The Court of the Stone Children* it comes alive in a museum, a reconstruction in San Francisco of rooms from a European house. "These rooms are from my home in France," says Domi, ". . . But it is *not* the same . . . ! This is a kind of strange, twisted dream of my home, the same and yet weirdly not the same" (p. 38). The novel is like its setting, the same as the English time fantasies it is modeled on, and yet weirdly not the same. The difference is that movement across time offers children in the English fantasies a satisfying sense of connection with a place where they already live; but Nina finds completeness by moving away from the jarring anarchy of contemporary San Francisco into Domi's alien and satisfyingly orderly rooms.

In *Beyond Silence* the homage to the order of the past and to the English fantasies that evoke it is even more explicit. Like Tolly in *The Children of Green Knowe,* Andrew hears children of another time sing nursery rhymes. Like Tolly and also like Tom in Philippa Pearce's *Tom's Midnight Garden,* his contacts with the past significantly involve a tree falling in a storm; and in both *Tom's Midnight Garden* and *Beyond Silence,* a woman from the past marries a man named Barty. Above all, Andrew actually leaves California and seems to feel more at home in Scotland; surrounded by relics of the past, he escapes his own confusion by moving across time.

In fact, *Beyond Silence* shares with *The Court of the Stone Children* and with the English time fantasies a

resolution that does literally what all novels do formally. In most novels, Frank Kermode says, "Mere successiveness, which we *feel* to be the chief characteristic of the ordinary going-on of time, is purged by the establishment of a significant relation between the moment and a remote origin and end, a concord of past, present, and future."[6] In both of Cameron's novels, meetings of past and present fortuitously solve problems caused by the past's insistence on being over, problems that have concerned characters in both the past and the present. Nina's discovery of the truth about Domi's father in *The Court of the Stone Children* both makes Domi happy and allows Nina to live with those aspects of herself that had previously defined her as a lonely eccentric; Andrew's encounters with Deirdre in *Beyond Silence* both save Deirdre's life and allow Andrew to face his guilt over Hoagy's death. By achieving resolution through such meetings of past and present, each novel literally denies mere randomness.

But for all that, *Beyond Silence* does not seem complete. A quick look back through the novel shows why: Cameron has carefully set up many potentially exciting confrontations that never take place. When Andrew first meets Beth McBride, he says, "I felt a kind of immediate recognition passing between us, some instantaneous knowledge that we were drawn to one another" (p. 7). When I first read that, I assumed Beth would figure prominently either in the mystery about Deirdre or in Andrew's self-recognition: she does neither. Cameron also dramatically sets the stage for Andrew to disburden himself to Dr. Fairlie; she sends him on an exciting trip to Fairlie's house involving missed buses and boats and then lets Fairlie make impressively bald statements about the novel's main themes. I expected Fairlie to perform a miracle, save Andrew, solve the mystery; instead, Cameron kills him off in an automobile accident.

That leaves Andrew with no one to confide in, and Cameron seems to have put Dunstan McCallum in the novel for just that purpose; but Dunstan's mere presence causes problems. Since Andrew meets Dunstan by chance, we can believe his wish to confide in him only if Cameron postulates an instantaneous empathy between the two; and in these cynical times, we tend to assume that all such attractions are sexual. So Cameron has to insert an otherwise pointless paragraph about both Dunstan and Andrew admiring a girl who passes them on the street, which establishes their heterosexuality. My first response was to wonder why she went to all this trouble, when she could easily have settled for one of the two confidants she had already set up and then not used, doing without Dunstan altogether.

Even odder is the way Cameron establishes Andrew's antipathy for Phineas Brock and then unceremoniously drops him completely from the novel. Andrew says, "Phineas became my enemy before I had the least glimmering of why he was. He was nosey, yes. Phineas annoyed the hell out of me. But I felt something deeper; instinctively I felt it" (p. 71). Andrew finds Brock grandly evil, even satanic; Cameron supports Andrew's fear of him even by the name she gives him. Phineas means "mouth of brass," like the biblical image for those who lack charity,[7] and a brock is a badger—it is not surprising that Andrew feels badgered by Phineas. Given all that, I expected a melodramatic revelation of Brock as a true limb of Satan, along the lines of characters in Susan Cooper's *The Dark is Rising* or various novels by Alan Garner, and then Andrew's glorious defeat of him. Alternatively, I thought Brock might turn out to be not dangerous at all, so that Andrew would have to face the cruelty of his false imaginings. But what actually happens is nothing at all. Professor Fairlie dies, and "Phineas had packed up and left before Dad and I got down to breakfast the next morning" (p. 168). He is not heard from again.

Cameron also creates unresolved expectations around the pictures of Deirdre of the Sorrows in the musicians' gallery. Deirdre Cames's letter reports the grandmother of the original Andrew saying that the pictures would mean something special to her; we expect something more than the accident of a name. But Deirdre Cames's life was not filled with sorrow, and she does not seem to have cuckolded her husband. And nothing special happens to Andrew in the gallery, either; when he goes to see those paintings that tantalizingly "had reached out to me when I'd first turned and looked up" (p. 99), all that happens is that Brock relates the story the pictures tell. While that story is about Deirdre Cames's namesake, it has nothing significant to do with events of the novel.

Cameron builds up and then thwarts similar expectations about Andrew's interest in the "Western Sea." He connects his first glimpse of it with the story of King Arthur's death told him by his mother and with his brother's death, for he had once planned to travel to that sea with Hoagy; he also connects it with his recurrent dream of drowning. But nothing remarkable happens when Andrew reaches the Western Sea. Instead of a major breakthrough, an understanding of the truth about himself, or about his brother's death, or a vision of Deirdre or King Arthur or even of Brock, Andrew simply has his old nightmare once more, decides anticlimactically that "I must go inland" (p. 177)—and, astonishingly, falls asleep.

Of course, both the paintings and the Western Sea allude to Andrew's situation, even if they come to nothing in terms of plot. Andrew himself connects them to the poem by Walter de la Mare that Dunstan recites to him; it evokes "the musicians' gallery at the end of the dining hall at Cames: its walls full of rich colors, trees and mountains and figures and, as I remembered, a glimpse of the sea" (p. 88). The end of the poem is, "Across the walls, the shadows / Come and go"; not surprisingly soon after hearing it Andrew overhears a conversation "about the space-time continuum and someone named Minkowski and about space and time vanishing into shadows" (p. 106). So the poem, King Arthur's sea, and the paintings all relate to Andrew's crosstemporal experiences. The problem is clear: what makes sense as an allusion to crosstemporal experience seems to create unresolved expectations is terms of plot.

Ironically, the biggest unresolved mystery in the novel is the easiest to accept. The unexpected death of Fairlie and the departure of Brock made me uneasy; but I had no trouble at all with the unexplained contact between Andrew and Deirdre. The whole point is that it is an infusion of wonderful inexplicability into the repressive understandability of normal reality. Andrew says, "Something had happened, something as impossible of explanation, as far outside the usual run of my life as that visitation on the plane" (p. 26). He asks himself, "Why couldn't I accept it and let all this searching for an unattainable solution sink away so that I would be left in peace?" (p. 131). Eventually he does accept it, and in finding peace beyond explanation, he comes to share an attitude expressed by Loren Eiseley in the novel's epigraph: "Nature contains that which has no intention of taking us into its confidence." It is also expressed by Cameron herself in *The Green and Burning Tree,* when she praises books that "let in almost everything; they make welcome the un-understandable."[8] *Beyond Silence* seems to do exactly that, but in two quite different ways.

First, *Beyond Silence* shows the limitations of understandable reality by describing experiences that transcend rational explanation and by making the rational scientist, Phineas Brock, the villain of the piece. Brock is called the Quark, "a busy little particle of matter" (p. 17); what Andrew resists most is Brock's attempt to explain, and therefore explain away, Andrew's strange experiences. Brock says, "It would be fatal for you to keep them hidden and unexplained" (pp. 134-35); in Cameron's scheme of things, someone who tries to explain the unexplainable is dangerous.

Cameron may also be confirming her faith in the un-understandable in *Beyond Silence* by deliberately leaving loose ends. All those thwarted expectations may be an attempt to make readers experience for themselves the unsettling state of not understanding something and to have no choice but the one Dr. Fairlie recommends to Andrew: "There's no use wracking yourself over a thing like that. Live with it, Andrew. Accept it. Take it as a wonder—there's so much we can't explain" (p. 158).

If Cameron is indeed doing that, however, there is a tension between her philosophical prejudices and her novelist's craft. For explanations of events and people give meaning to novels and therefore make them pleasurably different from the randomness of mere reality. Seen in this way, life itself is inexplicable, confusingly multifaceted, and novels satisfyingly explain it; Kermode defines a plot as "an organization that humanizes time by giving it form . . . a transformation of mere successiveness."[9] But in terms of Cameron's ideas about time, life is all too suffocatingly "humanized," all too constricted by the limited explanations of merely human scientists like Brock; deeper perception transcends mere cause-and-effect explicability. In her novels, Cameron transforms "mere successiveness" in two opposite directions, into the inexplicability of cross-temporal experiences and into the explanatory connections of story-telling. In *The Court of the Stone Children,* where there are no loose ends, she creates a satisfying unity that may weaken the unsettling wonder we should feel in face of the inexplicable. But in achieving unsettling inexplicability in *Beyond Silence,* she may have deprived it of its unity. Finally, its various threads do not come together; Brock has nothing to do with Deirdre, nor with Hoagy's death, nor with the separation of Andrew's parents. As a story, *Beyond Silence* seems something like Dr. Fairlie tells Andrew his own state of mind will come to be: "You must realize that even if you *can* connect, this might not be the end. That is, it would be an intellectual resolution while very possibly you would still have some way to go emotionally" (p. 158). The feeling of incompleteness *Beyond Silence* conveys, even though it solves the central mystery about Hoagy's death, is confirmed by the knowledge that Andrew tells his story "six years later" (p. 2). At that distance he should know what matters and what does not; but he continually misleads us, and ends up unsettling us, in ways that could easily have been avoided—if his creator had wanted to avoid them.

Apparently she did not want to. I believe that *Beyond Silence is* complete, but that the way the loose ends are tied together becomes clear only after a reader has been disturbed enough by its apparent incompleteness to look further.

The key to the unity of *Beyond Silence* is its main difference from *The Court of the Stone Children*—the fact that the story is told not by an omniscient narrator, but by its protagonist. Since Andrew is so disturbed by Hoagy's death, the novel is not just a time fantasy, but a psychological case study; it is similar to Judith Guest's numbingly realistic and thoroughly unconvincing *Ordinary People,* in which an ineffably wise therapist helps a boy confront his guilt over his brother's drowning by teaching this restrained child of restrained WASP parents to become open and responsive—as joyously Jewish as the therapist himself.

If the omniscient narrator of *The Court of the Stone Children* had left loose ends untied, we would have to accuse Cameron of bad craftsmanship. But when Andrew tells his own story, we can assume that Cameron's bad storytelling is quite deliberate—that it reveals his character and his situation. And it does. The central situation of the novel is Andrew's incomplete perception. He has forgotten the events leading up to his brother's death; in the imagery provided by his hypnagogic experience, he has built a wall around that memory. For most of the novel, Andrew does not know the whole truth, and it is his own honest reporting of his flawed perception that creates thwarted expectations. But as Andrew's own voice tells him in his hypnagogic experience, "You can't build the wall high enough—you never can. There'll be a crack in it somewhere" (p. 151). Eventually, the wall cracks; the whole truth Andrew perceives confirms that the apparent red herrings introduced earlier were traps, set by his unconscious to prevent him from making his breakthrough.

Seen in this way, Beth cannot figure importantly in the breaking down of Andrew's walls simply *because* he feels such sympathy with her; as he says himself,

"She might, in her good common sense, convince me of something I didn't want to be convinced of" (p. 177). She threatens the walls because her loving concern might break them down. On the other hand, Dunstan is no threat at all because he is so uninvolved with the rest of Andrew's life. Cameron seems to have introduced him so tenuously for just that reason. Andrew believes that Dunstan will listen to him without trying to help, so that he can safely unburden himself "just enough to ease the pressure" (p. 177) without actually cracking the wall. Furthermore, Andrew believes that Dunstan has also built a wall to protect himself: "Maybe he was all right as a man because he had the world he'd made for himself" (p. 87); such a person would understand and respect another's need for walls and do nothing to disturb them.

But Andrew's subconscious understands that Brock, the professional psychological investigator, might. What Andrew most hates about Brock is his desire to help him, which his subconscious sees as a matter of hunting him down. Brock really was only trying to help, and really did not have other things on his mind beside the torturing of Andrew; his unceremonious disappearance from the novel and from Andrew's life, for reasons unconnected with Andrew, is quite natural; and it shows Andrew how distorted his perception was: "I've often thought how I'd hated him—bitterly hated him! And so had been incapable of seeing him as anything but a cold, calculating, impervious little manipulator for his own ends" (p. 166).

Andrew is also blind to the fact that Dr. Fairlie, whom Brock worships, shares scientific prejudices and asks Andrew the same questions. Andrew worries that Brock would "break open the privacy, my secret life" (p. 148), but he allows Fairlie to do just that. Perhaps Fairlie, like Dunstan, is safely distant from Cames castle and can thus feel nothing but professional concern for Andrew. Fairlie's death once more shows Andrew that things are not, however, as he perceives them. Not only does he lose his proposed confidant, but Brock's grief over Fairlie forces Andrew to reevaluate Brock. Yet Cameron also allows Fairlie to die and Brock to disappear from the novel, I suspect, so that Andrew's breakthrough will ultimately come through inexplicable magic, not psychological science. The wall finally breaks down through the hypnagogic experience that provided Andrew with the image of a wall "with the break in it" (p. 187) in the first place.

The expectations aroused and not fulfilled by the paintings in the gallery and the Western Sea also re-

veal Andrew's unconscious at work, Andrew's flight from the sea as soon as he has his potentially revealing nightmare about drowning suggests how firmly the wall of his resistance stands; his unconscious tells him to leave before any serious crack develops and before he comes to understand what seas and drowning mean to him. But Andrew's unconscious also acts positively, in that it allows the mystical experiences that eventually do break down the wall. Since the paintings in the gallery seem to lose their potential for magic once Andrew hears Brock's dismissing explanation of the story they tell, thwarted expectations about them merely confirm Andrew's unconscious realization that Brock's explanatory mind is deadly to the one thing that can save him.

That one thing is what is still left unexplained—the inexplicable contact between Andrew and Deirdre. But while there is no logical explanation, there is a symbolic one. It involves the idea of going down. Hoagy died going downhill; drowning is going down, and Andrew's recurring nightmare is of Hoagy drowning. Andrew says, "How subtly our dreams express what is deepest: both of us had *gone down,* but only one had survived. As in the sea, so on the mountainside" (p. 189, my italics). On the mountainside, Andrew refused to drive the car, and "Hoagy had *gone down* alone" (p. 189, my italics); that is what Andrew is hiding from himself, and what his nightmare about going down in water expresses, in a disguised way that keeps him from the painful truth. But throughout the novel, Andrew's crosstemporal experiences take him down. When he first walks around Cames, he says that he, "*going down,* left the sunlight and submerged into a dense green shade like a swimmer sinking under water" (p. 36, my italics); once down, he passes Deirdre's house and then reads her letter to the earlier Andrew. Later on, he steps over a wall, and feeling "infinitely remote from all humankind" (p. 93), "*walked on down. . . .* I was lost, because of the gray, drifting, winding obscuring mist" (p. 94, my italics). This is almost like drowning again; but he hears a voice that guides him through the mist and realizes that it "had been Deirdre who'd *led him down*" (p. 96, my italics). Andrew connects the idea of going down underwater with the unconscious—"the unconscious would begin sending up illuminations, rising like bubbles to the surface of simmering water" (p. 186). Deirdre magically guides Andrew whenever he goes down past the wall into his unconscious, so that he does not drown after all. Rather, he comes upon the truth submerged there.

For Eleanor Cameron, the limited world that can be rationally explained is not true, but shifting, insubstantial, illusory. In that world, Cames is not as Andrew's father remembered it; Andrew's girlfriend's "whole life changed, and then she changed" (p. 38); and Beth says, "Never trust that everything will be the same, because it won't" (p. 195). The only permanent truth is in that inexplicable place Deirdre led Andrew down to, which is simultaneously beyond both time and ordinary consciousness. Paradoxically, the explicable workings of therapy do not restore Andrew's memory of the illusory world of reality; inexplicable magic does.

Andrew says of his crosstemporal experiences, "They were mine, of my deepest self" (p. 132). To find those deeps, he goes down into himself just as his mother did in her book, "with time peeled off in layers of reflection so that the whole range of herself as a reading, thinking, feeling, imagining animal was revealed by *going down* and back instead of along in time through the cycle of the year" (p. 112, my italics). And Andrew's father admits that though his "needs will have changed," he will be "always, *underneath,* the same Andrew" (p. 196, my italics)—permanent beyond time and change, beyond ordinary consciousness and beyond explicability. Selfhood is one with magic; both exist permanently outside mere shifting time. Finally, the wrong ideas Andrew has about people in the world of time, the ideas that created our unfulfilled expectations, are just further evidence of the illusory nature of the world we usually perceive.

Whatever one feels about Cameron's ideas of time, the cleverly paradoxical way she expresses them is admirable. Not only does she complete an apparently incomplete fiction, she also presents a psychologically convincing statement about the limitations of psychology. She does admirably what Kermode suggests good novels must do: she falsifies our expectations, and "the interest of having our expectations falsified is obviously related to our wish to reach the discovery or recognition by an unexpected or instructive route."[10] Kermode says we wish to do that because, in the midst of literary conventions, that things we do *not* expect create a sense of reality. But what is most unexpected about *Beyond Silence* is not the way Andrew's psychological difficulties realistically account for the novel's loose ends; rather, it is that inexplicable magic finally dismisses psychological explanations for being as illusory as the incomplete world they describe.

The title of *Beyond Silence* sums it up. The phrase occurs in Dr. Fairlie's statement of faith in wonders: "The thing is, Andrew, we live in a cloud of unknow-

ing, and who knows what lies beyond silence?" (p. 158). Beyond the phenomena we comprehend and therefore can name lies the inexpressible. Not surprisingly, Andrew's mysterious experiences are often voices moving out of the silence, like the voice of the wall builder, or Deirdre's voice in the dumbwaiter. Before Deirdre leads him home, Andrew experiences "utter silence" (p. 92), then moves past a wall into the unknown: "I heard nothing, and so presently I stepped over the wall and continued on down" (p. 93). Once down beyond silence, he is guided by her voice. Later, Andrew's despair about an American who speaks belligerently of Vietnam "stopped whatever words I might have managed to put together" (p. 124). But beyond this silence is an experience in which he shouts to warn Deirdre of danger. The wall Andrew builds around Hoagy's death silences the unspeakable; he remembers "no sound" (p. 32) as he recalls the accident. Dr. Fairlie suggests that Andrew might "see over the wall or through a crack in it" (p. 158); but the wall hides not sights but words, a conversation between Andrew and Hoagy. Other people in the novel also protect themselves with walls of silence. Andrew's mother, "the Quiet One," hides her grief for Hoagy in silence, and Andrew assumes that Dunstan, "big, *quiet,* wounded Dunstan" (p. 177, my italics), has also built a wall around his pain.

Andrew ultimately speaks to Dunstan and remembers Hoagy's words; Dunstan never gets beyond silence. But Nell Cames, whose name is similar to her creator's, finds a way beyond silence that says much about the making of fiction: "Now that Hoagy was gone," says Andrew, "when I'd come in from school at home the house would be silent, or there'd be the faint tapping from her study upstairs of my mother's typewriter: *tap, tap,* silence, *tap, tap, tap,* sometimes long silence—then the tapping again" (p. 55). What lies beyond speechlessness in the face of the pain and unknowing of being alive is the ordered language of imaginative discourse. George Steiner says, "Possessed of speech, possessed by it . . . , the human person has broken free from the great silence of matter."[11] To find the right words is to triumph over the random, chaotic world the words describe; what most truly lies beyond silence is eloquent fiction, fiction like *Beyond Silence.*

Notes

1. Frank Kermode, *The Sense of an Ending: Studies in the Theory of Fiction* (New York: Oxford Univ. Press, 1967), p. 8.

Andrew is for the first time brought face to face intellectually with an unanswerable proposition (unanswerable to him at his stage of understanding), one that is symbolic of the meaning of all he has experienced and absorbed emotionally, before the branch's falling, without the frantic, desperate questioning he now undergoes in his own mind. A crisis has been reached which forces him to seek help outside the circle of family and friends.

As for Deirdre in *Silence,* her marriage to a man named Barty assuredly echoes the marriage of Hatty in *Garden* to "young Barty"; and I will go even further in echoings. In all four novels, Boston's *The Children of Green Knowe,* Pearce's *Tom's Midnight Garden,* and my own *The Court of the Stone Children* and *Beyond Silence,* there is a *loved* place where the inexplicable events occur: the protagonists, Tolly, Tom, Nina, and Andrew, solitaries and newcomers every one, literally fall in love with a house (or the museum in *Court*) and with a garden (the wild hill country around Cames in *Silence*). The tremendous power of place over the imagination and sensibilities of a child or adolescent is evoked in each case. But always the love of place is deepened and enhanced by its ghostly and human inhabitants. Tolly falls so deeply in love with the children of Green Knowe that when Granny Oldknow tells him finally that they are dead, something he had not previously understood, he "sat dumbfounded, with his big black eyes fixed on her. He must have known of course that the children could not have lived so many centuries without growing old, but he had never thought about it. To him, they were so real, so near, they were his own family that he needed more than anything on earth. He felt that the world had come to an end."[2]

Tom, who hated the idea of leaving his brother Peter (ill with measles during vacation) to go and stay with his stuffy aunt and uncle in a stuffy apartment some distance from his own town, changes over a period of time after discovering his garden and Hatty. Eventually he works every device he can manage to put off the unhappy hour of departure for home, for he has become utterly devoted to a place out of his own time, a house as it once was, and a garden that no longer exists. And if he has not actually fallen in love with Hatty herself, he has certainly fallen wholly in love with the idea of her, of her situation, and with his relation to her and to the garden. So that when, just before leaving, he discovers that for some unexplainable reason he cannot recover his midnight garden, he screams, "Hatty, Hatty!" His uncle hears.

"Alan Kitson jumped the last few steps of the stairs and ran forward and caught Tom in his arms. The boy sobbed and fought as though he were being taken prisoner. Then his uncle felt his body go limp, and he began weeping softly now, but as though he would never stop."[3]

Nina in *Court,* like Tom, changes from positive dislike of the new place—in her case San Francisco—to the point where, because of the French Museum and its ghostly inhabitant, she is determined that she and her mother and father shall stay. Meanwhile, her father has gradually been changing the other way and has begun to think of leaving. Nina, upon realizing that Domi, in the end, will not return from some other level of existence or awareness, calls out to her in the silence of the court of the stone children:

> *"Domi . . . Domi, do you hear me? I'm ready. Let me come—"* Still with her arm around Odile, she held her body poised, willing herself over the brink, her breathing caught, in the concentration of her desire to follow Domi, without consciousness of need for breath, and her eyes opened to their widest while she waited for that moment when her angle of vision might be changed by the minutest degree and she could see Domi again.[4]

Andrew at the end of *Silence* is with Beth, the owner of Cames, to whom he has promised he will come again the following summer. But she reminds him of how he will change between the ages of fifteen and sixteen, of how his needs will change, and he thinks, in acute sorrow, "No, but it wasn't possible I wouldn't need to be here. I couldn't bear to think it would become unnecessary. Or—could it be it was Deirdre alone who was making me want to come back? Yet who knew if I would ever see her or hear her again, and why did I feel as I stood there with Beth that I probably never would?"[5]

Then there are the greenhouses. Surely both Green Knowe and the French Museum must have had greenhouses on the property, because no large gardens can be kept up through the seasons, with their changing flower beds, without them. But a greenhouse is central to place and in a way to story as well, in both *Tom's Midnight Garden* and *Beyond Silence.* I always saw the greenhouse behind Cames, at the back of it and up beyond the walk that led down to the lane where Deirdre's house stood. And the reason I knew it was there and always saw it in that particular location was because there *was* an old, broken-down, dilapidated greenhouse at the side of the path leading to a lane, there at the back of the huge house beside a loch where my Scottish husband and I stayed for our vacation in the lake country in the west of Scotland.

And there is one more parallel, this time again between *Tom's Midnight Garden* and **Beyond Silence**: in each the idea of relative time is acted out. As I have said, Tom is confused by seeing Hatty as a little girl in the beginning, then later as a very small girl, and even later as the girl he saw in the beginning. But over the period of the whole novel, while Tom himself remains a boy of about ten during the weeks he is with his aunt and uncle, Hatty grows to young womanhood—a change Tom is not really aware of until his brother Peter, on one strange occasion, points the fact out to him. And in **Silence** (though I did not think of *Garden* as I wrote my book), Andrew sees Deirdre, during his hypnagogic experience on the plane carrying him to the British Isles, as a young girl, hears her three times as a small girl later on, and sees her out in the hills as a young woman.

Indeed, quite unconsciously, I could have been paying tribute, as Nodelman suggests, just as Philippa Pearce could have been paying tribute to the art of *The Children of Green Knowe* in creating her own loved house and garden with its own ghostly presences (or was Tom the ghostly presence in Hatty's time?), after reading the story of Tolly and his much loved house and garden and the ghost children who came and went according to their own mysterious whims. *Children* was published in 1954 and *Garden* in 1958.

Furthermore, as in the writing of sonnets, where there are certain givens in structure, meter, and rhyme scheme, so there is a certain given in the writing of most time fantasies, apart from the intermingling of two or possibly three time periods. Yet this need not prevent each fantasy from being quite unlike every other in its overall plot structure, its meaning, in the impressions the place and the characters make upon us, and in the evocation of feeling. The given I speak of is that the protagonist, or the reader, or both, usually find out the truth about the past in one of three ways.

One way: in *The Children of Green Knowe* it is Granny Oldknow who is the communicator by means of the stories she tells Tolly throughout the book, just as in *Tom's Midnight Garden* old Mrs. Bartholomew tells Tom a fuller story of the past than he could ever have known without her when he ventures upstairs to say goodbye just before going home.

A second way: in *The Treasure of Green Knowe,* as also in K. M. Peyton's *A Pattern of Roses,* Nancy Bond's *A String in the Harp,* and William Mayne's *A Game of Dark,* scenes of the past alternate with scenes of the present, and the present, and the protagonist may or may not be a part of what is going on in the past. In Penelope Lively's *The House in Norham Gardens,* scenes of other times in the world of the hidden valley in New Guinea are given in brief paragraphs, indented, in smaller type than the text, and in italics, at the beginning of each chapter.

A third way: in Jill Paton Walsh's *A Chance Child,* Christopher goes to the local library to find out what eventually happened to Creep in records of the early part of the Industrial Revolution, records in the form of statements by various men and women who worked in the mines and potteries and mills in the area to which Creep went out of the present into the past. In **The Court of the Stone Children,** Nina at first learns of Domi's past during the French Revolution when Domi tells her the story of it (the first way), and then about Odile's past through her journal, which was published in France and the translation of which the curator of the French Museum has in her library. In **Beyond Silence,** Andrew learns of Deirdre's life through a letter she has written to the Andrew of her time, a letter which was among the rubbish Beth was clearing out of the old house when she and her husband bought it for a hotel. And the reason she kept it is a part of the philosophical-scientific problem enunciated throughout the book.

Ideally, this particular given, brought out by whatever method, speaks under the flow of movement of the feeling of inevitability the story had for its author: how it seemed to have grown as a part of the writer's private vision of his novel, characteristic of it, *right* for it, embedded so deeply within the structure that it could not be torn out and replaced by some other method of dealing with the problem of communication of the past without ruining the delicate net composed of all the elements of the novel interrelating. Delicate, yes, but a net which must at the same time be so firmly woven, with so satisfying an inner logic, that one never stops to think, as one reads, of the technique by which this firmness and sense of satisfaction for the reader were attained.

I come now to a third and last quibble: that of Nodelman's view of the Quark's—Phineas Brock's—relation to Andrew, his intentions toward Andrew. Nodelman says of Dunstan McCallum, Andrew's friend, that he "would understand and respect another's need for walls and do nothing to disturb them." This is quite true. However, Nodelman then adds, "But Andrew's subconscious understands that Brock, the professional psychological investigator, might. What Andrew hates most about Brock is his desire to help him, which his subconscious sees as a matter of hunting him down."[6] I would replace that word *might* with the words *was determined to.* And it wasn't a matter of Andrew's subconscious alone seeing Brock as the hunter, the cold, single-minded breaker of walls of privacy for his own self-centered ends; the consciously aware Andrew was fully convinced that Brock was on his trail, though he did not know why. And it took the words of Professor Fairlie to shed a hard light on just what Brock was up to.

Nodelman argues that "Brock really was only trying to help, and really did have other things in his mind beside the torturing of Andrew."[7] *But Brock is not benign.* Andrew does admit, after he hears Brock weeping over Fairlie's death, that he *had* "been incapable of seeing him as anything but a cold, calculating, impervious little manipulator for his own ends."[8] But then Andrew adds, "And he *was* that—he *was.*" Yes. That is the way Andrew and I see the matter. And Brock's grief over Fairlie does *not* force Andrew to reevaluate Brock. Andrew sees him in the end just as he had before. Of course Nodelman has every right to view the matter as he wishes, maintaining that Andrew isn't remembering correctly, but I am puzzled to know why he interprets Brock as he does, as a helpful little man of pure, comradely motives, when, as I believe, the text points to a quite different understanding of him.

Concerning *Ordinary People* by Judith Guest and its similarities to **Beyond Silence** in certain turns of the story—in both novels a boy loses his older brother, by drowning in *Ordinary People* (Andrew's nightmares in **Silence** echo this) and by a suicidal auto accident in **Silence,** and in both the boys are overcome by guilt and get help from psychologists—I can only say that I had not read *Ordinary People* at the time I was writing my novel, had never heard of it, nor have I seen the movie. I did finally read the book recently, feeling that I should know what two reviewers, a friend, and Perry Nodelman were talking about. In my estimation, aside from the likenesses mentioned above, the novels appear as different from each other as it is possible for them to be.

We go now, beyond quibbles, to Nodelman's comments on the naming of Phineas Brock and Nell Cames. The whole subject of names in novels is

fascinating. Roland Barthes tells of Proust who, in order to write *Remembrance of Things Past,* which had begun to blossom in his mind as early as his terms at the lycée, underwent years of "groping," as if the true and unique work were being sought, abandoned, resumed, without ever being found, "until at last he came upon that federation act which would permit Proust to write *Remembrance* without flagging, from 1909 to his death."[9] What was the "federation act"? Barthes answers that "the (poetic) event which 'launched' *Remembrance* was the discovery of Names; doubtless, since his *Contre Saint-Beuve,* Proust already possessed certain names (Combray, Guermantes); but it was only between 1907 and 1909, it appears, that he constituted in its entirety the onomastic system of *Remembrance:* once this system was found, the work was written immediately."[10]

Further along, Barthes speaks of the proper name "as sign . . . and a precious object, compressed, embalmed, which must be opened like a flower . . . a voluminous sign, a sign always pregnant with a dense texture of meaning."[11] And one of the most vivid examples of Barthes's conviction is the example Leon Edel gives in his essay on Hugh Walpole's last novel, *The Killer and the Slain.* It was a novel Walpole had had in mind for years before he was finally compelled to write it at the behest of an unconscious which perhaps knew that Walpole had not much longer to live.

Walpole dedicated it to Henry James twenty-five years after James died: "This macabre is dedicated in loving memory and humble admiration to the great author of *The Turning of the Screw* ."[12] And the error in that dedication, the misquotation of the title of James's novel, Edel reveals as central to the evidence that led Walpole to open out, as one might open out a flower, that "voluminous sign . . . pregnant with a dense texture of meaning," the name Walpole gave to one of his two protagonists. This is the initial villain of the novel, James Oliphant Tunstall. In other words, as Edel eventually came to understand, James Old Elephant Turnscrew was what Walpole's unconscious was actually saying deep beneath the level of his conscious hearing. The name James is obvious. And Old Elephant was the name Henry James had often given himself in letters to Walpole, whom he loved, but whose novels he always deprecated and was condescending about, acts which caused Walpole the deepest humiliation and which aroused in him a bitter, continuing resentment (that is, the *turning* of the screw). Turnscrew, melded into Tunstall, speaks of the title of the tale Walpole greatly admired and which held an element repeated in Walpole's novel, the corrupting of a small boy by a cynical elder.

Having set down the results of his detective work on that name, Edel was told, from evidence in Walpole's diaries, that he was indeed correct and that Walpole, in his last novel, had written out the submerged hostilities, harbored all these years of their friendship and afterward, toward the author he had loved in return. Walpole died on June 1, 1941, twenty-one days after reading the final type-script.

There is nothing at all so fascinating or mysterious in my own naming. Nodelman is quite right as to the meaning of Brock, the old Celtic word for badger; and also, as I came to find out, for a dirty fellow, a skunk. However, I hadn't realized that Phineas means "mouth of brass" in Biblical terms, apt as that is. In the beginning I had called him Alpheus but saw, as I got into the novel, that Andrew, Alpheus, and Alex would boggle the mind. Thereafter Phineas came to me, a much better name, I thought, and looked it up. Yes, Phineas blinded by his own ambition, as Phineus in mythology was blinded by Zeus. As for Nell Cames echoing Eleanor Cameron, that is very acute.

Why I chose Cames for the name of the castle, I have no idea. In 1971, my husband and I went to Scotland and stayed in the old residence, built in the 1700s, that became my castle. And while we were there a novel came to me, complete, but as the years passed the whole thing changed into its present version. Meanwhile my husband went back again some time later, while I stayed home because of a broken knee; he joined our son there and played golf with a young woman we had met on our first trip. But here everything falls apart as far as the novel is concerned: our friend is happily married and the Camerons and the Harknesses write to each other two or three times a year.

In Nodelman's perceptive discussion of the use of actual and symbolic walls in **Silence,** he speaks of inexplicable magic and psychological science, and their opposition. In the beginning I though that I was writing a time fantasy. But as time went on I could see that two other genres would come up as possibilities, and so it turned out. Ethel Heins, in her review in the *Horn Book,* said of it, "A kind of psychological science fiction, the novel presents a warping of reality, explained in terms of theories of the unconscious mind and precognition as well as of revised notions about space-time, cause and effect, and coincidence."[13] Others rejected the idea of science

fiction vigorously and said that it is a psychological study of a disturbed boy, while still others spoke of speculations as to the true nature of time. But a good many saw it, as I had in the beginning, as time fantasy.

Nodelman, apparently, sees it as fantasy, for he speaks of Fairlie's death as necessary because Andrew's breakthrough "will ultimately come through inexplicable magic, not psychological science." Yet, oddly enough, he goes on to say in the next sentence that "the wall finally breaks down through the hypnagogic experience that provided Andrew with the image of a wall 'with a break in it' in the first place."[14] For me, this is true. The break must come through his own efforts, his own perceptions, while he still keeps his secret. On the other hand, the break couldn't have come if Andrew hadn't heard Deirdre, as a woman, speaking of her own guilt, which brings us back either to "inexplicable magic" or possibly to a psychologically troubled boy hearing voices.

But of course there is a third possibility, with reference to speculations as to the true nature of time. If, actually, all of time *is* one time, all times being coexistent on a level of experience beyond our comprehension, and if Andrew, in a state of intense, vulnerable sensitivity, has been allowed briefly to experience that oneness and, because of this experience, is brought to a realization of the underlying truth of his own situation, then this is a book neither of fantasy nor psychological science fiction, but of time and reality.

In any case, I respond to Nodelman's words, "Beyond the phenomena we comprehend and therefore can name lies the inexpressible"[15] *Yes.*

Notes

1. Perry Nodelman, "Beyond Explanation, and Beyond Inexplicability, in *Beyond Silence,*" above, pp. 122-23.

2. L. M. Boston, *The Children of Green Knowe* (New York: Harcourt, Brace, 1954), p. 75.

3. Philippa Pearce, *Tom's Midnight Garden* (Philadelphia: Lippincott, 1959), p.212.

4. Eleanor Cameron, *The Court of the Stone Children* (New York: E. P. Dutton, 1973), p. 191.

5. Eleanor Cameron, *Beyond Silence* (New York: E. P. Dutton, 1980), p. 196.

6. Nodelman, above, p. 129.

7. Ibid.

8. Cameron, *Beyond Silence,* p. 166.

9. Roland Barthes, *New Critical Essays,* tr. Richard Howard (New York: Hill & Wang, 1980), p. 57.

10. Ibid., pp. 58-59.

11. Ibid., p. 59.

12. Leon Edel, *Stuff of Sleep and Dreams* (New York: Harper & Row, 1982), p. 309.

13. Ethel Heins, Review of *Beyond Silence, Horn Book,* 56 (Dec. 1980), 646.

14. Nodelman, above, pp. 129-30.

15. Ibid., p. 132.

TITLE COMMENTARY

A SPELL IS CAST (1964)

Bulletin of the Center for Children's Books

SOURCE: A review of *A Spell is Cast,* in *Bulletin of the Center for Children's Books,* Vol. XVIII, No. 5, January, 1965, p. 70.

Cory travels alone to the West Coast [in *A Spell is Cast*] to stay with the mother and brother of her adoptive mother, Stephanie; Stephanie is single, an actress who is seldom home. At Tarnhelm, Cory falls in love with the ocean, the house, and the inhabitants—even though Grandmother and Uncle Dirk seem ambivalent about her. Characterization is very good, the seaside atmosphere is described colorfully, and the possible contortions of plot are nicely avoided: there are logical explanations for all the events that seem to Cory mysterious or miraculous. The picture of Stephanie, selfish, impulsive, and generous, is sharp and vivid; she appears at the end of the book, reproaching the child she had always neglected, and just as quickly admitting her own culpability.

Helen E. Kinsey

SOURCE: A review of *A Spell is Cast,* in *Booklist,* Vol. 61, No. 21, July 1, 1965, p. 1028.

Cory Winterslow [in *A Spell is Cast*] comes to Tarnhelm convinced that it is an enchanted place and will offer a solution to her problem of loneliness. At first she is disappointed. No one is at the airport to meet her; she is shocked to learn that her supposed foster mother has never adopted her and so she is not really a part of Tarnhelm; and the local children are in no great hurry to include her in their ranks. How she faces her problems and helps to resolve some of them is told in a hauntingly poignant presentation that pictures the fears and anxieties of a small girl unsure of her place in the adult world. There is enough of a mystery to give the story appeal; more sensitive readers will appreciate the full depths of Cory's plight.

TIME AND MR. BASS (1967)

Ruth P. Bull

SOURCE: A review of *Time and Mr. Bass,* in *Booklist,* Vol. 63, No. 18, May 15, 1967, p. 988.

The fifth book [*Time and Mr. Bass*] in this science fiction series has the moral overtones of an epic. Chuck and David delve into Mycetian history and help their friend Tyco Bass overcome the power of a phantom murderer whose evil influence has plagued the Mycetians for centuries. Mushroom Planet fans will welcome these strange new adventures in which the three friends journey to Tyco's ancestral home in Wales and to Basidium in their search for lost relics and hidden secrets of the past.

Virginia Haviland

SOURCE: A review of *Time and Mr. Bass,* in *Horn Book Magazine,* Vol. XXXXIII, No. 4, August, 1967, p. 460.

To a fifth space fantasy involving David and Chuck and their Mycetian friend Tycho Bass [*Time and Mr. Bass*], the author has added new dimensions—a realm of magic reaching into Welsh mythology and a conflict between good and evil. Tycho is needed in Wales, for the ancient necklace of Ta and the historic scroll have been stolen. Part I describes a chase in which the three friends, racing from clue to clue, travel through Wales and as far as London on their mission to retrieve the stones of the necklace, a "hot, working, seething mass of magic." Out of the "working" of these glowing, brilliantly varied stones graven with hieroglyphs, the author has developed distinctly fresh story material. The quick pace continues in Part II, which carries the boys and Tycho to the Lost City on Basidium, where David discovers the isolated overgrown ruin containing the key to the scroll. And in the Welsh scenes the chilling designs of the evil Narrow Brain strengthen the impact of the book. The legendary background, drawn in part from the King Arthur story, is completely interwoven and essential to the fantasy, and the annual gathering of the eisteddfod is implicit in the scene of the Great Thronging.

THE GREEN AND BURNING TREE (1969)

Paul Heins

SOURCE: A review of *The Green and Burning Tree,* in *Horn Book Magazine,* Vol. XXXXV, No. 3, June, 1969, p. 294.

Although Mrs. Cameron states in the Foreword [of **The Green and Burning Tree**] that she is more "concerned with appreciation . . . than with criticism," it might be wise to remember that appreciation is a form of criticism. For who can appreciate anything unless he knows something about it—sees something that eludes the casual observer? The more that is known about any work of art or of literature, the surer the appreciation, especially if—like Mrs. Cameron—one is trying "to find the heart of the author's intent."

Some of the essays, two of which appeared as *Horn Book* articles, were first given as talks at workshops or symposia and have been further developed; but all of them, taken singly and together, reveal the range and depth of Mrs. Cameron's considerations. Running through the essays are explorations of the personalities and the works of well-known writers for children, *such* as E. Nesbit, Hans Christian Andersen, Eleanor Farjeon, and Laura Ingalls Wilder. Another stream of investigation includes judgments or evaluations of such current writers as Scott O'Dell, Joseph Krumgold, Paula Fox, and Jane Curry. And quotations from or allusions to H. G. Wells, Mark Twain, Katherine Anne Porter, or Eudora Welty—to name only a few—are constantly invoked to clarify or enrich Mrs. Cameron's commentaries on children's literature. She is concerned with the resonances and overtones of literature and is at her best in discussing the power of the evocation of place, as in the Little House books or in *The Wheel on the School,* or in presenting the ramifications of the human sense of time, as in the Green Knowe books or in *Earthfasts.*

If one had to single out one essay to emphasize, it would certainly be **"The Green and Burning Tree: A Study of Time Fantasy,"** in which the author develops the idea "that Time is not a thread at all, but a globe. . . ." The importance of the whole volume, however, lies in Mrs. Cameron's devotion to literature as art and experience. In her adherence to the credo that children's literature "does not exist in a narrow world of its own, but is enmeshed in a larger world of literature . . . ," she believes that "the highest standards of one hold good for the other." Rich in content, abundant and perceptive in treatment, the book celebrates the high estate of children's literature.

Kirkus Reviews

SOURCE: A review of *The Green and Burning Tree,* in *Kirkus Reviews,* Vol. 37, June 1, 1969, p. 605.

The author of the Mushroom Planet series and other outreaches has ruminated long and read widely on the nature of children's literature particularly on the characteristics of fantasy and its creators. The extended essays [in **The Green and Burning Tree**], some published in a briefer form in *Horn Book* and elsewhere, touch also upon such writers' concerns as style and setting, but most of the many examples, in these sections as throughout, are drawn from the great fantasists Nesbit, Potter, Boston, Grahame, Andersen. Mrs. Cameron states that she is writing "appreciation." not criticism, but she notes the mechanical quality of *Time Garden* and expands upon the failure, for her, of *The River at Green Knowe.* On the whole it is the practiced precision of her intense appreciation which renders it valuable for novice and initiate alike—that and the fact that she extends it to current writers like Curry *(The Sleepers),* Mayne *(Earthfasts).* Clarke *(Return of the Twelves),* etc. The title essay, exploring the concept of Timelessness under the umbrella of time fantasy, is particularly acute. Included are revealing glimpses of the gestation of her own books and two lengthy portraits—of Wanda Gag and Eleanor Farjeon. As a tribute it is both respectful and urgent.

A ROOM MADE OF WINDOWS (1971)

Booklist

SOURCE: A review of *A Room Made of Windows,* in *Booklist,* Vol. 67, No. 18, May 15, 1971, pp. 796-97.

[In **A Room Made of Windows,**] Julia Redfern is a sensitive, talented girl who devotes all her energies to becoming a writer. Although friendly and outgoing by nature, she is so absorbed in her own thoughts and dreams that she often fails to see or understand the real life problems of those around her. As a consequence, she is shocked by her beloved widowed mother's decision to remarry and responds with open rebellion. Julia's emerging comprehension of life's complexities and her ultimate acceptance of her mother's remarriage are recounted in a discerning realistic story of personal relationships between engagingly characterized individuals.

Bulletin of the Center for Children's Books

SOURCE: A review of *A Room Made of Windows,* in *Bulletin of the Center for Children's Books,* Vol. XXIV, No. 10, June, 1971, p. 153.

Julia's room was at the top of an old, rambling house [in *A Room Made of Windows*] in which there also lived an old man who loved, as she did, to write. His death came as a blow to her at a time when she was already upset by her mother's plans to remarry and by the mysterious unhappiness of the recluse next door. The book has several minor plots, but they are skillfully woven together in a solid and mature approach to the development of an adolescent's growing understanding. Julia, self-centered and sensitive, responds to the needs of others with increasing perception. The characters are firmly delineated, the dialogue and interrelationships deftly conceived.

📖 THE COURT OF THE STONE CHILDREN (1973)

Kirkus Reviews

SOURCE: A review of *The Court of the Stone Children,* in *Kirkus Review,* Vol. 41, No. 20, October 15, 1973, p. 1159.

Cameron's delicate time fantasy [*The Court of the Stone Children*] is set in a San Francisco museum furnished with the transported appointments of an old French castle, right down to the ghost of Domi, a young girl who inhabited the castle in Napoleon's time. Thus the museum, tangibly evoked, functions as a seamless link between the already introspective everyday life of lonely, intense Nina on the one hand and the ghosts' 170 year-old burden on the other. On

reflection the Domi-Nina intersection concerns a disappointingly, ordinary problem: Domi's father was unjustly accused and executed by Napoleon, and as the ploddingly scholarly Mrs. Stayne at the museum is now writing his biography Domi enlists Nina's help in uncovering evidence that will clear him of the charges. This accomplished, the ghost of course fades from Nina's company forever. Nina's new friend Gil, a solitary boy consumed by his "project" of investigating the meaning of time, proves an effective device for exploring the theoretical implications of the girls' encounter; thus he quotes Bergson, his parents, and others on the subject of time and conducts rational discussions of such subtopics as prophetic dreams (experienced by both Domi and Nina). Sometimes the discussions illuminate the adventure less than they weigh it down with reminders of the author's intent, and when even Nina's new landlady enters quoting a passage about existing out of time, it's hard to suspend incredulity. Nevertheless, the Gil/Nina/Domi relationship constitutes the center of an impressively executed pattern—and, incidentally, a far more ambitious use of a museum background than Claudia's detective work in Konigsburg's *Mixed-Up Files.*

Mary M. Burns

SOURCE: A review of *The Court of the Stone Children,* in *Horn Book Magazine,* Vol. L, No. 2, April, 1974, p. 151.

When lonely Nina Harmsworth, newcomer to San Francisco, encounters lovely, mysterious Dominique in Mam'zelle Henry's private French museum, she senses—but does not immediately comprehend—that customary time barriers have been broached [in *The Court of the Stone Children*]. Impelled by her fascination with Dominique, who she gradually realizes lived in France more than a century before, Nina becomes involved in unraveling a generations-old mystery. In the process, she is forced to grapple with the concept of time itself. Based on the premise that time is not a linear succession of events but a circle or globe within which present, past, and future are held in everlasting equilibrium, the carefully constructed narrative is sufficiently detailed to provide a satisfying conclusion; and the loving evocation of the San Francisco setting lends credibility to the events described. A gentle yet compelling story.

📖 *TO THE GREEN MOUNTAINS* (1975)

Betsy Hearne

SOURCE: A review of *To the Green Mountains,* in *Booklist,* Vol. 72, No. 4, October 15, 1975, pp. 297-98.

An intense remembrance of things past, this novel [*To the Green Mountains*] flows through rich description, complex adult interaction, and probing examination of small-town southern Ohio life during World War I. The point of view is that of a young girl, Kathy, watching the dissolution of her parents' relationship, the difficulties her independent mother encounters managing a hotel and maintaining her deep friendship with a black couple, and the tensions among a wider circle of insiders and outcasts who occasionally explode the smooth surface of a habit-bound rural community restless for gossip. Kathy's dream of escaping from her mangy hotel room to the green mountains of her grandmother's Vermont home is realized in the fullness of time, which will demand too much from impatient readers and reward those who can bide a while to ponder the nuances of Cameron's perfect, exacting prose.

Paul Heins

SOURCE: A review of *To the Green Mountains,* in *Horn Book Magazine,* Vol. LI, No. 6, December, 1975, p. 602.

The author of *A Room Made of Windows* has written another realistic novel [*To the Green Mountains*] in which the sense of place is of paramount importance yet subordinated to the often harrowing experiences of the protagonist. At thirteen, Kath Rule dreamed constantly of returning to her grandmother's house in Vermont, since she detested sharing a room with her mother in the small-town Ohio hotel where beautiful, independent Mrs. Rule was the housekeeper. During what turned out to be her last summer in Ohio, Kath, ever aware of details and sensitive to impressions, became increasingly perceptive of sudden and dramatic revelations and events.

From early childhood, Kath had loved Grant, the black headwaiter of the hotel, and Grant's ebullient wife Tissie. Mrs. Rule, who had the highest regard for Grant's abilities and his desire to be a lawyer, brought him some secondhand law books from Columbus, and immediately the neighbors began to gossip. Tissie, on her part, resented the fact that her husband's zeal for study was spoiling their married life.

Kath's summer was filled with emotional ambiguities. The girl welcomed her mother's decision to divorce her indifferent, insensitive father but was struck by his dejection at the decision; she was alternately attracted and repelled by Herb, an albino boy who had been devoted to her since early childhood. Unhappily aware of Tissie's estrangement from Grant, she inadvertently learned of Tissie's marital faithlessness. When Tissie was killed by a train, Kath witnessed her mother's agony at having unsuccessfully tried to better Grant's life.

The author has created a noteworthy work of fiction, in which people and places have been endowed with concreteness; emotions and sensations have been vividly recorded; and events past and present have been significantly reflected in the consciousness as well as in the dreams of the chief character. She has skillfully arranged an interplay of thematic symbols to unify the emotional epiphanies in a young girl's life. But even more important is the author's sense that good and evil are often inextricably entangled—in things as well as in people. Mrs. Rule's good intention turned out to be an evil intervention, and the railroad which was the source of terror and death for Tissie brought release to Kath and her mother.

For, ultimately, Kath returned with her mother to Vermont, but as she went, the girl carried with her a strong memory of a community of distinct and often humorous personalities, a sense of the relentlessness of life, and a picture of the land she was leaving: "the train bears them away and away, out into the rolling open countryside to which they will never return."

📖 *JULIA AND THE HAND OF GOD* (1977)

Barbara Elleman

SOURCE: A review of *Julia and the Hand of God,* in *Booklist,* Vol. 74, No. 2, September 15, 1977, p. 159.

Julia, the sensitive heroine of *A Room Made of Windows,* appears [in *Julia and the Hand of God*] as a younger, less confident girl. Living in Berkeley, she worries about earthquakes, struggles over the inequities of her Aunt Alex and her grandmother's favoritism to her brother Greg, idolizes her uncle Hugh, and wants desperately to write. However, her uncle's gift to her on her eleventh birthday—a thick, leather-bound book of blank pages—is so beautiful that it overwhelms her. A calamitous incident when Julia and a friend attempt cremation of a mouse leads her to an acquaintance with Dr. Jacklin, a noted art collector. When a fire sweeps the area, nearly trapping Julia, she helps rescue several paintings, gets her name in the papers, begins to have a deeper perspective on people around her, and realizes the constant changes of life. Cameron draws a moving, perceptive picture of a young girl, subtly catching nuances of joy and sorrow and standing them in high relief against the daily occurrences of Julia's life. The writing is imbued with grace and each character finely carved.

Virginia Haviland

SOURCE: A review of *Julia and the Hand of God,* in *The Horn Book Magazine,* Vol. LIII, No. 6, December, 1977, pp. 659-60.

Eleven-year-old Julia [in *Julia and the Hand of God*] has the stuff of which favorite storybook heroines are made—vital forthrightness (sometimes to her own undoing) and imagination. She is determined to become a writer and has a startling capacity for visualizing past events. She imagines all too vividly the great fire of San Francisco, and the vision is actualized when she becomes a heroine in the Berkeley fire of 1923. Julia is understood by her patient mother, cherished by Uncle Hugh and by a neighboring professor, and despaired of by Aunt Alex and Gramma. The adults all play important roles in the well-unified story. The cast of individualized characters is especially strong; their conversations, set down with verisimilitude, enhance each dramatic crisis. With her mother and fourteen-year-old brother, Julia has been living in Gramma's cramped apartment, but at last the three move to more spacious quarters. The author treats the preadolescent world with depth and subtlety. At the end the reader learns that Julia's story was continued in a previously published book, *A Room Made of Windows.*

📖 *BEYOND SILENCE* (1980)

Ethel L. Harris

SOURCE: A review of *Beyond Silence,* in *The Horn Book Magazine,* Vol. LVI, No. 6, December, 1980, p. 646.

Eight months after the violent death of the older brother he loved and admired, fifteen-year-old Andrew Cames still suffers from a profound trauma and is both confused and terrified by a recurring nightmare [in *Beyond Silence*]. Andy leaves California with his father for a long-planned visit to Scotland—to stay at a loch-side glen in a somewhat run-down hotel, once the splendid ancestral home of the Cames family. Just before the start of the journey the boy begins to undergo hypnagogic experiences—seeing clearly articulated images of people and happenings—that proved to be forerunners of his equally uncanny experiences in Scotland. Andy is given a long-lost letter written, but never sent, to a previous Andrew Cames by Deirdre, a young woman who would one day become the American boy's great-great-aunt; and Andy moves in and out of visionary encounters with Deirdre through a kind of precognitive memory of past circumstances—manifestations outside reason, "beyond time." His confusion and misery deepen as he struggles to comprehend the seemingly illogical, unbroken circle of events; and a release from his agony seems possible only when he finally perceives the link between his recent experiences and his deeply submerged, irrational guilt over his failure to prevent his brother's death. A kind of psychological science fiction, the novel presents a warping of reality, explained in terms of theories of the unconscious mind and precognition as well as of revised notions about time-space, cause and effect, and coincidence. A definitive literary style flavors the book, which may not reveal until the very end the full significance of the prefatory quotation from Rilke: "The future enters into us, in order to transform itself in us, long before it happens."

Kirkus Reviews

SOURCE: A review of *Beyond Silence,* in *Kirkus Reviews,* Vol. 49, No. 2, January 15, 1981, p. 78.

Cameron's latest novel [*Beyond Silence*] quivers with the self-consciousness of serious fantasy, but the time-theories she skirts so vaguely are unoriginal; and though she evokes "the new hypotheses' of physics" and refers to "the hunting of the quark," these ideas aren't explored or their sense of excitement conveyed. Rather, they are borrowed to dress up fanciful ideas of the supranormal. Similarly, as if to borrow class, there are gratuitous references such as the comparison of a character's appearance to that of "the young D. H. Lawrence." The story concerns 15-year-old Andrew Cames, visiting in Scotland with his Scottish-born father and still disturbed over the sudden death of his Viet-vet older brother. (Even the family's anguish over Vietnam is woodenly predictable.) En route to Scotland Andrew has one of what will be a series of sharp visions of the past; they turn out to be linked with Deirdre, the young woman of 80 years ago whose undelivered letter to a previous Andrew Cames is now delivered to the young Andrew's hands. Through his growing preoccupation and fleeting contact with Deirdre, Andrew comes to terms with his long-suppressed guilt over his brother's death. To be sure, his pre-existing distress can help to explain his unusual susceptibility to his supranormal experiences. However, both hero and author seem to approach the Deirdre episodes with undue solemnity. There is one moment fairly late in the story when Andrew participates in a scene Deirdre had mentioned in the letter—thus occasioning his wonder at "the wicked, unanswerable, incomprehensible, unbroken circle" in which past and present act on one another. Otherwise there is little drama in Deirdre's own story: A pitiful cry for help Andrew hears early on echoes only her momentary terror when stuck in a dumbwaiter during childhood play with his namesake. The ideas these recurrences inspire are standard to time fantasy, and the writing is hackneyed (". . . I was aware of a sudden leap of the blood so sharp that it sent a stab of pain up through my body") and pseudopoetical (". . . when I first kissed her, off behind the trees in the rustling, laughter-filled dusk at a class picnic, and knew for the first time to the core of my being what maleness meant . . .").

📖 *THAT JULIA REDFERN* (1982)

Kirkus Reviews

SOURCE: A review of *That Julia Redfern,* in *Kirkus Reviews,* Vol. 50, No. 18, September 15, 1982, p. 1056.

First met as a 1920s adolescent in [*A Room Made of Windows*] (1971), Julia Redfern was a little younger in the 1977 volume *Julia and the Hand of God.* [*That Julia Redfern*] moves back further yet to a six-year-old Julia, high-spirited and sometimes heedless (hence the title) but engagingly open, imaginative, and spontaneous in her emotions as well as her actions. Early in the story, Julia's beloved father, an aspiring writer, goes off to World War I. His death is foreshadowed; but before it's announced, Julia, unconscious from a playground accident ("'You live too hard, Julia,' Mama would say"), dreams of climbing upward with Daddy, high in the Berkeley hills, until he insists on going on alone, leaving her lost in

the hills with the message "Remember to tell Mama to go through my papers." Julia wakens terrified to a real nightmare—she's being held prisoner by two old people who found her unconscious and expect a reward for saving her—but learns later that her father was shot down on the day of her dream. And in his papers Mother finds a story that's accepted by the "very best" literary magazine. And so, despite Grandma's lack of faith, Daddy was a writer after all. And Julia too, we know even without the other volumes, will be a writer; Daddy had expressed his faith by building her a wonderful desk before he left. But this is not all love and promise: In neighbor Maisie, Maisie's mother, and Julia's tight-lipped Aunt Alex, Cameron portrays the petty spite and meanness and partiality that can drive a child to seething rage. And of course it also makes readers all the more sympathetic with Julia, who can name a hated doll (a gift from Aunt Alex) Felony, and then offer Maisie the doll with the most innocent and reasonable intentions. A winning first acquaintance.

Ann A. Flowers

SOURCE: A review of *That Julia Redfern,* in *Horn Book Magazine,* Vol. LVIII, No. 6, December, 1982, pp. 647-48.

Julia Redfern appeared in *A Room Made of Windows* and in *Julia and the Hand of God* but the new story [*That Julia Redfern*] goes back to her childhood—to 1918, just before the end of World War I. A child who forgets what she is told—such as warnings to keep away from bears in Yosemite—Julia inevitably gets into trouble, engendering impatience in her family. Contrasting with the book's realism is a supernatural element. Her beloved father has gone to fight in France. Julia injures herself on a playground, and while unconscious she has a vivid dream of her father taking her for a walk and giving her a message for her mother. Eventually, it becomes clear to the family that he was killed in action at the very moment of Julia's dream. At another time when her mother is on the verge of death during the flu epidemic, the cat awakens the girl in time for her to summon help. Imaginative, sensitive Julia is well characterized, as is the whole family, although her Aunt Alex is almost too frightful to be believed. The story is told entirely through Julia's eyes, and the childhood lovingly recalled certainly has a ring of truth.

JULIA'S MAGIC (1984)

Kirkus Reviews

SOURCE: A review of *Julia's Magic*, in *Kirkus Reviews*, Vol. 52, No. 24, November 1, 1984, pp. J95.

That Julia Redfern! [In **Julia's Magic**,] she's a little younger than when last seen but just as sparkly and full of life. The story pivots on a single incident—she accidentally breaks one of her aunt's perfume bottles—and its unfortunate complications: Hulda the housekeeper is blamed. Before things are set straight, Julia has a disturbing dream (as signifying as the one in **That Julia Redfern**, 1982), takes a streetcar by herself, then gets lost and knocked down by bullies while trying to find Hulda's house across town. Though baffled by the mysteries of adult behavior, Julia at six is an astute observer who already knows to be wary of nosy neighbors and reserve her better self for better times—during Uncle Hugh's tailored revelations about his bachelor days or Aunt Alex's confession of a childhood wrongdoing far worse than Julia's. As before, Cameron conveys the untidy contours of family life with a sure hand, and offers in the irrepressible Julia a disarming, always likable young girl.

Bulletin of the Center for Children's Books

SOURCE: A review of *Julia's Magic*, in *Bulletin of the Center for Children's Books*, Vol. XXXVIII, No. 4, December, 1984, p. 63.

Another story about Julia; [**Julia's Magic**] is set just before and leading into **That Julia Redfern** (reviewed in the September 1982 issue) and has the same structure: a nicely flowing narrative into which linked episodes are woven. Julia's undiscovered misdeed precipitates a crisis in her uncle's household, and Julia makes amends; Julia's parents are told by a waspish landlady that she's sold their house (true) and that they'll have to move (untrue) and Julia begins to differentiate between reality and the magic of her imagination.

THE PRIVATE WORLDS OF JULIA REDFERN (1988)

Denise M. Wilms

SOURCE: A review of *The Private Worlds of Julia Redfern*, in *Booklist*, Vol. 84, No. 18, May 15, 1988, p. 1606.

At 15, Julia is well on her way to becoming a writer [in *The Private Worlds of Julia Redfern*]. Observant and insightful, she watches and responds to the changing relationships around her, recording her feelings in a journal and discussing her interests with those close to her. Confidants include John, a classmate who is a talented actor and seems destined for the stage; Rhiannon, an elderly composer whose son is a world-famous pianist; and her Uncle Hugh, who has become like a father to her since Julia's real father was killed in World War I. The story hasn't a well-defined plot, but moves forward in tandem with the lives of Julia and her friends: she and John ready themselves for a school production of *Romeo and Juliet* and become romantically involved; Rhiannon's sister hates Julia and intrudes into the special friendship Julia shares with the older woman; Uncle Hugh, meanwhile, is preoccupied with marital troubles that culminate in a break with Aunt Alex and a decision to take up with the woman he should have married in the first place. In the midst of all this, Julia is wrestling with her art, working out a cathartic story about her father and then seeing it published in *St. Nicholas* magazine. Cameron's story is introspective and perceptive, plumbing some deep emotions and placing Julia firmly on the edge of adulthood. Readers who have watched her grow through the previous books will find this portrait of an intense, talented young woman has been worth the wait.

Nancy Vasilakis

SOURCE: A review of *The Private Worlds of Julia Redfern*, in *Horn Book Magazine*, Vol. LXIV, No. 4, July-August, 1988, p. 500.

The author continues the odyssey of her impetuous heroine that began with the youngest Julia in **Julia's Magic** and followed through **A Room Made of Windows** [with **The Private Worlds of Julia Redfern**]. Julia is now fifteen, and her mother and Phil are married, though as the story opens, the girl has yet to accept the fact with good grace. Her friendship with Rhiannon Moore has strengthened into an outpouring of mutual respect, even love. Julia is, as ever, bursting with creative energy, not only beginning to realize her early promise as a writer, but exhibiting some acting talent as well; she takes part in high school productions of Shakespeare with varying degrees of success. The most important development in the novel, however, is her gradual discovery that she can play only a peripheral part in the intimate lives of those who are most dear to her. This sense of limits pervades the narrative. Julia's school nemesis makes a better Juliet than she; her devoted Uncle Hugh, involved in a romantic liaison, forgets a lunch date with her. In the light of this dawning awareness that she does not, always, inhabit the center of the universe, her own first love with a high school classmate is not without its difficult moments. The melodramatic plot is suited to the late 1920s period in which these stories are set, and although the book may not be the strongest one in the series, the heroine of the earlier books is no longer the "selfish kid" her brother has accused her of being. She comes to accept her limitations without losing the joie de vivre that is her unique and best trait.

THE SEED AND THE VISION: ON THE WRITING AND APPRECIATION OF CHILDREN'S BOOKS (1993)

Zena Sutherland

SOURCE: A review of *The Seed and The Vision: On the Writing and Appreciation of Children's Books,* in *Journal of Youth Services in Libraries,* Vol. 7, No. 3, Spring, 1994, pp. 301-02.

A collection of eleven critical essays, **The Seed and the Vision** explores aspects of the writing, appreciation, and analysis of fiction for children. Three of the essays have never before been published; the imprint page describes changes in title, original sources, and changes in text ("much shorter form," "slightly different form," and "entirely different form") for the other eight essays. This is the sort of information much appreciated by serious students of literary criticism.

The title essay is the first of four gathered under the rubric "On Writing," and it examines the influences on authors of their own experiences of places and people in childhood. Cameron shows convincingly how, in her own books and in those by other writers, the vision reflects the seeds. In other essays in this section she examines stylistic idiosyncrasies, with emphasis on clichés and characterization and with attention to such pervasive attitudes as feminism.

Section two comprises two essays on fantasy. The first discusses ways in which authors establish a convincing frame of reference that will make the story's magic believable; the second is concerned with the fascinating variants found in time fantasy.

In **"The Inimitable Frances,"** Cameron pays tribute to a friend and mentor, Frances Clarke Sayers. This is the first of a trio of pieces in part three, "Is It Good, Will It Last?" The second is **"On Criticism, Awards, and Peaches,"** a brief, occasionally barbed commentary on the subjectivity of criticism; the third is a more extensive examination of criticism and of the disagreement that exists between those who believe (passionately) that criticism should begin with emotion and those who believe (passionately) that it should begin with thought.

In **"Into Something Rich and Strange,"** which is the first essay in part four, "The Unconscious," Cameron explores the ways in which the unconscious absorbs one's experiences and may transmute them (even if they seem to be forgotten) into treasures that emerge in the work of creative artists. The final essay, **"Of Dreams, Art, and the Unconscious,"** is a disquisition on the work of Lewis Carroll, Sir James Barrie, E. B. White, and Ursula Le Guin as it reflected their awareness of the workings of the unconscious.

This is an impressive book, scholarly but not pedantic, occasionally prolix and occasionally—but less often—bending toward the conjectural ("perhaps here is the tie," in speaking of Lucy Boston's Hanno and Ping,") or making assumptions ("Does hearing the expression 'Quiet as a mouse' really make a child want to curl up and *be* a mouse . . ."). Last quibble: it seems a far reach to say, "And I wonder if Peyton ever happened to read *Journey from Obscurity,* by Wilfred Owen's brother, Harold. Sylvia Townsend Warner says of it. . . ." These *are* quibbles, small lapses in a book both thoughtful and provocative.

As she did in **The Green and Burning Tree** (1969), Cameron writes as a passionate advocate for the readers of children's fiction, showing a teacher's zeal for imparting the standards she champions and a scholarly approach to the body of literature being examined. J. D. Stahl, contributor of the book's foreword, comments on the fact that Cameron sought his opinion because she knew they had differing opinions on some theories of criticism, and he notes that this is typical of "her questing, courageous mind." In responding to a point made by another critic, Boyd Davis, Cameron says in her preface, "But what the finest essays on children's literature criticism *are* about is not simply evaluation but, most primarily, discovery." **The Seed and the Vision** is just that, a provocative exercise in discovery.

Lissa Paul

SOURCE: "Critical Blindness—Without the Insight," in *Canadian Children's Literature,* Vol. 21, No. 77, Spring, 1995, pp. 67-8.

It's true, as Thomas Wolfe says: "you can't go home again." Whoops. Cliché. Eleanor Cameron wouldn't approve. She devotes a whole chapter [in *The Seed and The Vision: On the Writing and Appreciation of Children's Books*], "The fleas in the cat's fur," to policing the clichés in fiction, though she pays scant attention to the ones in her own critical text. Someone must have forgotten to remind her that to praise a novel, in this case, *The House in Norham Gardens* by Penelope Lively, as being accomplished "in subtlety, in depth, in symbolic meaning . . . as well as sheer accomplished artistry . . ." (189) doesn't really convey much about the book. And as the rest of her lengthy discussion of the novel is little more than an appreciative plot summary, I didn't learn anything I didn't already know. Worse, I felt keenly the absence of current theoretical discussions on postcolonial theory that would have offered helpful insights into Lively's story of the follies of imperialist nostalgia.

It wasn't until I read *The Seed and the Vision* that I understood just how impossible it was to "go home" to ahistorical, atheoretical criticism. Eleanor Cameron denies emphatically that she is in sympathy with the mid-century fashions of New Criticism, but it is difficult to read her book without feeling frustrated by what is missing. She doesn't appear to recognize how her choices of discussions (characterizations for example), or choices of terms (a fuzzy division between "thought" and "emotion" as critical oppositions without any mention of reader-response theories which attempt to locate the instability of those terms), reflect the totalizing discourses of mid-century. And she doesn't appear to realize that "objectivity" is no longer regarded as desirable, or even possible. What she's written is not really a critical book at all. It is more like a "commonplace book": a collection of interesting observations and passages recorded in a journal.

Despite Cameron's protests, theory—or lack of same—is the main issue of the book. To her credit, she invites American scholar, J. D. Stahl, who is theoretically knowledgeable, to critique her work. And to Stahl's great credit, he is unfailingly patient and sensitive to where she's "coming from" (couldn't resist). He provides her with guidance on critical dis-

courses, like feminist theory, which she only peripherally understands. Like the naive viewer of an abstract expressionist painting who claims that a six-year-old could do better, Cameron is bemused by feminist discussions on "clitoral hermeneutics." In a footnote she includes her response from J. D. Stahl, who explains to her that the discussion is part of "a theoretical debate that begins with Freud and continues through Lacan, Cixous, Kristeva, Irigaray, and others about how to 'read' and more recently to 'write' the body (133)."

"Clit crit" (as one of my friends cheerfully used to call it), is partly a joke, an ironic way of exploding the seriousness of traditional criticism—from which emerging feminist critics recognized they were excluded. Though Cameron finds "clitoral hermeneutics" bewildering, she makes no connection with a masculine equivalent: "the pen is mightier than the sword" (another cliché), normally treated with deadly earnestness, yet open to at least two sexual jokes. "Pen is" without the space becomes "penis"; and both "pen" and "sword" are, of course, phallic symbols. None of this is in Cameron's book.

It is not just in accounts of esoteric terms like "clitoral hermeneutics" that Cameron reveals her lack of scholarship. She criticizes Roland Barthes's uses of "bricolage" and "Dasein" without recognizing the historical contexts of either term: "bricolage" from Levi-Strauss's theories of structuralist anthropology; and "Dasein" from phenomenology.

Even when I put aside Cameron's lack of theoretical knowledge, and try to look for some insights into the authors and books under discussion, I still find disturbing gaps. For example, when she tries to praise Sylvia Townsend Warner's constructions of metaphor, she cites two which have musical elements: one, about listening to Schubert and feeling "as though one were holding a wild bird" (95); the other on two cats sitting on a chair, looking like "they might have been composed by Bach for two flutes" (96). As Cameron focuses on what's on the page, she misses something that's important about Warner's use of those, and other, musical metaphors. Warner defines herself as a musicologist. Before she was a novelist, Warner was a gifted musician, and she was one of the original compilers of the first collection of Tudor Church Music. Surely, that bit of biographical information is helpful in understanding Warner's particular motives for metaphor. Cameron, consistent with formalist practices, is not particularly interested in contexts for texts, though it is impossible to speculate on the precise reasons for her omissions.

As I write about what Cameron doesn't know, I am annoyed with myself for being so ungracious. After all, Cameron is a respected American novelist and critic, and was one of the pioneers of children's literature criticism. It is because of her work, and the work of others from her generation like her, that children's literature exists as an academic discipline. Her 1969 collection of critical essays on children's literature, *The Green and Burning Tree* was highly regarded. In fact, the reason I'm reviewing an American book of criticism like *The Seed and the Vision* at all in *CCL* is because Cameron is so prominent. As a critic, I'm of a different generation, and, in my turn, realize that I will probably be displaced by critics with new sets of radical ideological concerns, ones that haven't been invented yet. I hope someone as sympathetic as J. D. Stahl will be there to chart my way through unfamiliar critical waters.

Additional coverage of Cameron's life and career is contained in the following sources published by the Gale Group: *Dictionary of Literary Biography,* Vol. 52; *Junior DISCovering Authors; Major Authors and Illustrators for Children and Young Adults; Major 20th-Century Writers,* Vol. 1; *Something about the Author,* Vols. 1, 25, 93; *Something about the Author Autobiography Series,* Vol. 10.

highly entertaining while teaching the value of appropriate social behavior and how to tell time. It consists of split pages that grow larger and larger as the animals challenged by the ladybug grow in size, beginning with insects and ending with a whale. Similarly, *The Very Busy Spider* spins a web that grows bigger on every page. Although constantly interrupted by the neighboring farm animals, the spider perseveres and finishes the web to finally catch the fly that has been bothering the others. This book is considered especially valuable for visually handicapped children since the web and the fly are raised on the page. Three similar titles are *The Honeybee and the Robber*, *A House for Hermit Crab* (1988), and *The Very Quiet Cricket*.

In *Pancakes, Pancakes* Carle uses his customary torn paper pictures to emphasize shapes and brilliant colors. It is a cumulative story that begins with Jack wanting a pancake. His mother sends him to the mill to grind corn and to the barnyard to feed the corn to the hen who lays an egg. Jack must then milk the cow, mix the ingredients together and toss the pancake. When his pancake is cooked at last, Jack needs no instruction on how to eat it.

Do You Want to Be My Friend? is a favorite of Carle's because he understands the importance of friendship to children. It is dedicated to a childhood friend who wrote to him after his move to Germany and greeted him warmly twenty years later when Carle showed up unexpectedly at his door. In the book, a mouse asks animal after animal to be his friend until at last he finds the perfect companion. Critics called this book ingenious and a visual delight of striking beauty in its color and design.

Papa, Please Get the Moon for Me is the demand of a little girl to her father, so at the full moon he begins to climb to the moon to bring it down. As the father goes higher and higher, the pages of the book fold farther and farther up and out. Reviewers were charmed by both the creative format and the relationship between the father and his daughter.

AWARDS AND HONORS

Carle has been the recipient of many awards, garnering a large number for *The Very Hungry Caterpillar*. In 1969 this book was named as one of the *New York Times* Ten Best Pictures Books of the Year, and in 1971 it received a citation for the Best Children's Book of England. In 1972 it was a Selection du Grand Prix des Treize, France, and it received cita-

tions in 1973, 1976, and 1977 as a Brooklyn Museum Art Book for Children. It won the Nakamori Reader's Prize from Japan in 1975 and the American Institute of Graphic Arts Award in 1979.

1,2,3 to the Zoo won the 1970 International Children's Book Fair first prize for picture books and a Deutscher Jugendpreis citation. In the same year, *Pancakes, Pancakes* won the American Institute of Graphic Arts Award and received a Child Study Association Book List citation.

Do You Want to Be My Friend? received an honor book citation at the 1971 Children's Spring Book Festival and the first prize for picture books at the 1973 International Children's Book Fair. It also won the Deutscher Jegendpreis award, an American Library Association Notable Book citation, and was a 1973 Selection du Grand Prix des Treize, as was *Have You Seen My Cat?*

"My Very First Library" series was named the 1974 New York Times Outstanding Book Of The Year. *The Very Busy Spider* made *Horn Book's* "Fanfare" list in 1986 and was named to the American Library Association's list of Best Books of the 1980s. *Papa, Please Get the Moon for Me* was a Young Critics Award special mention in 1986 at the International Children's Book Fair, and won the Parents' Choice Award in illustration and the 1988 Kentucky Bluegrass Award. *Animals, Animals* received the Silber Medal from the City of Milano, Italy in 1989 and was named by *Redbook* as one of the Top Ten Books of the Year. *The Very Quiet Cricket* was also named a *Redbook* Top Ten Book of the Year in 1990.

Carle has received numerous other awards including awards from the New York Art Directors Show, the New York Type Directors Show, the Society of Illustrators Show, and the Best Book Jacket of the Year Show.

AUTHOR COMMENTARY

Eric Carle

SOURCE: "Where Do Ideas Come From?" in *The Art of Eric Carle*, Philomel Books, 1996, pp. 52-62.

Ladies, Gentlemen, and Friends;

One of the joys of an author is to receive letters from children, teachers, and parents. Some of these letters are ordinary, some funny, some precocious, some touching, most endearing. Here are some examples that I would like to share with you.

Quite a few classes do variations on ***The Very Hungry Caterpillar.*** I especially like this letter:

> A kitten grew from his mom.
> On Monday he ate one mouse.
> On Tuesday he ate two lollipops.
> On Wednesday he ate three eggs.
> On Thursday he ate one cricket, one orange, a lemon, and an apple.
> On Friday the kitten felt full.
> He went to the bathroom and felt much better.
> The End.

Here are some others:

Elena writes: *Why do you make your animals act like people? Maybe you should write about kids.*

Brad: *I am eight years old. My dad is fifty-four years old. My mom is twenty-eight years old. How old is your wife?*

David: *I am glad that God made you. If he wouldn't have, the world wouldn't have the most famous author.*

Matthew: *Your book is like a little poem.*

Jessie: *I like how you show feelings with color.*

Lizzy: *Do you have a bodyguard?*

Chris writes: *We know that you have written a lot of books, even before we were born. They are still good, even though they are old.*

Marilyn: *I am in third grade. My teacher says all writers edit and revise their work. I find that hard to believe, so I am writing to you to find out if that's true.*

A teacher from Texas: *We read all your books we could find. My librarian accuses me of "Carlezing" my students.*

Tony: *Do you color your books or do you have an artist do that?*

Paul: *One reason I like your books is they do special things.*

Gabriel: *Do you have a wife? How old is your wife? Do you have a girlfriend?*

Rebecca: *Do you have a job?*

Adam: *I like **Do You Want to Be My Friend?** I like when the mouse asked of the animals to be his friend. I couldn't find any friends either when I was little.*

And Sandra: *You are a good picture writer.*

But "Where do ideas come from?" is the most often asked question. Indeed, only recently a child asked, *Where do ideas come from?* Unlike the others, however, this letter writer provided me with the answer. Here it is: "Some ideas come from the *outside,* and other ideas come from your *inside.*"

What is this *outside* and *inside?* Bear with me if in the pursuit of the answer to this elusive question I do not proceed in a straight line, if I jump from subject to subject.

Willem de Kooning, the eminent Expressionist painter, in whose work the critics have searched for deep meaning, simply says this about his work: "I start with a dab of red in the upper corner of the canvas, and it looks good. Then I add a dab of green to it, and it doesn't look so good. So I paint a dab of blue in the center of the canvas, and it looks good again."

Allow me then to paint my dabs of color. A dab of red here, a dab of green there. In the end these dabs of color, strung together, should form a picture. But even a finished painting remains open to interpretation.

Since this occasion has been made possible by the Ezra Jack Keats Foundation, let me begin with Ezra. I had been working in advertising as an art director for many years when, in my mid-thirties, I decided that Madison Avenue was not for me. And I quit my job in order to freelance as an illustrator and graphic designer. Portfolio under my arm, I made the rounds to advertising agencies, studios, TV stations, and publishers during the day, and worked on my assignments at night.

By the time I had done ***Brown Bear, Brown Bear, What Do You See?*** and began working on the first book I both wrote and illustrated, ***1,2,3 to the Zoo,*** a friend of mine said to me that he would like to introduce me to Ezra Jack Keats, a Caldecott Medal winner.

"Who? The what?" I asked. You see, I was still a greenhorn in the field of children's books. When the three of us met, I was struck by Ezra's gentleness, "gentlemanness," and his directness. I had just struck out on a seemingly insecure career. So far, working on ***Brown Bear*** and ***1,2,3 to the Zoo*** had been fun and fulfilling, but would this type of work pay the bills?

"Yes," Ezra reassured me. "One can make a living doing picture books." Then he showed me his studio, his books, his fan letters, and he showed me how he made his marbled papers.

He told me about contracts, royalties, and advances. But we never talked about *Where do ideas come from?*

Yet Ezra was a shiny dab of color on that canvas, and I am sure he would be pleased that his foundation has made this day possible.

But the "dabs of color that don't look so good" are part of the canvas as well!

I was born in Syracuse, New York, to German immigrant parents. I remember kindergarten there. I remember a large sun-filled room with large sheets of paper, fat brushes, and colorful paints. I remember that I went to school a happy little boy.

When I was six years old, my parents went back to Germany—where I would live for the next seventeen years. There I started school all over again. I remember a dark room with narrow windows. And I remember a cruel teacher who introduced me to a time-honored tradition: corporal punishment with a thin and relentless bamboo stick. A punishment which I have not forgotten. A punishment that stopped my enthusiasm for learning for the next ten years until I went to art school. After that painful and humiliating punishment I asked my parents: "When are we going home again?" (Home to Syracuse.) But when it became apparent that we would not return, I decided that I would become a bridge builder. I would build a bridge from Germany to America and take my beloved German grandmother by the hand across the wide ocean.

I have tried to convince myself that I should forgive, that that punishment should not last forever. However, I cannot help, even today, to view that physical and emotional shock through the eyes of a small, innocent, six-year-old child.

Painters, musicians, and writers create mainly for themselves. First and foremost, my books and my ideas are done to please myself. Could it be that my cheerful caterpillars, ladybugs, roosters, and spiders have been created to paint over, or even scratch out, those dabs of color, which have gone wrong so long ago? Do I still seek to re-create the sun-filled room and the fat brushes? Do I still search for that kinder-garten teacher in Syracuse who called in my mother to tell her that her son liked drawing pictures and that his talent should be nurtured?

Both my teacher in Syracuse and my teacher in Germany are dabs of color on that canvas. It seems, then, that ideas spring from the need to sort out, to reevaluate, to transform, and to build that bridge to one's childhood and innocence.

When, years later, Bill Martin Jr asked me to illustrate his **Brown Bear, Brown Bear, What Do You See?,** the happy days of my kindergarten came to my mind as I created those large and colorful animals for that book. A dab of color for Bill Martin Jr.

One day I was punching holes into a stack of papers, looking at the holes I thought of a bookworm; however, the bookworm would not yield to be shaped into an idea. So I turned the bookworm into a green worm. When I presented the hungry green worm to Ann Beneduce, she liked the concept but not the worm. "How about a this?" "How about a that?" we went back and forth. "How about a caterpillar?" asked Ann. "How about a butterfly?" I shot back. And the book was finished!

This exchange between Ann and me symbolized our relationship. Never did one impose on the other. Strong convictions, yes. Power or ego struggles, never.

Many authors, half in fun, half in pain, speak of their rejection slips. I have never received an official rejection slip from Ann. Not all my ideas were that ingenious, but in our give-and-take some ideas simply and quietly were never mentioned again. Tossing an idea back and forth in this give-and-take manner might compromise or water down an idea. Somehow, we never fell into that trap. We just strengthened each other. It never mattered whether it took one, two, or three years for an idea to ripen into a finished book. There never seemed to be a rush to meet a deadline for the spring or fall list.

Today I know that Ann has that added, special gift to protect her authors from such lowly and mundane matters. A big dab of color for Ann.

Naturally, when Ann left Philomel and Patricia Gauch took over, I was concerned. Would I be able to work with this new and unknown editor? Of course, I learned to accept Pat and to work with her with confidence.

With *Animals, Animals,* which was Pat's idea, she offered me an opportunity to unfold my full potential as an illustrator. Thank you, Pat.

Twenty years ago my *Pancakes, Pancakes!* was published only to go out of print within a year or two. One of my publishers recently wished to reissue this book. I decided to redo the illustrations when I realized that some of the original pictures had been damaged or lost, and that the reproduction methods have improved quite a lot since then.

As I was redoing the pictures, I was able to stand back somewhat and observe how an idea comes about and is shaped into a book. Let me try to share this process with you. The idea for *Pancakes, Pancakes!* has two "outside," or external sources.

Before I tell about the first source, let me explain that sometimes I feel like a man with one leg in the Middle Ages and one in the nuclear age. This might explain my love for Brueghel and Klee, my favorite painters: Brueghel, the painter of robust peasants, thatched roofs and country life; Klee, the seer of our times.

Pancakes, Pancakes! was for me not a nostalgic trip into the "Once Upon a Time" world. It was drawn from my own childhood experience.

My first source: Some of my summer vacations were spent in a tiny village in southern Germany untouched by modern life, a place right out of the Middle Ages. This village of perhaps a dozen farmers and their families, houses, barns, and stables, surrounded by their fields, was too poor to have its own church, but the farmers had built communally a milk house and hired a cheese maker.

In the early morning and again when the sun set, the farmers or their wives or children carried cans of lukewarm milk to the milk house. The only modern event was the weekly arrival of a large truck in a cloud of dust. The driver paid the cheese maker and left with a load of big round wheels of Swiss cheese. This was an exciting time for the children.

I stayed with my grandmother's friend, a sixtyish-year-old unmarried woman and her old, old father, a widower in his nineties. I slept next to this ancient man, who snored dreadfully, in an enormous bed. I can still hear him get up in the middle of the night, reach for the chamber pot, and noisily tinkle into it.

I don't know whether this old man noticed me much, but I liked this gruff remnant of the Middle Ages, who, before the sun rose, would get up, throw a

scythe over his shoulder, stick a whetstone into his belt, and walk to the neighboring village. There he'd lean his scythe against the church, go inside, and say his prayers. Then he went to his small field between the two villages to cut enough grass for his two cows and stuffed it into a sack, which he had brought along. They owned two cows, a pig or two, some chickens, and several hives of honeybees in their vegetable garden behind the house.

In the meantime his daughter had gone to the edge of the forest to pick wild blueberries. She'd wash them, place them neatly in a basket; then, riding on her old bicycle for an hour, she'd deliver the berries to her city client for a few *Pfennig.* When she returned, she pumped water from a well in the kitchen and made strong coffee—coffee from roasted barley—served with warm milk, dark bread, and homemade gooseberry jam. Before we ate, she dipped her fingers into a small vessel of holy water, crossed herself, and blessed us all. I remember her addressing her father in the third person. "Would father like his milk now?" for instance. This sounded very strange to me.

I was brought up a non-believing Protestant. Now here, in this one-hundred-percent-Catholic village, I experienced for the first time a rich and deeply held faith. I was told that if I didn't want to I didn't need to go to church with them. But I loved the thick-walled old church, the Latin voices rising to the vaulted ceiling, the ornate robes worn by the priest and altar boys, the intoxicating smell of incense floating among the believers, and the saints carved in wood, painted in gold and lovely hues of blue and pink and brown . . . looking benignly down on us.

Next door lived a rich farmer; he had about thirty cows. In the evening they were driven from their stables into a green field to feed. One of the farmer's children, a beautiful girl who was my age, perhaps ten or eleven, would guard the animals so that they wouldn't trample the adjacent fields. I joined this cowgirl to be her cowboy, and felt a strange sense of happiness. When I came back the next year to my tiny village and wanted to help with guarding the cows, my hosts told me I couldn't. After all, I was Protestant and she Catholic. How could a faith be both so inspiring and so cruel at the same time?

Source number two is also from my childhood, but from more of a "modern age" experience. During the war, when my father was away and my mother worked in a factory, she would tell me, "Make yourself a pancake when you come home from school."

But first she taught me how to make one: take an egg, some milk, butter . . . These two experiences shaped the **Pancakes, Pancakes!** book. Nothing of the old man, the church, my lovely cowgirl is in my book. (Perhaps these things will lend themselves for another story or two or three.) During these vacations I learned that pancakes did not come premixed in a box from shelves in a store. But most of all, I hope to have captured the essence of a bygone age, which I was lucky enough to have been part of. So the experience of the *outside* becomes tempered with one's feelings from the *inside.*

Many religions tell us about a happy afterlife in heaven or of fire and brimstone in hell. I strongly suspect that the concept of heaven and hell is based on the memory of our early childhood or perhaps on the experience of the unborn. I tend to think that most early childhood experiences are positive: the mother's love, a sense of protection and warmth.

Segovia tells us that his grandfather would sit the little boy on his knees and strum an imaginary guitar—an imaginary guitar because he was too poor to own a real one. That is when Andrés Segovia became the musical genius we know.

Henry Moore as a child applied healing salves to his mother's arthritic back. That is when Henry Moore began his beautiful sculptures.

Sendak speaks of his grandmother, who'd sit little Maurice on her lap and open and close the window shades to reveal the outside to him. In his beautiful books and now as a stage designer, the shades of his childhood have become the curtains of the theater.

Beethoven's father came home drunk, boxed little Ludwig's ears, and screamed, "Why don't you play like Mozart?" But Ludwig also had a loving grandfather. And Beethoven's music would be both defiant and full of sweetness.

Many dabs of color form that small child. Perhaps some of the dabs take a stronger hold than others.

After his dreary work as a clerk and on weekends my father would take me for long walks through the woods and fields. He would turn over a rock and show me the little creatures that scurried and slithered about. He would tell me about the ant queen who would snip off her wings after the maiden flight because once she had started a new colony, there no longer was a need for wings. He told me that trout always swim upstream. He would bend down and show me a small ball of fur with tiny bones that an owl had dropped.

He taught me that it was easy to catch a lethargic lizard in the cool morning before the warmth of the sun changed it into a swift lizard that would disappear into a crevice of a rock. He and I would mend the wing of a wounded bird.

If we did bring home a salamander or ladybug, it would be only for a short while. Soon we would release our little friends into their natural surroundings. He knew where foxes, badgers, and rabbits had built their dens. He told me why the Roman Street (*Römerstrasse*) was called Roman Street. Our region had been occupied by the Roman Legions hundreds of years ago, and under the modern pavement were still the remnants by these early road builders.

He showed me a heart with his and my mother's initials, carved many years ago into the bark of a mighty oak tree in the middle of the forest.

When I was ten years old, World War II broke out, and my father became a faceless soldier of that war that swept across Europe. And when he returned, weighing eighty pounds, a faceless survivor of that great catastrophe from a Russian POW camp, I was eighteen years old. All these years I had missed him, but when he returned, I was an art student, not much interested in the woods and fields.

Some of those dabs of paint are my father's, some mine. Together they pay homage to this gentle and interesting man, who, when he was a young boy wanted to become an artist, but whose father would not let him.

In *Gymnasium,* or high school, *Herr* Krauss taught art. As a young man he had belonged to a Socialist Youth Group, and he was a follower of the German Expressionist Movement. Socialists and Expressionism quickly fell out of favor when Hitler came into power. Many Socialists were marched off to Dachau. The Expressionists were called "degenerate artists" and they were forbidden to paint. It was forbidden to view their paintings.

Somehow *Herr* Krauss hung on to his job as an art teacher. However, because of his youthful "sins" he was never promoted, and he was told to keep a low profile. A compromise he seemed to have accepted. I can still see *Herr* Krauss up front in the art room. He was a chain smoker and always had traces of ash all over his tweed suits. Holding up in his tobacco-stained hand last week's assignment, he'd say: "Hans Schmidt, good composition, lovely colors, beautifully drawn trees, but I can see that Carle drew this for you. An F for Hans Schmidt."

And so it would go with several more art assignments. Even though I had tried hard to develop an individual style for each of my classmates, *Herr* Krauss unmasked my crimes every time!

Remember, I hated school. I hated math and Latin. And I was a poor student. Now, Hans Schmidt was good in math and Latin, so we simply traded our talents.

I am still ashamed to admit that I sold my talent for a bratwurst from the butcher shop of the father of my classmate, Paul. Last year, my friend, Dr. Paul Katz, and I met after many years, and we still chuckled about the bratwurst-for-art-assignment swap.

One day, *Herr* Krauss asked me to come to his house. There he showed me reproductions of the "forbidden art," done by "degenerate artists."

"I like your drawings and paintings," *Herr* Krauss told me. "I like the rough and sketchy quality of your work. However, I have instructions to teach realistic and naturalistic art and not to foster what they call sloppy work. Look at these paintings, look at their rough and sketchy quality." Then he packed his forbidden art away and told me not to tell anyone what I had seen. For having such trust in me and for opening my eyes to the beauty of the Expressionists, *Herr* Krauss deserves two dabs of color on that canvas.

Most of my books are done in collage. Collage is nothing new. I did not invent the collage; they have been done by Picasso and by nursery school children and many others in between.

In *Brown Bear, Brown Bear, What Do You See?*, my first book for children, I used plain commercially available tissue papers, which come in about forty shades. After that book, I decided to give these hues more texture and color. So I began to paint with all kinds of brushes, finger-paint, splash and splatter onto these colored tissue papers.

Then I found out that these commercially available color-hued papers began to fade in the sun. Now I paint on plain white tissue papers. These by-me-prepared tissues become my palette.

What I am slowly discovering is that I am almost obsessed in creating richer and richer and more and more colorful colors than ever before. I suspect that I am still attempting to re-create those large colorful sheets of my kindergarten days in order to obliterate the darkness and the grays of my first grade.

If a recipe on How to Make a Picture Book were possible, it would go something like this: Take thirty-two pages (most picture books are thirty-two pages). Confine your story within these limitations. These limitations are of a technical nature. Your creative possibilities are endless. It helps to have a beginning, a middle, and an end.

Here are some basic ingredients to a few of my books: In *The Very Hungry Caterpillar,* I started with the holes—accidentally, playfully. The holes were the given. Now the caterpillar needed to be invented.

In *The Very Busy Spider,* the spider was the given. Now all I needed was the raised web.

In *The Grouchy Ladybug,* I wanted to deal with the concept of size. Now all I needed was an interesting story.

To these basic ingredients the following are added: Your love for animals, big and small.

Your appreciation for Nature.

Your father's love and his sense for passing on existing knowledge.

What you have learned from *Herr* Krauss.

You forget about your bamboo-wielding teacher (on second thought, you counteract and modify and transform that negative influence).

You entertain, teach, and challenge.

You include your likes and dislikes, your view of the world, your feelings.

And add an editor who gently prods you on.

Then like a musician, you decide on a format: Should it be a symphony, chamber music, or solo? The music should rise and fall, flow and come to an end with a crescendo or, if you feel like it, the softest bow of the violin. Then you hope for an echo. Forgive my mixed metaphors. I not only mixed dabs of paint and food but also music. But why not!

Perhaps my Uncle August had the answer to our question. My Uncle August was a Sunday painter. Sunday painters usually work as postal clerks, insurance agents, or investment bankers during the week, and paint on Sundays. My Uncle August painted on Sundays, but he didn't have a regular job during the week because on Monday, my Aunt Mina would sell his painting, and then the two would lead the high life, drinking and eating—mainly drinking—until Friday, when they would sober up. On Saturday, Uncle August got his paints, brushes, and canvas ready to paint again.

Uncle August was also a wonderful storyteller. Some weekends—happy weekends for me—I was invited to stay with Uncle August and Aunt Mina. When I arrived at their house, one of the oldest buildings in the old section of town, I'd sneak into his studio, a small unused bedroom, wait for the right moment, and say: "Uncle August, tell me a story." Peering over his glasses, he'd say, "First you have to wind up my thinking machine." And, as I had done many times before, I began to wind an imaginary lever near his temple. After a little while—all along he had made whirring noises—he shouted, "Halt! I have a story for you."

I like my Uncle August's answer to where stories come from. They come from your thinking machine. All you have to do is wind it up. A dab of paint for my Uncle August, the Sunday painter.

My time is up, and I am afraid that I have been less than successful with my dabs of color and my attempt to explain where ideas come from. It seems that instead of a painting, I have produced only a small sketch. But I hope you like my sketch. Thank you.

GENERAL COMMENTARY

Audrey Laski

SOURCE: "Painting with Papers," in *The Times Educational Supplement,* Vol. 3713, No. 1086, August 28, 1987, p. 14.

The Inner London Education Authority once published a set of video-recordings called *Becoming a Reader;* almost the first moment in it is the sight of a five-year-old girl at the very beginning of the process, playing back to her teacher the dearly loved history of *The Very Hungry Caterpillar* as her finger follows the brilliant, splashy pictures of the caterpillar working its way through an amazing menu to the moment when, recovered from stomach-ache, it emerges a beautiful butterfly. Told about this, Eric Carle, who looks a little like a silver teddy-bear, is touched and bewildered as he has been again and again by the universal love inspired by his second picture book.

While teachers notice the powerful cognitive educational features like the sense of sequencing and the ritualized appearance of the days of the week, he suspects that the appeal for children may be to do with the subtext about the possibilities of life, and with the tactile experience; as he says, we talk about "grasping an idea", and *The Very Hungry Caterpillar* enables a child to do this, as, with its embossed web, does *The Very Busy Spider.* What Eric Carle is sure of is the importance of the emotional experiences his books provide; he believes that "small children are capable of an enormous range of feelings" and is much more concerned with the support his books can give to those than with their more often recognized cognitive features. It is no accident that the dustjacket of *Papa, Please Get the Moon for Me,* published earlier this year, says more about the reassurance of Monica's father's willingness to climb up to the moon at her request than about the technical ingenuity of the unfolding pages.

Thus, his new book, *The Tiny Seed,* while it does not tackle as many aspects of learning as, say, *The Bad Tempered Ladybird,* is designed to work at greater depth. *Ladybird* at the most obvious level teaches the hours of the day, the comparative sizes of a series of creatures, and that it is more productive to be good-tempered than bad-tempered; less obviously, it introduces the pleasures of alliteration and, for the really alert child, the notion of the sun's apparent passage through the sky. *The Tiny Seed,* with its simple narrative of the single seed which survives a long and hazardous journey to produce a giant flower and, eventually, many more tiny seeds, seems on the surface to teach only the principles of seed transmission and germination and the single distinction of "tiny" from "giant." But, as Eric Carle says, it carries an "awesome message" about the extravagance of nature, the difficulty of survival and the promise of continuity.

Like all his most popular books, its stunning pictures are collages of coloured paper and other fabrics, painted in rich and subtle colours and cut out in simple shapes: "they're my palette—I really paint with papers." It's a method which pleases him because children recognize that they can use it too. He experiments continually to find ways "to make it more interesting . . . to get a new texture"; sometimes, like the stippled endpapers of *The Tiny Seed,* the new texture is the result of a happy accident, a brush shaken out over waste paper, the creative eye spotted something worth keeping.

He has been trying to make early learning more interesting since he was 40. As a child, he had just begun to appreciate a good American infant school—"large paper, colours, enjoyment"—when, at the age of six, he was moved to Germany and an education involving "small paper, hard pencils, the sense that you had to get it right." Returned to America, he pursued a career in advertising until his mid-thirties, and did not consciously think about children's books, even when his own son and daughter were small. But when he became a freelance illustrator, he started noticing how bad most of the children's books he saw were, and experimenting with "ways to make it more interesting." Fortunately, these experiments, undertaken at first without thought of publication, came to the notice of an inspired editor, Anne Beneduce, who got his first book, *One, Two, Three, to the Zoo!* published; *The Very Hungry Caterpillar* followed, and his true career was established.

He speaks with particular tenderness of one of his smallest books, whose only words are the five which make up its title: *Will you be My Friend?* It took only a couple of days to devise and then "I spent two years on it to get it right." Like so many of his books, it strikes an adult immediately with the wit and charm of the pictures and the way they draw a child inevitably in the right direction through the book. But for him, and probably for all the children who respond to it, what matters is the theme of friendship; he has never forgotten the depth of feeling associated with being separated from his best friend at the age of six.

On the way is a new book, *It's Time to Move, said Hermit Crab,* which will dramatize the process of growth and change that is the very stuff of a child's life. I expect, when I see it, that my first reactions will be to do with a strong and engaging surface. But now that I have met Eric Carle, I shall know to look below that surface to the emotional element within.

TITLE COMMENTARY

A HOUSE FOR HERMIT CRAB (1987)

Ann A. Flowees

SOURCE: A review of *A House for Hermit Crab,* in *Horn Book Magazine,* Vol. 64, No. 4, July-August, 1988, p. 477.

Brilliant, vigorous color-splashed illustrations are the backbone of [*A House for Hermit Crab,*] a story about a year in the life of a hermit crab. In January he finds his present shell is too small, and he timorously moves out. He finds a larger shell, just the right size but feels it is a little plain. Throughout the year he collects other forms of sea life, gently asking if they wish to join him. He finds a beautiful sea anemone, a handsome starfish, and a coral to decorate his house; a snail to keep it clean; a sea urchin to protect it; and a lanternfish to light it; and he even arranges a pile of pebbles for a setting. But then he realizes he has outgrown this shell as well. Sadly he gives it up to a smaller hermit crab, exacting a promise to be good to all the friends. He moves on out into the ocean, soon finding another shell and becoming enthusiastic about what kind of entourage can be added to his new home. "'Sponges!' he thought. 'Barnacles! Clown fish! Sand dollars! Electric Eels! . . . I can't wait to get started!'" Simple and easily understood information on the life of a hermit crab and the various other species is provided. The bright illustrations in Carle's familiar style, which seems particularly suited to undersea scenes, and the cumulative story are splendid, and one of the book's greatest strengths is the encouraging, hopeful view that the outside world is full of exciting possibilities.

Jane Doonan

SOURCE: A review of *A House for Hermit Crab,* in *The School Librarian,* Vol. 45, No. 3, August, 1997, p. 130.

Eric Carle has a self-confessed abiding love for small insignificant animals which appear as his characters, mostly involved in their natural activities but often exhibiting human emotions and foibles. Hermit Crab first traveled the sea bed in 1987 [in *A House for Hermit Crab*], decorating his house with the single-minded passion which inspires architects like Gaudi and customers of Sainsbury's Homebase. We creep alongside Hermit for a year watching him find a temporary shell, decorating it with sea anemones, starfish and corals, and gradually outgrowing his domestic work of art.

Carle's exuberant style and adventurous colour complements the subject matter; in collages of tissue paper, embellished with oil, tempera, pastel, and crayons, he creates transparent waters and dark green lanternfish-lit depths, occupied by a genial community of sea creatures practising symbiosis and courteously obliging each other. It's a matter of life and death too; the very first image on the title page is of a hungry shark. Brilliant in conception and execution, the picture book will give juniors a satisfying fiction replete with a dash of danger, unforced humour, and admirable role models; an aesthetic experience; a natural history lesson; and a demonstration of how non-fiction books work.

📖 *PAPA, PLEASE GET THE MOON FOR ME* (1987, REISSUED 1997)

Books for Keeps

SOURCE: A review of *Papa, Please Get the Moon for Me,* in *Books for Keeps,* No. 103, March, 1997, p. 18.

[*Papa, Please Get the Moon for Me*] is an old favourite reissued with novelty flaps and pop ups which work well, are robust enough not to up the anxiety levels of teachers or parents, and are supportive of the text rather than a superficial gimmick. Carle's story of the little girl whose father *does* fetch her the moon is an interesting mix of fantasy and reality that appealed from Nursery to Year Two. (Note to teachers—with Year Two this book provided us with a copybook 'planned assessment' situation—where were the OFSTED Inspectors then?)

Anne Hanzl

SOURCE: A review of *Papa, Please Get the Moon for Me,* in *Magpies,* Vol. 12, No. 1, March, 1997, p. 26.

Reaching for the moon and its mysteries has long been a preoccupation of little children and those who care for them—and as children know, such discussions can help to delay bedtime! In the picture book

[*Papa, Please Get the Moon for Me,*] 'Papa' is very obliging and tries very hard to get the moon for his daughter so she can play with it. He gets a very long ladder, puts it on top of the very high mountain and climbs to the moon who kindly explains that Papa can take him down to Monica but he will have to wait till he (the moon) is much smaller in size. Little Monica then has a lovely time playing with the moon until he becomes so small he disappears altogether. But one night a little sliver of the moon reappears in the sky . . .

Eric Carle, as readers have come to expect, uses a combination of bold colours, paint strokes, and collage with various kinds of paper engineering to tell his story. To emphasise the length of the *very long ladder,* for example, extra pages fold out horizontally, and to show the size of the full moon the pages fold out in a *moon burst.* This book should become a great favourite with young children and will inspire them to watch for the different phases of the moon. Fathers, however, will find themselves under considerable pressure to follow the example of Monica's father!

📖 *ERIC CARLE'S FAIRY TALES AND FABLES* (1988)

Margery Fisher

SOURCE: A review of *Eric Carle's Fairy Tales and Fables,* in *Growing Point,* Vol. 27, No. 2, July, 1988, p. 5016.

Eric Carle's jagged, sharply coloured collages give an oddly similar look [in *Eric Carle's Fairy Tales and Fables*] to such diverse tales as the touching account of Elsa and her swan-changed brothers and the roistering social comedy of the two Klauses; then there is the incisive moral of the fisherman and his greedy wife, shown beside increasingly ornate dwellings, and the fantastic journey of the Marsh King's daughter, resplendent with stylised Egyptian decorations. One particularly striking full-page plate shows a brisk housewife Ant peering from a window while, beside her, her offspring deck a Christmas tree and, outside, a Grasshopper begs sadly with his fiddle. The illustrative style is less well suited to Andersen, perhaps, than to the robust tales of Grimm and the Aesop fables in which animals are energetically humanised; all in all, the familiar tales are refreshed in a sequence of gorgeously fanciful pages.

📖 *ERIC CARLE'S ANIMALS, ANIMALS* (1990)

Bulletin of the Center for Children's Books

SOURCE: A review of *Eric Carle's Animals, Animals,* in *The Bulletin of the Center for Children's Books,* Vol. 43, No. 2, October, 1989, p. 47.

This poetry anthology [*Eric Carle's Animals, Animals*] is a splendid showcase for Carle's dramatic double image. Two haiku by Demaru and Issa, for instance, make perfect companions in describing "butterflies dancing through falling snow" on one page, and facing it, the observation of "how sadly the bird in his cage/ Watches the butterflies." The front part of a whale stretches across two pages that illustrate two lines from Genesis: the tail, surrounded by fish, extends onto the next two pages, which contain an African Pygmy chant and a haiku by Koson, both about fish. Prelutsky's poem, "Long Gone," is perched beside a painted Tyrannosaurus Rex that looms over John Gardner's "The Lizard," under which hides a childlike miniature of a dinosaur in the same brilliant green. Carle's textures are unfailingly intriguing, his colors eyecatching, his designs bold, his patterns innovative. [Laura] Whipple's selection [of poetry] should be credited for its variety, quality, and appeal. It's a winning combination.

Elizabeth S. Watson

SOURCE: A review of *Animals, Animals,* in *Horn Book Magazine,* Vol. 65, No. 6, November-December, 1989, p. 785.

This collaboration [*Eric Carle's Animals, Animals*] by two people who know children well has produced an immensely attractive and engaging book of poetry for the very young child. The poems vary widely and include haiku, Native American poetry, short familiar poems, pithy weather sayings, and Bible verses. Eric Carle's familiar style produces animals that children will recognize immediately. Some are displayed in double-page spreads; some share a page with other animals. Sixty-two poems extol various members of the animal kingdom; insects are included, and an illustration of Carle's familiar caterpillar may be found. The compilation is fresh, rhythmic, and humorous. The illustration for "Electric Eel" by X. J. Kennedy is more complex than most of the others and is particularly striking. *Animals, Animals* has a sure place on the story hour shelf, where it will be

sought again and again. Although other books of animal poetry exist for young children, this volume brings together suitable poems from other anthologies that are a perfect match for the illustrations.

📖 *THE VERY QUIET CRICKET* (1990)

Bulletin of the Center for Children's Books

SOURCE: A review of *The Very Quiet Cricket,* in *The Bulletin of the Center for Children's Books,* Vol. 44, No. 44, November, 1990, p. 56.

Remember the very hungry caterpillar and the very busy spider? Well, guess what? "One warm day, from a tiny egg a little cricket was born." The little cricket tries to answer greetings from each of the insects he meets: a big cricket, a locust, a praying mantis, a worm, a spittlebug, a cicada, a bumblebee, a dragonfly, mosquitoes, and a luna moth, but when he rubs his wings together, nothing happens . . . until he meets a female cricket, whereupon "he chirped the most beautiful sound that she had ever heard." You'll hear it too, because when you turn that page, [*The Very Quiet Cricket*] emits a distinct and realistically musical chirp from a device bound into the book. Although the text is more repetitive than cumulative, it can be read with dramatic voices for each creature (or, as suggested in the jacket blurb, as a voice-and-response game). Similarly, the physical device is not integrated into the whole story as continuously as in Carle's earlier books, but the final payoff is worth it; cricket noises can be very soothing at bedtime. Consumers are assured that "the battery will have a long life (a few years) as along as the book is always closed after each use." Carle's paintings stand out as dramatically as ever, catching the iridescent gleam of the insects' colors against plenty of white space. Having engineered sight, taste, touch, and sound so aesthetically into book form, Carle should go for smell next.

Lynne Babbage

SOURCE: A review of *The Very Quiet Cricket,* in *Magpies,* Vol. 6, No. 3, July, 1991, pp. 25-6.

Eric Carle is famous for his picture books about insects, especially *The Very Hungry Caterpillar.* In [*The Very Quiet Cricket*], a little cricket hatches from an egg and on each subsequent page a different

Illustration from **Draw Me a Star**

insect greets him. But when he tries to reply, he can't produce a sound. However it becomes obvious to the reader that both he and his wings are gradually growing bigger and finally, when he meets a lady cricket, he successfully rubs his wings together and . . . a small electronic strip chirps as the reader opens the last page.

Is this art or is it gimmickry? There is no doubt that the text is of high quality as are the collage illustrations. The repetition on each page is exactly right for the youngest listener and there is no doubt at all that they would love the sound effects. The publisher claims that with care the book can be used many, many times before the strip will stop issuing chirrup noises but librarians will probably be wary.

However the story will stand on its own merit, noise or no noise. Perhaps the book doesn't have quite the appeal of **The Very Hungry Caterpillar** but it is certainly more scientifically accurate. But is it just a gimmick? I'll leave you to decide.

DRAW ME A STAR (1992)

Kirkus Reviews

SOURCE: A review of *Draw Me a Star*, in *Kirkus Reviews,* Vol. 60, No. 17, September 1, 1992, p. 1126.

[*Draw Me a Star* is a] remarkable, quintessentially simple book encompassing Creation, creativity, and the cycle of life within the eternal. Introduced on the title page as a toddler drawing the first of five lines to make a star, an artist ages until, at the end, he's an old man who takes hold of a star to travel the night sky. Meanwhile, the first star says, "Draw me the sun"; the sun says, "Draw me a tree," and so on: woman and man; house, dog, cat, bird, butterfly, flowers, cloud; a rainbow arching over the middle-aged artist's whole creation; and back to the night and the stars. Carle's trademark style—vibrant tissue collage on dramatic white—is wonderfully effective in expressing the joy of creation, while the economy with which he conveys these universal ideas gives them extraordinary power. Yet the story is disarmingly childlike, concluding with an ingenuous letter from the author with instructions for drawing an eight-point star. Thanks be to the book for asking Carle to "draw" it!

Publishers Weekly

SOURCE: A review of *Draw Me a Star,* in *Publishers Weekly,* Vol. 239, No. 40, September 7, 1992, p. 95.

During his youth, this gifted author-artist explains in [*Draw Me a Star*]'s afterword, his German grandmother would often draw him a star while chanting a nonsense rhyme. Taking that symbol as his foundation, Carle here creates a world pulsating with life and color—a world that bursts forth from "a good star" sketched by a young artist. This kaleidoscopic pentagram requests a sun from the artist's pen; the sun asks for a tree, and so on until a man and woman are living happily among Carle's characteristic collages—flora and fauna of all shapes, sizes and vivid hues. Meanwhile the artist, now a bearded old man, continues to draw and create. This unusual, practically plotless work seems to embody a personal scenario close to the artist's heart. His unadorned language, pulsing with a hypnotic rhythm, adroitly complements the familiar naive artwork. Though some may be disturbed by similarities between Carle's evolving world and the biblical creation story (the unclothed male and female figures, for example), this tale of imagination and creativity pays homage to the artist within all of us—and may well fire youngsters' imaginations.

LITTLE CLOUD (1996)

Kathy Mitchell

SOURCE: A review of *Little Cloud,* in *School Library Journal,* Vol. 42, No. 5, May, 1996, p. 85.

[*Little Cloud* has a] familiar story line involving the whimsical world of ever-changing shapes in the sky. Little Cloud drifts away from his wispy friends and entertains himself by changing into a variety of forms—a lamb, an airplane, a shark, a clown, etc.—before joining the others to form one big cloud that rains . . . explores a similar theme. While the concept is not unique, the style is definitely Carle's own. His trademark painted cut-paper collages are eye-catching and appealing. Children will enjoy the simple text and the colorful illustrations.

Trevor Dickinson

SOURCE: A review of *Little Cloud,* in *The School Librarian,* Vol. 43, No. 11, November, 1997, p. 184.

First published in the USA, this large-format picture story book [*Little Cloud*] comprises, almost entirely, double-page illustrations—all but two of these in blue and cloud-white. The large-print black text itself is printed against a blue background: it is not, therefore, perhaps, as clear as it might need to be for some visually impaired readers. That said, however, this is a beautiful, gently absorbing book. Its brief, simple, repetitive prose combines perfectly with the artwork in presenting Little Cloud's sky journey and his constantly changing shapes. A delight in its own artistic right, the book, well used in the early years, should encourage close and interested observation of the wider world.

Additional coverage of Carle's life and career is contained in the following sources published by the Gale Group: *Major Authors and Illustrators for Children and Young Adults; Something about the Author,* Vols. 4, 65; *Something about the Author Autobiography Series,* Vol. 6.

Beverly Cleary
1916-

American author of fiction for children and pre-teens.

Major works include the "Henry Huggins" series beginning with *Henry Huggins* (1950), *The Mouse and the Motorcycle* (1965), the "Ramona" series beginning with *Ramona the Pest* (1968), *Socks* (1973), *Dear Mr. Henshaw* (1983).

For further information on Cleary's life and works, see *CLR,* Volumes 2 and 8.

Major works about Cleary: *A Girl from Yamhill* (Beverly Cleary, 1988), *Beverly Cleary* (Pat Pflieger, 1991), *My Own Two Feet* (Beverly Cleary, 1995).

INTRODUCTION

For over fifty years Beverly Cleary has been writing books for children about "plain, ordinary children like the ones I knew," who lived in neighborhoods like hers, and faced the everyday fears and pleasures of children. Although she is praised by critics for her clear, direct, and disarmingly simple style and for her timeless depiction of a child's inner life, children enjoy Cleary's books because they are funny and full of action, and because they recognize the children in them—honest, inquisitive, and sometimes a little naughty.

Cleary's best known works are the series about Henry Huggins and his dog Ribsy and the series about his neighbor, Ramona Quimby, and her family. *Henry Huggins* came to be because Cleary, in her role as children's librarian, was asked by a group of eleven-year-old boys for books "about kids like us." Being unable to find such books to satisfy this young male audience, she wrote one. If fact, she wrote several, ending the series with *Ribsy* (1964) fourteen years after publishing *Henry Huggins*. As Henry grew and matured, other characters in the books about him also began to develop. Henry's friend Beezus and her pesty little sister Ramona, spotlighted in *Beezus and Ramona* (1952), soon had their own series, written primarily from Ramona's point of view, that follows Ramona from the age of four through age ten over the course of seven books. Ramona, as do the other

children in Cleary's books, faces the normal problems children encounter while growing up, but Cleary's children learn how to work within their own social sphere to solve their own problems without adult interference, although they do use the services of supportive adults when needed.

Over the years, Cleary has expanded the reality she presents in her books to make them more relevant to the modern world, although the children in them, and the problems they face, are still those common to childhood. This is best exemplified by *Ramona and Her Father* (1977) and her Newbery award winner, *Dear Mr. Henshaw*. In the first of these two books, Ramona's father loses his job and her mother must return to work to support the family. This causes revolutionary, and not particularly happy, changes in their family life, changes with which Ramona must learn to cope. *Dear Mr. Henshaw* introduces a lonely little boy with low self esteem coming to terms with his parents divorce and his difficult relationship with an irresponsible father. Despite these serious situations, Cleary's stories are far from dull or moralistic, for her characters recognize the humor of life, even in difficult situations, and there are many funny moments.

Cleary has said, "The writer of fiction for children must be, first of all, a story-teller; if he cannot tell a story, his books will not last with children." She "simply writes the books I would have liked to read as a child," books that skipped "all that tiresome description" and allowed something to happen on every page, but above all with problems that the children solve themselves. In Cleary's neighborhood, growing up is never easy, but it can be funny.

BIOGRAPHICAL INFORMATION

Cleary has provided a detailed picture of her early years in her two biographies, *A Girl From Yamhill* (1988) and *My Own Two Feet* (1995). Born on a farm in Oregon, she spent four seemingly idyllic years in exploring life in the country, but when her father found the income from farming inadequate to support his family, he moved them to the city. Cleary grew up in a middle class suburb of Portland that became the setting for her Henry Huggins and Ramona books. She was happy to be in a busy neighborhood where there were other children to play with, but her experience of school in first grade was traumatic and miserable. The teaching methods imposed upon her made her decide that reading was not fun or pleasant, and it was not until she was eight that she discovered on her own how enjoyable reading could be. This experience colored her attitudes about education for the rest of her life, and she was a great advocate for making education, especially the teaching of reading, a pleasure. She began writing while young. Her mother encouraged her, telling her to "make it funny" and saying, "Always remember, the best writing is simple writing."

Cleary formed her opinion early of what she did *not* want to read, or write. She wanted the children in stories to be children as they truly were, not as they should be in the opinion of adults. She despised "any book in which a child reformed at all, any book in which problems were solved by a long-lost rich relative turning up in the last chapter, any book in which a family was grateful for the gift of a basket of groceries, usually on Christmas Eve, or any book in which a child turned out to be lord of the manor or

heir to a fortune. These things did not happen in my neighborhood. Neither did I want to read about a noble dog who died in the last chapter after a long journey home on bleeding paws nor any book in which a pioneer girl ran through the forest to warn settlers of Indians." She was also irritated by stories that turned into a reading lesson. She felt that the author "had cheated me. He had used a story to try to teach me. I bitterly resented this intrusion into my life." She firmly believed that authors should stay out of their books, nor should lessons masquerade as stories. "No child wants to read for pleasure a book written in a controlled vocabulary, tested on other children the way detergents are tested on house wives, and designed to teach. I certainly would not want to write such a book. It sounds like a tiresome task. Books for children should be written out of the desire to tell a story. If the reading is to be satisfying to the child, the writing should be satisfying to the author who is collaborating with his child self." "Children," she declared, "would learn so much more if they were allowed to relax, enjoy a story, and discover what it is they want or need from books."

Although Cleary wanted to go to college, her family was unable to afford it. She was fortunate in that an aunt offered to have her come to California where she could attend junior college for free, and although her mother was not happy about her leaving, her father encouraged her to go, seeing it as an opportunity for her to gain a profession. She went because she wanted to become independent. She attended the University of California at Berkeley, earning a B.A. in English in 1938. She met Clarence T. Cleary while at college and married him in 1940. Together, they moved to Oakland where Cleary gave birth to twins and worked as a post librarian at the Oakland Army Hospital. A job in the children's department of a bookstore in Berkeley convinced her that she could write a better book than many she saw there.

After attending the University of Washington in Seattle where she earned a B.A. in librarianship, she became a children's librarian in Yakima, Washington. There, she learned to tell stories and was inspired to write her first children's book, *Henry Huggins*, when she was unable to help a group of boys find humorous books that they wanted to read "about kids like us." Using material from her own life, she began her first book on January 2, and since then has begun nearly all of her books on the same date. Her setting was the neighborhood where she had grown up in Portland, and thirteen of her books take place on or near Klickitat Street. William Morrow accepted *Henry*

Huggins immediately, and Cleary's relationship with the publisher continued for many decades and through several editors.

MAJOR WORKS

Henry Huggins was Cleary's first book and was an immediate success. Its episodic format follows the everyday adventures of Henry and his dog Ribsy. Henry never means to get into trouble, but somehow trouble just turns up, and Ribsy is usually at the heart of the trouble. *Henry Huggins* was followed by four more titles featuring Henry—*Henry and Ribsy* (1954), *Henry and the Paper Route* (1957), *Henry and the Clubhouse* (1962), and *Ribsy.*

Beezus Quimby is a friend of Henry. Both she and her sister, Ramona, appear in the "Henry" books, and were featured in their own book, *Beezus and Ramona,* but it was with *Ramona the Pest* that the "Ramona" series really began. Ramona does not think she is a pest; it is bigger people who call her that. She is just "a girl who could not wait. She just had to find out what would happen next." Used to getting her own way by making big noisy fusses, Ramona finds out that in kindergarten things are different. The experiences she has in school gradually begin to socialize her, but nothing can break her spirit. Cleary continued to document Ramona's growing up in six more books—*Ramona the Brave* (1975), *Ramona and Her Father* (1977), *Ramona and Her Mother* (1979), *Ramona Quimby, Age 8* (1981), *Ramona Forever* (1984), and *Ramona's World* (1999).

Not all Cleary's books are about children. One of her most popular books is *The Mouse and the Motorcycle,* with its sequels *Runaway Ralph* (1970) and *Ralph S. Mouse* (1982). Ralph lives with his large family in the walls of a busy hotel. He achieves distinction when he obtains a toy motorcycle and begins his travels through the world. His adventures eventually lead him back home to his family, but the thrill of the ride never leaves him. The more realistic *Socks* is the story of a spoiled cat whose position in the household is usurped by a new baby. Told from the perspective of the cat, Socks eventually learns to adjust to his new family and contents himself with his new position in the household.

Leigh Botts, the protagonist of *Dear Mr. Henshaw,* is lonely and unhappy. His parents have divorced; he seldom hears from or sees his father; and someone keeps stealing his lunch. By writing letters to his fa-

vorite author and answering the questions he poses, Leigh begins to come to terms with his situation and gains some self esteem by devising a method to catch the lunch thief. Cleary wrote a second book about Leigh, *Strider,* in 1991.

AWARDS

Cleary has been honored with a host of awards, both for her books and for her contribution to children's literature. In the "Henry Huggins" series, *Henry Huggins* (1950) received the New England Round Table of Children's Librarians Honor Book Award in 1972, *Henry and Ribsy* (1954) received the Young Readers' Choice Award from the Pacific Northwest Library Association in 1957, *Henry and the Paper Route* (1957) won the Young Readers' Choice Award from Pacific Northwest Library Association in 1960, and *Ribsy* (1964) won the Dorothy Canfield Fisher Memorial Children's Book Award in 1966 and the Nene Award from the Hawaii Association of School Librarians in 1968.

Fifteen (1956) won the Dorothy Canfield Fisher Memorial Children's Book Award in 1958, and *Jean and Johnny* (1959) received a Notable Book Citation from the American Library Association in 1961.

The Mouse and the Motorcycle (1965) received a Notable Book Citation from the American Library Association in 1966, the Young Readers' Choice Award from Pacific Northwest Library Association in 1968, the South Central Iowa Association for Classroom Teachers Youth Award in 1968, the William Allen White Award from the Kansas Association of School Libraries and Kansas Teachers' Association in 1968, the Nene Award from the Hawaii Association of School Librarians and Hawaii Library Association in 1969, the New England Round Table of Children's Librarians Honor Book Award in 1973, the Sue Hedley Award from the Louisiana Association of School Librarians in 1973, the Surrey School Book Award from the Surrey School District in 1974, and the Great Stone Face Award in 1983.

Other books in the series also earned awards. *Runaway Ralph* (1970) won the Nene Award in 1972 and the Charlie Mae Simon Award from the Arkansas Elementary School Council in 1973. *Ralph S. Mouse* (1982) was named to the *School Library Journal* Best Books of 1982 list and received the Parent's Choice Award in 1982, the Golden Kite Award from the Society of Children's Book Writers in 1982, the

Californian Association of Teachers of English Award in 1983, the Garden State Children's Choice Award in 1985, the Iowa Children's Choice Award from the Iowa Educational Media Association in 1985, the Surrey School Award in 1986, and the West Virginia Award for 1986-87.

Of course the "Ramona" books have garnered their share of attention. *Ramona the Pest* (1968) won the Georgia Children's Book Award from the College of Education of the University of Georgia in 1970, the Young Readers' Choice Award from the Pacific Northwest Library Association in 1971, the Nene Award in 1971, the Sequoyah Children's Book Award from the Oklahoma Library Association in 1971, and the Young Reader's Choice Award in 1971, and was nominated for the Massachusetts Children's Book Award in 1977.

Ramona the Brave (1975) received the Golden Archer Award in 1977 and the Mark Twain Award from the Missouri Library Association and the Missouri Association of School Librarians in 1978.

Ramona and Her Father (1977) was highly honored. In 1978 it won a Notable Book Citation from the American Library Association, inclusion on the *Horn Book* Honor List, was named a Newbery Honor Book by the American Library Association, and won the *Boston Globe-Horn Book* Honor Award, the International Board on Books for Young People Honor Book Award, the Tennessee Children's Book Award from the Tennessee Library Association, the Utah Children's Book Award from the Children's Library Association of Utah, and the Garden State Award from the New Jersey Library Association. In 1980 it received the Young Readers' Choice Award from the Pacific Northwest Library Association, and the Nene Award. 1981 brought the Land of Enchantment (New Mexico) Children's Award and the Texas Bluebonnet Award.

Ramona and Her Mother (1979) won the American Book Award in 1981, the Garden State Children's Choice Award from the New Jersey Library Association in 1982, the Surrey School Award in 1982, and the Buckeye Children's Book Award in 1985.

Ramona Quimby, Age 8 (1981) won the American Book Award in 1981, was named a *School Library Journal* Best Book of 1981, received a Newbery Honor Book Award from the American Library Association in 1982, and won the Charlie Mae Simon Award in 1984, the Garden State Children's Choice Award in 1984, the Charles Near Simon Award from

the Arkansas Elementary School Council in 1984, the Michigan Young Readers Award in 1984, and the Buckeye Children's Book Award in 1985.

Ramona Forever (1984) received a *New York Times* Notable Book Award in 1984, the Parent's Choice Award in 1984, and the Iowa Children's Choice Award in 1987.

Socks (1973) won the William Allen White Award in 1976 and the Golden Archer Award from the University of Wisconsin in 1977.

Besides winning the Newbery Medal in 1984, *Dear Mr. Henshaw* won many other awards. The *School Library Journal* named it a Best Book of 1983, and the same year it was named a *New York Times* Notable Book and received the Parent's Choice Award, and the Christopher Award. In 1984 it was named to the *Horn Book* Honor List, received the Commonwealth Silver Medal from Commonwealth Club of California and a Notable Book Citation from the American Library Association. It won the Dorothy Canfield Fisher Memorial Children's Book Award in 1985, and in 1986 the Garden State Award, the Massachusetts Award, and the Sequoyah Award. It received a FOCAL in 1987 and the Nene Award in 1989. Its sequel, *Strider* won the Reading Magic Award in 1991.

Cleary's autobiography, *A Girl From Yamhill* received the Reading Magic Award in 1988 and the Bay Area Book Reviewers Association Award in 1989, and *Muggie Maggie* won the Garden State Award for Younger Fiction in 1993.

Other awards won for her contribution to children's literature are the Distinguished Alumna Award from the University of Washington in 1975; the Laura Ingalls Wilder Award from the American Library Association in 1975, for substantial and lasting contributions to children's literature; the Children's Choice Election Award, second place in 1978; the Regina Medal from the Catholic Library Association in 1980, for continued distinguished contributions to literature; the de Grummond Award from the University of Southern Mississippi in 1982, for distinguished contributions to children's literature; the Medallion from the University of Southern Mississippi in 1982; the George C. Stone Award in 1983; the *Everychild* honor citation in 1985, for her 35 year contribution to children's literature; the CBC Honors Program in 1985; and the Jeremiah Ludington Award in 1987.

But the laughter of my children at the absurdity of *Beady Bear,* while telling me something about the sense of humor in infants, did not explain why schoolchildren found my early books funny and sad. The answer came from an incident involving my son and the refrigerator door. For several years he had aspired to open the refrigerator all by himself. (This was before the days of magnetic doors.) First of all, he had to grow tall enough to reach the handle. This took several years, very long years to him, for children are impatient to grow. When at last he was tall enough to reach the handle, he tugged and yanked, but the refrigerator door remained stubbornly closed until one day when he was five years old, he was so angry at the refrigerator that he gave the door an extra hard yank as he was passing by. The door opened. He stared in joy and astonishment, and with the light from the refrigerator shining on his face, he burst into laughter, his anger and frustration forgotten. For weeks, every time he opened that door, which was often, he laughed. Opening that door was the funniest thing that had ever happened to him. Aside from the initial element of surprise, always important in humor, he laughed because he had grown.

Growth is, I believe, the essence of humor that children enjoy in realistic stories. I now understand why *The Peterkin Papers* which librarians pressed upon me as a funny book when I was a child, did not amuse me one bit. I took adults seriously and felt that the Peterkins were stupid instead of funny. An overly conscientious child, I had not matured enough to see adults in their proper perspective and did not find the Peterkins funny until I was an adult.

Children laugh because they have grown. We all laugh if we have grown. That is why we are no longer ashamed—most of the time—by those embarrassing experiences of childhood or youth. The time we made the whole class laugh by pronouncing apPENdix as APpendix and the time in a high school English class when we were studying *As You Like It* and made the class titter by innocently asking the teacher the meaning of *maidenhead* now seem funny instead of embarrassing, because we have grown.

Psychologists tell us that humor is a way of relieving anxiety and that in every humorous incident someone is made to appear or become inferior. (This information has been plucked from my morning newspaper—I certainly don't want to give the impression that I spend my time reading psychological journals.) From what I have observed, it seems to me that children enjoy feeling superior to their younger selves and are relieved to know they have grown.

This explains why children find sad the parts of books that adults label "purely for amusement." Children are too close to some of the dilemmas of childhood to have resolved their feelings, so they are unable to feel superior to their younger selves. Children who cannot resolve these dilemmas as they grow are the ones who laugh at acts of cruelty done to others—which may be "fun" for the emotionally immature but which are never done "in fun."

Children have taught me much. They have not only told me my books were funny and sad, they were insistent about wanting a whole book about Ramona, the pesty little sister in the books about Henry Huggins. At first I paid little attention to this request, for in those days I still believed what we had been taught in library school: Children did not want to read about characters younger than themselves; and girls would read about boys, but boys would not read about girls. Gradually I saw that these generalizations did not hold if children found books funny. Many boys wrote telling me they had enjoyed *Ellen Tebbits,* and both boys and girls asked for a book about Ramona, who was younger than the writers of those letters.

As my own children reached the age of the children who read my books, I noticed that nothing was so funny to them as their memories of kindergarten and nursery school, which became the subject of many hilarious dinner table conversations. They both laughed at their younger selves, that now-amusing kindergarten pair who had wanted to be the wake-up fairy after rest time and to whom show-and-tell had been such serious business. How ridiculous to have been so childish, they felt by the time they were eight or nine. I began to understand that children would enjoy a book about a younger girl because they would recognize and enjoy feeling superior to their younger selves.

Ramona the Pest, a book I thought about for fifteen years before writing, was the result of listening to children's requests, and it has proven to be one of my most popular books with children from kindergarten through junior high school. Many children tell me they laugh at Ramona because they used to act like her or because they have a little brother or sister exactly like her, implying that they are now much too grown-up to behave like that little brother or sister. A few, who do not always mention laughter, say they feel like Ramona. These readers have not matured enough to see their younger selves in perspective.

A five-year-old girl, whom I once asked what she wanted to be when she grew up, looked at me as if I had asked a stupid question—which of course I had—and answered, "A grown-up." To grow up is the ambition of normal children; and they want, and are sometimes starved for, humorous books because they want the assurance they have grown. As Ann Nolan Clark once said in an interview: "Anyway you look at it, it's rugged to be a child. Often I think more of us did not survive the experiences than meets the eye." I feel that books that help children laugh at their younger selves are the books that help them survive.

Children need humorous books for another reason—to convince them that reading is a worthwhile experience. Today many children are doubtful, telling me that they don't understand most books they find in the library or saying they get lost in the first chapter and don't know what the author is talking about. Many write that they find most books rotten or boring. Those who are beginning to understand that reading is something more than schoolwork tell me it is good to know there are books they can like. Those who are convinced of the joys of reading write ecstatic letters saying they love books and can't get enough of reading.

Over the years the first books to catch the imagination of children who have escaped the reading circle and are ready to discover the pleasures of reading have been simply written humorous books. Lucy Fitch Perkins's twins and Dr. Dolittle in the twenties and thirties as well as Freddy the Detective, little Eddie, Pippi Longstocking, Paddington, Encyclopedia Brown, Henry Huggins, and Ramona Quimby are characters that children have taken to their hearts. These fictional friends have made translating the lines of little black symbols a pleasure and have freed readers to grow, to progress to books of greater depth and complexity.

The best humor, although it may be broad, leaves room for growth. The episode that is merely a pratfall or a pie in the face will make a child laugh and may even lure him into books because he can easily understand it. Such humor is, after all, another version of topsy-turvy or nonsense humor and is valuable because it *is* easily understood. Younger readers often tell me that the incident in which a bucket of green paint falls on Henry Huggins is the funniest part of the book. These children are often the writers of those sad little letters that say, "Most books I find I can't understand." We should not underestimate

slapstick humor, but as a reader matures, it will not be enough, because it does not help him gain insights into himself and the world around him. Eventually, slapstick will seem less hilarious and, in its lack of room for growth, may even seem tiresome.

A good children's book does not bore a child for a second, third, or many more readings. It does not, as teachers of children's literature tell us, bore an adult who shares it with a child. If the author has written from a double point of view, the reader will make fresh discoveries as he grows. A ten-year-old reading *Porko von Popbutton* by William Pène Du Bois (Harper) will probably read it as a funny-serious story about the triumph of a fat boy who attends a boarding school where students and administration are enthusiastic about ice hockey. A few years later, he will find the story even funnier and may laugh aloud, as my son laughed, at the satirical picture of team sports. A ten-year-old reading Marilyn Sachs's *Marv* (Doubleday) will see as something of a villain Marv's big sister Frances, who attends Hunter College and is so desperately serious about the plight of the world that she feels everything Marv invents must be practical. An older reader will find Frances touchingly funny because she *is* so desperately serious. The authors have allowed room for growth. Readers are amused and delighted to discover fresh insight, as happens when they read and reread such writers as E. B. White, Lloyd Alexander, and E. Nesbit.

To conclude, what can I say on a subject I try not to think about? Humor, that gossamer butterfly, is so elusive that some people catch only an occasional glimpse. Some, who see cruelty to others as funny, have never developed the imagination to put themselves in another's place and will never understand humor; I wonder if they will survive. Those around them may not. We read about their victims in the newspapers every day. Others, the fortunate ones, see humor all around them; few will agree on exactly what it is. Children, in a world grown grim, long for it. "Why don't authors write more books that will make me laugh?" they ask. We can only do our best to offer children books—first, books of nonsense humor and then books in which there is room for growth—in hopes that as they read, or are read to, they will laugh and think in secret triumph, I used to do that or, I feel that way or, I am too grown-up to act that way now. To be a grownup, as the five-year-old girl reminded me, is the ambition of every normal child. Laughter helps children on their way.

Beverly Cleary

SOURCE: "Waxing Creative," in *Publishers Weekly,*
Vol. 242, No. 29, July 17, 1995, pp. 138-41.

I recall my pleasure upon entering the first grade at
seeing above the blackboard a reproduction of Sir
Joshua Reynolds's painting *The Age of Innocence,* I
was filled with admiration for the pretty little girl
who was wearing, to my six-year-old eyes, a white
party dress. I loved that little girl, but by Thanksgiving my love had changed to resentment. There she
sat under a tree with nothing to do but keep her party
dress clean. There I sat itching in my navy blue serge
sailor dress, the shrunken elastic of my new black
bloomers cutting into my legs, struggling to learn to
read.

My first grade was sorted into three reading groups—
Bluebirds, Redbirds, and Blackbirds. I was a Blackbird, the only girl Blackbird among the boy Blackbirds, who had to sit in the row by the blackboard.
Perhaps this was the beginning of my sympathy for
the problems of boys. How I envied the bright, self-
confident Bluebirds, most of them girls, who got to
sit by the windows and who, unlike myself, pleased
the teacher by remembering to write with their right
hands—a ridiculous thing to do, in my six-year-old
opinion. Anyone could see that both hands were alike.
One should simply use the hand nearer the task. To
be a Blackbird was to be disgraced. I wanted to read,
but somehow I could not. I wept at home while my
puzzled mother tried to drill me on the dreaded word
charts. "But reading is fun," insisted my mother. I
stomped my feet and threw the book on the floor.
Reading was not fun.

By second grade I was able to plod through my
reader a step or two ahead of disgrace. Although I
could read if I wanted to, I no longer wanted to.
Reading was not fun. It was boring. Most of the stories were simplified versions of folktales that had
been read aloud to me many times. There were no
surprises left.

Then, in third grade, the miracle happened. It was a
dull rainy Portland Sunday afternoon when there was
nothing to do but thumb through two books from the
Sunday school library. After looking at the pictures, I
began out of boredom to read *The Dutch Twins* by
Lucy Fitch Perkins. Twins had always fascinated me.
As a small child, I had searched through magazines—my only picture books—for pictures of the
Campbell Soup twins. To me, a solitary child, the
idea of twins was fascinating. A twin would never be

lonely. Here was a whole book about twins, a boy
and girl who lived in Holland but who had experiences a girl in Portland, Oregon, could share. I could
laugh when the boy fell into the Zuyder Zee because
I had once fallen into the Yamhill River. In this story,
something happened. With rising elation, I read on. I
read all afternoon and evening, and by bedtime I had
read not only *The Dutch Twins* but *The Swiss Twins*
as well. It was one of the most exciting days of my
life. Grown-ups were right after all. Reading was
fun.

GENERAL COMMENTARY

Jean Streufert Patrick

SOURCE: "'I Am Just a Plain Boy': Leigh Botts'
Changing Conception of Self in Beverly Cleary's
Dear Mr. Henshaw," in *Proceedings of the Thirteenth
Annual Conference of the Children's Literature Asso-
ciation,* 1988, pp. 84-87.

When I think about Henry Higgins, Beezus and Ramona Quimby, I still imagine them as I did as a child.
Klickitat Street, where Beverly Cleary's characters
lived, was somewhere in Oregon, I knew. But in my
mind, Klickitat Street was my street, 4th Avenue, in
Maywood, Illinois—and somehow, all of Cleary's
characters lived on 4th Avenue, too. I liked Cleary's
books because they were about what I considered to
be "normal" everyday life, the less-than-glamorous
life that I was leading in a middle-class Chicago
suburb. I especially liked Cleary because she never
treated her characters—who were, in some sense,
myself—as average: average kids with average
problems. Her characters were important, special.
And, as I remembered, her characters always knew
this about themselves, too.

But I was disappointed when I first started to read
Dear Mr. Henshaw (1983). Initially, I suppose I was
disturbed because a Cleary "regular" was not receiv-
ing the Newbery Award. Not a Huggins, not a
Quimby. Not even Ralph S. Mouse. Rather, some
new kid—Leigh Botts—had stepped forward out of
nowhere, wearing the Newbery seal. Also, I couldn't
imagine this new character living on my Klickitat
Street. He did not live in suburbia. His parents were
divorced. And he told his own story, through a series
of letters and diary entries, unlike Cleary's earlier
characters.

I could make room for these changes. Cleary had lots of characters besides those belonging to the Klickitat tribe. Also, "normal, everyday life" now included single parent families. But another change *did* disturb me, that of the protagonist's character. Unlike other Cleary characters, whom I remembered as having strong self images, Leigh saw himself as an average kid, possessing no unique attributes. Part of Leigh's response to Mr. Henshaw's first question, "Who are you" was: "I am just a plain boy." To the question "What do you look like?", Leigh droned, "I am sort of medium. I don't have red hair or anything like that. I'm not real big like my Dad. . . . In first and second grades kids used to call me Leigh the Flea, but I have grown. Now when the class lines up according to height, I am in the middle. I guess you could call me the mediumest boy in the class" (*DMH* 15 Nov. 20).

After about forty pages, I put the book down. This character, who judged himself as less than special, less than unique, was clearly un-Clearyish. Leigh did not belong with children like Beezus, whose uniqueness disturbed her or Henry, originator of creative ideas. And certainly, Leigh Botts did not belong on the same shelf with Ramona, who constantly expressed her uniqueness with her signature.

Fortunately, I did finish reading **Dear Mr. Henshaw**. I watched Leigh struggle and grow through his interaction with his peers, through his writing, and through his relationship with his father. I watched Leigh acquire a positive self image, an assurance that he was a special individual. But more importantly, I carefully re-read the works of Cleary's canon, rather than relying on my memory to make that trip. Some differences I had noticed between **Dear Mr. Henshaw** and Cleary's other works were confirmed—setting, family, first person narration. However, I discovered that Leigh, as a character, is not drastically different from the Cleary characters of Klickitat Street. They, too, had struggled with their uniqueness. The self-assurance that I remembered and admired in each character was not a given. Although a journey as pronounced as Leigh's from "average" to unique had not occurred on Klickitat Street, that is not to say that Ramona's "logo" had never been threatened, or that Henry had never doubted his gifts of creativity. Leigh was not the first Cleary character who struggled to see himself as unique.

For example, in **Henry and the Paper Route** (1957), Henry initially sees himself as an exceptional ten-year-old, exceptional enough to hold a paper route,

although Scotter McCarthy and Mr. Capper think otherwise. When Murph, an agemate, moves to town, Henry tries to impress him by bragging about the open route that might soon be his. But Henry regrets his bragging. Murph, he knows, is a genius. Henry then begins to sound like the early Leigh. "'How dumb can I get?' . . . Now Murph would probably go after the route, and what chance did Henry have against a brain. . . . Not a chance. . . . Not a chance at all" (96-97). When Murph gets the route (because of past experience), Henry again elevates Murph to extraordinary heights and lowers himself to the helpless average. "Naturally," Henry thinks. "A genius can do anything—anything at all" (105).

However, after Ramona torments Murph, he offers the route to Henry, who gladly accepts it—surprised that a genius could be licked by a four-year-old. Henry is not immune to Ramona's antics either, but he devises a way to prevent her from delivering his papers (she says they are hers) by creating a robot mask from a hatbox, and suggesting that she be Murph's robot, Thorvo. Henry once again sees himself as unique: "It was pretty smart of him to think of it, Henry thought modestly. Maybe he wasn't a genius like Murph, but he wasn't so dumb, either. In some ways he was even smarter than Murph. Henry found himself pleased with the thought of being smarter than a genius" (120), his self image restored.

In **Ramona the Brave** (1975), Ramona enters first grade. To be different, she removes her name tag from her desk and adds her special logo, the trademark she created in kindergarten from the first letter of her last name. But her mark of uniqueness is ridiculed when Mrs. Griggs callously asks if she should call her Ramona Kitty Cat. Her individuality faces a more severe test when the first grade makes Halloween owls. Ramona decides to make her own different from her classmates'. She positions her owl's eyes to the left. She draws spectacles. She draws V's on the wings. But Susan copies each of Ramona's artistic moves, and as the final injustice, Mrs. Griggs holds up Susan's owl for the class to admire.

In **Ramona the Pest** (1968), Ramona feared she had lost her identity under her witch costume and mask. This Halloween, although she knows she is the original owl-designer, she fears that no one else in her class knows this. Furious, "Ramona looked at her own owl, which no longer seemed like her own . . . Now everyone would think Ramona had copied Susan's owl when it was the other way around. They would call her Ramona Copy Cat instead of Ramona

Kitty Cat" (52). Ramona squashes her owl and later scrunches Susan's.

Nothing is easily resolved. Although her dad empathizes with the artist's need to have his work be his very own, and her mother assures her that she is luckier than Susan since she has imagination, Ramona must still apologize to Susan in front of the class. But as first grade continues, she does regain confidence in her originality. When Ramona loses her shoe, after throwing it at a big dog, she creates a paper slipper. This ingenious slipper wins the attention of her classmates and even helps her win a battle with Mrs. Griggs. She persuades her teacher to excuse her from making Thanksgiving turkeys like everyone else in the class in order that she may perfect her slipper.

Ramona Quimby, Age 8 (1981) also follows this pattern. Ramona enters third grade at a new school, pleased that she will not be compared to Beezus. However, her individuality becomes a problem. After accidentally cracking a raw, rather than a hard-boiled egg against her head, attempting to follow the third grade fad, Ramona overhears Miss Whaley call her a nuisance. Ramona's response is to attempt not to stand out, to attempt to be, in Leigh's terminology, the "mediumest." In subtle ways, such as vowing not to write her Q's in cursive, she can still be an individual. But generally, Ramona tries not to draw attention to herself, not even volunteering answers in the classroom. Then all backfires when she says nothing when she feels sick to her stomach. Ramona throws up. That afternoon, she christens herself "Supernuisance."

Next, Ramona faces a critical decision. For a book report, Miss Whaley wants her to pretend to sell the book *Left Behind Cat*. Does she sell the book as a commercial would, revealing her creative self, but reinforcing her nuisance status? Or, does she give a safe, average sales talk, one as uninteresting as everyone else's, one which will ensure that she does not stand out? Ramona chooses the creative route. But the book report, performed in costume to the tune of a cat food commercial, is nearly catastrophic. Ramona blanks and blurts, "I can't believe I read the whole thing" (161). The event serves as the catalyst Ramona needs to confront Miss Whaley. Ramona survives. She is free to be her un-average self in the classroom.

Like earlier Cleary characters, Leigh Botts struggles with his individuality. However, the narrative structure of ***Dear Mr. Henshaw*** differs. In the earlier

Cleary works, the characters are primarily rediscovering or reaffirming their individuality. They fall from the security of being unique and then journey back from the nadir of being average to the assurance of being special. However, after a quick introduction to him through letters written in the second through fifth grades, Leigh's story begins at the bottom of the inverted arc. In the autumn of the school year, Leigh—lonely and depressed—believes that he might be "a boy nobody pays much attention to" (7 Nov. 25). The only thing about him that they pay attention to is his lunch. But this is no comfort, especially since this stamp of identity disappears each time the lunchbag thief strikes.

When Leigh discovers that he is not so medium, the adults at school—Mr. Fridley, the custodian, and the librarian begin to notice him. When he installs a burglar alarm on his lunch pail and it blasts across the cafeteria, Leigh receives instant recognition from the teachers and the students. Leigh writes, "I began to feel like some sort of hero. Maybe I'm not so medium after all" (101-102 March 5).

Leigh also realizes his individual worth through his writing experiences. Early in his sixth grade year, Leigh writes to Mr. Henshaw that he wants to write books exactly like his. But, in spring, Leigh submits an original piece to his school's Young Authors contest, and wins Honorable Mention. Angela Badger, the visiting author, praises the special value of his individuality. "I happen to like *A Day on Dad's Rig* because it was written by a boy who wrote honestly about something he knew and had strong feelings about. . . . You wrote like *you,* and you did not try to imitate someone else. This is one mark of a good writer" (119-120 March 26). Leigh no longer is the mediumest. Like Henry, who realized that he was smart in his own way, Leigh begins to understand that his experiences and his interest in trucking have special worth.

The steepest part of Leigh's journey involves his relationship with his father. Leigh perceives himself to be less than special. For example, Leigh's father always ends their conversations by saying, "Well, keep your nose clean kid." Leigh, frustrated, writes, "Why can't he say he misses me and why can't he call me Leigh?" (28 Dec. 1). He also wishes for visible attention, for companionship—that his dad would take him to school in his rig and would say, "So long, Leigh. Be seeing you." And in his log book, Leigh fantasizes, his father would write, "Drove my son to school" (29-30 Dec. 1).

Leigh also is frustrated by the mixed signals his father sends him. He sends support payments. He sends a great gift at Christmas. However, his father does not call when he writes that he will. Leigh's self image remains low. Once, when his father doesn't call, Leigh phones him, just wanting to be comforted by hearing the phone ring in what he assumes to be his father's empty place. But his father answers. When Leigh asks about his dog, Bandit, his dad begins, "Well, kid." Sparks of the growing individual flash when Leigh interrupts, "My name is Leigh. . . . I'm not just some kid you met on the street" (70-71 Feb. 4). This spark is extinguished, however, when he hears a voice in the background say, "Hey, Bill, Mom wants to know when we're going out to get the pizza" (72 Feb. 4). His father is taking another boy out for pizza when he, Leigh, is home alone. This substitution haunts him a month later in another phone conversation, when he asks his father if he has found a replacement for the missing Bandit. Leigh writes, admitting, "I think what I really meant was, Have you found another boy to take my place" (105 March 16).

Not until the end of March does Leigh discover how special he is to his dad. His dad drives up to the house in his rig (almost a dream come true), but greets him with the all-too-familiar, "How're you doing kid?" And he is depressed that his dad is only there because he is waiting for his reefer to be filled in Salinas. But Leigh reaches a peace on this spring day, even after his mother plainly rejects his father's hope for resuming the relationship. Leigh receives a verbal embrace as his father leaves. "So long, Leigh. . . . You're a good kid, Leigh. I'm proud of you, and I'll try not to let you down. . . . See you around" (132-134 March 31). His dad has called him son. . . . Leigh. Leigh knows enough now that he cannot count on visits or calls, but he knows that he is special. Leigh writes: "Maybe it was broccoli that brought Dad to Salinas, but he had come the rest of the way because he really wanted to see us. I felt sad and a whole lot better at the same time" (134 March 31).

As a reader, I felt better, too, especially after comparing my memories of Cleary's characters with my newly-acquired textual knowledge of them. Growing up in a "typical" suburban setting, I needed Cleary to give me the assurance—through the treatment of her characters—that I was not average. From the start of each book, I had this assurance that the characters knew they were special. When they fell, I knew they would return to the security of a positive self image.

As a result, I suppose my memory was selective; I chose to remember the uniqueness of the characters as a given. And perhaps the narrative structure encouraged this. A re-reading of the works, however, provided me with something much different from my memory's trip to the past. Leigh's story belongs with the stories of the others of my Klickitat Street, despite the narrative variations. Leigh, like the others, has struggled to understand his special worth as an individual. For none of Cleary's characters has it been a journey without challenge.

Works Cited

Cleary, Beverly. *Dear Mr. Henshaw*. New York: Morrow, 1983.

———. *Henry and the Paper Route*. 1957; rpt. New York: Scholastic, 1972.

———. *Ramona Quimby, Age 8*. 1981; rpt. New York: Dell, 1983.

———. *Ramona the Brave*. 1975; rpt. New York: Scholastic Book Services, 1975.

———. *Ramona the Pest*. New York: Morrow, 1968.

Bruce Chadwick

SOURCE: "A Theory of Writing for Young Children: Arguing for a Moffett-Vygotsky Reading of Beverly Cleary's *Dear Mr. Henshaw*," in *The Lion and the Unicorn*, Vol. 11, No. 2, November, 1987, pp. 141-63.

In a recent article in the *New York Times*, Daniel Goleman wrote about the importance of children writing letters to the relatives of the astronauts who died in the explosion of the space shuttle *Challenger* on January 28, 1986. The children, he explained, could not readily explain or accept the sudden, violent loss of life, nor, he implied, could they understand the *idea* of loss. "The very act of writing the letters was a way for many children to heal those emotional wounds, experts say" (6). One particular psychiatrist stated, "Writing a letter lets a child express and organize his feelings in a way he would be unable to face. . . . It's a way for a child to repair his inner hurt" (6).

Although Goleman was not specifically exploring nor advocating a particular theory of writing, he clearly demonstrated that the children's letter writing became more or less a cathartic experience in learning how to *process* catastrophe and trauma. Beverly Cleary's ***Dear Mr. Henshaw*** more explicitly advocates writing as a way of coping with loss. Cleary relates the story of a pre-adolescent boy, taking him from the second to the sixth grade, through the boy's writing. In fact, the reader gets to know Leigh Botts through Leigh's development as a writer who is using writing as a way of learning how to cope with his parents' divorce. Written for children, Cleary's story shows the way Leigh uses writing to cope with loss, to explore his own feelings and reactions to events as they occur. The message is that writing is a valuable tool that is intimately connected with psychological and emotional growth.

In addition, Leigh's writing allows him to grow linguistically. For while he learns to cope with loss, he also learns that his ability to write is a skill that he has gained and can keep, and that leads to knowledge. Writing helps Leigh to define himself as a person; concurrently, growing more mature as a person has helped him during his writing; the two processes of growth—as a writer and as a person—blend into one. Initially, he allows himself to write by accepting other people's structures. Later, as he continues to develop as a writer and a person, he internalizes those structures, which to the reader seem to disappear as he takes more and more initiative in making structure accommodate his growth. In short, Leigh learns that growth and structure are related and mutually reinforcible. One needs both. Second, he learns that writing is closely akin to living and that the two processes—which become closely associated as one—*never* end, never become a product to be completed; they are always a process to be continued. In very specific ways, ***Dear Mr. Henshaw*** illustrates the theories of James Moffett and Lev Semenovich Vygotsky; each theorist stresses the importance of language development in the maturing lives of young children. Beverly Cleary manages to invigorate the theories of both Moffett and Vygotsky by creating a young protagonist who links his intellectual development as a writer with his social, psychological, and emotional development. The impact of her story not only emphasizes the brilliance and relevance of each theory in relation to the education of young children, but also serves to clarify the importance of writing in the lives of young children, and to show how an adult can help a young child learn to write and to develop a positive attitude toward writing.

Early in the story, Leigh's writing is structured by others, as his mother, his teachers, and Mr. Henshaw all urge him to write. Mr. Henshaw offers Leigh the most important kind of encouragement, becoming not only a correspondent, but also a surrogate father to Leigh who, at a young age, must learn to grow up without a father, and without the compensation of brothers and sisters. Throughout the story, Mr. Henshaw encourages Leigh to write. But most important, he initially offers Leigh a structure—ten questions—that does not threaten Leigh but allows him to explore his feelings and perceptions. They are as follows:

1. Who are you?

2. What do you look like?

3. What is your family like?

4. Where do you live?

5. Do you have any pets?

6. Do you like school?

7. Who are your friends?

8. Who is your favorite teacher?

9. What bothers you?

10. What do you wish?

Personally as well as discursively, Mr. Henshaw carries Leigh from the center of himself expansively outward:

1. Leigh's identity and appearance—family and domicile—school, friends, and teachers—his feelings and thoughts.

2. Writing about himself—his family—his home—his educational and social life (reporting, recording). His "bothers" (generalizing)—his wishes (theorizing).

These questions move from the very specific and concrete to the general. This arrangement accomplishes several things. First, it allows Leigh to proceed from factual answers to answers requiring more abstract thought. Moreover, Leigh's answers can proceed from *what he has already written,* helping him to articulate what would have been very difficult if he had not first answered the simpler questions. Similarly, the questions initially take Leigh out from himself, into the outer world, proceeding to his family, his relationships at school and outside his family, ultimately bringing him back more deeply *into* himself to consider more abstract projections about his future life (questions 9 and 10). Thus, heuristically, Leigh moves from writing about concrete things and people in his life to writing about abstract projections based on the concrete information he has just written. Or, as Moffett would say, Mr. Henshaw has presented Leigh a formula for "decentering" his writing; moving from "recording" to "theorizing." As Mr. Henshaw understands, Leigh must learn to work in the narrative mode in order to begin the process of decentering. Moffett explains: "The young learner . . . does not talk and read explicitly about categories and theories of experience; he talks and reads about characters, events, and settings" (49).

Mr. Henshaw illustrates well Moffett's theory of discourse progression which allows Leigh to integrate and interrelate his growth as a *writer* with that as a child learning to function more independently. Moffett posits that an important characteristic of maturity is self-awareness, or, to be more precise, reflection upon one's historical situation: seeing at once the past and the future by way of knowing the present. This reflection can be achieved through writing, or, to be more precise, through language which assumes symbolic significance representing events and situations through memory. Memory works to mark past events as meaningful if they seem relevant to present-time experiences. Yet, such past events can be recalled and identified only by the mind's ability to imagine them as significant conceptually, i.e., abstractly, to present, concrete experiences. Thus, a growth of cognitive ability posits an ability to think conceptually in several different dimensions at once: time (past-present-future); place (self—the world outside the self); and personal knowledge (what is happening to me now—what has happened to me in the past). And as Moffett states, the ability to think abstractly relates to and points toward a widening linguistic capacity:[1]

> So although one could claim that they [elementary school age children] can write high-level discourses of generalization, and even theory, this would be true only of utterances so brief as to finesse the basic assumption underlying my whole analysis of discourse—that the linguistic capacity to sustain such monologues depends on a cognitive capacity to explicitly interrelate classes and propositions, and to embed lower-order abstractions, as samples or evidence, into higher orders. (56)

The child who grows in cognitive ability, in moving away from the comforting context of a limited egocentricity, acquires instead a more sophisticated, conceptual structure of abstract "classes and proposi-

tions," which, in bringing the child farther away from an egocentric viewpoint, actually expand the child's more socially coherent *self:*

> The primary dimension of growth seems to be a movement from the center of the self outward. Or perhaps it is more accurate to say that the self enlarges, assimilating the world to itself and accommodating itself to the world, as Piaget puts it. (59)

Thus, the child literally transforms the meaning of the word "structure." Rather than taking comfort in thinking that "structure" can be created only within the limited, concrete world of the egocentric mind, the child, if s/he is to grow, expands his or her awareness to include more abstract, conceptual "structures," which conform to new ideas about the world not of the self. This act of "decentering" assumes the child's willingness to posit other views and ideas as distinct from his or her own, and thereby to "see" more sharply an egocentric view *as* egocentric. "Decentering" also means implicitly accepting someone else's *way* of "structuring" a view as valid and possibly beneficial:

> Differentiating among modes of discourse, registers of speech, kinds of audiences is essentially a matter of decentering, of seeing alternatives, of standing in others' shoes, of knowing that one has a private or local point of view and knowledge structure. (57)

In *Dear Mr. Henshaw,* Mr. Henshaw provides Leigh with a way to "structure" his development as a writer and as a child who needs to understand how to decenter through "structure."

Mr. Henshaw helps Leigh to do this through a particular genre: the personal letter which Mr. Henshaw has implied may serve as a structure within which to experiment with other genres, i.e., diary writing, interviews, description, process analysis, narration. The letter is the form through which Leigh can grow out and away from a "local point of view," working from the Moffettian monologue/dialogue mode of writing outward toward a more detached, theorizing mode of writing. Implicitly, Mr. Henshaw has Leigh move outward expansively through Moffett's "spectrum of discourse": "recording"—"reporting"—"generalizing"—"theorizing" (47).

Throughout the story, Leigh's mother reinforces Leigh's growth as a writer and a person. In the interview sequence (51-53), in which Leigh heeds Mr. Henshaw's advice to "listen," he records a conversation with his mother verbatim wherein it becomes clear that she is willing to answer his rather penetrating questions honestly, directly, and unambiguously. This structure also helps Leigh and his mother in a specific situation: adjusting to a divorce. Gradually, ***Dear Mr. Henshaw*** intertwines Leigh's growing ability to write with his ability to sort out and to process the meaning of his life *vis-a-vis* his parents' divorce. The conversations with his mother diminish his feelings of isolation and alienation and help Leigh to understand that perhaps he is *not* to blame for his parents' divorce.

Other people also support Leigh and help him to grow. Mr. Fridley notices Leigh's habit of "walking backwards" to school, and, when Leigh asks why the bear on the flag was turned upside down, Mr. Fridley invites Leigh to raise the flag rightside up, asking him to come to school early to help him with the flags, so perhaps Leigh does not have to walk "slow" anymore. Leigh writes that "It was nice to have someone notice me" (35). Later, Mr. Fridley confronts Leigh, telling him that perhaps the reason he does not have many friends is that he "scowls all the time" (80), and encouraging Leigh to "think positively" (81). Honesty becomes something Leigh values, and later on Leigh is praised for writing in his own voice, honestly, what his thoughts and feelings have told him.

The librarian makes it a point to stop Leigh in the hall to give him Mr. Henshaw's new book, *Beggar Bears,* because she notices that he checks Mr. Henshaw's books out of the library so often. Thus, he is rewarded for his interest in books, and he *accepts* what the librarian has to offer, feeling glad that ". . . Mr. Fridley isn't the only one who notices me" (55). A little farther on, he states that his teacher says his writing skills are "improving" and urges him to write a story for a "book of work of young authors" (58). Leigh also reports that there is a steady flow of correspondence between Mr. Henshaw and himself— Mr. Henshaw continually urges him to write.

Leigh's willingness to accept other people's structures helps him to see structure as something beneficial. Specifically, he internalizes the structures of writing and uses them to experiment with new ways of expressing himself in writing. He learns not to censor anything entering his consciousness, and also decides not to censor anything emanating out of it. This process can be seen most clearly on pages 26 through 29 where Leigh lets words and phrases lead to ideas and thoughts which they seem to suggest.

He answers Mr. Henshaw's questions, adhering to structure, and he does not censor thoughts as he writes. The four paragraphs which comprise his answer to question 9 (27-28) are cumulative, almost in the Christensen sense in which one word generates an idea which in turn generates words generating other ideas, and so on.[2]

Briefly, Leigh's thought process can be described this way: what "bothers" him: stolen lunches—runny noses—walking "slow"—feeling lonely—"walking backwards"—hiding from Mr. Fridley—father's not calling. So, he has let his pen roam over the page moving from one thought to another to get to what was *really* bothering him: his father's not calling him.

When Leigh is asked to respond to Mr. Henshaw's question, he replies:

> What bothers me about what? I don't know what you mean. I guess I'm bothered by a lot of things. I am bothered when someone steals something out of my lunchbag. I don't know enough about the people in the school to know who to suspect. I am bothered about little kids with runny noses. I don't mean I am fussy or anything like that. I don't know why. I am just bothered. (27)

In the second sentence, he tries to avoid the question, but as so often happens in the course of his writing, he accepts the premise because he trusts Mr. Henshaw's external structuring for writing about his own thoughts. Leigh's "answer" thus simultaneously serves two purposes: (1) answering Mr. Henshaw's question; (2) learning (through writing) to direct the exploration and progression of his own thoughts. Thus, Leigh admits that he is bothered—upon spontaneous, initial reflection—by relatively inconsequential things: his stolen lunches and "little kids with runny noses." In this paragraph, after he has considered these two things that bother him, he reflects that he does not (at the precise moment he is writing) exactly know why they bother him. But he goes on in the next paragraph to recount other things that bother him. That is, he does not *stop* writing.

> I am bothered about walking to school *slow*. The rule is nobody is supposed to be on the school grounds until ten minutes before the first bell rings. Mom has an early class. The house is so lonely in the morning when she is gone that I can't stand it and leave when she does. I don't mind being alone after school, but I do in the morning before the fog lifts and our cottage seems dark and damp. (27-28)

Leigh's recognition that he walks to school *"slow"* probably occurred to him from what he wrote in the previous paragraph, in which he used the word "runny" to describe "noses." Since he is bothered by "runny noses," the word "runny" might have led him to think of the word "slow" (opposing the word "But") which must have occurred to him just after he finished the previous paragraph, "I am just bothered." Thus, the idea of "slow" has most likely been triggered off by the *written* expression of the idea of "runny noses." Furthermore, he reports *why* he is "slow": because he does not want to remain in a "lonely" house in the morning, as his mother must leave very early for an "early class." He admits that he feels most lonely in the early morning rather than "after school" when he is also alone in the house, because in the morning "our cottage seems dark and damp." The idea of walking *"slow"* is carried over into the next paragraph, but this time. Leigh reveals more about the unusual odyssey during his walk to school, setting up the last paragraph in answer to the question about what bothers him:

> Mom tells me to go to school but to walk slow which is hard work. Once I tried walking around every square in the sidewalk, but that got boring. So did walking heel-toe, heel-toe. Sometimes I walk backwards except when I cross the street, but I still get there so early I have to sort of hide behind the shrubbery so Mr. Fridley won't see me. (28)

What is apparent is that he seems embarrassed and does not want to be discovered. He narrates his journey to school, explaining his ideas about how to get there slowly. The paragraph begs for clarification which Leigh delivers in the paragraph immediately following. Obviously, Leigh has decided to risk discomfort and possibly embarrassment by leaving his house early instead of remaining until he can leave and make a normal journey to school. The oddity of walking "backwards," and hiding "behind the shrubbery" causes him less pain than remaining in his empty house. Leigh thus prepares his readers (and himself) for the real reason why he leaves the "dark and damp" cottage early: he misses his father who is heavily responsible for the "lonely" house:

> I am bothered when my dad telephones me and finishes by saying, "Well, keep your nose clean, kid." Why can't he say he misses me, and why can't he call me Leigh? I am bothered when he doesn't phone at all which is most of the time. I have a book of road maps and try to follow his trips when I hear from him. When the TV worked I watched the weather on the news so I would

know if he was driving through blizzards, tornadoes, hail like golf balls or any of that fancy weather they have other places in the U.S. (28)

In the first paragraph, Leigh admits that he does not like "little kids with runny noses." The word "noses" reappears as "nose" in the final paragraph: he states that his father is always telling him to keep his "nose clean." Thus, the phrase "runny noses" triggers another association for the word "nose." That is, the word "nose" (in "runny noses") seems to have vitalized a thought, unexpressed in writing (or even within Leigh) about his father. Furthermore, the discomfort at seeing "little kids with runny noses" foreshadows the deeper, more painful discomfort of being told by his (distant) father to keep his "nose clean." In a sense, the dislike of "runny noses" prepares Leigh to face the perhaps consciously repressed dislike of his father's rather clichéd remark about his "nose" which becomes, for Leigh, repugnant because it defines the rather pathetic terms of communication between them. On a deeper psychological level, however, Leigh perhaps does not like "little kids with runny noses" because *they* do not keep *their* noses "clean" as Leigh obviously must do, as his father tells him he must do. That is, even though he does not *like* what his father tells him, he *values what his father says.* (A psychologist might say that Leigh, in his preadolescent way of thinking, translates his father's advice literally, changing it from an affectionate sign-off into an internalized value.)

Secondly, Leigh admits that what bothers him a lot is that he misses his father. He has taken three paragraphs to admit this feeling because he has difficulty directly expressing his feelings. Obviously, this is one of Cleary's underlying assumptions in *Dear Mr. Henshaw,* and her advice to Leigh (and to her readers) is that growth in writing can foster emotional growth. Leigh has used his writing to bring to the surface of his consciousness anger and frustration about what really bothers him. By allowing the progression of his writing to work from the most vividly conscious to the least conscious, he has uncovered unarticulated feelings and thoughts. That is, his writing has become meaningful because he has discovered he has something to say, and he has discovered that what he thinks and feels can be expressed through his writing. He has *trusted* his ability to let the writing process help him work toward expressing his deepest frustrations.

His thoughts and feelings move, through his writing, toward a center, as outer layers peel away, exposing an inner core. Thus, in the four paragraphs on pages

27-28, a pattern becomes evident. He is bothered by having his lunch stolen. Having something "stolen" is, in a larger sense, losing something. Thus, the loss of his lunch, which he articulates in paragraph 1, parallels the greater loss—of his father—which he is able to articulate in paragraph 4. In looking at the progression of paragraphs 1 through 4, the discerning reader can infer the most general theme of the pain of loss: loss is, in itself, painful, but is a part of being human; however, a way of coping with loss is to write about how it feels to lose something or someone. Secondly, in paragraph 2, he admits he does not like being in the house during the early morning "before the fog lifts and our cottage seems dark and damp." Thus, he associates loneliness with bad weather to which he alludes in paragraph 4 when he imagines his father (a truck driver) "driving through blizzards, tornadoes, hail like golf balls." For Leigh, being in a "fog" means he cannot see his father because he does not know where his father is. Bad weather separates Leigh from his father, causing loneliness. Thus, he feels most lonely when it is early morning during a "fog": bad weather seems to lengthen the distance between Leigh and his father causing him to feel more acutely the painful reality of his father's loss (i.e., the "lonely" house early in the morning when his mother has left). In addition, it is notable that the actual, *concrete* fact of bad weather, "fog" in the early morning, has triggered off the generalized *concept* of bad weather-lengthening-distance-causing-more-acute-loneliness: Leigh is imagining his lost father being more unreachable because of (imagined) "blizzards, tornadoes, hail like golf balls." Leigh's only contact with his father is by telephone, a form of communication which does not allow Leigh to *see* his father. The importance of identification through sight is brought up at the end of paragraph 3 when Leigh mentions that he hides in the shrubbery so Mr. Fridley will not see him when he arrives early. The theme of paragraph 4 is Leigh's frustration at not being able to *see* his father. He cannot see him because he cannot find him: father thus seems to be "hiding" from Leigh, an idea perhaps triggered off when he expresses the *concrete,* real act of "hiding" from Mr. Fridley. In Leigh's mind, then, his father's occupation of driving a truck is a way of "hiding" away from Leigh, of *avoiding* Leigh. Later on, Leigh's mother admits to Leigh that one of the reasons she divorced Leigh's father was that "he loves the excitement of the road, when I don't" (76). Thus, Leigh's father, indeed, was never home, and must have appeared to be "hiding" from Leigh. Leigh gradually begins to understand, then, in adult terms, the reasons for his parents' divorce.

Cleary's emphasis on writing as a vehicle for social, intellectual, and emotional growth is also supported by Vygotsky's views. Vygotsky emphasizes the general axiom that "learning and development are interrelated from the child's very first day of life" (*Mind* 84). The relationship between learning and development is crucial as a key to understanding the full range of Vygotsky's theories. For this relationship posits that the intellectual growth of a child cannot proceed without the specific help of another person to act as a guide, whether that person is a peer or an adult who possesses more knowledge than the child. In Vygotsky's view, learning always "marches ahead of development"; the child's internalized history of development encounters new ideas and concepts from other people who, in a sense, challenge the child's understanding of knowledge, offering new stimuli and considerations: thus, the key to a Vygotskian conception of intellectual growth lies with the value of instruction:

> In the child's development . . . imitation and instruction play a major role. They bring out the specifically human qualities of the mind and lead the child to new developmental levels. In learning to speak, as in learning school subjects, imitation is indispensable. What the child can do in cooperation today, he can do alone tomorrow. Therefore the only good kind of instruction is that which marches ahead of development and leads it; it must be aimed not so much at the ripe as at the ripening functions. (*Thought* 104)

An inference concerning this close relationship between learning and development is that, in order for learning to influence the child's development, the child must learn to trust the person or people from whom s/he learns. That is, the child must not only accept the offer of help from other people but must also be willing to adapt to the milieu and behavioral responses that the kind of help demands. Resistance to help can only hinder growth. Vygotsky posits cooperation as essential to growth:

> We propose that an essential feature of learning is that it creates the zone of proximal development; that is, learning awakens a variety of internal developmental processes that are able to operate only when the child is interacting with people in his environment and in cooperation with his peers. Once these processes are internalized, they become part of the child's independent developmental achievement. (*Mind* 90)

The social dialogue between peer and peer or between peer and adult stimulates an inner dialogue in the child which then influences social dialogue, and so on. Thus, the ability to use language increases as social interaction and internal thought act upon one another so that one type of dialogue stimulates and reinforces the other. As I have indicated earlier, Leigh's growth as a writer and as an emotionally healthy individual proceeds because he trusts Mr. Henshaw as a mentor, a guide. He implicitly accepts Mr. Henshaw's "structures": the format of the correspondence between them, and the strict format of question-and-answer response. (It is significant that the last question, "What bothers you?" is open-ended and can be answered in many different ways.) Leigh faithfully tries to answer each question *even though he may not know, nor has he previously considered the answers*. Yet, as he answers each question, he discovers that he knows more than he thought he did: his discoveries occur through his own writing.

In Vygotsky's terms, Leigh has answered the question, "What bothers you?" considering it in more abstract terms based on the knowledge gained from personal experience; the question as asked implicitly contained within it the possibility of an infinitely considered response, while positing a more limited one. If Mr. Henshaw had asked Leigh, "How do you feel about not having your father around?" or "Does not having your father around bother you?" Leigh would not have had the opportunity to answer the question in the way which felt most comfortable. The question itself was designed to allow Leigh room to consider an answer taking into account what Leigh had already revealed in answers to the previous eight questions, and what he was prepared to consider beyond what he already knew. Mr. Henshaw implicitly accepted any answer Leigh wished to give; yet he *already knew* that Leigh trusted him enough to answer the first eight questions which heuristically guided Leigh to deeper considerations beyond the most familiar. Vygotsky expresses concisely the phenomenon achieved through Leigh's relationship with Mr. Henshaw:

> One might say that *the development of the child's spontaneous concepts proceeds upward, and the development of his scientific concepts downward,* to a more elementary and concrete level. (*Thought* 108)

In Vygotskian terms, Leigh's progress as a writer depends upon Mr. Henshaw to provide, as Vygotsky states, "a related scientific concept" (108). Leigh works to understand that his stolen lunches as things that he has lost will signify more meaning than he can presently identify. Thus, he allows this "spontaneous concept" of lost lunches to serve as a focal point for apprehending a greater awareness which he knows he has not yet discovered, but which he works through with Mr. Henshaw's help. That is, he needs the help of someone who has already worked through some problems to understand the meaning of loss in conceptual, "scientific," terms. Thus, Mr. Henshaw's *words* contain within them a history of mature, conceptual thought beneath and beyond Leigh's immature, concrete thought. By using the key word, "bothers," Mr. Henshaw allows Leigh to expand the meaning of the word into the region of unformed conceptual ideas, touched off by a willful investigation of the word's deeper meaning—*if* Leigh feels ready to do so. Thus, Mr. Henshaw *guides* Leigh to the possibility of considering a greater sense of self-knowledge without actually presuming *what* that knowledge *should be*. Vygotsky explains:

> In working its slow way upward, an everyday concept clears a path for the scientific concept and its downward development. It creates a series of structures necessary for the evolution of a concept's more primitive, elementary aspects, which give it body and vitality. Scientific concepts in turn supply structures for the upward development of the child's spontaneous concepts toward consequences and deliberate use. (*Thought* 109)

Mr. Henshaw presents the concepts of "bother" and "wish" as focal points of mediation—contexts for conscious thought. Leigh accepts the use of the words "bother" and "wish" as relevant and as a way of trying to fulfill the need to communicate with Mr. Henshaw. (Both Mr. Henshaw and Leigh presume writing as a form of intimacy, communion because of its inherent ability to link both reader and writer.) Leigh, then, expands upon his "spontaneous concepts," brainstorming in the four paragraphs on pages 27-28 to "clear a path" for getting at what really "bothers" him the most: the loss of his father. This identification occurs on the basis of the "more primitive, elementary" identification of something more familiar, and less threatening: Leigh's stolen lunch. But, by the *end* of the four paragraphs, Leigh is able to successfully link the pain of losing his lunch with the more acute pain of losing his father, grouping both kinds of pain under the heading of what "bothers" him.[3] Leigh consciously links the two kinds of losses in his answer to Mr. Henshaw's tenth and final question: *"What do you wish?"*

> I wish somebody would stop stealing the good stuff out of my lunch bag. I guess I wish a lot of other things, too. I wish someday Dad and Bandit [the family dog] would pull up in front in the rig. (29)

Leigh realizes—in three sentences (as opposed to four paragraphs in the previous question)—that both his lunch and his father represent losses in his young life. What is also significant is that Leigh's discovery and developing articulation of his pain at his father's loss has arisen through Leigh's *collaboration with Mr. Henshaw*. Mr. Henshaw has provided the "instruction," i.e., the heuristic ten questions, to which Leigh has brought his "personal experience" (his "spontaneous concept" has met and merged with Mr. Henshaw's unstated "scientific concept") so that his previously formed development has been challenged by and has flourished under Mr. Henshaw's adult guidance. Mr. Henshaw did not have to know anything about Leigh to help Leigh learn; but, he *did* have to know how to provide structures through which Leigh could guide his *own* learning.

Beverly Cleary makes clear that Leigh's learning occurred, in a Vygotskian sense, from his desire and capacity to socialize, and that Leigh has progressed toward becoming an intellectually mature adult. What Leigh does is truly Vygotskian: as he grows and develops as a child into an adult, he simultaneously develops as a *writer* so that the two forms of development become intertwined and indispensable. Here is Vygotsky:

> *An interpersonal process is transformed into an intrapersonal one.* Every function in the child's cultural development appears twice: first, on the social level, and later, on the individual level; first, *between* people *(interpsychological),* and then *inside* the child *(interpsychological),* This applies equally to voluntary attention, to logical memory, and to the formation of concepts. All the higher functions originate as actual relations between human individuals. *(Mind* 57)

The book is thus Leigh's version of his own development as an adult and as a writer: his reader sees an inextricable link between his inner, intellectual life and his outer, socialized world both of which create and define Leigh Botts. Leigh's writing has helped him integrate himself into the lives of other people whom he then *integrates into his writing.* For language unites Leigh's "interpersonal" and "intrapersonal" *conscious* life which can exist only through the mergine of thought and language. According to Vygotsky: "The relation between thought and word is a living process; thought is born through words. A word devoid of thought is a dead thing, and a thought unembodied in words remains a shadow" *(Thought* 153). Leigh's intrepid devotion to his communication with Mr. Henshaw (an "interpersonal process") becomes his key to developing his growing ability to

think-through-writing (an "intrapersonal" process) as he gradually decenters his own egocentric thought and speech (written and oral), thus stimulating his ability to see his life in terms of concepts, i.e., loss as a part of his life; therefore, his "higher functions" of reasoning occur by way of his relationship with Mr. Henshaw.

Cleary makes clear that the developing, collaborative relationship between Leigh and Mr. Henshaw might not have evolved into "a living process." Leigh might not have accepted the structure (i.e., the ten questions) as a way to stimulate the growth of his own thought: He might have resisted the opportunity to stimulate his thoughts by answering the ten questions more superficially, by responding with rote answers, not bothering to scrutinize his own writing for keys (and key words) to further development. Or Leigh might well have decided not to answer the questions at all. In fact, Cleary indicates that Leigh was actually considering this possibility:

> Well, I got to go now [he writes Mr. Henshaw]. It's bedtime. Maybe I'll get around to answering your ten questions, and maybe I won't. There isn't any law that says I have to. (12)

Yet, Leigh chooses to answer them. The fact that he says there really is no "law" which states he has to answer questions indicates that his (temporary) interpretation of freedom is to do what *he* wants, not what *someone else* wants him to do. Yet, gradually he begins to understand that his "freedom" must involve the help of other people (Mr. Henshaw, Mr. Fridley, his mother, his friends), and that his "freedom" really is a state of mind, and that this state of mind is tied to his ability to think and that in a true Vygotskian sense, his freedom of thought cannot flourish without *interpersonal* relationships. Thus, the feeling of intellectual expansion he experiences, evolving into his "inner speech," cannot occur without his first experiencing socialized, externalized exchanges of words-into-concepts, which he does in his communication with Mr. Henshaw. "Inner speech," as Vygotsky asserts, is virtually unlimited, infinite, untranslatable: "inner speech is to a large extent thinking in pure meanings. It is a dynamic, shifting unstable thing, fluttering between word and thought, the two more or less stable, more or less firmly delineated components of verbal thought" *(Thought* 149). "Inner speech" allows Leigh to become *creative,* as it fuels his imagination (spurring and honing his writerly intuition); the testimony to his creative ability is the expansion of Leigh's letters into what Cleary has established as Leigh's book. Thus, Leigh's *concept* of freedom has been borne out as inherently a process of infinite expansion, a state of mind which posits and implicitly links the social, psychological freedom of communicating with other people with the intellectual, spiritual freedom of feeling able to evolve the most versatile, highly developed form of written and oral discourse. The latter part of *Dear Mr. Henshaw* shows clearly Leigh's expanding awareness of himself not only as a child maturing, but also as a child-maturing-as-he-writes. In fact, for Leigh, the ability, the capacity, and *freedom* to write become signs of emotional well-being.

Epilogue: Leigh's Growing Awareness of Himself as a Writer

Throughout the book, Leigh gradually grows more confident. He becomes more able to express his feelings about his loss, and to articulate more fully the meaning of that loss for his future development. Leigh's openness is evident, for Mr. Henshaw has indeed *urged* him to "write like *me*" (81) and in so doing, Leigh expresses how he feels: "Maybe I can't think of a story because I'm waiting for Dad to call. I get so lonesome when I am alone at night when Mom is at her nursing class" (61). In fact, the more open Leigh is about his feelings concerning the loss of his father, the more his writing becomes a possession that is uniquely his, and which he can *never* lose. Leigh's writing allows him to become more comfortable with himself as a person, which, in turn, allows his writing to become more individualized and original.

From the middle of the book onward, Leigh's writing increasingly expresses thoughts and feelings about his father. He is able directly to admit feelings about his parents:

> Dad still hasn't phoned. A promise is a promise, especially when it is in writing. When the phone does ring, it is always a call from one of the women Mom works with. I am filled with wrath (I got that out of a book, but not one of yours). I am mad at Mom for divorcing Dad. As she says, it takes two people to get a divorce, so I am mad at two people. I wish Bandit was here to keep me company. Bandit and I didn't get a divorce. They did. (64)

Later, he progresses in his writing to the point of shouting his feelings through his writing: "*I hate my father*" he states at the beginning of a letter (67). Shortly after this written entry, when Leigh talks to his father on the telephone, all the practice Leigh has had in expressing his feelings in writing becomes the basis of a test. In other words, in a Vygotskian sense, writing has become meaningful for Leigh, has become "incorporated into a task that is necessary and relevant for life." The task in this sense has been Leigh's ability to accept his parents' divorce, and specifically his father's absence from his life. When Leigh feels ready to confront his father directly (shortly after he writes so plainly about his feelings toward him), he calls him on the telephone. Overcoming a fleeting desire to hang up, he *communicates* directly with his father: "You promised to phone me this week and you didn't" (68). His father explains, or offers an excuse for, why he did not call Leigh, and asks Leigh if anything is on his mind. Leigh reports:

> I didn't know what to say, so I said, "My lunch. Somebody steals the good stuff out of my lunch." (69)

After his father tells Leigh to find the culprit and "punch him in the nose," Leigh responds a little more directly to his father about what is really bothering him: "'I hoped you would call,' I said. 'I waited and waited'" (69). His father explains that he could not call because he was delayed by "heavy snows in the mountains," which, to Leigh, has a ring of truth:

> From my map book I know Highway 80 crosses the Sierra. I also know about putting chains on trucks. When the snow is heavy, truckers have to put chains on the drive wheels—all eight of them. Putting chains on eight big wheels in the snow is no fun. I felt a little better. (69)

Thus, what occurs in this colloquy is reported by Leigh in his letter. That is, there is noticeable, fluid Vygotskian movement between Leigh's written speech and his oral speech. The reader sees, especially in this last passage, how each kind of speech affects—and complements—the other. Although Leigh is not yet able to say to his father, "I miss you and I feel lonely without you," the pattern of his oral responses to his father (paralleling a similar pattern of growth in expressing his feelings in writing seen on pages 27-28) indicates that he is *working toward* expressing to his father exactly how he feels. Thus, the reader is reminded once again of the importance of *process* in the mastery of written and oral discourse, as well as the interdependence of both kinds of discourse.

What is most important in these pages is that Leigh's writing has become nearly completely personalized. For, at this point in the book, Leigh is completely comfortable *writing for himself*. The writing is no longer *to* Mr. Henshaw, but to "Mr. Pretend Henshaw." He had previously decided to keep a diary, at Mr. Henshaw's urging, but did not know, at first, to whom to address his writing:

> When I started to write in it, I didn't know how to begin. I felt as if I should write "Dear Composition Book," but that sounds dumb. So does "Dear Piece of Paper." The first page still looks the way I feel. Blank. I don't think I can keep a diary. I don't want to be a nuisance to you, but I wish you could tell me how. I am stuck. (36)

But, later on, during the time he decides to phone his father, he discovers something important about keeping a diary:

> I don't have to pretend to write to Mr. Henshaw any more. I have learned to say what I think on a piece of paper. (73)

That is, Leigh has discovered the *raison d'être* of writing. He no longer needs the externalized structure of an immediate audience, nor does he need a guide who will provide a *structure* through which to respond. Leigh has *internalized* Mr. Henshaw's structure, as is evident from Leigh's remarkable statement, "I have learned to say what I think on a piece of paper." What Leigh actually says is that his ability to "think" has grown out of his developing ability to write; *writing* has stimulated his thinking, as Leigh gradually begins to move from plain narrative reporting to another person to Moffettian "abstracting from experience" *for himself*. Also, in Moffett's terms, Leigh has become more *of* himself by focusing less exclusively *on* himself: "in moving outward from himself, the child becomes more himself" (59). In Vygotsky's terms, Leigh has made the language of oral and written speech interdependent, as well as representative of his ability to solve problems which he must confront in order to develop further:

> The specifically human capacity for language enables children to provide for auxiliary tools in the solution of difficult tasks, to overcome impulsive action, to plan a solution to a problem prior to its execution, and to master their own behavior. Signs and words serve children first and foremost as a means of social contact with other people. The cognitive and communicative functions of language then become the basis of a new and superior form of activity in children, distinguishing them from animals. (*Mind* 28-29)

To "think on a piece of paper," for Leigh, is to move from socialized, externalized speech to "inner speech" back out toward re-externalized speech which is itself an externalized linguistic form of thought.

After this breakthrough, Leigh begins to think with more power and authority as a writer. He notices things more acutely, pays attention to other people, and to occurrences around him, not knowing just what relevance they may have at the moment, yet realizing that his writer's intuition tells him that they ought to be stored in his *memory* because they may become useful later on. Thus, he learns to begin making connections between events and ideas. He scrutinizes his environment for "signs" that may trigger something in his memory which has become active in developing concepts and ideas. For, as Vygotsky says, *"For the young child, to think means to recall; but for the adolescent, to recall means to think"* (*Mind* 51). And so, he becomes interested in the "alarm system" on the side of the gas station near his house, not explaining why initially, but retaining it in his memory. He also notes the name of the gas station attendant as "Chuck," because he sees Chuck's name written on his uniform. Leigh later connects "batteries" used in the "alarm system" to an idea about rigging a burglar alarm for his lunch box, which, in turn, leads him to try out a story called, *The Great Lunch Box Mystery* (108). He does not succeed because he does not know who the thief is, and he does not yet realize that he is free to *create* an ending. As Angela Badger later points out to Leigh, "the ability to write stories comes later, when you have lived longer and have more understanding" (119). Nonetheless, Leigh has begun to see how the writer's imagination may work to create a story.

Another idea about writing occurs to Leigh in the section on "butterfly trees" (81). In a descriptive passage, he writes about how he gets the idea for a story by observing butterflies, but does not mention what the idea *is* right away, for he still seems to be adding to the idea: the next day he notices the "alarm system." Thus, Leigh begins to "decenter" his awareness, growing in his cognitive ability to synthesize seemingly disparate events and occurrences into meaningful concepts later on, focusing his attention subjectively away from himself, and more objectively toward noticing things and people in the world which he then filters back through his consciousness. The details he notices may not all be relevant, but they are evidence that he is developing the ability to select from his experience and attempt to combine observations into a coherent idea. This is the essence of abstraction. Thus, although Leigh fails to write a story about a *Ten-Foot Wax Man,* or about his lunchbox experiences, he learns the *process* of creating a story, and, eventually, through trial-and-error, creates a successful piece of writing, *A Day on Dad's Rig.*

He mentions that this "story" evolved from his going back over old trains of thought (107). He goes back to the butterfly trees, and allows associations to occur, practicing what he has learned to do: develop an idea from a specific train of thought, i.e., a word which forms an idea which in turn envelops other words, putting into motion the words as living entities. It is as he is thinking about "butterflies" that Leigh begins thinking about his father and a day "when he was hauling grapes to a winery" (107-8), perhaps associating migration or movement of butterflies with the movement of hauling grapes. The important point is that he fed his thoughts with words which in turn influenced and awakened his thoughts.

At the end of his story, Leigh recognizes his growth—"I wrote a true story which won Honorable Mention in the Yearbook" (123)—but at the same time he also realizes that he is not yet ready to write an imaginary story. However, this is all right, since the idea is that growth is a *process* which never really ceases, and writing, for Leigh, becomes closely identified with his intellectual, emotional, and moral development. Thought has become verbal—Leigh has verbalized his *thoughts* and feelings about his father; and speech has become rational—his *written* speech has helped him to make his oral speech to his parents more articulate, and this oral, socialized speech has influenced and helped crystalize his written speech. Thus, in Vygotskian terms, Leigh has associated his intellectual development with his linguistic ability. Writing for Leigh is his own "history" in the world, in itself an ongoing process, always being written. *Dear Mr. Henshaw* is thus Leigh's "text," and the "history" of his linguistic, cognitive, as well as social and emotional development.

The implications of Leigh's development as an author are enormously significant. Not only has Leigh intertwined his life as a writer with his life as a boy maturing into an adolescent, but he has implicitly defined the meaning of literacy in relation to his future life as an adult. For Leigh Botts, life can have greater meaning through literacy; he has learned to solve his growing-up problems by becoming increasingly more proficient as a writer. He has made reading and writing indispensable to his personal life. Thus, *Dear Mr. Henshaw* proposes a theory of writing and a program for literacy which recommend and illustrate a successful, *logical* rationale for making a child's school life relevant to his or her personal life. *Dear Mr. Henshaw* effectively empowers the theories of Moffett and Vygotsky who clarify and stress the relationship between thought and language, thus re-

emphasizing the importance of teaching young children the value of literacy.[4]

Notes

1. As will be discussed later, Vygotsky elaborates upon the relationship between linguistic and cognitive capacity by showing that the increase of the first directly affects the second.

2. Christensen, in his text, *Notes Toward a New Rhetoric,* states that proficiency in language arises from "syntactic dexterity" which accrues from practicing the "narrative-descriptive sentence" out of which ideas spring and from which other sentences generate. He is concerned with the interrelation of the different kinds of content (the "general" and the "specific") which form and define the structure of the paragraph. "Coordination and subordination" become rhetorical techniques for stringing together "general" and "specific" sentences; "coordination" defines a sequence of sentences "at the same level of generality," and "subordination" defines a sequence of sentences in which "each (sentence) is at a lower level of generality than the one above it" (103). Christensen is concerned with describing grammatically the external structure of written discourse which, he posits, "generates" into particular, discernible sequences. For Christensen, good writing is equivalent to full, rich paragraphs with a "density of texture" (75). Such richly textured paragraphs epitomize a healthy interrelationship between abstract—"general"—and concrete—"specific"—sentences although Christensen makes clear that "a description of the internal structure of any given paragraph" (101) does not necessarily imply that a paragraph always moves from the "general" to the "specific" or vice versa.

Where Christensen is content to discuss the anatomy of paragraphs in terms of the generative pattern of their sentences, I would go one step further and contend that the seemingly free-written sentences of Leigh Botts on pages 27-29 conform to a pattern of thought in which the "density of texture" of the sentences signifies a mixture of conscious knowledge and discovered (or, more precisely, *un* covered) unconscious thoughts. Specifically, conscious knowledge serves as a path to follow in order to probe beneath it. Leigh uses his sentences "cumulatively" to probe and expose his thoughts and feelings which move downward then upward: from his conscious thoughts down to his unconscious then upward again.

Leigh's ability to make his writing work in this way, especially in the paragraphs on pages 27-29, seems to expand the scope of Christensen's theory. Leigh shows his readers how he uses his conscious knowledge to "generate" previously unconnected thoughts *as* his conscious thoughts proceed onto the page, shaping them into a structure *as* he writes. Thus, Leigh allows his readers to share in his creative process by making that process conform to his readers' expectations of how to read systematically: he does not need to revise his writing into a *product* before his readers can make sense of what he is writing. He "structures" his thoughts as he proceeds and as he thinks about them in a sort of lively dance of form-with-content. Therefore, Leigh clarifies and empowers Christensen's theory of "generative" rhetoric in several ways. First, Leigh's paragraphs indicate that writing has an implicit, discernible structure evident *as* the writing appears on the page. Second, writing can serve as a clue to the internal thought processes of the writer as well as to a description of the externalized written product. Leigh "generates" his sentences in a deeper Christensenian sense to indicate his use of writing as revealing a pattern of psychological thought formation not only *by* his writing but also *as* his writing. The formation of the four paragraphs on pages 27-29 reveals a psychological pattern of thought distinguishable as a grammatical pattern of written discourse.

Christensen's theory of rhetoric then serves to help define—in rhetorical terms—cognitive thought processes. For, in addition to viewing the structural relationship between a "general" sentence and its "specific" counterpart *grammatically,* where the two kinds of sentences are described, as if they represent thoughts transferred *en masse* from the writer's cognitive domain onto a blank page, one can also view the relationship historically, in the sense that the structure reveals a writer's thought-formation operating as rhetoric. Christensen's system of "generative" rhetoric suggests that not all thoughts evident on the page (as words within a paragraph) were consciously present in the writer's mind when he or she set out to write. "Generative" rhetoric connotes thoughts-in-writing generating other thoughts in writing. The connection between consciously present thoughts and subsequently generated *other* thoughts occurs to the writer as he or she writes. Thus, Christensen seems close to Moffett in providing a rationale as well as a method for abstracting: he presents a procedure of writing for the young writer like Leigh to follow which will help him to stimulate cognitive development. What is so amazing about Christensen is that he actually defines thought grammatically. Christensen shows the writer that any thoughts he or she forms into writing can *themselves* not only form

the basis for other, further thoughts, but also reveal a thought pattern and identify it as capable of having a grammatical structure. Most importantly for Leigh, it does not matter how much cognitive structuring he must do before writing, i.e., in his head; Christensen suggests that a pattern evolves as rhetoric progresses.

Writing then, if practiced as an evolving *process* of revealing hidden thought, can not only lead to (and imply) a greater sense of self-knowledge, but also reveal and record a history of the evolving self. Writing can thus record the origins of thought processes and reveal them as having a recognizable structure which *in itself* may serve as the focal point for "seeing" thoughts-made-conscious and for working with them to see how they fit into a discernible context and make sense. Christensen's theory of "generative" rhetoric seems to me then very important not only in locating and describing the structure of thought processes in rhetorical terms, but also in defining the interdependent relationship (1) between content and structure in writing, and (2) between thought and writing. Whereas many theorists stress the importance of generating thoughts to fit into an empty "structure," i.e., a paragraph of an essay, Christensen—among others—posits the structure itself as contributing toward the generation of thoughts. He stresses the indivisibility of structure and content by stating that the "methods of paragraph development . . . are the channels our minds naturally run in whether we are writing a sentence or a paragraph or planning a paper" (77). In this way, he bridges the gap between the structureless "free-writers" on the one hand, and the product-oriented traditionalists on the other. Writing, as well as thought, is ongoing, and structure in writing signifies not closure, but, rather, more writing, as it "generates" more rhetoric which becomes "cumulative."

3. Thus Leigh, as a child, through Mr. Henshaw's guidance, has learned how adults explain (i.e., abstractly) the *concept* of being "bothered." That is, he has explained in terms he thinks Mr. Henshaw is helping him to work toward how to learn to think less as a child and more as an adult. The lesson is that an adult thinks in conceptual, abstract terms which require a Moffettian decentered vantage point so that to know oneself is equivalent to standing away in order to "see." In other words, Leigh intuits and directs himself to learning not only the *form* of structuring content in adult (written) communication, but also the mode of structuring *thought* in adult intellectual life.

4. I would like to thank Professor Dan Moshenberg of Georgetown University for his support and encouragement in the preparation of this paper.

Works Cited

Christensen, Francis. *Notes Toward a New Rhetoric.* 2nd ed. New York: Harper, 1978.

Clearly, Beverly. *Dear Mr. Henshaw.* New York: Dell, 1983.

Goleman, Daniel. "Children's Letters Voice Sorrow About Astronauts Who Died." *New York Times* 29 March 1986: A6.

Moffett, James. *Teaching the Universe of Discourse.* Boston: Houghton, 1983.

Vygotsky, Lev Semenovich. *Mind in Society: The Development of Higher Psychological Processes.* Cambridge: Harvard UP, 1978.

———. *Thought and Language.* Ed. and trans. Eugenia Hanfmann and Gertrude Vakar. Cambridge: MIT, 1985.

Suzanne Rahn

SOURCE: "Cat-Child: Rediscovering Socks and Island Mackenzie," in *The Lion and the Unicorn,* Vol. 12, No. 1, June, 1988, pp. 111-20.

There are far more cat than dog protagonists in children's books. In dog stories the dog-owner, not the dog, tends to provide the primary point of view; a typical story like Jim Kjelgaard's *Big Red* or Mary Stolz's *A Dog on Barkham Street* centers on a boy's desire for a dog or problems with it, and most of the better-known exceptions—*Lad, Lassie, White Fang, The Call of the Wild*—seem to have been originally written for adults.[1] In cat stories the cat sits at the center. The reader sees through the cat-eyes of Jenny Linsky, Tom Kitten, Buttons, and Orlando. Cats often dominate even a human protagonist; they run the show in *The Cat in the Hat* and *Time Cat,* and in *Millions of Cats* overwhelm by sheer numbers.

The comparative rarity of dog protagonists can be accounted for by the common view of dogs as wholly dependent on human beings for their fulfillment. The classic boy-wants-dog story is a kind of proto-love story, in which the dog's unquestioning devotion is highly satisfying to the (usually male) protagonist; most children naturally prefer to identify with the

power position in this relationship. The cat-human relationship is ambiguous, and cats play more varied roles in children's literature. A cat may be a magical guide, an urbane adult, a toughminded nonconformist, or perhaps most often, the child itself.

The common view of cats as essentially independent of human society as well as the traditions linking cats with witches and sorcerers are reflected in the cat's literary role as magical guide or intermediary. In cat stories of this type, the cat dominates the young protagonist—whether providing for his welfare as an animal helper (as in "Puss in Boots"), initiating him into another world (as in Lloyd Alexander's *Time Cat* or Nicholas Stuart Gray's *Grimbold's Other World*), or simply inciting magical anarchy in this one (as in Dr. Seuss's *The Cat in the Hat*).

Other cat stories, in which human beings are often of peripheral importance, give cats a society parallel to ours. The British folktale "The King of the Cats" suggests that the cat drowsing by the fireside may have a secret, even royal identity in its own world. The "Cat Club" stories of Esther Averill and Kathleen Hale's "Orlando" books portray cat societies in tireless and loving detail, as does Tad Williams's recent fantasy *Tailchaser's Song.* In *Old Possum's Book of Practical Cats* by T. S. Eliot, cats simply enter human society on equal terms. Stories such as these allow children to identify with protagonists who are in charge of their own lives, like adults, yet who also suggest alternatives to adult supremacy.

In still other stories the cat's role is that of the nonconforming individual. Kipling, in "The Cat Who Walked by Himself," shows how such an individual, who insists on making his own terms with society, faces inevitable hostility from leaders (the Man) and followers (the Dog) alike. Lewis Carroll's Cheshire Cat also deserves mention here. It is the only inhabitant of Wonderland that Alice calls "friend" (in introducing it to the Queen), and William Empson suggests in *Some Versions of Pastoral* that the Cat and Alice are in fact "the same sort of thing" (274), representing Carroll's own "ideal of intellectual detachment." The Cat

> can disappear because it can abstract itself into a more interesting inner world; it appears only as a head because it is almost a disembodied intelligence, and only as a grin because it can impose an atmosphere without being present. In frightening the king by the allowable act of looking at him it displays the soul-force of Mr. Gandhi; it is unbeheadable because its soul cannot be killed. . . . (273)

Unlike Kipling, Carroll presents his nonconforming cat as invulnerable even to the highest social authorities, the King and Queen.

In addition to political and intellectual nonconformists, yet another type is the creative artist, symbolized by a blue cat in Catherine Cate Coblentz's *The Blue Cat of Castle Town*. The blue cat listens to the river singing, "'Riches will pass and power. Beauty remains. / Sing your own song'" (16), and sets out to find a home with some person who will sing the song with him. After several wrong choices, the cat comes to live with a bitter but talented young woman who weaves its portrait into her carpet—a real carpet, now hung in the Metropolitan Museum as a masterpiece of American folk art. In this tale the typical independence of the stray cat, which chooses its own home, is equated with the artist's need to protect creative integrity by refusing to settle down with the shoddy or commercially successful.

But most often the stray cat seems to represent a child in search of the love and security of a family. Tom Robinson's picture book *Buttons,* about a tough alley tomcat who must overcome his distrust of all humanity, is a good story of this kind. Wanda Gag's *Millions of Cats* tells it from the viewpoint of the adopting family. Paul Gallico's *The Silent Miaow,* though for adults, also belongs in this (sorry) category, taking the form of advice to strays on how to choose and ingratiate oneself into a suitable household. The happy endings of such cat-orphan stories must be reassuring (or, if need be, comforting) to young readers, for whom loss of home and family is probably the ultimate imaginable disaster.

And yet, some cat stories are not so reassuring— those in which the feline protagonist seeks love and security, but finds rejection. As a motif it is even traditional; all "Puss in Boots" variants begin with the disappointment of the youngest son who has received "only a cat" as his inheritance, and with the cat's need to prove its usefulness. In Perrault's version, the miller's son is ready to kill and skin his new pet, who hastily offers a more profitable suggestion. Nor is "Dick Whittington," from the cat's point of view, an edifying legend; the apprentice seems only too willing to turn his faithful pet into an investment. Among more recent stories, Elizabeth Coatsworth's *The Cat Who Went to Heaven* also makes use of this motif, adding a religious dimension; the little cat Good Fortune must prove herself worthy not only of a place in the artist's household but of one by Buddha's side as well. Despite her sweet temper and vir-

tuous behavior, the artist repeatedly insults and rejects her. Even the happy ending, with its assurance of her salvation, is qualified by her death.

Paul Gallico's *The Abandoned* (in Britain, *Jennie*) makes the motif explicit even in its title. Its protagonist is a small boy named Peter, transformed after a near-fatal accident into a white cat and driven by his own nanny out into the city streets. As a boy, Peter has already been rejected by his mother, who "never seemed to have much time for him" (5). And Jennie, the cat who befriends him in his cat-form, has also been abandoned by her human "family" and has sworn that she will "'never again trust a human being or give them love or live with them'" (61). Indeed, the entire story is revealed, in the end, as the delirious fantasy of the neglected boy, whose mother now promises that "'There is nothing I will not try to do to make you happy if you will just get strong and well once more'" (303).

Such stories as these are derived from the cat's unique position in human society—now valued, now vilified, with an ambivalence directed toward no other animal. On the child's level, however, their import is human and universal. No child escapes some experience of rejection. Thus the cat protagonist becomes cat-child; its sufferings express the child's worst fears of being unloved, abandoned, cast out into a hostile world.

Two stories of this type seem to me worth examining in detail—for their interesting treatments of this cat-child theme, and because both deserve more critical attention that they have yet received. *Socks* (William Morrow, 1973) is a popular book by a very popular author—nearly a quarter of my current undergraduates recognized and remembered it—but Beverly Cleary is only beginning to be taken seriously by the critics, and *Socks* in particular, falling outside her main territory of the humorous family story, has been especially neglected. *Island Mackenzie* (Morrow 1960; first published in Great Britain as *The Nine Lives of Island Mackenzie* in 1959) is by Ursula Moray Williams, an author well known in Britain but not in America; none of my students recognized or had even heard of it, and I have seen no criticism of it either.

Socks is adopted by a young couple, the Brickers, and becomes "the center of the Bricker household" (36), till a baby arrives. Then he is ignored, unpetted, underfed (in his opinion), and finally (after biting Mrs. Bricker's ankle) forced to live outdoors, where a mean tomcat bullies him and steals his food. After he is beaten up by the tomcat, the Brickers allow him to stay indoors again. But the real solution lies in a new alliance between Socks and the fast-growing baby, Charles William. Alone for the first time one afternoon, they discover each other as playmates, make a thorough mess of the bedroom, and curl up to sleep together, friends for keeps.

Socks is truly both cat and child. As cat, his behavior is authentic in every pungent detail. When shut into the laundry room for the night for example,

> Socks lay yowling on the hard floor and groped under the door with his paw. He sat up and threw his shoulder against the door. When nothing, absolutely nothing would free him, his last act before settling down on the sweat shirt was to plow Kitty Litter over the floor so someone would have to sweep it up in the morning. (105-6)

Socks's story can be taken literally; it is not uncommon for a cat or dog in a previously childless household to cause difficulties when a new baby comes. But his feelings are human and described in human terms—the feelings of a child displaced by a new brother or sister:

> Sad and confused, Socks went back to lapping up the formula in the bowl. The warmth and sweetness of the milk comforted him. He lapped every drop and then licked the empty dish so hard that he moved it across the newspaper until it bumped the wall. Socks needed every drop of consolation he could get. His owners loved the baby more than they loved him. (54)

"Sad and confused," "comforted," and "loved" encourage the young reader to empathize with Socks as directly as with a human protagonist. At the same time, Beverly Cleary maintains a careful distance between child reader and cat character by making Socks's behavior so wholly catlike, and by her pervasive, ironic humor. For a young reader, this balance between distance and involvement is especially delicate; while an adult reader can take the story lightly and may perceive it as pure comedy, a young reader may find Socks's problems too true to chuckle at. When I asked my students if they remembered *Socks* as "sad" or "funny," they looked doubtful. They remembered that they "felt sorry" for Socks—but that there was "a happy ending"!

It is characteristic of Beverly Cleary—this balance between emotional involvement and ironic detachment, that makes her books read differently for adults and children, even for older and younger children; one finds it in the "Ramona" books as well.[2] Equally characteristic is the complexity of her point of view, her insistence that children and adults make an effort to understand each other. In *Socks* the reader is always aware of Socks's feelings, but the Brickers are not seen simply through his eyes. The reader hears Mrs. Bricker's "small, scared voice" when she realizes that her labor has begun, and the anxiety of the young parents over the first home feeding and burping of Charles William: "'Are you sure you know how to feed him?' she asked. Both parents spoke of the baby as 'he,'" observes the author wryly, "as if he were a stranger whose name they had not caught" (45). When the Brickers banish Socks from the house—a crucial scene—the viewpoint shuttles rapidly between them and him. Even the young reader not used to empathizing with a harried mother is forced to see how "A fussy, teething baby, a husband in a hurry to leave for his classes and his job in the University library, the strain of a mother-in-law in a house too small for guests, papers waiting to be typed, and a nipping cat were all too much for Mrs. Bricker" (117). Charles William, too, acquires his own perspective as soon as he begins to discover the world around him:

> Charles William stared at his toe in astonishment. Never before had he experienced Scotch tape on his toe. He lay back and waved his foot. The tape stuck fast. Fascinating! "Ah-gah-gah," he said. (90)

Awareness of the Brickers' and Charles William's points of view makes the final reconciliation of all parties in a new family configuration particularly satisfying. But it also encourages young readers to move beyond natural egocentricity toward a mature regard for the rights and feelings of other people, even to recognize one's own self-regard for what it is. Socks, with whom the reader must identify, is not simply a victim of injustice and insensitivity (although to some extent he is); he is spoiled, greedy, inconsiderate, and thoroughly self-centered. Beverly Cleary, however, is too cunning to describe him in these words. She tells us, for example, that Socks was "affectionate toward his loving owners but firm about getting his own way" (36), or that Socks liked to distract Mrs. Bricker from her typing because "Her typewriter was his rival for her attention, and Socks did not like rivals" (35)—using language that Socks himself might choose. It is left to the reader to see beneath this surface that Socks is not behaving well.

But Beverly Cleary's refusal to label Socks "spoiled" and "selfish" is more than a technique for disarming and educating the young reader. It is also a way of acknowledging the real suffering of the displaced child. She knows that what the child is afraid of losing is not pampering, but love:

"He was filled with jealousy and anger and a terrible anxiety. The Brickers might love the new pet more than they loved him" (43).

"His owners loved the baby more than they loved him" (54).

"Mrs. Risley"—a baby sitter who cuddles him— "loved him more than she loved his rival" (95).

And with special force, for Socks has just been cast out of the house: "'Oy-doy-doy!' shouted Charles William, happy to be eating breakfast at last and secure in the love of his family" (119).

Again, readers of different ages may be differently affected. Adults may be reminded of the need for love that underlies the child's most obnoxious behavior. Children may be reassured by the open acceptance and kind understanding of their most painful feelings—and especially when the story reaches them through a parent's voice, read aloud and shared.

Beverly Cleary offers sympathy, but no easy way out. From the hour of Charles William's arrival, it is clear that never again will Socks be "the center of the Bricker household." The Brickers will always love Charles William more than they love him. He must content himself with whatever love they have left over, and by learning to care for the child who has displaced him. As a solution, it is neither wishful nor sentimental but rather almost grimly realistic.

In *Socks* the cat-child identification is obvious; the situation is a common family problem. The same cannot be said of *Island Mackenzie,* a more complex and fantastic variation on the theme. Its opening sentence propels the reader into a dramatic and exotic world:

> One August afternoon a little shipwrecked cat called Mackenzie was swimming for his life toward a desert island, pursued by eight hungry sharks. (11)

Mackenzie's ship, the pleasure cruiser *Marigold,* has been sunk by a typhoon, separating him from his beloved master, Captain Jupiter Foster. Having reached the island just ahead of the sharks, Mackenzie finds a surviving passenger, Miss Mary Pettifer; unfortunately, Miss Pettifer hates cats, and the fact that she

is in love with Captain Foster only makes her jealous of Mackenzie. She drives him away with well-aimed coconuts, and when he accidentally unravels her knitting—a striped sweater she has been making for Captain Foster—she decides to kill him, traps him in her knitting bag, and plunges it into a tide pool. She repents in time to fish him out alive, however, and they slowly become friends. They save each other from an enormous python, from cannibals, and they survive a fire that burns the island bare. When Captain Foster, seeing the smoke, arrives in his new ship to rescue them, all three are ready to settle down together and live happily ever after.

Like *Socks, Island Mackenzie* is best read aloud to younger children who probably would not be able to handle it on their own—children just beyond the picture book stage and ready for a "real" book, with chapters. Good books for these five-to-eight-year-olds are rare, and few are as thrilling as *Island Mackenzie.* Socks, a more typical protagonist for this age group, is at worst beaten up—quite vividly—by the tomcat. Mackenzie is nearly devoured by sharks, nearly drowned by Miss Pettifer, actually swallowed and all but digested by the python, captured after a fierce battle by the cannibals, and half boiled alive in their pot. And the style is designed to match. Borrowing the ornate language of Victorian popular fiction, it achieves a kind of heroic elevation—"His natural intelligence told him that land was not far away, while his stout heart and strongly thrashing claws served to keep him just beyond the range of the terrible danger on his tail" (12)—but mock-heroic, because this is a cat, after all. Sentences are far longer and more intricately structured than is usual in young children's books, and vocabulary larger and more interesting, with words like "impervious," "gratification," and "promontory." The author, moreover, has an expert's knowledge of what young listeners can comprehend, and deftly varies her mixture with short sentences and punchy verbs; hair-raising adventures, too, alternate with pleasant details of life on the island, Mackenzie's fishing and Miss Pettifer's gardening. And despite all the violent action, the changing relationship of Miss Pettifer and Mackenzie is what remains most important, a solid and complex emotional core that makes the book much more than a funny adventure story.

A crucial difference between *Socks* and *Island Mackenzie* is the developmental stage represented by the protagonist. Socks's emotions and thought processes are those of a young child (or even, plausibly, a real cat), while Mackenzie's, though characterized by a childlike simplicity, are closer to those of a boy in his teens, or even a young man. Unlike Socks, who expects to be looked after, Mackenzie feels duty-bound to protect Miss Pettifer. He resolves to guard her while she sleeps, even after she has thrown coconuts at him:

> "For this human being is not kind," said Mackenzie to himself, "but she is one of the passengers from the *Marigold*. I must see that no harm comes to her, even if I don't sleep a wink myself till morning." (46)

Next morning he provides fish for her to eat; after they have become friends, he even risks death to save her from the python and the cannibals.

In fact, though he first crawls into her lap (while she sleeps) for comfort, like a child, his relationship with Miss Pettifer at once becomes that of a man romantically—even sexually—in love. When his initial advances are rudely repulsed, and she throws him from her lap and hurls coconuts at him, he is "miserably humiliated" (43) and thinks, "What a way for a lady to behave!" (44) Yet he cannot stop following and watching her from a distance. He feels respect for her courage on the crocodile-infested beach, and for her ability to swim and throw (89) (for Miss Pettifer is no standardized old maid). His impulse to "play and show off a little" (54), when she first allows him to approach her, leads to a predatory leap, which not only unravels the sweater but plunges his claws into the lady's thigh (58). Again, he has gone too far, and again she recoils with anger. In her vengeful attempt to murder him, however, she learns that she does care for him after all, and after she has rubbed him back to life with her skirt, they sleep "side by side by the light of the great tropical moon" (67). Significantly, a few nights later Mackenzie dreams vividly of mermaids who try to lure him into the sea, and of how Miss Pettifer rescues him from them and then slaps him soundly, exclaiming, "'Can't a man *ever* tell a hussy when he sees one?'" (73) "But the mermaids," Mackenzie remembers afterwards, "had been very beautiful and charming," and he lies half awake, "thinking about them for some while . . ." (75).

The love growing between Miss Pettifer and Mackenzie is not sweet and simple; it is an intense and often difficult relationship. Mackenzie is still tempted by "other women" in his dreams. And Miss Pettifer is unfaithful to him in another fashion; she finds a baby parrot with a broken wing, nurses it back to health, and becomes for a time totally absorbed in the "ugly little creature" (85). Mackenzie is extremely

jealous, and it is not until he nearly dies in the python's belly, and she rescues him, that they are reconciled once more.

The developing relationship thus roughly parallels a human courtship and marriage—but only roughly. While Mackenzie's jealousy can be compared to the feelings of some young fathers, the parrot is in no sense "his," or really even Miss Pettifer's, and can be disposed of guiltlessly in the next thunderstorm; recovered from her infatuation, Miss Pettifer does not even "turn a hair at finding the parrot lying dead on the edge of the jungle" (98). And the final *ménage à trois* of Mackenzie, Miss Pettifer, and Captain Foster has no imaginable adult human equivalent. Both these "solutions" suggest a level at which *Island Mackenzie* becomes instead wish-fulfilling Oedipal fantasy; the child Mackenzie, finding the mother (Miss Pettifer) temporarily separated from the father (Captain Foster), eventually overcomes her irrational hostility and wins her love; vanquishes its one rival, a younger sibling (the parrot); and finally reforms the family unit with itself at the center, as Captain Foster, "Taking her in his arms, with only Mackenzie to separate the beating of their two hearts," asks Miss Pettifer to marry him and she replies, "'Love me, love my cat!'" (126). Her use of animal characters allows the author—and reader—to make the book work both ways.

If Socks holds a mirror to the young reader, Mackenzie lets children see themselves as at once still small and vulnerable, yet older and more heroic than they are; it speaks less of present problems than of love-relationships that still lie ahead—yet in ways that children can relate to the loves they know. But both tales, despite their humor, make painful reading, as Socks and Mackenzie suffer rejection, indignity, and neglect from those they care for. Both authors show young readers a "dark side" of love—that those we love are also those who make us suffer most.

Indeed, both stories—and other similar cat stories, like *The Cat Who Went to Heaven* and *The Abandoned*—reveal a dark side of human nature itself, which could not be shown so easily to children through a human protagonist. In Beverly Cleary's "Ramona" books, Beezus is sometimes resentful of her little sister and feels (wrongly) that their parents favor Ramona over her. In Socks the older "child" is right; we see that the Brickers do care more for Charles William, and we share Socks's jealousy and distress. The animal fantasy actually brings into prominence negative aspects of parenting and family relationships that are played down by the "realistic" family story, but are nonetheless often "real," whether literally or simply as experienced by a child. And *Island Mackenzie* moves further down the scale, from mere neglect to violent hostility. As **Socks** exposes the unhappiness that can thrive even in happy families, so the jungle island reveals dark and primitive passions lurking even in the most ladylike; crocodiles, pythons, and cannibals prove less savage than Miss Pettifer. The grimmest "problem novels" generally stop short of murder. Yet the cat-mask enables the young reader to contemplate these frightening aspects of human nature with equanimity—as an animal's "flight distance" is decreased by the interposition of a pane of glass.

Such cat stories, of course, do not stand alone.[3] Other species of animals have been used to display the human dark side as it affects both animal and human victims. Stories of hunting and other animal-slaying sports, like *Bambi* and *Ferdinand,* may call into question the human need to kill not only animals but one's own kind. Horse stories like *Black Beauty* and *King of the Wind* show how cruelly society treats all helpless creatures. But stories of the cat-child, centered on the most intimate relationships—those of the family—are closest to home. What happens to Socks and Mackenzie can happen to anyone.

Both cats begin (as we all do) by taking love for granted. And both must prove themselves worthy of it by long, humiliating, even dangerous ordeals. And yet, after all, both stories also end well. Love may never again offer that first careless security—but a wise cat can live happily with the family that is still its own.

Notes

1. A rule-proving exception is Dodie Smith's *The 101 Dalmations,* which depends for its humorous effect on the reversal of the standard dog-human roles. Sirius, in Diana Wynne Jones's *Dogsbody,* is, of course, not really a dog at all.

2. Take for example the scene in *Ramona and Her Father* in which Ramona's father comes home so late that Ramona, waiting alone, thinks that he may have deserted her. An adult knows that Ramona is being melodramatic and finds the scene funny; a child would not be so sure. For both, however, there is a moving undertone; it is at this point that Ramona realizes how deeply she needs her father.

3. The prototype is in fact "The Ugly Duckling," whose protagonist represents both the artist-nonconformist and the abandoned child.

Works Cited

Cleary, Beverly. *Socks.* New York: William Morrow, 1973.

Empson, William. *Some Versions of Pastoral.* London: Chatto and Windus, 1950.

Gallico, Paul. *The Abandoned.* New York: Knopf, 1950.

Wiliams, Ursula Moray. *Island Mackenzie.* New York: William Morrow, 1960.

James Zarrillo

SOURCE: "Beverly Cleary, Ramona Quimby, and the Teaching of Reading," in *Children's Literature Association Quarterly,* Vol. 13, No. 3, Fall, 1988, pp. 131-35.

Beverly Cleary is one of the most popular and honored writers of contemporary children's fiction. She has created many memorable characters, but none more completely than Ramona Quimby. There are six books with Ramona as protagonist: **Ramona the Pest** (1968), **Ramona the Brave** (1975), **Ramona and Her Father** (1977), **Ramona and Her Mother** (1979), **Ramona Quimby, Age 8** (1981), and **Ramona Forever** (1984). In addition to twenty-two other books for young readers, Cleary has written nonfiction pieces which include remembrances of her childhood (Cleary, 1969, 1970, 1971, 1975a, 1984a). After reading the Ramona books and her articles, I am convinced she has a great deal to say to elementary school teachers who want to create a stimulating reading environment for their students. Beverly Cleary offers a child's perspective of elementary reading programs in both her autobiographical recollections and her Ramona stories. Her writing gives us revealing descriptions of the negative effects of misguided reading instruction on children who come to school able and eager to read. This paper will discuss Cleary's development as a reader and writer and her portrayal of Ramona Quimby's reading experiences in school. Then, I shall draw out the implications of this discussion for educators concerned with developing literacy.

FROM BLACKBIRD TO BESTSELLER

Beverly Cleary's literary development is a remarkable story. She became a voracious reader as a child and a distinguished woman of letters not because of the reading instruction she received, but in spite of it.

Cleary was born in McMinnville, Oregon. After six happy years on an eighty-acre farm in the Willamette Valley, economic misfortune forced Cleary and her parents to move to Portland. She first entered school in a public first grade classroom.

Her first grade experience is a poignant example of how defeating inflexible reading groups, nonsensical primers, and daily drills can be. Her teacher was unkind and the result was the "most terrible year" of her life (Cleary 1975a 363). The teachers had three reading groups—the Bluebirds, Redbirds, and Blackbirds. Cleary was a Blackbird and "to be a Blackbird was to be disgraced" (1970 2). She had come to school fully expecting to read. Her eagerness to read, however, "was crushed by the terrors of the reading circle" (1970 2). She described life as a Blackbird: "At school we Blackbirds struggled along, bored by our primers, baffled when our reading group gathered in the circle of little chairs in the front of the room to stumble over phonic lists. 'Sin, sip, sit, red, rill, tin, tip, bib, bed.' The words meant nothing" (Cleary 1969 288). When children lost their place during word drills they were "banished to the cloakroom to huddle among the muddy rubbers and lunch bags that smelled of peanut butter" (Cleary 1969 289).

Her reading text was as inappropriate as her teacher's methodology. Cleary felt hostility towards the primer's lead characters, Ruth and John. She considered John a sissy. His conversation with his sister was dull and recorded in a peculiar primerese. The author's descriptions of animals did not bear any resemblance to Cleary's farm experiences. The Blackbirds were bored and desperately "wanted action. We wanted a story" (Cleary 1969 288). Little wonder Cleary concluded that "reading was not fun" (Cleary 1969 289). Things improved in second grade. Cleary had a gentle and patient teacher. The first reader was something of an improvement over the primer, and the pressures of the reading circle decreased. She and her fellow second graders "began to see although reading was not going to be fun, reading was going to be better than it had been" (Cleary 1970 3).

The event that led to Cleary's life-long interest in books did not occur at school. On a rainy Sunday afternoon when she was in the third grade, she went to the Portland public library. She discovered *The Dutch Twins* (1911) by Lucy Fitch Perkins. She was enchanted with the illustrations. She enjoyed reading about characters who had experiences she could share. This was the first "real book" Cleary had read;

it was "story all the way through and did not end with word lists or contain the dreaded word, *Review*" (Cleary 1970 5). Cleary remembers, "It was one of the most exciting days of my life. Shame and guilt dropped away from the ex-Blackbird who had at last taken wing" (Cleary 1969 290). As a proficient reader. Cleary found books at a branch of the public library with the assistance of a caring librarian. Cleary became a discriminating reader, bored with books that contained needless descriptions, stereotypical heroines, and moral lessons. At school Cleary found a way to cope with the dreariness of her reading texts. She recollected, "Teacher and textbooks had to be put up with, but one could get around them by reading the entire reader the first week of school and after that hiding *Heidi* or *The Secret Garden* inside the cover" (Cleary 1970 6).

As Cleary grew older she thought seriously about becoming a writer. She received encouragement from "a succession of aloof, exacting English teachers" (Cleary 1984a 429). Her mother had a great influence, encouraging her only child to use "imagination" and "ingenuity," and to remember "the best writing is simple writing" (Cleary 1984a 430-431). Cleary went on to receive bachelor's degrees from Berkeley and the University of Washington. She became a children's librarian. In 1948 Cleary and her husband moved to California. In that year she began her first book, *Henry Huggins* (1950). Cleary has written twenty-seven books since then (Mercier; Reuther).

Most of her stories are about the every day lives of ordinary children. Cleary has achieved wide popularity with children. She has been the recipient of fourteen separate awards voted by school children. Professional response to her work has been equally enthusiastic. Cleary received the 1984 Newbery Medal for *Dear Mr. Henshaw* (1983). Two of the Ramona books, *Ramona and Her Father* and *Ramona Quimby, Age 8,* were Newbery Honor Books. She has received many other awards, most notably the 1975 Laura Ingalls Wilder Award (Shaw), and she continues to write at her home in California.

RAMONA THE READER

Ramona Quimby's school adventures are of particular interest for two reasons. First, Beverly Cleary has written one book about each of Ramona's years in school from kindergarten to grade four. (There are two books, *Ramona and Her Father* and *Ramona and Her Mother,* about second grade.) The books stand as a longitudinal case study of one fictional child's development. Second, there is a consistent response among a variety of critics that Cleary is uniquely perceptive, both in her ability to enter a child's mind, and in her ability to write about home and school life (Burns; Flowers; Ellen Goodman; Heins; Hunt; Lewis; List; McDaniel). Ethel Heins has described her perceptions as "uncannily accurate" (535) and Peter Hunt has described Ramona Quimby as "quietly humorous and immensely real" (771). Ellen Goodman, reviewing *Ramona the Pest* in the *New York Times Book Review,* concluded Cleary's "familiarity with both children and school produces some lively, authentic scenes" (34). Goodman found that Ramona's "adventures, the small ones that lace every school day, ring as true as the recess bell" (34). As a teacher with ten years experience in the elementary school, I found Cleary's school episodes amazingly accurate. Cleary cites the experiences of her children and letters school-age children write to her as important sources when writing about school (Reuther; Roggenbuck).

Cleary's Ramona, like so many kindergarteners, comes to school with three attributes that should lead to successful encounters with the printed word. She is eager to learn, she has extensive verbal ability, and she has a background with some literary works. Ramona "was a girl who could not wait. Life was so interesting she had to find out what happened next" (1968 11). She is familiar with fairy tales, and knows what type of books she likes. *Mike Mulligan and His Steam Shovel* (1939) is a favorite because it is "neither quiet nor sleepy, nor sweet and pretty" (1968 22). Ramona enters school expecting, from the first day, to learn to read and write. She learns, though, that she will spend a great deal of her time doing assignments which require her to sit quietly at her desk and complete a variety of skill-oriented exercises.

Like virtually all elementary students, Ramona's day includes assignments in her reading workbook. This bright child finds the workbook boring and confusing. In *Ramona and Her Mother,* second grader Ramona finishes a worksheet, becomes bored, and fills "all the double oo's she could find with crossed eyes and frowns" (64). Cleary provides another example that is typical of what happens when a child encounters a context-free exercise in a workbook. Ramona's first grade reader includes characters named Tom and Becky. They have a dog, Pal. Mrs. Griggs is Ramona's teacher. The following transpires:

> One day the reading workbook showed a picture of a chair with a wrinkled slipcover. Beneath the picture were two sentences. "This is for Pal."

> "This is not for Pal." Ramona circled "This is for Pal," because she decided Tom and Becky's mother had put a slipcover on the chair so that Pal could lie on it without getting the chair dirty. Mrs. Griggs came along and put a big red check mark over her answer. "Read every word, Ramona," she said, which Ramona thought was unfair. She *had* read every word. (1975b 121-122)

Ramona is frustrated again when "she explored her reader to see if she could find the grown-up words she knew: *gas, motel, burger.* She could not." In *Ramona the Brave* Cleary describes a situation many young readers face. The basal fails to build upon each child's unique pattern of development. Ramona's experiential background, her knowledge of words and phrases, and personal interests are special, and different from the other children in her class. Unfortunately, Ramona's basal reader attempts to meet the needs of a generic first grader. Later in this book, Cleary tells us Ramona is learning to read. The material that stimulates her, though, does not come from school. Rather, Ramona was learning to read from "newspapers, signs, and cartons" and "the world was suddenly full of words that Ramona could read" (129).

There is an excellent example of how children develop as language users by using writing to communicate in *Ramona and Her Father.* Second grader Ramona and her older sister mount a campaign to convince their father to stop smoking. Together they make signs and write notes to their dad. Ramona learns to read and write words like *pollution* and *hazardous* by including them in messages to her father. Ramona and her sister paint about a dozen signs. They include "Stop Air Pollution," "Cigarettes Start Forest Fires," and "Smoking Is Hazardous to Your Health" (95). During the afternoon Ramona learns to spell words she can say, and becomes acquainted with the meanings of several others.

In her fourth year of school, Ramona is exposed to a school reading activity she likes, Sustained Silent Reading (SSR). Ramona finds refuge from her reader and workbook as her teacher, Mrs. Whaley, allows her to read whatever she wants for a few minutes a day. Cleary tells us how Ramona feels about SSR and elementary school reading:

> How peaceful it was to be left alone in school. She could read without trying to hide her book under a desk or behind a bigger book. She was not expected to write lists of words she did not know, so she could figure them out by skipping

and guessing. Mrs. Whaley did not expect the class to write summaries of what they read either, so she did not have to choose easy books to make sure she would get her summary right. Now if Mrs. Whaley would leave her alone to draw, too, school would be almost perfect. (1981 42-43)

It is difficult to say how many of our students share Ramona's perspective. Certainly the elaborate instructional systems used in most elementary classrooms, complete with texts, work-books, dittos, and prescriptive-diagnostic tests, create formidable obstacles to be overcome by children who want to read books of personal interest.

LESSONS TO BE LEARNED

Two sources have the greatest influence on curriculum and pedagogy in elementary reading: tradition and the standardized test. It is time educators looked to other sources, such as the child's point of view, to determine the efficacy of reading programs. Cleary offers vivid descriptions of children whose development was frustrated, rather than facilitated, by the reading instruction they received. Those responsible for helping students become readers should learn from Cleary's accounts of how children are affected by basal-oriented reading instruction. Reading programs that better serve the needs of children can, and should, be created.

In Cleary's writing we read about specific instructional methods that are not in the best interests of children. Most notable for its lasting, damaging impact on students is the practice of organizing a class into inflexible ability groups. No child should suffer through the year on the bottom rung of a reading caste system. Cleary's descriptions of her days as a Blackbird provide an eloquent testimony of life as a reading untouchable. Sadly enough, a generation later Cleary's son suffered from the same stigma when he trudged off to school with the other poor readers an hour earlier than their classmates who were good readers (Cleary 1969). The influential report, *Becoming A Nation of Readers* cited the prevalence of ability grouping in contemporary classrooms and called for educators to "explore other options for reading instruction" (91). Indeed, teachers need to consider the many legitimate ways to group children for reading. For instance, children can be grouped by their shared need for specific instruction, by their desire to share what they have written, by their common interest in a book, or by their desire to work together on a project in response to what they have read. There is a good example of the latter in *Ramona Quimby, Age 8*. Ramona and two classmates work together and present a most unusual and entertaining book report (see chapter eight, "Ramona's Book Report").

It is equally important that educators view reading as a meaning-seeking endeavor, rather than as the mastery of a sequence of subskills. Beverly Cleary and Ramona Quimby were forced to resort to subterfuge to read silently a book of personal interest in school. Theirs is not an uncommon experience, for teaching hundreds of skills in the name of teaching reading has created classrooms where children have little time to read. After reviewing evidence collected from 134 elementary classrooms as a part of The Study of Schooling, Goodlad concluded, "The state of reading in the classrooms we observed seemed quite dismal. Exclusive of the common practice of students taking turns reading orally from a common text, reading occupied about 6% of the class time at the elementary level" (106). It is this ubiquitous classroom scenario, a small group of children seated in a "reading circle" laboring over a skills lesson or reading aloud, that Cleary has so realistically portrayed. She could well be describing the feelings of today's elementary children when, recalling her childhood, she wrote, "Reading was a stomach tied into a knot of dread . . . Reading was sitting very still, hoping to become invisible, so that one might be skipped" (1970 2).

Though abolishing ability grouping and providing more time for silent reading are important, they are superficial reforms of a system of reading instruction that is fundamentally unsound. To provide a reading program that is truly worthy of the Beverly Clearys and Ramona Quimbys in our classrooms, teachers, administrators, and teacher educators must accept a redefinition of the relationship between children and basal reading systems. Such systems, used in over 90% of American elementary school classrooms (Anderson et al.), supposedly exist to serve the needs of our students. In practice, however, it is the basal that takes control and becomes the reading program. As a result instructional materials and practices frequently are chosen because they serve the needs of a commercial program, not because they foster the development of literacy.

It would seem a program utilizing children's literature would have suited Cleary and Ramona far better than the basal-oriented instruction they received. A word of caution is in order, however. These increasingly-popular programs are usually referred to as "literature-based" (California State Department of

Education 3). We need, however, reading programs that are "child-based." Cleary has written eloquently of the great "diversity of the lives of children" (1984a 432). As committees at the state, district, and school-site level consider preparing lists of required novels to replace the basals, they should pay attention to this statement by her: "The rallying cry of my library training was 'the right book for the right child.' In a world in which children's lives vary so widely, there is no reason why every child should like every book" (1984a 438).

Beverly Cleary, Ramona Quimby, and millions of children like them come to school with an eagerness to read, with five or six years of unique life experiences, with some level of literary awareness, and with sophisticated oral development. Elementary reading programs need to build on these strengths. The basals would be replaced with children's literature, since the great diversity of the children in our classrooms is matched by the great diversity of wonderful children's books available in any good library. Teachers would lead each child to the books Cleary and her fellow Blackbirds eventually discovered. "the books that every child needs, the books to read for pleasure, the books from which we could go on" (1970 5). Cleary states that "The discovery that one can at last turn lines of printed words into meaning and enjoy doing so must surely be one of the most exciting moments of a lifetime" (1970 5). This discovery will occur with less pain, at an earlier point, and with greater frequency if teachers develop a literature-based program that respects the individual differences in children.

In place of the workbook and skills lessons, the reading program should allow children to write extensively, and share the stories, plays, and poems they have composed. Drama, in several forms, would enliven the school day. Children would have daily experiences in using reading to learn concepts from social studies. science, health, music, and art. Artificial barriers separating reading, writing, listening, and speaking would disappear. Teachers would view language as a tool to give and get meaning. Children would have a high degree of control over what they read and write. I think, then, that the Beverly Clearys and Ramona. Quimbys in our classrooms would be well served by teachers with a "whole language" orientation to literacy development (Goodman: Newman). Reading programs would be literature-based and similar to a model of individualized reading (Veatch).

Yes, there are lessons to be learned from the writing of Beverly Cleary. She has provided us with a perspective we in education frequently overlook, insight from the child.

Works Cited

Anderson, Richard C., Elfrieda H. Hiebert, Judith A. Scott, and Ian A.Q. Wilkinson. *Becoming a Nation of Readers: The Report of the Commission on Reading.* Washington, D. C.: The National Institute of Education, 1984.

Burns, Mary M. Rev. of *Ramona and Her Father,* by Beverly Cleary *The Horn Book* 53 (1977): 660.

Burton, Virginia L. *Mike Mulligan and His Steam Shovel.* Boston: Houghton Mifflin. 1939.

California State Department of Education. *English-Language Arts Framework.* Sacramento: 1987.

Cleary, Beverly, *Dear Mr. Henshaw* New York: William Morrow, 1983.

———. *Henry Huggins.* New York: William Morrow. 1950.

———. "Laura Ingalls Wilder Award Acceptance." *The Horn Book* 51 (1975a), 361-364.

———. "Low Man in the Reading Circle: Or, a Blackbird Takes Wing." *The Horn Book* 45 (1969): 287-293.

———. "Newbery Medal Acceptance." *The Horn Book* 60 (1984a): 429-433.

———. "On Talking Back to Authors." *Claremont Reading Conference Thirty-Fourth Yearbook.* Ed. Malcolm P. Douglass. Claremont. CA: Claremont Reading Conference, 1970. 1-11.

———. *Ramona and Her Father.* New York: William Morrow, 1977.

———. *Ramona and Her Mother.* New York: William Morrow, 1979.

———. *Ramona the Brave.* New York: William Morrow. 1975b.

———. *Ramona Forever.* New York: William Morrow. 1984b.

———. *Ramona the Pest.* New York: William Morrow, 1968.

————. *Ramona Quimby. Age 8.* New York: William Morrow, 1981.

————. "Writing Without Stretch." *PNLA Quarterly 36* (1971): 23-24.

Flowers, Ann A. Rev. of *Ramona and Her Mother,* by Beverly Cleary. *The Horn Book* 55 (1979): 412.

Goodlad, John I. *A Place Called School.* New York: McGraw Hill. 1984.

Goodman, Ellen. Review of *Ramona the Pest.* by Beverly Cleary. *The New York Times Book Review* (Part II). May 5, 1968: 32. 34.

Goodman, Ken. *What's Whole in Whole Language?* Portsmouth, NH: Heinemann. 1986.

Heins, Ethel L. Rev. of *Ramona Quimby, Age 8,* by Beverly Cleary. *The Horn Book* 57 (1981): 533.

Hunt, Peter. Review of *Ramona and Her Father,* by Beverly Cleary. *Times Literary Supplement* (London), July 7, 1978: 771.

Lewis, Marjorie. Review of *Ramona and Her Father,* by Beverly Cleary. *School Library Journal* 24.3 (1977): 54.

List, Lynne. Review of *Ramona the Brave,* by Beverly Cleary. *The Reading Teacher* 29 (1976): 511-512.

McDaniel, Jessica. Review of *Ramona the Pest,* by Beverly Cleary. *Library Journal* 93.12 (1968): 2531, 2536.

Mercier, Jean F. "Beverly Cleary." *Publisher's Weekly* 209.8 (1976): 54-55.

Newman, Judith M. *Whole Language: Theory in Use.* Portsmouth, NH: Heinemann, 1985.

Perkins, Lucy F. *The Dutch Twins.* Cambridge, MA: Riverside Press, 1911.

Reuther, David. "Beverly Cleary." *The Horn Book* 60 (1984): 439-443.

Roggenbuck, Mary J. "Profile: Beverly Cleary—The Children's Force at Work." *Language Arts* 56 (1979): 55-60.

Shaw, Ruth J. "Beverly Cleary: A Collection of Biographical Sources." Unpublished paper.

Veatch, Jeannette. *Reading in the Elementary School* (2nd ed.). New York: John Wiley and Sons, 1978.

Susan Stan

SOURCE: "Conversations with Beverly Cleary," in *The Five Owls,* Vol. 3, No. 6, July-August, 1989, p. 87.

In homes across America, Beverly Cleary is almost as well known as Henry Huggins, Ellen Tebbits, Beezus, Ramona, Ralph, and the other characters she has created. Of the countless children who know and love her books, some didn't even enjoy reading until they encountered a Cleary book.

Cleary's own rocky start in becoming a reader is fully described in **A Girl from Yamhill,** her memoir published by Morrow last year and just out in paperback. Her enthusiasm for learning to read was quickly squelched in the first grade when, due to two illnesses, she ended up in the Blackbirds, the "slow" reading group composed mainly of boys. Understandably, this experience had a lasting effect. Even after she learned to read, she no longer wanted to, and she could not comprehend adults who said that reading was fun.

Beverly's conversion to reading occurred two years later. Her mother, harboring the ongoing hope that Beverly would change her mind about reading, had checked out two books by Lucy Fitch Perkins, *The Dutch Twins* and *The Swiss Twins.* Bored and stuck indoors on a rainy day, Beverly picked one up, intending only to look at the pictures. Instead, she found herself reading the book, and miraculously she understood the magic of reading.

Perkins wrote twenty-five of these books from 1911 to 1935, and a 1926 survey showed them to be the most popular books among young readers. "They appealed to me because they were books at my reading level at that time," says Cleary, "and although I know the backgrounds are considered inaccurate, I didn't care that much about the background. I just liked the stories. I reread *The Dutch Twins* when it was brought out twenty years ago for sentimental reasons, and I thought the little stories held up quite well."

While in school, Beverly eventually discovered the pleasures not only of reading but also of writing. In fourth grade, she won a contest for her essay on the beaver "because no one else entered," and in seventh grade, she was inspired by the reading teacher (who doubled as the librarian). This energetic teacher offered imaginative assignments and frequently praised Beverly's work; it was she who first suggested that Beverly should become a writer of children's books when she grew up. Cleary's mother did not disagree but, being practical, advised her to have another, more stable career as well. In that way Beverly decided to become a librarian. She earned two B.A. degrees, one in librarianship, and took a job as children's librarian in Yakima, Washington.

This year marks the fortieth year of Beverly Cleary's writing career, which began in 1949 with *Henry Huggins.* The book was published by Morrow in 1950. "When I sat down to write the book I was always going to write, I expected to write about a girl. But I got to thinking about those little boys in Yakima who couldn't find books they wanted to read. This started me thinking about the boys I went to school with and the boys in the neighborhood. I found myself writing *Henry Huggins.* I was really quite surprised."

Henry lived in Portland in a neighborhood soon to become familiar to Beverly Cleary's readers. He had a dog, Ribsy, and among his neighbors on Klickitat Street were Scooter, Robert, Beezus, and Ramona. In all, Cleary has written thirteen books about the children in this neighborhood, but no doubt the best known of these—due in part to a recent television series—are the books that feature the irrepressible Ramona. *Ramona,* a ten-part series aired on public television last fall, was based on the stories in three books in which Ramona is approximately the same age: *Ramona and her Mother, Ramona Quimby, Age 8,* and *Ramona Forever.*

Cleary retained the right of script approval for *Ramona* and was also involved as story consultant. The project occupied her for two years. "Considering the pressures of time and money, and the fact that it had to be moved to Canada instead of the United States," says Cleary of *Ramona.* "I think it turned out quite well." For various reasons, the scriptwriters were not always able to remain true to the original Ramona books. In one instance, over Cleary's objections, they put Ramona's words into the mouth of Beezus. Cleary actually received letters from astute readers who recognized this error.

Young people have recognized Cleary more than thirty-five times with such cherished accolades as the Young Readers' Choice Award, and in 1975 she received the Laura Ingalls Wilder Award for her body of work. She is winner of the 1984 Newbery Medal for *Dear Mr. Henshaw,* and two of the Ramona books were named Newbery Honor Books. With the publication of *A Girl from Yamhill,* Cleary has unintentionally developed a new readership: "I've had stacks of letters from adults," she notes, "and many of them tell me the story of their lives."

When young Beverly won that essay contest in fourth grade, she learned a lesson that turned out to be far more valuable than the two-dollar prize. "Go ahead and do something—maybe nobody else will," she explains. "Particularly after I became a writer, I met many people who were planning to write when they had time. I think if you really decide to write, you find time."

Geraldine Deluca

SOURCE: "'Composing a Life': The Diary of Leigh Botts," in *The Lion and the Unicorn,* Vol. 14, No. 2, December, 1990, pp. 58-65.

Recently I came across a book by two psychologists, David Feinstein and Stanley Krippner, entitled *Personal Mythology: The Psychology of Your Evolving Self* (Jeremy Tarcher, 1988). It is a New Age guidebook in Jungian psychology that asks its readers to find their inner story through dreamwork, body work, and through locating an "inner shaman," or wise person who can give them some connection to their own best knowledge and intuition. The story that readers are instructed to write has three parts: the first is a personal recollection—usually an early memory—of paradise, when one felt happy, safe, peaceful. The second part is a memory that represents the loss of the paradise—when something changed, when one began to feel frightened or angry or bereft, perhaps when one began to distrust life. The third part of the story is to be based on a projected image of paradise regained. Readers are asked to imagine how one moves toward a better life—where the losses are compensated for, where the strengths developed during periods of pain are recognized and used, where wounds begin to heal.

This is a helpful, therapeutic structure for conceptualizing the journeys we all make. Its essentially comic movement assumes we have some power over our lives, and it corresponds to the shape of many works of literature, particularly children's literature, where there is a strong pull toward resolution. Sometimes we enter the story "after the fall," but the movement is usually toward finding some way back to a condition of understanding and regeneration.

Beverly Cleary's *Dear Mr. Henshaw,* a deceptively plain but wise book, is an attempt, I think, to take one protagonist, Leigh Botts, through such a journey. It is perhaps her most somber work and it handles in a small space (134 pages of very large print) many matters that the bulk of her work avoids.

Cleary is no doubt best known for her books about Henry Huggins, Beezus, and especially Ramona— *Ramona Quimby, Age 8, Ramona the Brave, Ramona and Her Mother, Ramona and Her Father,* etc. As her characters have grown—very slowly— maybe a year for every decade of their fictional existence—into the eighties, Cleary has allowed them to reflect the changing status of the family in suburban America. In the fifties, a typical dilemma might be that Henry Huggins's dog eats the neighbor's lambchops. By the eighties, life has become more complicated. Ramona's father loses his job and her mother has to get one. But there is an upbeat, comic spirit to the books that prevails throughout. In the episodic world of the Ramona novels, life always ends with a Christmas pageant or a ride with Mom and Dad in the car to a friendly restaurant for a burger and fries, some image of life lived within the paradise. It is never really threatened and so it doesn't have to be regained.

But as Cleary recognizes, such stories do not even come close to telling the truth for many children. Summarizing the author's observations about what readers write to her, Pat Pfleiger says:

> Though Cleary had noticed an increasing surface sophistication in her readers . . . she also noted that their "deepest feelings remain the same." Her readers enjoy books they "can understand"; they want pets and they want teachers who like them . . . and, most important, they "want to love and be loved by two parents in a united family." . . . For there has been an increase, too, in letters "filled with sorrow": "parents were divorced, a father had been murdered, children who were alone after school were sad and frightened." (145)

Dear Mr. Henshaw is Cleary's answer to such letters, a novel whose protagonist, Leigh Botts, loses his paradise of two parents and a dog early in the story—its existence is only briefly recorded through Leigh's letters to an author, Boyd Henshaw. Leigh's struggle is to understand the loss and regain something from it by the story's end.

Leigh's father is a trucker who drives large hauls cross-country. His mother has tired of his not being home, and has asked him to leave. The father has taken the dog with him, and Leigh and his mother have moved to a small town in California, the final spot on the map of the American dream. They live in a tiny house behind a gas station. Leigh's mother works for a caterer who makes canapés for rich people's luncheons, and she studies at night to become a nurse. Leigh, meanwhile, is possessed of delicious lunches, compliments of the catering business, but someone is stealing them. Moreover, he is lonely in his new school, in his new neighborhood, and he misses his dad who, though a responsible worker, is basically an irresponsible husband and father. Leigh's mother tells Leigh that she used to ride in the truck with him before Leigh was born, and understood the excitement of

> controlling a mighty machine . . . of never knowing where his next trip will take him. He loves the mountains and the desert sunrises and the sight of orange trees heavy with oranges and the smell of fresh-mown alfalfa. I know, because I rode with him until you came along. (63)

This, of course, leads Leigh to believe, "Maybe I'm to blame for everything" (64). Later, however, his mother reassures him that she had tired of that life: "'I didn't think playing pinball machines in a tavern on Saturday night was fun anymore. Maybe I grew up and your father didn't'" (76).

The novel is written as a series of letters to an author, Boyd Henshaw, whom Leigh admires. The correspondence begins when Leigh writes to ask Mr. Henshaw some questions to which he needs answers for his book report. The author writes back to him asking him ten important questions about his life. As the story progresses, Leigh comes to understand that Henshaw cannot answer all his letters, but that Leigh must continue writing anyway. For a time he writes to a "Dear Mr. Pretend Henshaw," then finally he crosses that out, writing, "I don't have to pretend to write to Mr. Henshaw anymore. I have learned to say what I think on a piece of paper" (73). He begins to keep a diary, and several parts of the book including the last part are "from the Diary of Leigh Botts." Thus the book is like a journal in which Leigh discovers what he knows by writing about it, remembering, selecting, and exploring the details of his life to find his own inner story.

In Leigh's answers to Mr. Henshaw's ten questions, he sets forth at first begrudgingly but nonetheless faithfully the major issues of his life. The first question is "Who Are You?" which is, of course, a question to which the answer never ends. Leigh answers,

"I am just a plain boy." He continues, "The school doesn't say I am gifted and talented" but he adds, "I am not stupid either" (14-15). He doesn't know yet who he is; he feels somewhat oppositional about school and to his credit knows the difference between who he is and who the authorities have decided he is or is not. To the second question, "What do you look like?" he answers that he is not "real big like my dad. . . . I guess you could call me the mediumest boy in the class" (15). Question three, "What is your family like" allows Cleary to outline the circumstances of Leigh's life without his father and his dog, Bandit, as Leigh sees it. He doesn't have a favorite teacher, but he does mention the custodian, Mr. Fridley, a kindly man "who didn't even look cross" when a child threw up in school (26). Regarding friends, he says,

> I don't have a whole lot of friends in my new school. Mom says maybe I'm a loner, but I don't know. . . . Maybe I'm just a boy nobody pays much attention to. The only time anybody paid much attention to me was in my last school when I gave the book report on *Ways to Amuse a Dog* [Henshaw's book]. . . . The kids here pay more attention to my lunch than they do to me. (25)

He knows, no matter how offhanded his acknowledgment, that his writing has an effect on people. In answer to question nine, "What bothers you?" he answers, "I am bothered when my Dad telephones me and finishes by saying, 'Well, keep your nose clean, kid.' Why can't he say he misses me, and why can't he call me Leigh? I am bothered when he doesn't phone at all which is most of the time" (28). To the final question, "What do you wish?" he answers:

> I wish somebody would stop stealing the good stuff out of my lunchbag. I guess I wish a lot of other things too. I wish someday Dad and Bandit would pull up in front in the rig. . . . Dad would yell out of the cab, "Come on, Leigh. Hop in and I'll give you a lift to school." (29)

Everyone would see them. At the school, they'd exchange some ritual goodbyes and then "Dad would take a minute to write in the truck's logbook, 'Drove my son to school.' Then the truck would pull away from the curb with all the kids staring and wishing their Dads drove big trucks, too" (30). His desire is for circumstances to reverse themselves, for his father to come closer to some ideal. But he feels powerless to effect these changes, as of course he is. He needs to discover the power he does have to make his life happier.

The rest of his book chronicles the events that lead to that discovery. Soon after this entry, he realizes that the custodian, Mr. Fridley, notices him. And on a day when Leigh is ready to start kicking other kids' lunches in frustration, Mr. Fridley stops him, warning him that he's going to turn into a kid who gets into trouble. "'So you've got problems. Well, so has everyone else, if you take the trouble to notice.'" (80). It is appropriate—and characteristic of the way this book quietly reverberates—that it is the custodian who is there when Leigh's lunch is continually ripped off. He is a shadowy, almost underground figure, a caretaker, who stands by the garbage at lunch time to make sure kids don't throw out their retainers—don't lose what's valuable. He is someone you might not pay attention to but who looks out for you, almost a kind of spirit guide, who understands that Leigh is lacking some basic nurturing. Someone is ripping off the essentials in his life. Next, however, Leigh discovers that the librarian notices him, too. The librarian lets him know when a new Boyd Henshaw book arrives at the library. Leigh is surprised and grateful but at the same time he is angry that although these peripheral men take note of him, his own father can't remember to telephone. Other people call him "Leigh" or "son." His own father calls him "kid."

The day of Leigh's angry assault on the lunches, he writers,

> I felt so rotten I decided to go for a walk. I wasn't going any special place, just walking . . . when I came to a sign that said BUTTERFLY TREES. I had heard a lot about those trees where monarch butterflies fly thousands of miles to spend the winter. . . .
>
> The place was so quiet, almost like a church, that I tiptoed. The grove was shady, and at first I thought all the signs about butterflies must be some kind of ripoff for tourists . . .
>
> Then the sun came out from behind a cloud. The sticks began to move, and slowly they opened wings and turned into orange and black butterflies, thousands of them quivering on one tree. Then they began to float off through the trees in the sunshine. Those clouds of butterflies were so beautiful I felt good all over and just stood there watching them until the fog began to roll in, and the butterflies came back and turned into brown sticks again. They made me think of a story Mom used to read me about Cinderella returning from the ball.
>
> I felt so good I ran all the way home, and while I was running I had an idea for my story.
>
> I also noticed that some of the shops had metal boxes that said "Alarm System" up near their roof. . . . (82-84)

This is the symbolic center, the turning point of the novel. Emotionally, spiritually, Leigh is at sea. He is beginning to let his energies move him to destructive acts, beginning to throw himself away. Then he finds himself walking toward what he characterizes as a sacred place, and the butterflies, traditional symbols of transformation, of transcendence, turn out not to be ripoffs, but real. The grove functions as what Northrop Frye called a "house of recognition" (77), what Angus Fletcher saw as a temple in the labyrinth (259), informing Leigh and healing him so that when he leaves, he is ready to begin solving his problems.

He is ready, first of all, to take Mr. Fridley's suggestion to think positively and make an alarm for his lunch box. When he does so he wins the admiration of all the kids in the lunchroom, and he makes a friend. He has learned to notice the resources around him, to listen to the suggestions that come his way, and to take his fate into his own hands.

The other major challenge of his life is to write a story for a school contest. When he leaves the grove he has an idea for a story called "The Ten Foot Wax Man" about a trucker made of wax who melts a little every time he crosses the desert. The feeling that his father is a person of ever diminishing stature—not real big anymore, and as insubstantial as wax—is certainly understandable, but the story doesn't "work." This symbolic destruction may serve to express Leigh's anger, but it doesn't really deal with the complexity of his father's life or the relationship between them. So he writes to Mr. Henshaw, a real letter this time, describing his dilemma, and Henshaw answers him. Leigh reflects on his answer:

> I understand what you mean. A character in a story should solve a problem or change in some way. I can see that a wax man who melts until he's a puddle wouldn't be there to solve anything and melting isn't the sort of change you mean. (91)

His second attempt is much more successful. It is in effect his "paradise" story, his memory of a happier time when he and his father were together. He calls it "A Day on Dad's Rig." Technically, it's not a "story," and Leigh doesn't win any prizes, but he finally gets to have lunch with a famous author—not Boyd Henshaw—and she goes out of her way to compliment him on his work.

> "I just got honorable mention," I said, but I was thinking, She called me an author. *A real live author called me an author.*
>
> "What difference does that make?" asked Mrs. Badger. "Judges never agree. I happened to like *A Day on Dad's Rig* because it was written by a

boy who wrote honestly about something he knew and had strong feelings about. You made me feel what's it was like to ride down a steep grade with tons of grapes behind me."

> "But I couldn't make it into a story," I said, feeling a whole lot braver.
>
> "Who cares?" said Mrs. Badger. . . . The ability to write stories comes later, when you have lived longer and have more understanding. *A Day on Dad's Rig* was splendid work for a boy your age. You wrote like *you,* and you did not try to imitate someone else. This is one mark of a good writer. Keep it up." (119-20)

This episode suggests that what one must do with experience, whether joyful or painful, is face it, remember it, transform it—use it to shape one's life, use it to create something. Once that happens, once one figures out what one can do, rather than getting stuck at what one can't, other things begin to happen. Leigh finds that other men will sometimes watch out for him. A real author writes to him, and another real author praises his work. His mother has encouraged him all along—which is not something every artistic child can count on (witness Jess in *Bridge to Terabithia*). She is also honest with him about the reasons for the divorce. He finds a creative solution to his lunchbox problem, and once he does he no longer cares who the thief is. "Maybe," he writes, "he was just somebody whose mother packed bad lunches" (103).

Leigh's father does show up again at the end of the novel, almost as Leigh had wished him to do early in the work, asking Leigh's mother for another chance. But he is still driving long hauls and so Leigh's mother says no: "'Too many lonely days and nights not knowing where you were, too much waiting for phone calls you forgot to make because you were whooping it up at some truck stop'" (132). When his father promises to "'get over to see you more often,'" Leigh says, "'Sure, Dad,'" and then writes, "I had learned by now that I couldn't count on anything he said" (132). At least he knows what he knows.

Our lives may seem simple, ordinary, lacking the luster of fairy tales. The only sound may be the sound of the gas pumps ringing up their sales, and the only voice may be our own, sometimes cranky, sometimes just flattened out and bewildered. But Cleary conveys the inherent dignity of such a life, of Leigh's struggle, of his voice in writing, which is all we really hear. He has made a commitment to recording his life, has taken on the task of selecting and shaping it in writing. Mary Catherine Bateson recently published a book called *Composing a Life* about the patchwork lives of five women and how the events lead to something approaching a work of art. Cleary does this for her fictional character Leigh. And Leigh, with his recording, and with his final achievement of writing about his own lost paradise, his own decision to recollect a joy of his past that is now gone, does the same for himself. And by dealing with his sadness, transforming it into a record, he also reclaims his present and his future. He composes his life and he becomes an "author." Thus, Cleary makes a statement to her readers about the value of memory, about facing what you've lost. She is also suggesting that while the nuclear family of our dreams may be a most desirable condition when it exists, it is inevitable that some of us will be without it. To know that is to deal with pain but it's also an important step toward finding something to replace it. As Leigh writes in the last line of the book, "I felt sad and a whole lot better at the same time" (134).

Works Cited

Bateson, Mary Catherine. *Composing a Life*. New York: Atlantic Monthly Press, 1989; rpt. New York: Penguin, 1990.

Cleary, Beverly. *Dear Mr. Henshaw*. New York: Morrow, 1983; rpt. New York: Dell Yearling, 1984.

Feinstein, David, and Stanley Krippner. *Personal Mythology: The Psychology of Your Evolving Self*. Los Angeles: Jeremy Tarcher, 1988.

Fletcher, Angus. *The Prophetic Moment: An Essay on Spenser*. Chicago: U of Chicago P, 1971.

Frye, Northrop. "The Structure of Imagery in *The Faerie Queene*." In his *Fables of Identity: Studies in Poetic Mythology*. New York: Harcourt, 1963.

Pflieger, Pat. *Beverly Cleary*. Twayne Series. Boston: G. K. Hall, 1991.

Heather Vogel Frederick

SOURCE: "And to Think That I Saw It on Klickitat Street," in *Publishers Weekly*, Vol. 240, No. 41, October 11, 1993, p. 31.

In the mellow glow of an Indian summer evening, Portland's Grant Park neighborhood looks like many such quiet corners tucked away in cities across the United States. Tidy homes anchor tree-lined streets, and the shady, well-kept park welcomes a steady flow of families. It's a neighborhood as American as Ramona Quimby, say. Or Henry Huggins.

And that's not particularly surprising, given that this section of Oregon's largest city *is* their neighborhood, immortalized by Beverly Cleary in her perennially popular books for children. It was here in Grant Park that Henry Huggins dug for night crawlers; Klickitat Street, home to both the Huggins family and the Quimby family (Ramona and her big sister, Beezus), is just a few blocks away. In fact, there are Cleary landmarks in just about every direction one looks.

And if all goes as planned, a statue and fountain commemorating Ramona, Henry and his dog Ribsy, will be dedicated in Grant Park next June. The project has been "fermenting" for about 15 years, says Doris Kimmel, co-chairwoman of The Friends of Henry and Ramona. The seeds were originally sown when Kimmel and her husband, Eric, a children's book author and professor of children's literature at Portland State University, bought a house in northeast Portland, only to discover that they were just four block away from Klickitat Street—which they immediately recognized as Beverly Cleary country.

At the time, Doris Kimmel was adjunct faculty at PSU, teaching a children's literature course in which she used Cleary's books. Over the years, Kimmel and her husband talked about how nice it would be to have something for children in Grant Park to celebrate Cleary. Then, a few years ago, Eric Kimmel mentioned the idea to one of his students, Heather Johnson (now co-chairwoman of The Friends of Henry & Ramona). Johnson was intrigued, and when she later took a job at Powell's Books, she found herself in a perfect spot to get things rolling.

The Kimmels and Johnson first collaborated on a walking map of sites from Cleary's stories. "Henry Huggins' Neighborhood" maps were an immediate hit, and their success gave them enough confidence to form The Friends of Henry & Ramona, a nonprofit corporation, and begin raising money for a larger-scale project.

Cleary fans (who now stretch across at least two generations, as her books have been continuously in print for over 40 years) have rallied to the cause with contributions ranging from penny drives by elementary classrooms and a read-a-thon in the Portland public schools to donations from individuals across the U.S., neighborhood associations, and corporate sponsors both large and small. A major boost was a grant from the Hearst Book Group, owner of William Morrow, Cleary's publisher.

With just $50,000 to go, the group is bullish about remaining on schedule. An artist, Lee Hunt, has been chosen, and local architect Nancy Merryman is helping the group plan the site. Although the final design has yet to be determined, the sculptures will be organized so that they'll be next to a wading pool or fountain, and the figures will be set up in an interactive format, much like the ducks in Boston's Public Garden. "Kids will be able to go up and pet Ribsy and sit on him, and so on," says Johnson. And Ramona, of course, will appear in her rain slicker and rubber boots.

When asked her thoughts on the project, Cleary says she's "terribly pleased. If I had known [that any of this would have happened] when I was a first-grader swinging on the swings, I would have been astonished!"

Cleary, who now lives in Carmel, Calif., has returned numerous times to her old neighborhood—at least three times accompanied by television cameras. "I think it must be one of the most stable neighborhoods in the United States," she says. "I'm really very fortunate to have it as the setting for my books, because it has not changed a great deal since I've been there."

With any luck, perhaps the new attraction at Grant Park will foster a renaissance of the idyllic childhood Cleary remembers, and of which she so fondly writes in her inimitable stories.

Margaret Mackey

SOURCE: "Ramona the Chronotype: The Young Reader and Social Theories of Narrative," in *Children's Literature in Education*, Vol. 22, No. 2, June, 1991, pp. 97-109.

Meanings are made socially. Every child has to learn a language that already exists; the completely personal, idiosyncratic language, by definition, cannot communicate until a second person cracks the code. One of the many challenges of childhood is to master the social network of meaning making. Learning the mother tongue is a huge part of that process, but there are other complexities to comprehend as well.

At the same time, children gradually have to locate themselves in the world. Where are they? When are they? What is the impact of time on their existence?

What belongs to the social network and what is exclusive to the individual? What is constant and trustworthy? What shifts and disappears?

These issues are at the heart of major questions raised by those theorists who look at how narrative connects with and feeds into the society which surrounds it.

Mikhail Bakhtin, writing "notes towards a historical poetic," makes some remarks about the development of the novel as a form of narrative which, by implication, cast considerable light on what young readers may gain from a story. He comments on the role of story in establishing individuals in time and space, borrowing the word *chro-notope* from mathematics to describe "the intrinsic connectedness of temporal and spatial relationships that are artistically expressed in literature."[1]

As Bakhtin expounds his ideas about the history of the novel in its earliest forms, he also draws attention to a problem of the Hellenistic era:

> A contradiction developed between the public nature of the literary form and the private nature of its content. . . . The quintessentially private life that entered the novel at this time, was, by its very nature and as opposed to public life, *closed*. In essence one could only *spy* and *eavesdrop* on it. (p. 123)

Artistic forms that overcome this contradiction have long been available, but the clash between what is private and what is public still is an issue of major importance to children who are learning to distinguish between themselves and their own private thoughts and the public world which creates and shapes their existences.

A different thinker starts with questions about the psychology of learning. Jerome Bruner discusses another element in narrative which makes it a force in the lives of even very small children: its ability to let us comprehend deviations from the socially acceptable norm, from the canons which govern social life.

> Folk psychology is invested in canonicality. It focuses upon the expectable and/or the usual in the human condition. It endows these with legitimacy or authority. Yet it has powerful means that are purpose-built for rendering the exceptional and the unusual into comprehensible form. For . . . the viability of a culture inheres in its capacity for resolving conflicts, for explicating differences and renegotiating communal meanings. The "negotiated meanings" discussed by social anthropolo-

gists or culture critics as essential to the conduct of a culture are made possible by narrative's apparatus for dealing simultaneously with canonicality and exceptionality. Thus, while a culture must contain a set of norms, it must also contain a set of interpretive procedures for rendering departures from those norms meaningful in terms of established patterns of belief. It is narrative and narrative interpretation upon which folk psychology depends for achieving this kind of meaning. Stories achieve their meanings by explicating deviations from the ordinary in a comprehensible form.[2]

Between them, Bakhtin and Bruner offer a powerful set of roles for stories: finding a location in space and time, distinguishing between the private and the social, establishing the norm and explaining the deviations.

Reading narrative fiction or listening to it read aloud is a specialized subset of story exchange, but it is an important one in Western cultures. Given the immense significance of narrative as outlined above, we can look at the importance of childhood reading in a new way. Children establishing their own place in the world find narrative speaking to that challenge; at the same time, lured by the appeal of that narrative voice, they learn about how to process a story.

RAMONA: AN EXAMPLE OF THE SOCIAL IMPORT OF
NARRATIVE

To see how this duality works, let us look at one example. In the account of Ramona Quimby by Beverly Cleary, we have a story which highlights many of the points made above. As a useful bonus, there happens to exist a description of how one child met, enjoyed, and benefitted from Ramona, as well as an account of the social network within which her reading took place.

Ramona's story is actually told over several books which are accessible to children as young as six or seven. They meet all criteria of positioning the individual in a particular time, place, and culture, and they treat the importance of all these issues with respect. The books are lighthearted and funny, but their themes are as significant as those of many more weighty adult books.

The Ramona books, published over several decades, delight and comfort children who already know that growing up takes time and effort. The passage of time is the dominating theme of all of them. Like many other people, Ramona wants to get bigger and smarter herself, but she would like this to happen

without any other ramifications of change impinging on her security. One of the reasons for Beverly Cleary's enduring popularity is her rigorous honesty in insisting that it can't be done. By the end of the last book, Ramona is finally "winning at growing up," but the costs have been measured faithfully throughout the series.

Time is a major issue in narrative fiction. The Ramona books, however, do not make a feature of sophisticated arrangements of events by the narrator. By and large, Cleary sticks to a straightforward chronology; the passage of time is a topic and a theme in the Ramona books, rather than a tool for narrative manipulation.

Readers of the Ramona books will find Bakhtin's substantial narrative projects given proper importance. Part of the challenge of growing up is to get a sense of your place in time and space, and to establish what is private and what is public. Through all her engagements with authority, Ramona is establishing who, when, and where she is, and also what distinctions she must learn to make between her own personal convictions (all very strongly held) and the social norms which govern public life in school, at home, and on the neighborhood streets.

Narrative's role in explaining deviations from canonical expectations is a feature of almost every chapter. Ramona wants to grow up and she wants to make sense of the very specific social network in which she lives, at the same time developing an idea of what private beliefs and opinions are important to her. She engages in the real work of childhood and finds it stimulating and exhausting. What children have to do is important and difficult, and this understanding feeds every paragraph of the Ramona books.

Bruner's account of the role of narrative in establishing what is canonical expresses a vital ambiguity in elegantly but deceptively simple terms. Narrative not only establishes cultural norms and explains deviations from those norms; it also establishes ways of looking at and talking about such things. At one and the same time, it involves a cultural subject and a way of talking about that subject. Children reading books like the Ramona stories learn about themselves and their surroundings and at the same time learn more about ways of making stories.

Although the Ramona books seem simple to read, a great deal is going on on each page. Again, Bakhtin has a description:

In the literary artistic chronotope, spatial and temporal indicators are fused into one carefully thought-out, concrete whole. Time, as it were, thickens, takes on flesh, becomes artistically visible; likewise space becomes charged and responsive to the movements of time, plot and history. (p. 84)

One of Cleary's strongest points is her talent for "thickening time." Her observation of how time works for children is acute and subtle; her artistic representation of time is fascinating.

RAMONA IN TIME

Much of what children learn, they take in by a process of accretion through repetition. Novelists are often inclined to describe once an event which recurs many times. Beverly Cleary makes inverse use of that custom: she describes recurring events again and again, building up layers of reference to commonplace thoughts and conversations. The familiar and the consistent in Ramona's world take on new texture from this technique.

Take an example: Ramona's ongoing envy of her classmate Susan's thick, springy curls. At several points, this envy causes incidents which get Ramona into trouble with her teacher, but many of the references are passing ones. Here is the introductory sequence, in **Ramona the Pest,** on Ramona's first day of school:

> The other interesting person was a big girl named Susan. Susan's hair looked like the hair on the girls of the old-fashioned stories Beezus liked to read. It was reddish-brown and hung in curls like springs that touched her shoulders and bounced as she walked. Ramona had never seen such curls before. All the curly-haired girls she knew wore their hair short. Ramona put her hand to her own short straight hair, which was an ordinary brown, and longed to touch that bright springy hair. She longed to stretch one of those curls and watch it spring back. *Boing!* thought Ramona, making a mental noise like a spring on a television cartoon and wishing for thick, springy *boing-boing* hair like Susan's.[3]

Over the next chapters of the book, Ramona has no fewer than three substantial confrontations with Miss Binney, the teacher, over her inability to resist tweaking Susan's curls and shouting, "Boing!" Furthermore, almost every time Susan is mentioned, Ramona notices the curls and thinks, "Boing!" to herself in passing.

Such repetition serves a number of ends. Susan is not a major character compared to Ramona's family and her neighbors, the Kemps; on the other hand, she and

her curls are vital to the plot. Young readers are helped to remember Susan and keep her distinct from other classmates, even if they are reading the book slowly, over a lengthy period of time. Repeated explicit reference to Ramona's utter fascination with Susan's curls reinforces the idea that Susan's hair is important to the plot and encourages new readers to make use of a standard ingredient of story making: repetition as a mark of emphasis.

Beverly Cleary also observes a rule that is more often seen in life than in fiction: even after a crisis ties up the ends of many plot strings, some things just don't go away. In the subsequent book, Ramona has reluctantly learned that tweaking Susan's curls is just not worth the aggravation, but she carries on thinking:

> . . . Susan with her fat curls like springs touching her shoulders. *Boing,* thought Ramona as always, at the sight of those curls. This year she promised herself she would not pull those curls no matter how much they tempted her.[4]

There are at least three more mentions of Susan's curls, spread throughout the second book. Here, they serve no real plot purpose, but they help to maintain the consistency of Ramona's environment as outlined in the first story.

Also, and very importantly, all the references to Susan's curls help to establish a distinctive sense of time in Ramona's world. Children are more likely than adults to notice and remember even very similar occasions as separate events. Where adult memories may lump together and blur into a general category such repetitive experiences as watching Susan's curls bounce on her shoulders day after day, children are likely to notice each time as an individual event. Reiteration also emphasizes that much of a child's life is very repetitive indeed, and that to the child, routine is more likely to be a positive than a negative feature of life. It is one way for Cleary to focus on and express Ramona's own perceptions of the world, an artistic tool very deftly used.

In later books, Cleary uses repetition to even more subtle effect with her reiteration of Ramona's great burden in life: the obligation to spend time after school in the care of Howie Kemp's grandmother and his infuriating little sister, Willa Jean. This arrangement first comes into effect in the early pages of **Ramona and Her Mother,** when Mr. Quimby gets a new job (he later goes to teacher training college) and Mrs. Quimby works full time as a doctor's receptionist. Many features about the afternoon hours at the Kemps' are identical, day after day. Mrs. Kemp watches soap operas on television. She always gives the children graham crackers and apple juice, which bores Ramona to distraction. Howie often escapes to play with his friends on his bike (Ramona does not own a bike because the Quimbys cannot afford one). Beezus arrives as late as possible and buries herself in her homework. Ramona is expected to entertain the small but bossy Willa Jean, who can do no wrong in her doting grandmother's eyes.[5]

There are references to this situation all the way through *Ramona and Her Mother* and *Ramona Quimby, Age 8.* No magic solution appears in either book, and day after day is shadowed for Ramona by the prospect of the Kemps' house after school:

> Ramona . . . liked being big enough to be counted on, but sometimes when she went to the Kemps' she felt as if everything depended on her. If Howie's grandmother did not look after her, her mother could not work full time. If her mother did not work full time, her father could not go to school. If her father did not go to school, he might have to go back to being a checker, the work that made him tired and cross.[6]

Ramona does her best to cope, but the unremitting dailiness of the problem gets her down. "Even though her family understood, Ramona still dreaded that part of the day spent at Howie's house in the company of Mrs. Kemp and Willa Jean" (p. 29). Even by the end of the book, Ramona is still struggling. Her mother says to her:

> "Ramona, Mrs. Kemp did not come right out and say so, but she did drop a hint that you are not playing as nicely with Willa Jean as you might."

Ramona heaved a sigh that seemed to come from the soles of her feet. . . .

> Mrs. Quimby ignored the sighs . . . and continued. "Ramona, you know that getting along at the Kemps' is your job in this family. I've told you that before." (p. 137)

By the last pages in the book, Ramona has worked out a temporary solution: "She would try reading her Sustained Silent Reading books aloud because Willa Jean was old enough to understand most of them. That should work for a little while" (p. 153).

Finally, in *Ramona Forever,* enough time has passed so that Beezus is old enough to look after Ramona at home after school, as long as they can be trusted to be good. Cleary herself has observed:

> The stories I write are the stories I wanted to read as a child in Portland, Oregon—humorous stories about the problems which are small to adults but which loom so large in the lives of children, the sort of problems children can solve themselves.[7]

Ramona and Beezus finally solve for themselves the problem of afterschool care, but only with the aid of time; and Cleary uses that time to shape the books and simultaneously to show us the world from Ramona's perspective.

Repetition is not Cleary's only tool for measuring time. When it suits the needs of the story, she can describe time slowed to a crawl—again emphasizing the perceptions of Ramona herself. In this example, Ramona has been forbidden to visit her mother and her new baby sister because hospital rules say she is not old enough and might be carrying germs; she must wait downstairs:

> Ramona sat gingerly on the edge of a couch. If she leaned back, she might get germs on it, or it might get germs on her. She swallowed hard. Was her throat a little bit sore? She though maybe it was, way down in the back. She put her hand to her forehead the way her mother did when she thought Ramona might have a fever. Her forehead was warm, maybe too warm.
>
> As Ramona waited, she began to itch the way she itched when she had chickenpox. Her head itched, her back itched, her legs itched. Ramona scratched. A woman sat down on the couch, looked at Ramona, got up and moved to another couch.
>
> Ramona felt worse. She itched more and scratched harder. She swallowed often to see how her sore throat was coming along. She peeked down the neck of her blouse to see if she might have a rash and was surprised that she did not. She sniffed from time to time to see if she had a runny nose.[8]

RAMONA IN SPACE

The establishment of Ramona in space is also built up in a series of accretions. We know the Quimbys live in Klickitat Street in the rainy city of Portland, Oregon. For the most part, however, Ramona establishes her location not geographically, but socially. Her place is created in a network of other people, and she positions herself among them.

Ramona first appeared in stories about her sister Beezus and Beezus's friend, Henry Huggins. She got her first book to herself because readers begged Beverly Cleary to write it. Ramona thus begins as a child observed by others, particularly by Beezus, who often dislikes her little sister for being such a noisy nuisance.

When that little sister takes over her own books, Cleary sticks very close to Ramona as the central consciousness. She uses a third-person narrative but does not exploit this to give other perspectives on Ramona—except, crucially, as Ramona occasionally perceives them for herself. Ramona's relationships with family, teachers, and classmates are all filtered through Ramona's own awareness. Nevertheless, Cleary uses many techniques to show young readers that Ramona may be limited or mistaken in what she sees. Ramona's position in her world is thus created by reciprocating rather than one-way ties, but Cleary has the opportunity to be explicit to her readers about how this works.

For example, Ramona sometimes leaps to new awareness in confrontations with Beezus. Beezus has complained bitterly to their mother about Ramona's behavior in the park:

> Ramona was suddenly subdued. She had thought Beezus was angry at the boys, but now it turned out she was angry with her little sister, too. Maybe angrier. Ramona was used to being considered a little pest, and she knew she sometimes was a pest, but this was something different. She felt as if she were standing aside looking at herself. She saw a stranger, a funny little six-year-old girl with straight brown hair, wearing grubby shorts and an old t-shirt. . . . A silly little girl embarrassing her sister so much that Beezus was ashamed of her. And she had been proud of herself because she thought she was being brave. Now it turned out that she was not brave. She was silly and embarrassing. Ramona's confidence in herself was badly shaken.[9]

Sometimes she is jolted out of her image of herself by the reaction of others. One such example occurs when Ramona, obsessed with cute little children in television advertisements, quotes a cheeky child from a commercial and is actually quite rude to her teacher. The reaction of the teacher and her classmates rapidly brings her down to earth:

> Suddenly Ramona was no longer an adorable little fluffy-haired girl on television. She was plain old Ramona, a second-grader whose own red tights bagged at the knee and wrinkled at the ankle. This wasn't the way things turned out on television. On television grown-ups always smiled at everything children said.[10]

Sometimes Ramona's parents take a hand and improve her understanding by spelling things out for her:

> "Did you ever stop to think, Ramona," said Mrs. Quimby, "that perhaps Mrs. Kemp would rather not be a sitter for you or her grandchildren?" No, Ramona had not thought of that.
>
> "Women her age were brought up to keep house and take care of children," explained Mrs. Quimby. "That's all they really know how to do. But now maybe she'd rather be doing something else." She looked thoughtful.[11]

Very occasionally, Ramon has a flash of insight for herself:

> Ramona was suddenly struck by a new and disquieting thought. *Mrs Kemp did not like her.* Until this minute she had thought all adults were supposed to like all children. She understood by now that misunderstandings were to be expected—she had had several with teachers—and often grown-ups and children did not agree, but things somehow worked out. For a grown-up to actually dislike a child and try to shame her, she was sure had to be wrong, very, very wrong.[12]

A PLACE IN THE WORKING WORLD

Ramona's relationship to the world around her is also affected by economic forces. Mr. Quimby loses his job early in the series; he eventually gets a job he detests; he subsequently goes to teacher-training college, which puts further pressure on the family budget; and then he cannot find a teaching job because there are cutbacks in the State of Oregon and he has to settle for something else. Scrimping and pinching are a feature of many of the incidents in the books. Tempers fray under pressure, and the Quimby family sometimes quarrel out of sheer fatigue and frustration. Ramona's ability to persevere at the Kemps' house is important to everyone just because family finances are so precarious. She cannot escape with Howie from the appalling Willa Jean because he is always off on his bicycle and the Quimbys can't afford one for Ramona. That lack of a bicycle impinges on much of Ramona's life and affects her relationship to the specific geography of the neighborhood as well as to the other children. The network which sustains Ramona in her place in the world is indeed a complex one.

Work is not something done only by parents either. Ramona works hard every day. There are many references to tidying bedrooms and setting tables, but Ramona's main work is schoolwork, and Cleary gives her full credit for it. This adds verisimilitude to the accounts of Ramona's daily existence, gives balance to Ramona's home and street life, and, very importantly, shows Ramona actively engaged in establishing her own awareness of the canonical workings of narrative. Ramona spends large parts of the books reading and writing. Learning to write her name, first in squiggles, then in print, finally in cursive, is a major project in three different books. However, reading is the dominant task. Ramona masters words, stories, chapters, books. She reads when things are unbearable elsewhere. She reads for duty and she reads for fun. She judges books:

> The book . . . was divided into chapters but used babyish words. . . . Medium-boring, thought Ramona, good enough to pass the time on the bus, but not good enough to read during Sustained Silent Reading.[13]

Ramona learns to read in **Ramona the Brave,** which marks her progress in detail. Reading gives her a new language, which works at first according to its limits. Ramona, unhappy on the way to bed and with the unsympathetic Mrs. Kemp babysitting, writes her first note to her mother:

> Come here Moth er. Come here to me. No need to sign the note. Her mother would know who it was from because Beezus wrote joined-up letters.[14]

The language of the basal reader actually functions for a real purpose here. Later, Ramona uses its limitations as a lament. She has had a row with Susan, but Mrs. Griggs refuses to get excited:

Mrs. Griggs, finished with mittens, had the class counting balloons. Unexcited Mrs. Griggs. Mrs. Griggs who did not understand. Mrs. Griggs who went on and on about counting and adding and taking away, and on and on about Tom and Becky and their dog Pal and their cat Fluff, who could run, run, run and come, come, come. Mrs. Griggs, always calm, never raising her voice, everything neat, everything orderly with no paste wasted.

> Ramona wished she could run, run, run, out of that classroom as she had the day before and never come back.[15]

Ramona also considers *how* to read. She is the source of the great unanswerable question which stops Miss Binney in her tracks on the first day of school:

> "Miss Binney, I want to know—how did Mike Mulligan go to the bathroom when he was digging the basement of the town hall?"[16]

Miss Binney's attempts to answer the question are not successful:

> "Boys and girls," she began, and spoke in her clear distinct way. "The reason the book does not tell us how Mike Mulligan went to the bathroom is that it is not an important part of the story. The story is about digging the basement of the town hall, and that is what the book tells us."

Miss Binney spoke as if this explanation ended the matter, but the kindergarten was not convinced. Ramona knew and the rest of the class knew that knowing how to go to the bathroom *was* important. They were surprised that Miss Binney did not understand, because she had showed them the bathroom the very first thing. Ramona could see there were some things she was not going to learn in school, and along with the rest of the class she stared reproachfully at Miss Binney. (pp. 20-21)

READING WITH RAMONA

As it happens, there is a study of a reader of Ramona: seven-year-old Claire, who was observed during the process of becoming a confident reader within the reading community of her own family. For Claire, the crucial turning point in her reading development was her active engagement with the stories of Ramona. In the account of how Ramona made an impact on Claire's life, we find considerable insight into how reading works as a social process.[17]

Claire first turned to the Ramona books on the recommendation of her mother, who was already engaged in making a detailed study of her child's literacy growth. Claire's first reaction to the stories was described by her mother as "passionate attention," a phrase of Auden's:

> That Claire loved the Ramona books was evident within two weeks after her introduction to them. For the next several months she was so completely captivated by the lives of the characters in the books, and particularly by the lively, imaginative Ramona, that they became almost a part of our own family. Her enthusiasm for them affected others in the family as her sisters [aged twelve and fifteen] began to reminisce about hilarious incidents from the books and then began taking the books to their rooms for a quiet reread. (p. 620)

Claire read funny bits out to her family; she asked questions about the meaning of words and the significance of plot developments; she made comparisons between her own family and Ramona's. After she had reread all the books at least twice, she began to comment more reflectively about what made the books so attractive to her. She remarked more than once that Ramona resembled her and extrapolated incidents to apply to her own life, quizzing her father, for example, about what would happen to the family if he lost his job as Mr. Quimby had. As time passed, Claire's comments became more analytical and specific; she assessed particular phrases and what made them successful or otherwise.

> Through her deep engagement with these books Claire became an amateur critic quite naturally. I did not have to force talk about literary form because she initiated such discussions. She wanted to extend her experience of these books at a variety of levels and so at various times she: shared amusing incidents from the stories, related them to her own life, saw patterns in common between these and other books she read, explored new experiences and feelings, and examined the form of the writing to discover why it was so successful. (p. 626)

From Ramona, Claire moved on to other books, securely established as a reader. Her mother comments on her development:

> Claire's immediate response to the stories she read was a subjective one, a feeling one. But the interplay between affect and cognition was clearly observable, and it is ultimately the workings of both together that contribute to her reading of the world and to her growth as a literate person, and indeed as a human being. (p. 631)

What is also clearly observable in this account is the linkage between the social and the private. In this description of a child making sense of Ramona making sense of the world, we can perceive the dynamic of story at work. Because Ramona takes so seriously the social and personal project of growing up, in which Claire is also actively involved, she engages Claire's enthusiasm and enables her to comment both on how the story sheds light on her own life *and* on how the story works within itself. Claire's absorbed reaction, and the enthusiasm of countless other readers, testifies to the subtlety and precision of Cleary's observation of childhood and the skill with which she shapes that observation into story.

We have come full circle. Meaning making is indeed social. Ramona engages all her social connections with her own private perceptions and attempts to make sense of the world she lives in. Her young readers not only see Ramona's involvement with this process but also see story used to explain, describe, and account for that process in action at the symbolic level where, despite her graphic vividness, Ramona really lives. Young readers interact with Ramona and also in a different way with Beverly Cleary. They

read about someone else's perceptions of time and space and compare them with their own; they see narrative shaping those perceptions; they see narrative affecting themselves. Reading is both private and social. Ramona's challenge to grow up illuminates more lives than her own.

Notes

1. M. M. Bakhtin. *The Dialogic Imagination: Four Essays,* p. 84

2. Jerome Bruner. *Acts of Meaning,* p. 47

3. Beverly Cleary. *Ramona the Pest,* p. 15

4. Beverly Cleary. *Ramona the Brave,* p. 41

5. Beverly Cleary. *Ramona and Her Mother*

6. Beverly Cleary. *Ramona Quimby, Age 8,* p. 13

7. Beverly Cleary. "The Laughter of Children," p. 557

8. Beverly Cleary. *Ramona Forever,* p. 146

9. *Ramona the Brave,* pp. 11-13

10. Beverly Cleary. *Ramona and Her Father,* pp. 31-32

11. *Ramona Forever,* p. 32

12. *Ramona Forever,* pp. 25-26

13. *Ramona Quimby, Age 8,* pp. 119-120

14. *Ramona the Brave,* p.

15. *Ramona the Brave,* pp. 79-80

16. *Ramona the Pest.* p. 19

17. Maureen Sanders. "Literacy as 'Passionate Attention,'" p. 620

References

Bakhtin, M. M., *The Dialogic Imagination: Four Essays.* Michael Holquist, ed., Caryl Emerson and Michael Holquist, trans. Austin: University of Texas Press, 1981.

Bruner, Jerome, *Acts of Meaning.* Cambridge, MA, and London: Harvard University Press, 1990.

Cleary, Beverly, *Beezus and Ramona.* Louis Darling, illus. New York: Dell Yearling, 1955.

Cleary, Beverly, *Ramona the Pest.* Louis Darling, illus. Harmondsworth: Puffin Books, 1976. (First published 1968.)

Cleary, Beverly, *Ramona the Brave.* Alan Tiegreen, illus. Harmondsworth: Puffin Books, 1978. (First published 1975.)

Cleary, Beverly, *Ramona and Her Father.* Alan Tiegreen, illus. Harmondsworth: Puffin Books, 1981. (First published 1978.)

Cleary, Beverly, *Ramona and Her Mother.* Alan Tiegreen, illus. New York: William Morrow & Company, 1979.

Cleary, Beverly, *Ramona Quimby, Age 8.* Alan Tiegreen, illus. Harmondsworth: Puffin Books, 1984. (First published 1981.)

Cleary Beverly, *Ramona Forever.* Alan Tiegreen, illus. Harmondsworth: Puffin Books, 1986. (First published 1984.)

Cleary, Beverly, "The laughter of children," *The Horn Book Magazine,* October 1982, pp. 555-564.

Sanders, Maureen, "Literacy as 'passionate attention,'" *Language Arts,* October 1987, *64* (6), pp. 619-633.

Pat Pflieger

SOURCE: "Beverly Cleary: An Ordinary Life," in *Twayne's United States Authors,* on CD-ROM, G. K. Hall & Co., 1997.

"If my books are popular with children," Cleary wrote in 1957, "it is because my childhood was bounded by the experiences of an average American child."[1] Cleary's childhood, spent first on a small family farm and then in Portland, Oregon, has provided a wealth of material for her books, from experiences to emotions. The reader of Cleary's 1988 autobiography, **A Girl from Yamhill,** cannot help but realize the richness of her childhood memories, in a 279-page work that explores only the first eighteen years of her life. Memories of the specific events—fears, joys, and confusions—of her childhood fill Cleary's works with authentic emotions and with "the little everyday experiences that do not seem important to adults, but which are so terribly important

to children." Cleary remembers that children's "lives do not seem eventful, but they are eventful in the little ways that loom large to a child" (**"Writing,"** 11).

YAMHILL

Cleary's life began on 12 April 1916, in McMinnville, Oregon. Born to Chester Lloyd and Mable Atlee Bunn, Beverly was descended from Oregon pioneers, whose fortitude and courage Beverly came to resent being reminded of each time she found something difficult.[2] But Beverly loved the house her grandfather had enlarged from a wheelwright's house into the "first fine house in Yamhill, with the second bathtub in Yamhill County" (*Yamhill,* 8); she loved the eighty-acre farm her father worked; and, especially, she loved life in Yamhill, Oregon.

Writing of those first six years of her life, Cleary has called them "exceptionally happy."[3] The only child on the farm, she learned quickly to amuse herself and was given the run of the place because her father had taught her the rules she was to follow for her own safety—rules which Beverly obeyed, but which did not preclude such activities as picking flowers, feeding baby birds the worms out of Bing cherries, throwing rotten eggs, or tripping chickens with a long pole (*Yamhill,* 24). The rules Beverly's mother taught her seemed more arbitrary, dealing as they did with etiquette and social graces. But it was her mother who told Beverly, "Never be afraid" (*Yamhill,* 39), and it was her mother who instilled an early love of a good story. Though Yamhill did not yet have a library, Mrs. Bunn sparked Beverly's imagination with remembered recitation pieces and fairy tales as well as with stories of her own Michigan childhood. The lack of a library did not mean that young Beverly did not know of the magic of books. In fact, she had loved her first book at age four:

> My first experience with a book was fraught with peril. When I was four years old and lived on a farm outside Yamhill, Oregon, a neighbor showed me a picture book which so delighted me that she invited me to look at it any time I pleased. Unfortunately her bachelor son had made a deal to sell me for a nickel to another neighbor, Quong Hop, who was planning to return to China to die. To reach the book I had to pass Quong Hop's house, and since I did not want to go to China, but I did want to see that book, I snaked on my stomach through tall grass and arrived damp with spitbug spit. Alert for the son's footsteps so I could hide in the pantry, I perched on a kitchen chair and studied the pictures of red-coated men on horse-

back chasing a fox with a pack of hounds. At the end of the book they held the fox's tail triumphantly aloft. Fascinating! Nothing like this went on in Yamhill. The crawl home left me even damper with spitbug spit and longing for more books.[4]

Beverly's own books were a Mother Goose and a copy of *The Three Bears* printed on linen (***Yamhill,*** 60).

More books came when Beverly was five; her mother launched a campaign for a town library "when other homesteaders would come for miles around just to borrow her one book" (Ernest Thompson Seton's *The Biography of a Grizzly*)—sent from Michigan (***Yamhill,*** 20).[5] The library, housed in the Commercial Clubrooms over the Yamhill Bank, was a "dingy room filled with shabby leather-covered chairs and smelling of stale cigar smoke" ("Writing," 7), but it was the means of a revelation to Beverly: that there were other books for children, exciting books such as Jacobs's *More English Fairy Tales* and Beatrix Potter's *The Tailor of Gloucester, Johnny Crow's Garden,* and *The Curly-Haired Hen.* That charming and gruesome story of the Hobyahs—who "run, run, run," "creep, creep, creep," and "trip, trip, trip" up on the peasant's house—was a favorite, with Beverly insisting on taking Jacobs's work to bed with her "instead of my teddy bear" (**"Writing,"** 7); the mouse embroidery in Potter's work intrigued Beverly, who was learning needlework (**"Books"**).

In Yamhill, Beverly felt a part of everything since her uncle was mayor, her father was on the town council, and her mother was the librarian. Children were expected to be a part of everything in Yamhill, so Beverly acted in pageants and went to church picnics, dances, and the Fourth of July parade (***Yamhill,*** 43-44). All of this changed when Beverly turned six: the good harvest brought little money, and Mr. Bunn decided to quit farming. He was probably the only one in his family distressed at the prospect of moving: Mrs. Bunn, unprepared to be a farmer's wife, disliked the hard work of farming, and Beverly looked forward to moving to the big city of Portland, Oregon. Although she could amuse herself on the farm, Beverly longed to play with other children, making do with her stolid cousin, Winston; her mother's pregnancy when Beverly was four had ended in miscarriage, so Beverly had remained an only child. Now she would "have children close by to play with, school, a real teacher who would teach me to read. Even though adults had troubles, I was secure. Yamhill had taught me that the world was a safe and beautiful place, where children were treated with kindness, patience, and tolerance" (***Yamhill,*** 64-65).

PORTLAND

Portland taught her different. Excited by the wonders of the city, by the enormous children's room of the Portland Library Association, and by the joy of playing with the many neighborhood children, Beverly was eager to plunge into her new life. School was interesting but sometimes puzzling and arbitrary: Beverly did not understand why she was wrong to pick up a pencil in the closest hand (her left) and why she suddenly had "a right or wrong hand" (***Yamhill,*** 75-76); Beverly already knew how to add and subtract but was taught again. Reading was "dull but easy" (***Yamhill,*** 77) until a bout of chicken pox put Beverly behind the other students. Now "the boundaries of childhood closed like a trap" (**"Wilder,"** 363). Used to the freedom of the farm, Beverly hated the classroom, which was crowded by forty students, hated the primer which bore "the symbol of a beacon light, presumably to guide us and to warn us of the dangers that lay within,"[6] and was confused by Miss Falb, her teacher, who punished without explaining. Smallpox seemed wonderful, for it meant Beverly did not have to go to school. However, it put her even farther behind in reading, and when Beverly returned to school the class had been divided into reading groups: Bluebirds, the best readers; Redbirds, the next best; and Blackbirds, the worst readers. Beverly was a Blackbird, which meant sitting closest to the blackboard and farthest from the windows, reading from flashcards, and learning monotonous word lists; Beverly also learned that, despite her mother's assurances, reading was *not* fun (**"Low,"** 288). Afraid at school, Beverly also became afraid at home. Beverly was afraid that the earthquake that had ravaged Japan would be repeated in Portland, that something would happen to her father as he worked nights, that (as her nightly prayer hinted) she might die before she woke, and afraid to tell her mother, who had taught her to be brave (***Yamhill,*** 81). When Mrs. Bunn visited the classroom to find out why her daughter begged to stay home from school, Miss Falb "was so kind to me that my mother was reassured, and I learned a bitter lesson of childhood—an adult can be a hypocrite" (**"Wilder,"** 363).

During the summer between first and second grades, Beverly regained her self-confidence; in second grade, Beverly loved her teacher and learned to read. But she refused to read outside of school, though while ill with tonsillitis Beverly was languidly surprised to learn that a book could tell her something she did not already know (*Yamhill*, 87). It was on a boring afternoon when she was eight that Beverly picked up Lucy Fitch Perkins's *The Dutch Twins* "to look at the pictures" and realized that, not only was she reading, but she was enjoying it (*Yamhill*, 93). In Perkins's work about two ordinary children and their often-humorous adventures, Beverly found a "great feeling of release"[7]; suddenly she "felt young, and it is a marvelous thing to feel young at the age of eight" (*"Wilder,"* 363). Soon Beverly was devouring Perkins's entire series, then all the fairy tales in her branch of the library, and, finally, *all* the works for children in her library, working her way from Alcott to Zwilgmeyer (*"Books"*). She also turned her new-found love to practical use: a review written for the *Oregon Journal* earned Beverly a copy of *The Story of Dr. Dolittle* (*Yamhill*, 93).

School life improved as Beverly moved through the grades, despite multiplication tables and an incident in which a beloved teacher called her a "nuisance" (*Yamhill*, 100). Having moved once, the Bunns moved again, to a lively neighborhood in which Beverly felt comfortable. However, now Mrs. Bunn decided to "mold Beverly's character," a process seemingly designed to make her independent; now she was exhorted to "Try" (*Yamhill*, 105). Trying earned Beverly $2 when hers was the only entry in a contest "for the best essay about an animal"; trying earned her $1 from the *Shopping News* when it published a letter from her (*Yamhill*, 105). However, Beverly's contribution was rejected by the St. Nicholas League ("Writing," 9).

Now there was tension at home because Mr. Bunn, educated to work a farm and not to work in the city, was unhappy in his indoor job. Mrs. Bunn prayed that the family would not go back to the farm. Tensions began, too, between Beverly and her mother, with battles over woolen underwear and high brown shoes (*Yamhill*, 116). These tensions escalated when the inflation of 1927 brought new money worries to the family. Mrs. Bunn took the only job she could find, telephoning for subscribers to *McCall's* magazine: "When I came home from school that dark and dreary winter, I felt as if Mother, bundled up in an old sweater, had shut me out by endlessly repeating the merits of *McCall's* to strangers over the telephone" (*Yamhill*, 124). Beverly's relationship with her mother was not openly affectionate. Surprised once to find that her best friend's mother kissed her daughters, Beverly confronted her mother and received a hug and a kiss in "a sweet, isolated moment" that "was never repeated" (*Yamhill*, 113-14).

Feeling shut out, Beverly took refuge in books, reading Carroll Watson Rankin's *Dandelion Cottage* over and over and finding comfort in a story of a mother devotedly searching for her daughter, the story of Demeter and Persephone: "In my imagination I became Persephone. . . . At home, the wet Oregon winter with its sodden leaves became the dark underworld, and somehow Mother's telephone soliciting kept the world from blooming" (*Yamhill*, 124-25). Demeter found Persephone only as Beverly was "emerging from the dark underworld of anesthesia" after a tonsillectomy, with Mrs. Bunn calling her by endearing names for the first, and only, time (*Yamhill*, 126-27).

The possibility of going back to the farm vanished when Mr. Bunn sold it, and for a time the Bunns enjoyed a certain amount of prosperity, buying a car, getting Beverly's teeth straightened, and buying a house near Klickitat Street. Now, Beverly began to find pleasure in writing, especially after she was encouraged by a seventh-grade teacher whose assignments required imagination. "Journey through Bookland," in which Beverly wrote about her favorite characters, brought the comment that Beverly should write for children when she grew up, a comment Beverly took seriously, vowing to write "the kind of books I wanted to read" (*"Writing,"* 9). Encouraged by her mother to think about a steady job as well, Beverly blithely decided to become a librarian (*Yamhill*, 147).

An incident in the summer before Beverly entered eighth grade left her more bewildered than anything, when an uncle made sickeningly clear to Beverly that his feelings toward her were more than avuncular. On the other hand, eighth-grade boys were not confusing; they were "horrible" (*Yamhill*, 161). Graduation from the eighth grade marked the beginning of adulthood, when each graduate was given an adult library card as she or he crossed the stage.

In the summer of 1930, another tense time began in Beverly's life, when her father lost his job. Suddenly, the depression was upon them (*Yamhill*, 173). Feeling claustrophobic from the effort to live as cheaply as possible and from the pain of seeing her father so defeated, Beverly revelled in a week spent with a friend away from home. Mindful of her possible career in librarianship, Beverly took college preparatory classes in high school, though there was no possibility that the family's dwindling resources would cover the costs. Domestic tensions had deepened after Mr. Bunn decided, and failed, to sell the house.

This was balanced by Beverly's success in writing, when, taking her mother's advice to be funny and to keep things simple, she wrote stories that her teachers praised. One —"**A Green Christmas**," about a boy accidentally dyed green—was published, though under another's name (*Yamhill,* 186-87).

As the depression deepened, Beverly's father found a job, though the family's skills in making do still were tested. Once Mr. Bunn was working, Beverly and her mother began to disagree openly, as Beverly began to resent her mother's attempts to dominate her life and compared Mrs. Bunn with her best friend's mother, who did not pressure or "interfere" (*Yamhill,* 205). High school was fun for Beverly, though she disagreed with the emphasis some students put on being popular. Her view of boys, too, had improved, though Beverly had no thoughts of dating. One evening, however, while delivering Christmas decorations to the local lodge during a dance, Beverly—most unsuitably dressed and painfully aware of her lack of skill—was astonished to be asked to dance, and Mrs. Bunn had her take a class in ballroom dancing as a result.

Dancing class resulted in something more, when Beverly met a young man of whom her mother approved. Though the man, whom Beverly calls "Gerhart" in her autobiography, had nothing in common with Beverly and though Beverly found that her dates with him—and his kisses—were not that enjoyable, they continued to go out together, for Gerhart gave Beverly an escape from her mother (*Yamhill,* 225). As their relationship continued, Beverly began to find school more interesting than did Gerhart, who poked fun at her articles and who grew more and more possessive. Beverly's dates with another boy made her realize that there were boys more interesting than Gerhart, and a fumbled kiss at the end of the junior play—co-authored by Beverly—proved to her that there were kisses better than his as well (*Yamhill,* 232, 236).

That summer brought several realizations: Beverly learned how much she disliked Gerhart and also saw that her mother would always make her feel guilty and would always feel the need to be right (*Yamhill,* 250). She resisted both realizations during her senior year, breaking up with Gerhart but having to endure his visits, which were engineered by her mother. Beverly wanted to go to college but knew that her family could not afford it. The answer to everything seemed to lie in an invitation from Beverly's great-aunt to come to California for the winter and attend junior college tuition-free—an invitation that was at first dismissed as impractical. Mr. Bunn, however, seeing a chance to have his worries about Beverly's future allayed and to help her break off completely with Gerhart—whom he had never liked—decided to let her go.

Beverly was sent to college "not to catch a husband, as was the custom for young women of that time and place, but to become independent."[8] Studying at the University of California—Berkeley, she earned a B.A. in English in 1938; in 1939 she earned a B.A. in librarianship from the University of Washington—Seattle. Her first job as a librarian was as children's librarian in Yakima, Washington, which was important to Cleary's development as a writer. Here she met the children who wanted to read humorous books about children like themselves, and here she learned to tell stories to children.[9]

At college she had met Clarence T. Cleary ("**Newbery**," 431), whom she married in 1940. Then she gave up her job and moved with her new husband to Oakland, California. The Cleary family, which doubled in the 1950s with the birth of twins Marianne Elisabeth and Malcolm James, has lived in California ever since. Cleary used her librarian's skills again during World War II when she worked as post librarian at the Oakland Army Hospital.[10] Still interested in writing for children, Cleary bided her time. A job in the children's book department of a Berkeley bookstore seems to have provided the final incentive for her writing: "Surrounded by books, she was sure she could write a better book than some she saw there, and after the Christmas rush was over, she says, 'I decided if I was ever going to write, I'd better get started'" (**Reuther**, 441).

THE AUTHOR AT WORK

Cleary's working methods seem to have changed little since she wrote that first book in pencil on typing paper that previous owners had left in the linen closet of her home. *Henry Huggins* was begun on 2 January; she has begun most of her works on the anniversary of that date.[11] Writing longhand on a legal pad, Cleary begins the story wherever it starts: "I often begin books in the middle or at the end and play about with my characters in my poor handwriting until I am satisfied with their behavior, which is often a surprise to me."[12] There are no outlines, for Cleary learned as a sophomore in high school that outlining was no help to her (*Yamhill,* 213). Working on weekday mornings, Cleary may take six months to a year to complete a book (Reuther, 442). Then it is typed

The books Cleary did and did not enjoy as a child have influenced her writing: "In my own books I write for the only child I really know and that is the child within myself. I simply write the books I wanted to read as a child" (**"Writing,"** 11). Though *Down-right Dencey* and *Dandelion Cottage* reflect their times—as Cleary's do hers—there are parallels in their themes of ordinary children looking to themselves to solve their problems, children who are neither very good nor very bad, living lives that are not perfect but that are filled with family love. In her works, ordinary children lead ordinary lives, though these lives have changed since publication of **Henry Huggins** in 1950. Cleary's characters solve their problems by themselves, though they are clever enough to accept adult help if offered.

One of the chief delights of Cleary's work is her writing style: clear, direct, and disarmingly simple, it is the essence not only of good humorous writing, but of good writing in general. Though the words and sentence structure Cleary uses are simple and straightforward, there is no sense that Cleary is stripping her writing to accommodate her audience; instead, there is a sense that these are simply the right words for what Cleary wants to say. In part, this simplicity is a legacy from Cleary's mother, who advised her in high school to "[a]lways remember, the best writing is simple writing" (*Yamhill,* 186). Remembering the child who loved *Dandelion Cottage,* in writing her own books, Cleary also has remembered the child who disliked books in which the main character conceitedly told the story, books with too much description, books with a message, books with an author who kept popping in to harangue the reader. **Dear Mr. Henshaw,** the only work in which a child essentially tells his own story, is basically epistolary: Leigh's letters and diary are reproduced as if edited by Cleary herself. Description is sparse in Cleary's works, especially since Beverly's eighth-grade teacher handed back a paragraph of description "inflamed with red pencil corrections," having "changed almost every word": "For years I avoided writing description, and children told me they liked my books because there isn't any description in them" (*Yamhill,* 169).

There isn't any author, either, or any explicit message in Cleary's books. She does not lead her readers to the right reading of the work. Wryly pointing out that adults who insist to children that reading is fun also seem to insist to authors of children's books that a message is essential, she has answered their claims

again and again in her fiction for children, with its implicit messages, and, more bluntly, in her speeches and articles aimed at adults:

> The writer of fiction for children must be, first of all, a story-teller, and if he cannot tell a story his books will not last with children. A story, according to my dictionary, is "a narrative, either true or fictitious, designed to interest or amuse the hearer or reader." The definition does not include the word "teach." Any message conveyed by the story must be implicit in the story, and this implicit message stems from the personality of the author, from his experience, his emotions and his convictions and not from any desire to teach or to get into a market. . . .

> No child wants to read for pleasure a book written in a controlled vocabulary, tested on other children the way detergents are tested on housewives, and designed to teach. I certainly would not want to write such a book. It sounds like a tiresome task. Books for children should be written out of the desire to tell a story. If the reading is to be satisfying to the child, the writing should be satisfying to the author who is collaborating with his child self. (**"Talking,"** 7-8)

Besides, Cleary maintains, "[c]hildren would learn so much more if they were allowed to relax, enjoy a story, and discover what it is they want or need from books.[17]

Because Beverly wanted stories that were funny (**"Low,"** 290), because Mrs. Bunn advised her to "Make it funny" (*Yamhill,* 186), and because Cleary finds that "[f]unny or sad, or even funny and tragic, describes my view of life," she has emphasized humor (**"Laughter,"** 558). Believing that "comedy is as illuminating as tragedy," Cleary also is aware that her readers "may be frightened or discouraged by tragedy in realistic fiction" (**"Laughter,"** 558). The world of Cleary's books is one in which a boy's lunchbox alarm keeps his lunch safe but proves noisy to disarm, in which talcum powder turns the white spots on a dog's coat pink, in which a girl's first kiss is interrupted by a gopher-bearing cat, and in which a little girl crowning herself with cockleburs discovers that un-crowning herself is not quite so easy. Though some of the humor in Cleary's books is slapstick— Ribsy dumping paint on his owner, Ramona giving herself and Howie an unexpected blue bath—most of it is more subtle, for Cleary has noted that "children laugh because they have grown," because they have grown past the embarrassment and can see their younger selves in perspective (**"Laughter,"** 562).

Readers close to the problems Cleary's protagonists encounter may not find them funny, but as they resolve the dilemmas of their childhoods they are able to enjoy the humorous aspects of the growing up of Henry and Ramona and Ellen and Leigh; "the best humor," Cleary reminds us, "leaves room for growth" (**"Laughter,"** 561, 562). This humor may be the main reason for Cleary's continuing popularity, a popularity she never has actively sought. Children love humor, Cleary notes, and they long for it "in a world grown grim" (**"Laughter,"** 563). Humor captures the early reader, helping her or him to realize that "reading is a worthwhile experience": "Over the years the first books to catch the imagination of children who have escaped the reading circle and are ready to discover the pleasures of reading have been simply written humorous books" (**"Laughter,"** 562). And more experienced readers enjoy looking back on and feeling superior to their earlier, less mature selves. Like the books Cleary cites in an article on humor, her own works reward more than one reading, amusing and delighting readers who are "discovering fresh insight" each time they reread a book (**"Laughter,"** 563).

The real popularity of Cleary's work lies both in their timeless qualities and in the way Cleary has responded to her readers. In print since 1950, **Henry Huggins** seems as fresh for young readers now as it did then. Dealing with the ordinary fears and pleasures of childhood, which do not change, Cleary's works are timeless in their depiction of the inner life of a child and in what will entertain that child. On the other hand, Cleary has responded to the changing world of her readers by expanding the reality she presents. Moving from Henry Huggins, who lives with two parents in a suburban house and deals only with the problems he gets into himself, to Ramona Quimby, who lives with two parents but is aware that parents can divorce and deals with her father's layoff and the tight economic times that follow, to Leigh Botts, who lives with his divorced mother in a tiny cottage and is beset by loneliness, Cleary has kept the situations contemporary even as she emphasizes the unchanged essentials. Henry is as much a product of his time as Ramona is of hers and Leigh is of his, but they share the same needs for love and acceptance, and they all struggle with the confusing process of growing up, as Beverly Bunn did. Drawing on her own ordinary life and the lives around her, Cleary shows her readers that growing up is never easy, but it can be funny.

Notes and References

1. Beverly Cleary, "Writing Books about Henry Huggins," *Top of the News,* December 1957, 11; hereafter cited in the text as "Writing."

2. Beverly Cleary, *A Girl from Yamhill* (New York: Morrow, 1988), 11; hereafter cited in the text as *Yamhill.*

3. Beverly Cleary, "Laura Ingalls Wilder Award Presentation," *Horn Book* 51 (1975):362; hereafter cited in the text as "Wilder."

4. Beverly Cleary, "Books Remembered," *Calendar,* July 1982-February 1983, n.p.; hereafter cited in the text as "Books."

5. Deborah Churchman, "Children's Literature: A Source of Hope and Morality," *Christian Science Monitor,* 6 June 1983, 17; hereafter cited in the text.

6. Beverly Cleary, "Low Man in the Reading Circle, or, A Blackbird Takes Wing," *Horn Book* 45 (1969):287; hereafter cited in the text as "Low."

7. In David Reuther, "Beverly Cleary," *Horn Book* 60 (1984):443; hereafter cited in the text.

8. Beverly Cleary, "Newbery Medal Acceptance," *Horn Book* 60 (1984):431; hereafter cited in the text as "Newbery."

9. Shirley Fitzgibbons, "Focus on Beverly Cleary," *Top of the News,* Winter 1977, 168; hereafter cited in the text.

10. Paul C. Burns and Ruth Hines, "Beverly Cleary: Wonderful World of Humor," *Elementary English* 44 (1967):744; hereafter cited in the text.

11. "Beverly Cleary: A Practicing Perfectionist," *Early Years,* August—September 1982, 25; hereafter cited in the text as "Perfectionist."

12. Beverly Cleary, "Why Are Children Writing to Me Instead of Reading?" *New York Times,* 10 November 1985, 42; hereafter cited in the text as "Why."

13. Mary June Roggenbuck, "Beverly Cleary—the Children's Force at Work," *Language Arts,* January 1979, 59; hereafter cited in the text.

14. Beverly Cleary, *Ramona the Pest,* illus. Louis Darling (New York: Morrow, 1968), 75; hereafter cited in the text.

15. Beverly Cleary, Regina Medal Acceptance Speech, *Catholic Library World* (1980):23; hereafter cited in the text as "Regina."

16. Beverly Cleary, "On Talking Back to Authors," *Claremont Reading Conference Yearbook* (1970):4; hereafter cited in the text as "Talking."

17. Beverly Cleary, "The Laughter of Children," *Horn Book* 58 (1982):556; hereafter cited in the text as "Laughter."

Pat Pflieger

SOURCE: "Beverly Cleary: A Boy and His Dog," in *Twayne's United States Authors* on CD-ROM, G. K. Hall & Co., 1997.

As a young reader in Portland, Oregon, Cleary longed for stories "about American children in moderate circumstances who lived with two parents in plain square houses on fifty by one hundred lots in a medium-sized city and who walked a few blocks to a red brick schoolhouse like the one I attended . . . [and who acted] like the children in my neighborhood who were only moderately well-behaved and who were often naughty" (**"Writing,"** 8). As an adult librarian in Yakima, Washington, she found herself fielding requests from young readers for—as boys from a local parochial school put it—"books about kids like us" (**"Regina,"** 23). The result, published in September, 1950, was *Henry Huggins,* the first of six works about an ordinary boy and his dog, both of whom find themselves getting into most unordinary situations.[1]

A DOG AND HIS BOY

Henry Huggins

Henry's first story seems to have been written in that half-haphazard way in which many first books are produced. Having spent the years of World War II as an army librarian, Cleary found herself with more time for herself after she and her husband moved to Berkeley, California—time, and typing paper in the linen closet. Now, she remarked to her husband, "I'll have to write a book":

"Why don't you?" he asked.

"Because we never have any sharp pencils," I answered.

The next day he brought home a pencil sharpener and I realized that if I was ever going to write a book, this was the time to do it. (**"Writing,"** 10)

The book was begun 2 January, the date on which all her subsequent works would be begun (**"Early,"** 25). Cleary had intended to write "a book that was to be a girls' story about the maturing of a sensitive female who wanted to write" (**"Regina,"** 23). What came out was somewhat different, for she found herself "remembering the boys of St. Joseph's and the children who had once come to Saturday afternoon story hour and my own childhood reading" (**"Regina,"** 23). Cleary, at a table in the spare bedroom, "began a story based on an incident that had once amused me about two children who had to take their dog home on a streetcar during a heavy rain. This turned into a story about a boy who would be allowed to keep a stray dog if he could manage to take him home on a bus. When I finished the chapter I found I had ideas for another chapter and at the end of two months I had a whole book about Henry Huggins and his dog Ribsy" (**"Writing,"** 10). Cleary sent the finished work to William Morrow and Company "because I had heard that Elisabeth Hamilton, who was then editor, was one of the best and because I had once heard an author remark that Morrow was kind to authors" (**"Writing,"** 10). The work—then titled "Spareribs and Henry"—was accepted six weeks later (Reuther, 441), and Cleary realized her ambition to be an author.

Henry Huggins set the episodic tone of most of Cleary's work for younger children, though in this book the chapters are more loosely connected than are those in Cleary's later novels. This is because, Cleary admits, "when I began *Henry Huggins,* I did not know how to write a book, so I mentally told the stories to that remembered audience and wrote them down as I told them. This is why my first book is a collection of stories about a group of characters rather than a novel" (Fitzgibbons, 168). The book concerns Henry's growing relationship with Ribsy, the dog he finds on the street, and also his solutions to the problems of everyday life, which, in Henry's case, mysteriously exaggerate themselves.

Henry is the type of boy to whom nothing much seems to happen—until he meets Ribsy. Just getting Ribsy home after the two first meet involves a hair tonic box, a melee on a bus, and the police. Suddenly, life is exciting. The weekly trip to the pet shop for Ribsy's horsemeat leads to Henry's buying a pair of guppies on sale; and, since guppies beget guppies beget guppies, Henry soon has a roomful of jars of tiny fish. He is surprised and relieved to learn that the pet shop owner will take them in exchange for enough credit to buy a tank and a pair of fish that do not breed in captivity. Distracted by Ribsy as he and Scooter McCarthy toss Scooter's new football back and forth, Henry throws the ball into the back seat of a passing automobile and must buy a replacement, which costs $13.95 (plus 41¢ tax). Catching night crawlers for neighbor Mr. Grumbie proves to be the key, and, with his parents' help, Henry comes up with the necessary 1,331 crawlers. Even better, the driver of the passing automobile returns Scooter's ball, leaving Henry with money to buy his own football.

Ribsy comes to Henry's rescue after Henry gets the part of the little boy in the school's Christmas pageant; teased about the sappy role, Henry is wild to get out of it but cannot until Ribsy manages to knock a can of indelible green paint on Henry's head, leaving him to play the Green Elf instead. Ribsy himself becomes a pale pink dog at a dog show. After a thorough bath, Ribsy is still wet when he and Henry arrive at the show, and so when Ribsy takes a nice, long roll in a flower bed, he ends up muddy. When he sprinkles talcum powder on the white parts of Ribsy to re-whiten them, Henry finds that the powder itself is pink—and so is Ribsy. However, after a memorable show in which Ribsy entangles Henry in the leash, refuses to obey commands, and involves Henry in a dog fight, Henry and Ribsy go home with a silver cup for the "most unusual dog" in the show.

As a result of Ribsy's picture's being in the paper, another boy claims him as his own runaway. Henry feels sorry for the boy, but he cannot give up Ribsy; finally, the boys decide to let Ribsy choose. Ribsy picks Henry, to the delight of Henry and the entire neighborhood, because neither the neighborhood nor Henry's life would be the same without him.

Both young and adult readers apparently felt as enthusiastic. "Probably no reviewer of children's books has forgotten the excitement and fun of reading the first of Beverly Cleary's Henry Huggins books in 1950," May Hill Arbuthnot later recalled.[2] Reviewers also expressed that excitement, praising the humor and simplicity of the work. "This story of Henry Huggins and his dog, Ribsy, is written for younger boys and girls but we defy anyone under seventy not to chuckle over it," said one,[3] while another emphasized that "there is not a dull moment but some hilariously funny ones in the telling of Henry's adventures at home and at school."[4] Most im-

portant, Cleary began to receive letters from her young readers.[5]

Readers' responses to the work point up Cleary's success in presenting the everyday concerns of everyday life: "reality twisted to the right into humor rather than to the left into tragedy" ("Laughter," 558). The emphasis of the book is on Henry's misadventures, which arise naturally out of things of everyday life: finding a stray dog, keeping guppies, attending a dog show, acting in a school Christmas pageant. It is real life that shapes Henry's adventures, and while these everyday situations are taken to the limits, it seems logical and inevitable; the ultimate events are not forced but, rather, grow naturally. Trying to carry a lively, adult dog like Ribsy onto a city bus naturally is difficult, and the resulting slapstick is the natural outcome of a panicked dog on a crowded bus; guppies are programmed to multiply, and a softhearted boy naturally would have hundreds to care for before a few weeks pass.

These events are inevitable because of Henry's personality. Though the episodic, action-filled chapters leave Cleary little room for characterization, Henry emerges as a believable boy who is not above ridiculing girls or arguing hotly with his friends and accustomed to taking care of his own problems—whether it is earning money to replace a friend's football or getting out of playing a sappy role in a Christmas pageant. Henry's allowance for several weeks goes for fish supplies, and the pet shop owner is impressed with Henry's success with the hundreds of tiny fish. Earnest and responsible, Henry seems the sometimes-hapless pawn of absurdity: he never instigates trouble but is somewhat passive. After all, it isn't *Henry's* fault that guppies reproduce so quickly, or that an automobile races past just as he throws a football, or that the city transit authority allows only boxed dogs onto buses. But Henry is not passive for long. Once things begin to happen to him, he takes charge and solves his own problems in a way that is logical to a young boy. Need to have a dog in a box? Fine. Put him into the biggest box possible. The box needs to cover the dog? Fine. Wrap the dog in paper and put him into a shopping bag. Need to clean a dog that has rolled in the mud? No problem. Use a little talcum powder on the white parts, and hope the fact that the powder is pink will not show in the bright sun. Henry's middle name seems to be "perseverance."

Tested throughout the book, Henry's skill at persevering seems to grow stronger by the last chapter. The rules of the transit authority prove too much for him in the first chapter, and he must be rescued by the police; even Henry finally cracks under the strain of taking care of hundreds of guppies. But he is unswerving in his attempts to earn money for Scooter's football, to get out of playing the little boy in the Christmas pageant, and to win a prize for Ribsy in the dog show. This strengthened perseverance stands him in good stead in the book's final chapter, when his relationship with Ribsy is threatened. Episodic as the book is—as we have seen, Cleary called it "a collection of stories . . . rather than a novel"—it takes as its theme the growing bond between the boy and his dog. The last chapter works to reaffirm their relationship, as Ribsy chooses Henry over his old master in a tense but hilariously undramatic scene. Stopping, lying down, sighing, and biting a flea, Ribsy chooses Henry in a way that is realistic and that repudiates melodramatic scenes in other works too numerous to mention. It is the kind of scene few of Cleary's readers will experience firsthand, but it is firmly rooted in reality.

It is just this rooting in reality that soon set up a puzzle for Cleary: while her adult readers found Henry's adventures humorous, many of her younger readers found them "'funny and sad.'" ("Laughter," 558). It was years before Cleary realized what they meant. Planted in everyday life, Henry's adventures strike a bit too close to home for some of her young readers to find humorous; too young to put Henry's problems in perspective, they do not always see the humor in his troubles. It is those who can feel superior to their younger selves who laugh at Henry, and this is mostly adults and older children (**"Laughter,"** 561). This dichotomy has remained for almost all of Cleary's works.

Henry Huggins not only introduced readers to Cleary's style of humor and view of real life; it showed them a large cast on which Cleary could base subsequent books. From Henry and Ribsy to Scooter to Beezus and Ramona Quimby, all are introduced here; the cast is large and varied enough to support the thirteen works Cleary would set on Klickitat Street.

Henry and Beezus

Though Cleary's next book was *Ellen Tebbits,* she "continued to have ideas about Henry Huggins" (**"Writing,"** 10); and on 2 January Cleary began her next book about the boy and his dog. Though the book still focused on Henry and his relationship with Ribsy, Cleary brought forward two children who had

been minor characters in the earlier work and gave them new emphasis: Beatrice (Beezus) Quimby and her preschool-age sister, Ramona Geraldine Quimby. *Henry and Beezus,* published in 1952, paved the way for Cleary's Ramona series, so popular in the 1970s, for in this work Ramona begins to show her true colors.

At the center of *Henry and Beezus* is Henry's desire to own a bicycle, which he cannot afford. The lack of both bicycle and funds is emphasized in the first chapter, when Ribsy steals a roast the neighbors are planning to barbecue. Henry can only look on in envy as Scooter McCarthy chases Ribsy on his bicycle and rescues the roast. More determined than ever to get his own bicycle, Henry also now must pay for the chewed-up roast.

Finding forty-nine boxes of bubble gum dumped by a businessman who has gone out of business leads Henry into his own business. But selling the gum at school soon becomes a problem: the principal outlaws gum chewing on school grounds, Henry's customers demand more than the one flavor he has, and Henry finds himself reducing the price until he is giving the gum away and has given up keeping track of delinquent accounts. Henry, too, goes out of business, dumping the gum, with Beezus's help, exactly where he found it earlier.

Beezus also helps when Henry gets into trouble by teaching Ribsy to fetch. Scooter, who will pay Henry to take his paper route while he goes to Scout camp, suddenly finds that the papers he has delivered are vanishing: it turns out that Ribsy, enthusiastically practicing his new paper-fetching skills, is fetching the neighbors' papers as well. Inspired by Ramona's squirting of everything in sight with her water pistol, Henry and Beezus "untrain" Ribsy by squirting him with water each time he goes after a newspaper.

Henry believes his moment will come—he will finally get a bicycle—at the police auction of bicycles, but in reality his troubles have just begun. He and Beezus are accompanied by Ramona, who is pretending to be a windup toy and who must be wound up what seems like every five minutes. Ramona's demand for food leads to Ribsy being tied to a parking meter and getting a ticket, which an amused policeman "fixes" for Henry. Once they get to the noisy, crowded auction, it looks as if Henry must leave without his bicycle, for he cannot get in a bid, and Ramona, bored, announces loudly that she is going to throw up. Quelling her with a sisterly threat, Beezus must later go up front to claim her when, having gotten lost in the crowd, Ramona is held up by the auctioneer. Here, though, Beezus can bid, and she bids $4.04 for a bicycle—but a girl's bicycle, not a boy's. Henry tries to make do by tying a broom-handle in the appropriate place, but this subterfuge does not work, for his new bicycle has too many structural faults.

The opening of the Colossal Market provides the neighborhood with free entertainment in the form of samples and doorprizes. Even Henry wins a prize—$50 worth of work at the market's beauty salon, which he doubts he will ever live down. However, when Beezus offers to buy a coupon, Henry realizes that his prize has value after all; and he sells the coupons for almost enough money to buy the fancy red bicycle he has coveted. At last he can pass Scooter with calm assurance.

The Henry of *Henry Huggins* is growing up, and in this second Henry Huggins book Cleary emphasizes the ways in which Henry is expanding his relationships and his world. Having created a neighborhood full of children for Henry to play with, Cleary emphasizes his growth by showing him in action with his friends. Where the first book focuses on the growing bond between Henry and Ribsy, the second highlights Henry's relationships with his peers, particularly Beezus and Ramona. The increased mobility a bicycle provides is important to a child forging ahead into the wider world.

Still responsible and persevering, Henry continues to fall into one troublesome situation after another. Working to alleviate his bikeless state, Henry rarely anticipates the somewhat-exaggerated, but always natural, outcome of his actions. But who could predict that a dog taught to fetch the evening paper would fetch every paper in the neighborhood? Or that simply selling bubble gum could get so out of hand? Still beset by events, Henry, nevertheless, does not let himself be defeated by them; he takes charge of the situation as best he can.

But this time Henry has help. Whereas in the first work he was able to take care of his problems himself, in the second he often finds himself calling upon Beezus. It is Beezus's and Ramona's wagon that Henry must use to transport his bubble gum from and to the empty lot; Ramona's squirting of everything in sight with her water pistol inspires him in his quest to untrain Ribsy. Beezus tells Henry of the bicycle auction; Beezus bids for Henry's bicycle;

Beezus makes up for the fact that it is a girl's bicycle by showing him that the coupons he wins in the last chapter are more valuable than he thought. Henry is often reluctant to have Beezus's help, for she is, after all, only a girl, interested in gardenias and in having her hair waved. But having proved his independence in the earlier book, he now learns to accept the aid of others, at the same time forging more complex relationships with his peers.

Complex is the word when dealing with Ramona, who provides much of the book's humor. In love with slugs and with getting her own way, yelling when she does not get what she wants, and embarrassingly blunt, Ramona is the typical bratty younger sister, descendant of many a bratty younger sister in earlier works for children—the kind of character whom we would rather read about than know. Here, she is not so much a character in her own right as she is an impediment to Henry: she must be placated before he and Beezus can pick up his bubble gum; pretending to be a windup toy, she runs down at inopportune moments when Henry is impatient to be at the bicycle auction; demanding food, she is the reason Henry ties Ribsy to a parking meter and gets a ticket; and her bored announcement that she is going to throw up almost gets them sent home before Henry can bid on a bicycle. She is both hilarious and irritating in her unpredictability. Older sister Beezus, used to these difficulties, takes them in her stride, giving in to Ramona or quelling her with sisterly threats; only-child Henry, who is most emphatically *not* used to them, has no such defenses and must deal with Ramona by dealing with Beezus. In her first presentation, Ramona is dominated by Beezus, but her liveliness shines through; and it is easy to see why she eventually became protagonist of her own series.

Focused on Henry, this work introduced another of Cleary's most enduring characters. But, more importantly, it presents its readers with a character who succeeds in growing up. Dealing with Beezus, earning the money for his bicycle, Henry is definitely moving into the larger world—a movement Cleary emphasizes in the later works about Henry Huggins.

Henry and Ribsy

After *Henry and Beezus* came *Otis Spofford,* but Cleary continued to have ideas about Henry and his dog, and on 22 September 1954, *Henry and Ribsy* was published. The book sprang from an idea Cleary's father had that "it would make a funny story if Henry and his father took Ribsy salmon fishing and Ribsy was so frightened by a salmon flopping around in the boat that he jumped out and tried to swim away" ("**Writing,**" 10). Inspired by incidents of her daily life, Cleary found that *Henry and Ribsy* "was an easy book to write and I had a good time writing it" ("**Writing,**" 11).

Just as funny as the first book, *Henry and Ribsy* is equally episodic. The work emphasizes Henry's attempts to keep Ribsy out of mischief to earn a promised trip salmon-fishing. The trouble begins with Ribsy's theft of a policeman's lunch right out of the police car; Mr. Huggins extracts from Henry a promise to keep Ribsy out of trouble until salmon season. Excited by the prospect of catching an enormous fish, Henry agrees and then realizes what a job he has landed for himself.

The promise even complicates taking out the garbage, for Ribsy defends the garbage so ferociously that the garbage collectors skip the Huggins's house. When Ribsy growls at Scooter as he wheels Henry's bicycle out of the garage, Henry realizes that Ribsy is protecting his bicycle and has been protecting the garbage. Because Ribsy did not "protect" the garbage until Henry took it out, he bargains with his father to take over clipping the edges of the lawn, which is a harder job but which will make it difficult for Henry and Ribsy to get into trouble.

After Henry's mother helps him out after a disastrous home haircut, Ribsy helps him pull his loose canine teeth. Now Henry discovers a new talent: spitting double through the holes in his mouth. His care to keep Ribsy out of trouble almost comes to nothing when Ramona gets revenge for Ribsy's stealing her ice cream by putting his bone into her lunchbox. Following Ramona closely, Ribsy ends up at the bottom of a jungle gym on the school playground, with Ramona screaming at the top. The sight convinces two PTA members that Ramona has climbed the gym out of fear. After a confusion created by Ribsy's barking, Ramona's howling, a spontaneous game of catch, and the PTA mothers trying to decide what to do, the school principal—a friend of Ribsy—takes charge and gets Ramona down.

Ribsy gets into trouble even on the promised fishing trip, when he inadvertently helps Mr. Grumbie's hooked salmon escape before jumping into the river. Henry's chance to catch a fish vanishes, for he and his dog are put ashore. His humiliation deepens when he realizes that Scooter is out fishing, too, and sure to catch a salmon. Strolling along the beach, how-

ever, Ribsy finds a fish for Henry: a Chinook salmon trying to swim up a shallow stream, when Henry holds on to long enough to be rescued by a man attracted by Ribsy's barking. The man clubs the salmon and helps Henry carry it back. Henry's salmon weighs twenty-nine pounds, and his triumph is complete when he learns that Scooter has caught nothing and that Mr. Grumbie has caught a fish to replace the one he lost.

Henry and Ribsy delighted both reviewers and its intended audience. Reviewers enjoyed the humor: *Booklist* said it was "better, if possible, than its predecessors" and praised its "natural characters and . . . unhackneyed, genuinely funny situations,"[6] while *Publishers Weekly* called it "one of Mrs. Cleary's most hilarious books."[7] Yet another reviewer felt that this work "has more real child humor than some of the earlier Cleary books have had."[8] The young readers voted to give it the Young Readers' Choice Award of the Pacific Northwest Library Association in 1957.

After emphasizing the relationship between Henry and his peers in *Henry and Beezus,* Cleary refocuses in *Henry and Ribsy* on the relationship between Henry and his dog. As before, the situations Henry finds himself in are not of his own making, and he sometimes seems to find himself the pawn of circumstance; but once again, he takes charge and solves his problems himself. Having introduced the idea in the first book that having a pet is not easy, Cleary returns to this topic in the third book, focusing on the difficulties of keeping a lively dog out of trouble—the kind of trouble only a Huggins could get into. Difficulties seem to follow Ribsy as they do Henry: the lawn he chases a cat across is the one freshly seeded yard in the neighborhood; like his owner, Ribsy has his own problems with Ramona. As in earlier books, Cleary allows these humorous problems to grow naturally out of the situation. But the problems the two encounter strengthen their bond.

Having set up the trouble Ribsy can get into as her major theme, Cleary does not allow anything to distract her readers from this problem. Though this work takes Henry farther afield than the earlier two works and though we see him interacting more than before with those around him, Cleary uses this broader scope to focus on his main problem with Ribsy.

Henry always has interacted with the children in the neighborhood, but now Cleary makes his interaction part of his main problem. The neighborhood children spread the story of Ribsy's growling at the garbage collector until it is exaggerated beyond recognition. Ramona may have been a pesty little obstacle in *Henry and Beezus,* but here she is a real danger to Henry's fishing trip when she takes Ribsy's bone in retaliation and ends up screaming at the top of the jungle gym with Ribsy below in what looks like a classic case of a child's fear of a vicious dog. Even Mr. Grumbie, during a memorable day fishing with Ribsy and Henry, manages to cause them as much trouble as Ribsy causes him. But Henry's love of his dog is solid, and trouble from other sources does not dent it. In spite of the problems Ribsy causes, their relationship emerges stronger than ever.

As in *Henry Huggins,* the two support and help each other, though more in this third book than in the first. Henry defends Ribsy from all critics, from his parents to his neighborhood friends to the ladies of the P.T.A., as he struggles to keep Ribsy out of trouble or to undo the trouble Ribsy has caused. This can be difficult when Ribsy threatens the garbage collectors or seems to threaten Ramona in front of the P.T.A. For his part, Ribsy helps Henry in more ways than before. In *Henry Huggins,* he had merely accidentally dumped paint on Henry at an appropriate moment. Now he incidentally saves Henry from a chore by proving that he will guard the garbage from all comers if Henry takes it out, he plays tug-of-war with a piece of string and thereby pulls Henry's canine teeth in an appropriately doggy and dramatic way, and—after their disastrous morning of fishing—finds for Henry a salmon even bigger than those Henry had dreamed of catching. Without meaning to, Ribsy shows Henry tangible expressions of his devotion. While their relationship has never been one-sided—Henry counts on Ribsy's love as much as Ribsy counts on Henry—it seems to become more equal here; the boy whose favorite song is a dog food jingle has a dog worthy of such devotion.

Henry and the Paper Route

The next Henry book was not published until 1957, after Cleary had published her first adolescent novel, *Fifteen,* and the first of her series of books about Ramona Quimby, *Beezus and Ramona.* Though three years had passed between books, Henry has aged only one year: in *Henry and the Paper Route* he is ten, and his interests have widened to include having his own paper route.

When the book opens, Henry decides to take a paper route. Undaunted though he is a year too young to have a route, Henry sets off to talk Mr. Capper—who

is in charge of the routes—into giving him the route. Henry's professionalism loses its edge when he ends up with four rummage-sale kittens in his jacket, and an amused Mr. Capper asks Henry to come back in a year or two.

At home that night, Henry has another problem, for his parents and Ribsy object to having four kittens in the house. Henry decides to solve both problems with ease: he will sell subscriptions to the newspaper, offering a free kitten with each subscription; and the list of new subscribers will persuade Mr. Capper to give him a route. This does not go as planned, however, and Henry ends up giving the kittens to the local pet shop owner to sell. The house is quiet that night without the kittens; Mr. Huggins sends Henry to buy the most audacious of the four, Nosy, who quickly settles into the household.

More determined than ever to get his own route, Henry folds papers for Scooter once a week. The week that Henry's school starts a paper drive, Scooter has Henry deliver the papers for him one evening; Henry seizes this chance to advertise the paper drive by enclosing an advertisement in each newspaper. The advertisements' success causes problems, for Henry receives many calls, and the magazines and newspapers soon fill the Huggins's garage and overflow into the driveway. Bundling the paper is less fun than collecting it, and hauling it to school is even less fun. Though Henry's room wins due to his efforts, next time he will not advertise: it was too successful.

Henry's eleventh birthday is wonderful, especially since now he is old enough for a paper route, and the new family who has moved in might include a boy. Then Scooter gets the chicken pox, and Henry must take his route. That day he finally meets the new boy in the neighborhood: Byron Murphy ("Murph"), who is building a robot and who probably is a genius. Ramona is the only child in the neighborhood who is not awed by Murph, and she imitates him, wearing sunglass frames to mimic his glasses. Scooter takes back his route when he gets well, and the route Henry had hoped to take over goes to a boy who is shifting his route to Henry's neighborhood—Murph. It is not fair, Henry thinks, that Murph not only is a genius, but he also has the paper route. On the other hand, he has humiliating battles with Ramona, who has decided to be a "paper boy" like Murph and who insists on "delivering" Murph's newspapers. Bested by Ramona, Murph gives up his route to Henry, and Ramona becomes very good—too good, Henry finds,

mona, he does not believe her until the end of the work. Then, displeased because of all the trouble she has caused him and pleased because she has told Mrs. Peabody Henry's real name, Henry finds himself feeling sorry for Ramona as she stands tired, cold, and pathetic in the deep snow. Seeing her suddenly as the small child she is, Henry finds himself helping her, though he does not want to. Henry receives an immediate reward in the form of a letter of praise from a customer and his father's resulting pride in him, but having found compassion even for Ramona, Henry is clearly on his way to real maturity.

Though *Ramona the Pest* would not be published for another six years, *Henry and the Clubhouse* is important in Ramona's career as an independent character. Identifying with Beezus in *Beezus and Ramona* and with Henry in the earlier Henry Huggins books, the reader cannot be blamed for viewing Ramona with little sympathy. But now, seeing her as a small child eager for Henry's attention, it is easier to feel sympathy even for a child who locks another person in a clubhouse. Sympathy is just what we come to feel for Ramona in her own series. Then, too, Ramona has some of her best scenes in this work, as she interviews herself with a cardboard-tube microphone and, especially, in her infatuation with Sheriff Bud.

Cleary uses this chance to get in her say about the burgeoning influence of television. While television is not mentioned in Cleary's earlier works, by 1962 its impact was being felt in American culture in general, and Cleary satirizes its influence and the commercial-saturated cartoon shows. Sheriff Bud's program, in which he seizes every opportunity to insert pitches for Nutsies and for Crispy Potato Chips, is the essence of avaricious advertising; even Henry's letter provides an opening for a potato chips advertisement. Wearily and warily listening as her daughter is directly asked for help by a character on television, Mrs. Quimby informs her, "Whatever it is, I'm not going to buy it" (160). Ramona proves the perfect recipient of all this advertising, enthralled by what she sees on the television. Enamored of television commercials, she repeats them everywhere, sternly informing Mrs. Peabody that only she can prevent forest fires, singing the Crispy Potato Chips song when asked to do a trick on Halloween, and joyously reciting the Nutsie candy bar commercial word for word in honor of the candy bar she receives. Searching for a hero, Ramona finds one through most

of the book in Sheriff Bud, whom she imitates by wearing disguises; she shifts her allegiance to Henry primarily because he can communicate with Sheriff Bud.

Though *Ribsy* was yet to be written, it is possible to see in *Henry and the Clubhouse* the appropriate winding down of the Henry Huggins series and the beginning of the Ramona series. Here, Ramona comes into her own as a believable and lively force of energy. Once a boy to whom nothing much happens in the first book, Henry now has become more confident and ready to find a place in the larger world, a responsible and determined boy who somehow gets himself into surprising difficulties—and gets himself out of them as well.

Ribsy

The Henry books came full circle with the last one, published in 1964, after Cleary's fourth novel for adolescents. In *Ribsy*, the most popular dog on Klickitat Street is the focus of his own adventures. Cleary already had written part of a scene in *Henry and the Clubhouse* using Ribsy's point of view in the scene of his fight with Ranger. Now she devotes half a book to Ribsy's feelings and thoughts as, in his own version of *Lassie Come Home*, a lost Ribsy makes his way back to his boy in a reaffirmation of the love between the boy and his dog. However, as a child, Cleary did not want "to read about a noble dog who died in the last chapter after a long journey home on bleeding paws (**"Regina,"** 23), so Ribsy's journey has a few twists to it that never would have occurred to Lassie.

Ribsy's troubles begin with a flea, a new car, a Pomeranian, and a shopping center parking lot. His collar must be removed so he can get the flea; the automatic window of the new car opens when he accidentally triggers it barking at the insolent Pomeranian; and the parking lot confuses scents so that Ribsy jumps into the wrong car. The Dingley family is startled to find him here, but they take him home until someone claims him. Home is on the outskirts of town, far from Klickitat Street, and Ribsy is miserable.

So is Henry, who begins a search for his dog. Given a bath by the Dingleys, Ribsy hates his new smell and seizes the first chance to run away from it, though he cannot outrun or get rid of the scent. As Henry, miserable, advertises for Ribsy, Ribsy is finding the world a frightening, uncongenial place. A lonely widow adopts him for a while, and life with her is pretty comfortable for Ribsy. But he longs to run with the boys he sees playing, and doing tricks for the widow's little club is humiliating. He is a dog, not a person, and he wants to do dog things. When the club leaves, Ribsy bolts.

Hearing from the Dingleys, Henry runs his advertisement for three more weeks. Ribsy, meantime, is in the city, scrounging for food and looking for Klickitat Street. For a time he is the unofficial mascot of the second grade. But now that Ribsy has been gone for a month, he is getting used to being lost, finding much to enjoy in his new life. One day he finds his way into a football stadium during a game, joining the players at a critical moment and tripping the quarterback about to make a touchdown. Joe Saylor, grabbing Ribsy, sees a chance to be important and claims Ribsy as his; after the game, Ribsy follows Joe home. Henry, seeing Ribsy's picture in the newspaper, calls Joe, who lets him talk to Ribsy on the telephone. Ribsy is off again, into the night, looking for Henry.

Henry is confused, unaware of what has happened at the other end of the telephone conversation; Ribsy is confused, recognizing Henry's voice but unable to find him. In front of an apartment building, he meets Larry, a bored latchkey child who tries to smuggle Ribsy into his apartment—an operation that goes awry when Ribsy's barking draws the attention of the building's manager. Then Larry tries to smuggle Ribsy *out* of the building but must hide him on a cold, uncomfortable fire escape. Frantic, Ribsy barks for attention and is answered by Henry, who has talked his parents into searching Joe Saylor's neighborhood. Soon Ribsy is off the fire escape and in Henry's arms. All are happy: the reward is enough for Larry to buy a new ball, and Ribsy has come home.

Reviewers enjoyed this work just as much as they did the first Henry book, emphasizing the humor of this work, as they had of all the others. "The characters are real, the dialogue is lively, the humor is unquenchable," wrote the reviewer for the *Bulletin of the Center for Children's Books,*[9] while *Horn Book* called Ribsy's adventures "an exceedingly fast-moving, varied, and original sequence of adventures in being lost" with "high comedy and pathos."[10]

In its reaffirmation of the relationship between Henry and Ribsy, *Ribsy* neatly parallels the first Henry book, *Henry Huggins;* in both works, the two characters' belonging to each other is tested and affirmed. In *Henry Huggins* it is Ribsy who must decide to be-

long to Henry in the book's climactic scene, whereas in *Ribsy* Henry's determination to belong to Ribsy gets as much emphasis: Ribsy's journey home is paralleled by Henry's efforts to find his beloved dog, and their reunion owes more to Henry's determination than it does to Ribsy's, for it is Henry who finally finds Ribsy, not the other way around.

Using alternating points of view, Cleary presents the reader with both searches, emphasizing Ribsy's. Ribsy's point of view not only helps advance the plot but adds a layer of humor and emphasizes Ribsy as a lively personality. In many of Cleary's other books—most notably, the Ramona books—the humor works on two levels, with the child reader finding something to laugh at and the adult reader laughing at something else. *Ribsy'*s humor works on two levels, too, as the reader understands from a human viewpoint what Ribsy sees from a dog's-eye view and enjoys the difference. Thus a football game becomes for Ribsy a gathering of yelling, hotdog-eating children around a smooth, green field where boys chase a football in a kind of dog paradise; hearing Henry's voice over the telephone is confusing, for no Henry is in sight.

Using Ribsy's point of view also emphasizes his ordinariness. Having seen Ribsy only from Henry's point of view in the first four books, the reader gained insight into him in the scene told from his point of view in *Henry and the Clubhouse*. Now, privy to many of Ribsy's thoughts in a work told mostly from his viewpoint, the reader sees him as very much his own dog, a vital personality and an ordinary dog. Intolerant of squirrels and more than tolerant of boys, hotdogs, and balls to chase, Ribsy is very much the everyday dog no brighter or more loyal than any other—the kind of dog who could lose his master's scent in a big parking lot and who must take up with the humans he meets in order to survive more comfortably. Ribsy's devotion to Henry is never in question, but even a loving dog can get used to being lost and—while not happy—can be comfortable in his aimless wandering. Cleary makes it clear to the reader that this is not a dog who is obsessed with crawling home to wag his tail feebly and lick his master's hand, but, rather, a dog reacting to a wide, complex world full of excitement and adventure. Like Henry, Ribsy is acted-upon more than the actor: he finds himself led by his appetite and his search into most of his adventures. But, like Henry, Ribsy needs determination to get out of his difficulties (though it is Henry's determination to find his dog that leads to the final happy ending).

This ending highlights the bond between the boy and the dog as it emphasizes that Ribsy's place in the family is both real and secure. At the beginning of the book, Henry's parents are reluctant to allow a wet Ribsy into the new family car. But they become as caught up in the search for Ribsy as Henry is, and by the time they find the dog, it is clear that Mr. and Mrs. Huggins have come to think of Ribsy as part of the family. Having found each other in the first book, Ribsy and Henry re-find each other in the last. Ribsy's place in the Huggins household is thereby confirmed, and he rides in the Huggins's new car, along with the rest of the family.

An Ordinary Boy

The popularity of the Henry books was assured from the start, and that popularity has not dimmed. Beginning in 1964, the Henry books were translated into Swedish, with German, Dutch, and Finnish editions to follow; Norwegian, Danish, and Japanese editions followed in the early 1970s, and a Chinese edition of *Ribsy* was copyrighted, though never published. The books were made available in Great Britain in the late 1970s. The works were the basis of a series of television programs that ran in Sweden, Denmark, and Japan in the 1970s.[11]

In the United States, the Henry books have been in print since 1950; in 1979 Henry was one of the rather limpid-eyed paper dolls featured in *Cutting Up with Ramona*. Their audience has accepted them wholeheartedly. "Henry is almost a catalyst," librarian Margaret Novinger found. "Give one book to a youngster and he will be back to finish the series" (Novinger, 73). Cleary herself noted that "many boys write to me. Their most frequent comment is that one of the Henry books . . . was the first book the boy enjoyed reading" (Roggenbuck, 60). Since the first eight-year-old girl wrote to Cleary soon after publication of *Henry Huggins,* scores of others have written fan letters to their favorite author, describing their families and their lives (**"Dear,"** 22; **"Writing,"** 11).

What readers are responding to is Cleary's presentation of the events of an ordinary life: the "little everyday experiences that do not seem important to adults, but which are so terribly important to children" (**"Writing,"** 11). Cleary's skillful blend of the stuff of ordinary life and her understanding of children make Henry an "Everychild," whom we watch grow through the trials and triumphs of daily life. After the first book, Cleary worried about her presentation of a young boy: "At that time I had no children. What *had* I done? I didn't know a thing about small boys." But, reading Arnold Gesell, she "was enormously relieved to find that Henry Huggins was psychologically sound, and that I really did know quite a bit about boys" (**"Writing,"** 10). The center of the books is Henry himself, a boy like other boys, who lives with his parents in a "square white house," and to whom "[e]xcept for having his tonsils out when he was six and breaking his arm falling out of a cherry tree when he was seven, nothing much happened" (*Huggins,* 7). Henry's life is not high drama: he does not solve mysteries or find himself in life-or-death situations. He does the things that many children do: he gets a dog and a paper route, builds a clubhouse, and makes friends. As the series progressed, Henry's friends and neighbors began to take more important parts in the action, but Henry was still their focus.

In all the books, adults and their concerns generally are kept in the background, because, according to children Henry's age, that is the proper place for adults. Since children usually are involved with their own lives and their circle of friends, adult concerns are not that important to them. "Children wanted to read about children; adults should mind their own business and stay out of the story as much as possible," according to Cleary, who, as a child, "found disappointing, even objectionable, any book in which a child accepted the wisdom of an adult and reformed"; adults "were there to be supportive when needed" (**"Regina,"** 23). Henry's parents are supportive without being pushovers. In all the books, they are in the background, a loving stability on whom Henry can rely, but, especially in the early books, they rarely take part in the action. Bundling and delivering paper during the school paper drive, crawling in the dewy grass to catch night crawlers, loaning Henry the money he needs to buy his bicycle, climbing up a fire escape to bring down Ribsy—Henry's parents do help him when the occasion demands it. They also support Henry emotionally when Ribsy is lost, suggesting that Henry advertise in the newspaper and driving around in what might be a futile gesture to find his dog. However, they insist that Henry stand on his own feet and take responsibility for his actions. Henry must keep Ribsy out of trouble, and when Ribsy jumps out of the boat during the fishing expedition, Henry must give up his fishing to take care of the dog on land. Henry earns $50 of the $59.95 he needs for his bicycle, for his parents cannot afford to buy him a new one. Henry must take total responsibility for his paper route, collecting the money and delivering the newspapers himself—something his father makes clear to him when Henry is late one day and his mother begins his delivery route for him. Having worked hard on the school paper drive, Henry is pleased that his room has won, but he also realizes that his parents worked almost as hard as he did, and he thanks them for all they have done, "sorry that he had not thanked them sooner"; because they all helped with the paper drive, the family goes to a movie to celebrate (*Paper,* 131). Henry can depend on his parents for love and moral support, but he must not take for granted that they will help him out of his difficulties.

As a result, Henry is independent and determined, and he takes his concerns into his own hands without appealing to his parents. Having discovered how fast guppies reproduce, Henry makes their care his responsibility, and it does not occur to him to ask his parents for their advice; having lost a friend's football through no fault of his own, Henry takes it upon himself to earn the money to replace it; when he has earned $50 for his new bicycle, Henry is ecstatic that he has almost achieved his goal, and he does not think to ask his parents for the rest of the money. To an adult, the problems with which Henry finds himself contending are not earthshaking; they are, nevertheless, important for Cleary's audience, not just because they are Henry's, but because they are the readers'. Henry deals with the matters of everyday childhood: trying to be grown up and learning to be responsible, relating to friends and neighbors, occasionally having difficulties with school and adults. Impatient at being too young for his own paper route, Henry attempts to seem grown up enough to impress the district manager into giving him one; the two months he must wait to be old enough for his own route seem endless. Taking responsibility is a major matter in the works, as Henry is responsible not only for Ribsy but for himself and his paper route.

A major subject of the books is relationships and the inherent difficulties therein. Henry must cope with the tantrums and hero-worship of preschooler Ramona, with the fact that Beezus—though a good friend—is "only" a girl, and with the awe-inspiring genius of Murph. Henry has the kind of problems with school and adults with which almost any child can identify. He is embarrassed by being chosen to play the little boy in a "dumb" Christmas pageant—something adults cannot understand. He is nonplussed by how to tell an adult customer that she is calling him by the wrong name. All these problems may seem small, but they loom large in the average child's life, and they are the kind of problems that every child must solve ("**Laughter,**" 557).

The problem-solving is appropriate, for Cleary had set out to write about ordinary children solving ordinary difficulties, and much in the works is from everyday life. Keeping in mind the boys of St. Joseph's who only wanted funny stories about ordinary children, Cleary tried to oblige and found she had "a collaborator . . . a rather odd, serious little girl, . . . who sat . . . reading for hours, seeking laughter in the pages of books"—herself as a child ("**Laughter,**" 557). What that child wanted to read about was "children, preferably children in my own neighborhood, as they were, not as they should be in the opinion of adults. An avid reader of all sorts of books, . . . I wanted most of all to read about problems children could solve themselves" ("**Regina,**" 23). These are the kinds of problems Henry faces. Having been "brought up to believe that if you wanted to do something, you went and did it," Cleary gave Henry the determination and imagination with which he tackles his problems and usually solves them ("**Perfectionist,**" 25).

In the Henry books, as in almost all her work, Cleary used the stuff of ordinary life. Some of that stuff is from her own childhood: that "collaborator" within Cleary has kept her "from writing down to children, from poking fun at my characters, and from writing an adult reminiscence about childhood instead of a book to be enjoyed by children" and has provided some of the material in the works ("**Laughter,**" 10). Cleary's childhood was "bounded by the experiences of an average American child and I have been fortunate enough to make stories out of the ingredients such a childhood provides—trips to the beach or the mountains, classroom experiences, neighborhood play, family relationships" ("**Writing,**" 11).

Henry himself is a "composite of boys Cleary had known as a child."[12] The Christmas pageant that he is so desperate to get out of in *Henry Huggins* was Cleary's fourth-grade pageant, complete with line of tin soldiers being knocked over by a basketball cannon ball (*Huggins,* 98; *Yamhill,* 107, 108). The solution to Henry's problem with that pageant already had appeared in "The Green Christmas," a story Cleary wrote as a freshman in high school (*Yamhill,* 186-87); the story provided not only the plot, but the title of the chapter. Having decided that Henry should get a bicycle at the end of *Henry and Beezus* but unable to figure out how, Cleary saw the solution in a newspaper story "of a raffle in which someone had signed a ticket in the name of the Little Sisters of the Poor. They had won fifty dollars worth of beauty work at Elizabeth Arden. Suddenly my problem was

and being so badly misunderstood. In so many things that they do, Beverly Cleary's characters are so recognizably like our childish selves, with all of our worries and fears, that—many years after my own childhood experience—they continue to exert this powerful pull on young readers.

I recently talked with some fourth graders in a Chapter One pullout program at a local school. Their two favorite authors are R. L. Stine and Beverly Cleary, especially the Ramona books. How's that for a modern contradiction? They like R. L. Stine because they can be scared and read very fast and know that it is just "fantasy," as one girl told me. And why do they read Beverly Cleary? They tell me the books are funny; "they're hilarious," one child said. The pictures are funny—especially the inside ones (they noted that the modern covers were done by a different artist from the inside pictures and liked the skinny, untidy, grimacing Ramona of the inside pages better). And one astute young man told me, "Well, they are funny but what I like is that you can look back and remember things when you read them." This boy recognized in Ramona not a girl in a book only girls could read, but instead a child who represented something of his younger, less polished self.

Do these modern children notice that some of Cleary's books were published as much as thirty-five years before they were born? Third graders noticed the low prices in the early Henry books, but they didn't assume automatically that this was because the books were old. Some readers said that Mrs. Cleary must not know very much about how much bikes and guppies and newspapers cost—"Maybe she didn't do her research," said one child. Others said it was just a story and so prices didn't have to be realistic. After this discussion, their teacher sent them home to ask how much these items cost in their parents' childhoods, and the children were scandalized to discover inflation.

Elementary school students who had read *Ramona the Pest* were surprised when I told them it had been first published more than twenty-five years ago. They hadn't noticed as they read, but they gamely looked for things that might have changed. They told me that they don't have crossing guards anymore—now police officers or senior volunteers do this; they don't have little trash cans at schools (like the ones where Ramona hid when she had a substitute teacher in kindergarten)—they have dumpsters that you can't play on; they have "show and share," not "show and tell." But, they told me, all of those things were easy

enough to figure out, and they knew what Mrs. Cleary was talking about. A more telling comment is one I receive from children regularly. Although they like Cleary's books, the children feel that they are not realistic. Things don't always work out very well in real life, and they seem to in these books. Several children suggested Cleary ought to put sadder things in her stories to make them "more real." Others liked them because they weren't sad. A third grader whose family was going through a painful divorce read and reread the Ramona books because they were stories about the way her family used to be, and she could laugh and remember; and, she said wisely, "They comfort me." Another group of third graders told me they liked the characters in Beverly Cleary's books because they did a lot of the things kids do and because they were funny. While young readers don't necessarily notice, Beverly Cleary's Oregon stories—from *Henry Huggins,* published in 1950, to *Ramona Forever,* published in 1984—provide a kind of chronicle of changes in middle-class American life over the past forty years. Seven of the Oregon stories were written in the fifties and reflect the values and activities of that decade. This was my own childhood, and reading these books brought it back to me. This was a time when ice-cream cones were a nickel, and you could buy several pieces of bubble gum for a penny. The tooth fairy still left a dime or, at most, a quarter under your pillow. (The tooth fairy began leaving quarters instead of dimes "because the cost of living has gone up," Henry's father told Henry in *Henry and Ribsy.*) It was a time when children of eight and nine could play on the playground equipment after dark in the park unattended by parents; could ride buses alone to go to the Y to swim or to the rink to skate. It was a time when parents listened to the news on the radio; when people read on Sunday afternoons, and children were fooled by the most basic of adult psychology—the mischievous Otis Spofford finds himself easily outwitted by his teacher in a spitball episode. Children visited libraries, collected stamps, and rode bikes; wore coonskin caps with snap-on tails, participated in paper drives, and did spool knitting. It was a time when swearing included such lurid phrases as "None of your beeswax," "Gee whillikers," and "Oh, for goodness sake." It was also a time of unconscious racism: Henry and Otis love to play at "wild Indians," dressing up in blankets, painting their faces, war-whooping, and attacking innocent wagon trains.

But even in the fifties a character in *Otis Spofford* foreshadows things to come. She is Valerie Todd Spofford, a single parent who runs the Spofford

School of Dance. She is a professional woman who must leave her son to be supervised by a landlady; they live in an apartment above a store rather than a house. A subtle judgment is passed upon her—Otis, though bright, is mischievous and bored. His mother feeds him canned dinners and, because she is pressed for time, puts off ironing and neglects sorting the laundry so that Otis's underwear turns an embarrassing pink. Alone among Cleary's middle-class families with mothers staying home, she represents the future. She was also, for me—the daughter of a working mom, a child who sometimes wore pink underwear herself (in our house the children helped with the wash)—a recognizable figure.

Three of Cleary's Oregon novels, *Henry and the Clubhouse, Ribsy,* and *Ramona the Pest,* were published in the sixties. In these stories, boys are still playing at wild Indians; girls are still wearing dresses to school; kids are still playing safely in the streets and neighborhoods; and Halloween is a blessedly uneventful holiday. But television has entered the picture. Ramona is quite susceptible to children's programming, especially the advertising wiles of Sheriff Bud, but her mother is unswayed by this commercial persuasion. In *Ribsy,* published in 1964, the first shopping mall appears, a clump of stores where you can stay dry surrounded by acres of parking without meters so you don't have to run out every half hour and put in a nickel. Who knew in 1964 that malls would become a subculture in their own right?

Cleary's three Oregon novels published in the seventies, *Ramona the Brave, Ramona and Her Father,* and *Ramona and Her Mother,* reflect some of the changes that hit our society during that decade. In the first of these, Ramona's mother goes back to work. In Beezus's words, her mother is going to be "liberated," but at this point she is only working part-time, to pay for an addition to their too-small house. By the next novel, Mrs. Quimby is forced to bear the brunt of the family finances when Ramona's father loses his job. Parental time with children is cut drastically, and Ramona's father is clearly somewhat depressed. When her father takes a job he is unhappy with in *Ramona and Her Mother,* the family chores are shared, Ramona goes to not-entirely-satisfactory after-school daycare with a neighbor, and, for the first time, Ramona's parents begin to argue, and she and Beezus worry about divorce. But behind these outer stresses lies a solid family in which Ramona is supported for being a "spunky gal," there is lots of time for imaginative play, and television is cut off at an eight-thirty bedtime.

In *Ramona Quimby, Age 8,* one of the last two Ramona books, there are further signs of modern stress. The quarreling continues in the Quimby family, though part of the problem is that Beezus is now a somewhat surly adolescent. The family has to live on a very limited income as Mr. Quimby returns to school; the family eats fast food and pizza more often; and television influences Ramona's book reports. Cleary knows the good times can't last forever. In the last paragraph of this novel she writes:

> "That man paying for dinner was sort of like a happy ending," remarked Beezus, as the family, snug in their car, drove through the rain and the dark toward Klickitat Street. "A happy ending for today," corrected Ramona. Tomorrow they would begin all over again.

Because Beverly Cleary was so responsive to the times in each of her Oregon novels, the astute reader might guess that *Ramona Forever* was indeed the last story about this family because it seems to return to the themes of the fifties novels. In this novel, the strength of the Quimby family is re-insured; Mr. Quimby will graduate and, although he returns to work in the supermarket, will certainly find a teaching position; Aunt Beatrice is married off; a new baby enters the Quimby household; and poor old Picky-picky dies and is buried with practical dispatch. The romance has reemerged in the Ramona books.

Readers first met these lovable but believable children in 1950 when Henry Huggins and Beezus Quimby, third graders, lived near each other in a Portland neighborhood and were somewhat hampered by the mischief of Beezus's three-year-old sister, Ramona. In the last book, thirty-four years later, Ramona is in third grade, and the stories have come full circle to the good times and small worries of American middle-class childhood. Ramona has had a very full five years in between.

Not only do the books chronicle American life, they also provide real insights into language and learning from the perspective of the child. Ramona is clearly going to be a reader. Her sister reads, and Ramona desperately wants to learn, too. She has regular visits to the library, with kind librarians who know their books, and an older sister and parents who (mostly) patiently read her favorite book, *Big Steve the Steam Shovel,* over and over to her. Ramona has her first hint of "booklinks" when she hits kindergarten and finds out about *Mike Mulligan.* Her question about this book—"Miss Binney, I want to know—how did Mike Mulligan go to the bathroom when he was digging the basement of the town hall?"—provides some of my students with their first hint that response to literature on the part of young children is personal and immediate.

Mrs. Cleary also shows readers the power words have for children. A second grader I know is very fond of an onomatopoetic word, *boing,* which she discovered in **Ramona the Pest** when Ramona imagines the noise Susan's curls would make if they were pulled. Actually, *boing* must be one of Mrs. Cleary's favorite words—it first appears in **Henry and Beezus** when Beezus drops a baton and Henry and his friends make fun of the sound. In **Ramona the Brave,** Ramona makes up the "swear word" which her family doesn't take seriously but which I am enjoying using myself these days—"Guts, guts, guts." One of my favorite Ramona words is *yeep.* When Ramona hears the expression "Make a joyful noise unto the Lord," she decides *yeep* is the most joyful noise she knows, and she says it regularly.

The other kind of power that words have in Cleary's novels is when miscommunication takes place. Some examples—when Miss Binney tells Ramona to "sit here for the present" on her first day of kindergarten; when she talks about the "dawnzer" song (i.e. "The Star-spangled Banner"); and, most painfully, when in third grade she overhears her beloved teacher Mrs. Whaley saying, "I hear my little show-off came in with egg in her hair. . . . What a nuisance." Fortunately, Ramona is gifted with teachers and parents who are aware that miscommunication occurs and are glad to come more than halfway to assure Ramona that her listening "miscues" are natural.

In **Ramona the Pest** we watch Ramona become a reader. In first grade she discovers environmental print: "Ramona shoved aside her stuffed animals and threw herself on her bed with *Wild Animals of Africa,* a book with interesting pictures but without the three grown-up words, gas, motel, and burger, which she had taught herself from signs but was unable to find in books." But Ramona keeps on trying with books at home and with the newspaper at her sitter's house, and finally the miracle of reading happens: "Best of all, Ramona was actually learning to read. Words leaped out at her from the newspapers, signs, and cartons. Crash, highway, salt, tires. The world was suddenly full of words that Ramona could read." In third grade Ramona is introduced to the joys of Sustained Silent Reading by her beloved Mrs. Whaley, who, to Ramona's delight, calls her students "you guys." Of course, in Mrs. Whaley's class this blissful

time when Ramona can read what she wants is called DEAR, for "Drop Everything And Read." Ramona prefers "Sustained Silent Reading" because it sounds more grown-up, and when the time comes to "Drop Everything And Read," Ramona sits quietly doing her "Sustained Silent Reading." SSR becomes her rescue and solace at daycare when she can read instead of playing with Willa Jean and get lost in the land of "princesses, kings, and clever youngest sons."

Ramona struggles with writing—especially its mechanical aspects. Unlike her more serious sister, Ramona doesn't have any problem with being imaginative in art, in her play, or in her ideas for writing. She has some trouble with over-generalizing on her letters. Her kindergarten teacher's descriptions of letters as looking like witches' caps and cats with tails curled and robin redbreasts result in some highly calligraphic efforts on Ramona's part. But even this becomes part of her unique identity, as she gleefully invents her distinctive signature cat Q. Ramona's second-grade teacher, Mrs. Rudge, insists that with her newly acquired cursive skills, the capital Q should look like a 2—an idea that strikes Ramona as absurd. But she bows to her teacher's wishes and, thrilled with grown-up writing, writes her name, with 2 in place, in the dust on the top of the television, in the steam on the bathroom mirror, and on the backs of old arithmetic papers and around the edge of the newspaper.

Ramona also struggles with spelling. She has been told she can't spell and is willing to live with it. But Mrs. Rudge tells her there's no such word as can't. Once Ramona has thought about how there can't be such a word as can't when her teacher has just said it, and why relief is spelled "r-o-l-a-i-d-s," she struggles with spelling traps: "blends and silent letters and letters that sounded one way in one word and a different way in another."

But Ramona has come a long way since those first episodes in **Henry Huggins** and **Henry and Beezus** when she was the difficult little sister. It has been a wonderful long visit with our neighbors on Klickitat Street. Our society has changed. We are more diverse; we recognize that life for many children is far more difficult than Ramona or Henry or Beezus or Ellen could even imagine. What stays true about these books—what rings true for the child who reads them and looks back to the time when learning to ride a bike, read, or print her letters seemed impossibly challenging—is that these children are alive in all of us. One last quote from **Ramona the Brave** says it all: "Beezus gave her sister a look of disgust. 'Ramona, grow up!' Ramona lost all patience. 'Can't you see I'm trying?' she yelled at the top of her voice. People were always telling her to grow up. What did they think she was trying to do?" For thirty-four years we've watched these children in a small Portland neighborhood, and we—children and adults alike—can indeed see they are trying. Their efforts have enriched us all.

Linda Benson

SOURCE: "The Hidden Curriculum and the Child's New Discourse: Beverly Cleary's *Ramona Goes to School*," in *Children's Literature in Education,* Vol. 30, No. 1, March, 1999, pp. 9-29.

THE HIDDEN CURRICULUM

Long a favorite with readers young and old, Beverly Cleary's **Ramona** series provides far more than mere entertainment. The series also provides a study in shifting subjectivity as Ramona Quimby grows from an irrepressible kindergartner to a more responsible and socially aware third-grader. Readers enjoy the humor born of Ramona's conflicts with rules, educational processes, other students, and teachers, but her school experiences reveal ways the school setting socializes the child by modifying, even reconstructing, a child's subjectivity. As Ramona adapts to the social norms of the educational community, she must internalize the external restrictions on her behavior or suffer the consequences of remaining at odds with the system. Readers who love and identify with Ramona's resistance to authority may enjoy thinking of her as untameable, but Ramona much prefers her teachers' approval than their (real or perceived) disapproval. She therefore usually conforms to the strictures of her new surroundings so that her teachers' approval will make her feel loved, especially in the earliest grades. As she progresses from kindergarten through third grade, her either/or mentality leads her to think that her teachers either like/approve of her or dislike/disapprove of her. When she thinks they do not like her, she literally (as she does during her kindergarten year in **Ramona the Brave**) or figuratively drops out (as when perceived disapproval silences her in later grades). Conformity, however, is not easy for Ramona. For her, as for almost any child, the system both coerces through various social punishments or convinces through equally effective social persuasions.

Like Ramona, most children soon learn that certain behaviors lead those who perform them to feel a sense of agency. Michael Apple identifies those behaviors as "the norms and values that are implicitly, but effectively, taught in schools" as part of the "hidden curriculum," though they are "not usually talked about in teachers' statements or end goals."[1] This hidden curriculum teaches the "basic rules" that dictate "the choices one has within the rules of the game" children come to know as school (p. 86). There, "students tacitly learn certain identifiable social norms mainly by coping with the day to day encounters and tasks of classroom life" (p. 87). The hidden curriculum, Peggy Orenstein points out in her study of middle-school girls, "once used to describe the ways in which the education system works to reproduce class systems in our culture, . . . has recently been applied to the ways in which schools help reinforce gender roles, whether they intend to or not."[2] Because the hidden curriculum tends to represent passive ideologies, most of the "rules" represent a culture's least examined assumptions about what constitutes a civilized child within the constructs of race, class, gender, and religion.

When Ramona does not understand the basic rules of her new behavioral boundaries or, understanding, transgresses them anyway, there are at least three results. One is the humor for which the Ramona books are famous. Another is a subtle communication about what social boundaries are. The third is that sympathetic recognition on the reader's part, which Cleary refers to when she writes that, "We can only do our best to offer children books . . . in which there is room for growth—in hopes that as they read, or are read to, they will laugh and think in secret triumph, I used to do that or, I feel that way or, I am too grown-up to act that way now."[3] With her emphasis on growth and the self-recognition of the progress it represents from a more mature perspective, it is not surprising that Cleary's books trace Ramona's school experience from the first day of kindergarten through her days as a third-grader headed into the fourth grade. The meeting of opposing forces—the egocentric, willful Ramona and the rules of home, neighborhood, and, now, school—produces the humor in the series even as it emphasizes the child's developmental process and reveals ways that Ramona internalizes the lessons within which social norms are encoded. Examining some of the hegemonic forces at work in the complex social dynamics of the traditionally feminized elementary school setting demonstrates how the dominant culture manipulates at least this one young female, who if not silenced or entirely subdued by the end of this series, is at least much more civilized according to the norms of the classroom.

LESSON ONE: SQUELCHING THE GREAT BIG NOISY
FUSS

If Ramona Quimby had known about the painful lessons in store for her on her first day of kindergarten, she might have pitched one of her famous great big noisy fusses to stay home, but Ramona's excitement about going to school is, of course, innocent of any such prior knowledge. Always acutely conscious of her subordinate position as the youngest child in the Quimby family, she is overjoyed to think that she will at last "catch up" with her sister Beezus and the other neighborhood school children. She feels "grown-up in a dress instead of play clothes" and joyfully expects that "Today she was going to learn to read and write and do all the things that would help her catch up with Beezus."[4] What would not have excited Ramona is the realization that behind the overt curriculum designed to develop her skills as a literate citizen lies the "lessons of the hidden curriculum [which] teach girls to value silence and compliance, to view those qualities as a virtue" (Orenstein, 1994, p. 35). Since Ramona is just entering kindergarten and Orenstein's study focuses on eighth-grade middle-school subjects, the lessons on "silence and compliance" seem quite a prediction to make for a strong personality like Ramona. Nevertheless, as early as the first day of kindergarten, Ramona's behavior conflicts with the norms of her school community, and readers see the beginnings of the socialization process.

Up to the day Ramona enters kindergarten, the basic rules of her home and neighborhood have allowed her to exercise a remarkably effective control over those around her by means of the tantrums her family euphemistically dubs the "great big noisy fuss" (*Ramona the Pest*, p. 12). While such disruptive tantrums can hardly be viewed as appropriate or positive behavior, they certainly allow Ramona to dominate the moment. Readers of Cleary's Henry Huggins series (1950-1962) see an example of Ramona's preschool power in *Henry and Beezus* (1952). In that narrative, the three-year-old's tantrum changes the older children's plans at a bike auction.[5] Ramona is four in *Henry and the Paper Route* (1957) when one of her outrageous public fits embarrasses Henry, who cannot control her.[6] One indication of Ramona's usual success is the rueful observation made by the two older children most affected by Ramona's behavior; at the bike auction in *Henry and Beezus,* "Beezus and Henry exchanged unhappy looks. It looked as if Ramona was going to get her own way. She usually did" (*Henry and Beezus,* p. 135). Ramona continues to manipulate adults and older children with her tantrums in the first books of the Ramona series. The child obviously has mastered a means of communication that empowers her in her home and neighborhood, the community that has thus far shaped her behavior and allowed her great big noisy fusses to work by silencing those who would silence her.

When at last Ramona arrives at kindergarten, the five-year-old has already said "No!" "stamped her foot," and considered that "she would make a great big noisy fuss" to avoid walking to school that first morning with Beezus and her friend Mary Jane instead of her own mother (*Pest,* p. 12). Since everyone capitulates to forestall the tantrum, the victorious Ramona cancels the performance and happily walks to school with her mother at her side. Ramona has no reason to suspect that the techniques that have served her so well will not continue to work at school. But that very day begins the socialization process imposed by the classroom experience. Researcher and elementary schoolteacher Isabel Beaton sympathizes with children facing what she calls "school culture" for the first time: "school culture is . . . school language . . . school behaviors . . . school politics . . . school economics"; it[7] most likely represents an alien environment to which children must adapt and in which they must become "proficient." For Ramona, this new culture involves a complex exchange of power as she begins to internalize the external rules imposed by the teacher and the group. In the beginning, following the basic rules of the teacher and the social group makes Ramona feel diminished as her sense of agency is undermined. This repositioning begins when she misunderstands, then defies Miss Binney, a teacher "so young and pretty she could not have been a grownup very long" (*Pest,* p. 16).

Cleary begins the process with a "present" that allows readers a look back at a younger self's linguistic naivete. Ramona is five, and her understanding of "present" is of the birthday and holiday kind, not the temporal kind Miss Binney means when she directs Ramona to a desk by saying, "Sit here for the present" (*Pest,* p. 17). Ramona's misunderstanding keeps her in her seat through the "Star Spangled Banner" (which, in another example of linguistic inexperience, Ramona immediately misunderstands to be about the "dawnzer lee light"). She would have kept her seat through recess if Miss Binney had not asked her why she had not gone to the playground with the other children. Both teacher and student are greatly embarrassed by the miscommunication. Miss Binney may be unhappy that she momentarily forgot that children Ramona's age tend to view the world in terms of objects and nouns—the literal rather than the figurative. The egocentric Ramona is more irked by the slipperiness of "puzzling" words than humbled by her lack of experience: *"Present* should mean a present, just as *attack* should mean to stick tacks in people" (*Pest,* p. 27). This initial confusion and its ensuing disappointment about there being no present foreshadows the deeper lesson that recess provides.

Even as Ramona concentrates on sitting in place for the present, one of the chief fascinations of the morning is her classmate Susan's hair:

> Susan's hair looked like the hair on the girls in the pictures of the old-fashioned stories Beezus liked to read. It was reddish brown and hung in curls like springs that touched her shoulders and bounced as she walked. Ramona had never seen such curls before. All the curly-haired girls she knew wore their hair short. Ramona put her hand to her own short straight hair, which was an ordinary brown, and longed to touch that bright springy hair. She longed to touch one of those curls and watch it spring back. *Boing!* thought Ramona, making a mental noise like a spring on a television cartoon and wishing for thick, springy *boing-boing* hair like Susan's.[8]

Establishing Ramona's longing for the tactile experience of touching Susan's boingy hair sets up what Pat Pfleiger identifies as one of Ramona's "difficulties" as she moves "into a world of complex relationships" outside her family and neighborhood.[9] Ramona's mental repetition of the word *"boing,"* revealed by the omniscient narrator and focalized through Ramona, resonates with young readers and brings a smile of recognition to older readers. The duality of the appeal creates an understanding sympathy for Ramona's longing to experience that tempting, evocative *"boing."* It is no surprise that when the students play the tag game Miss Binney teaches them, Ramona tries "to stand next to the girl with the springy curls" (*Pest,* p. 28). Her plan does not work, but Ramona's desire to touch Susan's curls becomes so strong that when her turn comes to run around the circle,

> She ran as fast as she could to catch up with the sneakers pounding on the asphalt ahead of her. The *boing-boing* curls were on the other side of the circle. Ramona was coming closer to them. She put out her hand. She took hold of a curl, a thick, springy curl—
>
> *"Yow!"* screamed the owner of the curls. Startled, Ramona let go. She was so surprised by the

scream that she forgot to watch Susan's curl spring back.[10]

Stemming from a preoperational impulse that does not consider consequences or the feelings of others, Ramona's desire "to touch that beautiful, springy hair" is thwarted by Susan's reaction (*Pest,* p. 30). Moreover, just as Ramona willingly lets Miss Binney shoulder the responsibility for the confusion about the present, she immediately blames the shrieking Susan for the scene that follows the hair-pulling. When Miss Binney makes clear that "in our kindergarten we do not pull hair," Ramona attempts to sidestep responsibility for violating Susan's body by accusing the complaining victim of being a "baby," the highest insult possible for a kindergartner (*Pest,* p. 30).[11] Miss Binney, however, cannot allow such behavior; she tells Ramona to "go sit on the bench outside the door while the rest of us play our game" (*Pest,* p. 30).

What happens next signifies the beginning of the end for Ramona's great big noisy fusses as well as an effectively public beginning of her perception of "what is private and what is public" behavior:

> Ramona did not want to sit on any bench. She wanted to play Gray Duck with the rest of the class. "No," said Ramona, preparing to make a great big noisy fuss, "I won't."
>
> Susan stopped shrieking. A terrible silence fell over the playground. Everyone stared at Ramona in such a way that she almost felt as if she were beginning to shrink. Nothing like this had ever happened to her before.
>
> "Ramona," said Miss Binney quietly. "Go sit on the bench."
>
> Without another word Ramona walked across the play-ground and sat down on the bench by the door of the kindergarten. The game of Gray Duck continued without her, but the class had not forgotten her. Howie grinned in her direction. Susan continued to look injured. Some laughed and pointed at Ramona. Others, particularly Davy, looked worried, as if they had not known such a terrible punishment could be given in kindergarten.[12]

Surrounded by her teacher, classmates, and that "terrible silence," Ramona "shrink[s]" into a conscious decision not to throw a tantrum. Her subject position takes a radical shift as she retreats to the bench. Out of the circle but not out of sight, she can see the range of the other children's responses. These responses include one that she probably cannot know or articulate through projection: the epiphany for Davy and other children that kindergarten and "terrible punishment" can go hand-in-hand for the child who steps out of bounds. This shift in focalizer, infrequent in the Ramona series, underscores for the reader the significance of this event. School and punishment become inextricably linked, especially as they serve to repress behavior deemed antisocial. For the first time in her life, Ramona learns a lesson that her family has not succeeded in communicating: Her own very personal desires cannot be expressed freely or with impunity. Most emphatically, she learns her great big noisy fuss will no longer make her effectively the center of a world that works mostly her way. Other powers, those represented by Miss Binney's quiet voice, now begin to supersede the child's impulses. Readers see no more great big noisy fusses at school throughout the rest of the series.

Ramona, however, would not be Ramona, the willful child with whom so many readers identify, if even "terrible punishment" brought about an instant transformation; Cleary allows her to *boing* Susan's hair two more times. The first time—which I will explore more fully below—she gets away with her defiant misbehavior because she is one of several children in witch costumes for Halloween, so Susan cannot identify which witch pulled her hair. The second time invokes a punishment worse than time-out on the bench when Miss Binney tells Ramona, "If you cannot stop pulling Susan's hair, you will have to go home and stay there until you can" (*Pest,* p. 163). Again a silence descends on the children, "and Ramona could almost feel their stares against her back as she stood there looking at the floor" (*Pest,* p. 163). This time, the focus is on Ramona. Readers see only what Ramona sees, but perhaps that silence, echoing Ramona's first silencing, evokes for readers the shock from the first episode when Davy and the other children are aghast that so terrible a punishment as bench time could be meted out. To be sent home is far worse. Ramona becomes an unforgettable example of what happens to children who cross socially imposed boundaries. She becomes "That girl [who] has been bad again" to the observant preschoolers in the yard next to the school (*Pest,* p. 165). Most significantly, Ramona does choose to go home, to drop out of kindergarten, "because Miss Binney did not love her anymore" (p. 165).

Later, after several more confrontations, Ramona internalizes these external rules governing social behavior and is proud when she exercises what she perceives as self-control. Margaret Mackey sees Susan's curls and Ramona's enduring response to them as "one way for Cleary to focus on and express Ramona's own perceptions of the world"[13] (Mackey, 1991, p. 102). Drawing on Bakhtin's theory of the chronotope as "the intrinsic connectedness of temporal and spatial relationships that are artistically expressed in literature" and Bruner's ideas about the power of the narrative to establish "negotiated meanings," Mackey concludes that the combination "offer[s] a powerful set of roles for stories: finding a location in space and time, distinguishing between the private and the social, establishing the norm and explaining the deviations" (1991, p. 98). In the Ramona narratives, Susan's curls serve as a chronotope which helps young readers negotiate what constitutes proper conduct in a social setting. Ramona is tempted by those curls; that she repeatedly thinks of Susan's curls through both ***Ramona the Pest*** and ***Ramona the Brave*** reveals Ramona's evolving sense of public behavior and that behavior which is best confined to the privacy of one's own imagination.

In a different context, Vivian Gussin Paley also addresses the power of the narrative to shape behavior.[14] After a year-long study of her kindergarten class, she comes to view the superhero play of the boys and the doll-corner play of the girls as narratives through which the children explore, define, and practice their cultural (e.g., gender) roles. The boys construct "serious drama" based on Star Wars and other contemporary superhero tales; the girls play at the "single drama" of the doll corner, which often becomes a Cinderella tale; together they reenact *The Boxcar Children.* Paley concludes that girl-play and boy-play are strikingly similar in that whether the "play" is Cinderella or Darth Vader, girls and boys are equally noisy, equally messy, and equally interested in "social order" (pp. 82, 23). Her observations bear out claims such as Bruner's about the importance of narrative in the lives of children. Both boys and girls build on fictions they know to construct their own highly specialized dramas in which the characters they assume act out appropriate masculine or feminine behavior as the children understand it. Tellingly, that understanding places the girls, by choice, in the doll corner, a site few boys enter as playmates.

As with Paley's kindergartners, Ramona's fictive experience carries the message to readers that negotiating socially constructed meanings is neither easy nor immediately achieved. On the first day of first grade, a year after her first encounter with the boundaries represented by Susan's curls, Ramona again sees "Susan with fat curls like springs touching her shoulders. *Boing,* thought Ramona as always, at the sight of those curls. This year she promised herself she would not pull those curls no matter how much they tempted her."[15] The hard-learned lessons of kindergarten prevail. Although this is by no means the last time Ramona thinks about *boinging* those springy curls, she does not again act on the thought. She has effectively internalized at least the rule of the institution which insists that children keep their hands off other children. The conflicts and lessons young readers see in the Ramona books bring to mind Brian V. Street's assertion that, "Whether we attend a course or school . . . , we are doing more than simply decoding script, producing essays or writing a proper hand; we are taking on—or resisting—the identities associated with those practices."[16]

Has Ramona, as Orenstein suggests young girls do, already begun to assimilate the rules about compliance and less aggressive behavior? Can she be identified as a tamer, more feminized child as a result of the persuasive punishments meted out by the school? In Paley's kindergarten classroom, Ramona's behavior would have violated the last of Paley's four play rules.[17] The first three admonish girls and boys to let others play without disturbance, to share, and to avoid "excessive noise and careless running" (pp. 82-83). The last rule singles out the aggressive play behavior of boys, which Paley struggles to accommodate and reshape: "There is a final rule, applicable only to boys; no grabbing, pushing, punching, or wrestling" (p. 83). According to Paley's rules, Ramona's grabbing of Susan's curls marks her as crossing a gender boundary; Paley's designations construct only boys as physically aggressive. Ramona's action, then, masculinizes her and thereby makes the girl's behavior even less acceptable in the feminized classroom. But it would be difficult to argue that this lesson in controlling one's urges is gender specific. In the culture of the feminized classroom, such behavior would be discouraged regardless of the child's gender. If a five-year-old boy had capitulated to the same ego-centered impulse and then refused to obey the teacher, it seems reasonable that he also would have been punished with bench time. In our culture, however, aggressive behavior such as Ramona's willful *boinging* of Susan's curls is identified with masculine behavior. As Paley's rules demonstrate, it appears that Ramona's inappropriate behavior and the strong example the ensuing punishment sets for her classmates (and readers) also provides an example of socializing Ramona into a more civilized female child.

LESSON TWO: READING, WRITING, AND THE
EMPOWERED CHILD

Dedicated as Ramona is to the idea of "catching up," she enters school ready to work hard "to learn to read and write" (*Pest* p. 73). Her own inability to read and write becomes entangled in her mind with the general unfairness she feels is her burden as the younger child. Literacy, as Ramona might define it, promises a big girl position for a child weary of being regarded as little; she intuits that learning to read and write will empower her by leveling the playing field. Though she is a preschooler, the child already thinks in terms of what Janet Carey Eldred and Peter Mortensen term "the literacy myth."[18] Their theories suggest that even as a prekindergartner, Ramona has internalized the idea that learning to read and write will lead to personal, social, and economic improvement. In Eldred and Mortensen's term, this is a "narrative of socialization," a phenomenon in literacy narratives when children willingly attempt to shift their "discursive arena" (p. 512). Ramona is so absorbed by the idea of herself entering the discursive arena of literacy that she gives little thought to how all those older children learned to read and write; she knows they go to school, so Ramona perceives school as a source of empowerment. In this case, Ramona is correct: Reading, writing, and the communication skills associated with them do give her the means to improve her standing with teachers and in her family, and, most important, these skills allow her a more potent means than the great big noisy fuss to negotiate power in her culture.

James Zarrillo pays close attention to the process by which Ramona, as a representative child, learns to read.[19] He discusses Cleary's own miserable first-grade experience with an unkind teacher whose martinet methods so paralyzed her that she could not learn to read. He cites Cleary herself saying that the first grade was "the most terrible year" of her life because she was consigned to the lowest reading group and literally terrorized by her teacher's practices, which included isolating children in the cloakroom for making mistakes in their reading. Luckily, Ramona is not made to replicate her creator's trauma. Though often constrained by the rules of the classroom to which her teachers insist she conform, Ramona suffers from boredom rather than tyranny.

The combination of Cleary's real and fictive narratives, Zarillo says, demonstrates that "the elaborate instructional systems used in elementary classrooms, complete with texts, workbooks, dittos, and prescriptive-diagnostic tests, create formidable obstacles to be overcome by children who want to read books for personal interest" (p. 133). Such practices, he concludes, mostly disappoint and frustrate students like Ramona who "come to school able and eager to read" (p. 131). Zarrillo does not mention how Ramona's opinion of the basals is influenced by the kind of stories she chooses to have her family read to her, but it takes no great imaginative leap to conclude that a child who loves books about steam shovels with invigorating action that inspires her to honk ("Beep-beep"), wail ("A-hooey, a-hooey"), and shout ("Clunk! Clunk!") would find "Tom and Becky and their dog Pal and their cat Fluff, who could run, run, run and come, come, come," downright boring no matter what skills such repetition develops (**Pest,** p. 13; **Brave,** p. 119). Though the acquisition of those abilities, as Zarrillo suggests, sometimes proves tedious, Ramona does feel powerful when, "Words leaped out at her from the newspapers, signs, and cartons. *Crash, highway, salt, tires.* The world was suddenly full of words that Ramona could read" (**Brave,** p. 129).

Mackey also pays attention to the literacy narrative inherent in Ramona's reading process, saying that in these books, "reading is the dominant task. Ramona masters words, stories, chapters, books. She reads when things are unbearable elsewhere. She reads for duty and she reads for fun. She judges books" (1991, p. 106). Mackey examines reading acquisition to demonstrate the importance of stories, of Ramona's growing "awareness of the canonical workings of narrative" (p. 106). In **Ramona Quimby, Age 8,**[20] Ramona, assigned a book on which to report, knows by the third grade the critical differences between this "medium boring" book with chapters but "babyish words" chosen for her by her teacher and a book she herself would choose to read for pleasure. The report book she tags as "good enough to pass the time on the bus, but not good enough to read during Sustained Silent Reading" (**Age 8,** p. 149). By age eight, Ramona has become a discriminating reader; she has at least moved beyond the stage Lillian Smith suggests centers on "the immediate allure" of "what happens" from one moment to the next in a story as the only basis of her judgment.[21]

Most important, in connection with Zarrillo's and Mackey's assertions, Ramona has also developed a sense of the difference between reading for herself and reading for school, between pleasure and responsibility. She finds "duty"—as the teacher-selected book report book represents it—is not always as satisfying as self-selection, although she ful-

fills her responsibility as a dutiful student when she reads the book her teacher assigns her. That school reinforces for her the lesson between the pleasure principle and the reality principle so early in her education provides one more example of how school socializes Ramona into societally sanctioned behaviors.

Moreover, Cleary demonstrates how thoroughly texts embrace young readers who, as Mackey argues, look to texts for exemplars.[22] The Ramona books' use of intertextuality invariably demonstrates Ramona's passion for narratives. At age four, Ramona, influenced by *Hansel and Gretel,* bakes her doll, filling the house "with a horrid rubbery smell" and ruining for the second time in one afternoon her mother's efforts to produce a birthday cake for Beezus.[23] A year later, when Henry Huggins rescues her and her new red boots from a muddy quagmire, she obviously thinks of fairy tale princes who rescue princesses when she declares she will marry Henry (**Pest,** pp. 112-127). First grade brings a direct encounter with Red Riding Hood's wolf in the form of a territorial German shepherd. Though in a state of panic, Ramona's mind catches onto the one literary referent she has to a little girl and a big canine: "He had teeth like the wolf in *Little Red Riding Hood.* Oh, Grandmother, what big teeth you have! The better to eat you with, my dear. Ramona took another step back. Growling, the dog advanced. He was a dog, not a wolf, but that was bad enough" (**Brave,** p. 168). Reminding herself that her situation is neither a dream nor a story and that she can expect no rescuing woodchopper, she rescues herself by throwing first her lunch box, then her shoe at the dog. She emerges from this encounter as Ramona the Brave, her actions and self-image underscored by her classmates, teacher, and the school secretary, who all call her brave. Readers, who have been in on Ramona's struggles to be brave about sleeping alone in her new bedroom and overcoming nightmares brought on by the picture of a gorilla in *Wild Animals of Africa* (another affective reading experience), likely celebrate with her and applaud her spunk.

Though Ramona certainly enjoys reading and, as exemplified above, finds intertextual exemplars in narratives, it turns out that the power she craves lies in writing:

> Come here Moth
> er. Come here
> to me[24]

In this plaintive missive, "here" is Ramona's new bedroom and "me" is Ramona. It represents the six-year-old's first written message, her first effort in writing to convey her needs to her mother. Ramona knows her parents will learn at a school open house they are attending that she has scrunched Susan's paper bag owl, news that she does not much want them to hear. The handwriting—printing, actually—is childish but clear. The style, as Mackey notes, mimics the "language of the basal reader" (1991, p. 106). But it effectively summons the family support the anxious Ramona needs. The note, in all ways a successful communication, represents a first reward for Ramona's dedication to "catching up" with Beezus and the other, always older neighborhood children.

The payoff comes in *Ramona and Her Father.* Zarrillo cites this, saying,

> There is an excellent example of how children develop as language users by using writing to communicate in *Ramona and Her Father* Second grader Ramona and her older sister mount a campaign to convince their father to stop smoking. Together they make signs and write notes to their dad. Ramona learns to read and write words like *pollution* and *hazardous* by including them in messages to her father. Ramona and her sister paint about a dozen signs. They include "Stop Air Pollution," "Cigarettes Start Forest Fires," and "Smoking is Hazardous to Your Health" (95). . . . Ramona learns to spell words she can say, and becomes acquainted with the meaning of several others.[25]

While this campaign certainly fosters Ramona's language skills, it also accomplishes something Zarrillo does not mention as a component of that development: It empowers her within her family. Perhaps it also indicates Ramona's intuitive appropriation of the didactic impulse to socialize behavior that dominates texts of all kinds. Most specifically, although it is Beezus who makes Mr. Quimby's smoking an issue in *Ramona and Her Father* it is Ramona who instigates the campaign to make her father quit.[26] She makes several signs, including one that reads,

NOSMO

KING

printed "in big letters" and she and Beezus eventually put signs condemning their father's smoking all over the house. Although her efforts do not work immediately, in part because she has not paid attention to the conventions her new medium and her new audience demand, Mr. Quimby ultimately promises he will try to quit smoking. This elates Ramona; her signs have been convincing. The text—her text—is as persuasive as any other. She feels so powerful that she takes charge and dumps all her father's cigarettes in the garbage. The success of her campaign, impossible without her writing skills, demonstrates to her and readers the power of literacy. Zarrillo points out that the act of making the signs is an effective learning experience. Because Ramona has a real reason to write, she willingly and meaningfully extends her vocabulary and spelling skills in this extracurricular setting (*Father,* p. 133). School, with its attendant pressures and conflicts, finally pays off when Ramona assumes the role of the child who guides the adult.

Ramona's biggest reward comes later, on "the terrible afternoon" she discovers her father has cheated:

> Mr. Quimby sat down on the couch and leaned back as if he were very, very tired, which made some of the anger drain out of Ramona. "Ramona," he said, "it isn't easy to break a bad habit. I ran across one cigarette, an old stale cigarette, in my raincoat pocket and thought it might help if I smoked just one. I'm trying. I'm really really trying."
>
> Hearing her father speak this way, as if she really was a grown-up, melted the last of Ramona's anger.[27]

Having her father speak to her as an equal validates Ramona's sense of herself as a competent agent in her family. With that validation, which she has earned through exercising her new literacy skills, Ramona can, as the text explains it, become "a seven-year-old again" (*Father,* p. 157). Now that Ramona has the means to move beyond what she has always considered her inferior status as the youngest member of the family, it appears that she no longer has to be quite so impatient to grow up. If, as Cleary says, "To grow up is the ambition of normal children" ("**Laughter,**" p. 562), then the reading, writing, assertive Ramona is now secure in the knowledge that she is on the way to acquiring skills that have always seemed the province of people older than she is. She can be content in this moment when her father speaks *with* her and a little more patient than the Ramona who has always felt so far behind everyone else. But it cannot be overlooked that Ramona, institutionally manipulated into socially acceptable behaviors, uses the lessons she has learned in her literacy narrative in turn to manipulate someone else into behavior she considers acceptable.

LESSON THREE: MASKS, IDENTITY, AND ASSERTIVENESS

Social institutions have powerful effects on children's developing sense of themselves as gendered people. For example, Carol Gilligan, Nona P. Lyons, and

Trudy J. Hamner demonstrate in *Making Connections: The Relational World of Adolescent Girls at Emma Willard School* that even girls (like Ramona) who have had a good sense of themselves and have had no qualms about asserting their ideas and needs lose that self-esteem as they enter adolescence.[28] *Shortchanging Girls, Shortchanging America: A Call to Action* (1991), the study conducted by the American Association of University Women, as well as subsequent studies, supports their findings, so it is not surprising that Ramona, still of elementary age, remains assertive.[29] At age eight, Ramona is three or four years younger than the eleven or twelve most of these studies mark as the crucial age at which pubescent girls begin the behavioral shift indicative of their assimilation of gender constructs demanding that females be acquiescent (Gilligan, Lyons, and Hamner, 1990, p. 11; Pipher, 1994; Orenstein, 1994, p. xiv). But signs within the series point to a similar conclusion for even the assertive Ramona.[30]

Within the context of the school culture, Ramona senses losing her identity as early as the first few months of kindergarten. Halloween precipitates the identity crisis when, as one of several children dressed as a witch, Ramona comes to fear that if no one can name her, then she does not exist. At first Ramona is wild with the freedom she feels her costume gives her from the constraints normally imposed by the school setting; the five-year-old revels in her sense of herself as "the baddest witch in the world!" (*Pest* p. 137). Caught up in the power of the moment, Ramona "yelled and screamed and shrieked and chased anyone who would run" (p. 137). Emboldened by her status as "the baddest witch" among the many on the playground, Ramona finally achieves a goal she has pursued since the first day of school—she catches and kisses Davy (p. 137). Cresting on having achieved this object of desire, Ramona moves in on Susan's forbidden curls. *Her* excitement, *her* actions create a *boinging* frenzy in which several other masked children join. Within the context of the narrative, this scene is one of the funniest in the book because it humorously depicts Ramona and the other children caught up in the carnivalesque holiday freedom of Halloween. Isolated, this passage carries disturbing overtones. The children, led by the unknown and unknowable Ramona, act on desires they also must have harbored. Ramona's transgression frees them to become a tiny mob of children taunting someone whose curls mark her as different.

As it is depicted, the scene offers an unflinching look at an unthinking, unintended cruelty. The result terrorizes Susan, who cannot identify the witch who started the whole episode or any of her other assailants. Still bold, Ramona shouts scary hellos to Miss Binney, who clearly does not recognize her. This in turn terrifies Ramona. It is one thing if Davy and Susan do not recognize their masked tormentor, but when Miss Binney does not identify her, the power drains from Ramona. She enjoys the freedom the mask allows; when she violates the school codes, she finds the anonymity exhilarating. When the same mask does not allow her to receive the personal responses she values, it becomes a threat to her sense of self. The following passage traces the escalation of her growing fear that the very mask and costume she felt so empowered by have somehow subsumed her:

> Nobody knew who Ramona was, and if nobody knew who she was, she wasn't anybody. . . . The feeling was the scariest one Ramona had ever experienced. She felt lost inside her costume. She wondered if her mother would know which witch was which, and the thought that her own mother might not know her frightened Ramona even more. What if her mother forgot her? What if everyone in the whole world forgot her? With that terrifying thought Ramona snatched off her mask, and although its ugliness was no longer the most frightening thing about it, she rolled it up so she would not have to look at it.[31]

Does she intuit that her fear that she does not know herself well enough to exist independently of others' naming her is even greater than her fear that others will effectively erase her if they do not name her? At five, she cannot articulate such thoughts about the power of the name and the self, but her dependence on the recognition of others underscores how acutely she has come to depend on relationships as a means of self-definition: Without them, she has no identity. She does know she wants more than anything to be recognized as Ramona Geraldine Quimby. To ensure that her mother and others will indeed recognize her as that entity, she retreats from the playground to the classroom. There, armed with crayon and paper, "As fast as she could Ramona printed her name, and then she could not resist adding with a flourish her last initial complete with ears and whiskers, RAMONA Q" (*Pest,* p. 147).

Has she used her literacy to effectively identify herself? Ramona thinks so. She carries her hand-lettered sign; now that she is self-signified, others can complete the process by naming her. Miss Binney calls her by name; her mother recognizes her and waves. Feeling "very grownup," Ramona Q. can again claim the mask and her position as "the baddest witch in the world!" (*Pest,* p. 148). Her own ability to write allows her to name herself, to rescue herself from the dangerous anonymity the mask threatens. Claiming herself as Ramona Q. means relinquishing something of the aggressive self who can terrorize Susan, but it is a trade-off Ramona embraces to make herself *the* Ramona Q., complete with ears and whiskers on her Q., among the otherwise anonymous throng of kindergartners parading around the school ground.

A few years later, when Ramona is eight and in the third grade with Mrs. Whaley as her teacher, the power of the school as a socializing institution is again underscored when Ramona consciously creates a persona she hopes will please her teacher more than she thinks she does as the person she actually is. Toward the end of *Ramona Quimby Age 8,* Ramona assumes another mask. This one, however, provides the power she now needs to assert herself because the eight-year-old Ramona no longer possesses the sense of an assertive self owned by the five-year-old Ramona. Although the narrative and characters (notably Beezus) in the series have identified Ramona as a pest, she always adamantly rejects this label. This rejection shifts to a form of acquiescence throughout most of *Age 8,* where Ramona suffers from her perception that she is a nuisance to her teacher. On some level, she recognizes "nuisance" as a synonym for "pest." The identification makes her distinctly uncomfortable, but she no longer confronts with a direct denial the status of pest/nuisance. When Ramona, anxious to be part of the third-grade fad of cracking hard-boiled eggs from their lunches on their heads, cracks on her head a raw egg her hurried mother has accidentally packed in Ramona's lunch, the mess embarrasses and angers her. She has to go to the front office where the secretary, Mrs. Larson, helps her clean up. Left alone, Ramona works on her hair, listening with fascination to the conversations between Mrs. Larson and teachers who stop by. She realizes for the first time that teachers talk about their students and classes. Soon she over-hears her own teacher, Mrs. Whaley, in a conversation that marks a shift in her self-perception almost as profound as the silencing she experienced the first day of kindergarten:

> Then Mrs. Whaley said, "I hear my little show-off came in with egg in her hair." She laughed and added, "What a nuisance."
>
> Ramona was so stunned she did not try to hear Mrs. Larson's answer. Show-off! Nuisance! Did Mrs. Whaley think she had broken a raw egg into her hair on purpose to show off? And to be called a nuisance by her teacher when she was not a

nuisance. Or was she? Ramona did not mean to break an egg in her hair. He mother was to blame. Did this accident make her a nuisance?

> Ramona did not see why Mrs. Whaley could think she was a nuisance when Mrs. Whaley was not the one to get her hands all eggy. Yet Ramona had heard her say right out loud that she was a show-off and a nuisance. That hurt, really hurt. . . . Her body felt numb and so did her heart. She could never, never face Mrs. Whaley again. Never. . . .
>
> Ramona was forgotten, which was the way she wanted it. She even wanted to forget herself and her horrible hair now drying into stiff spikes. She no longer felt like a real person.[32]

The episode again underscores Ramona's dependence on and vulnerability to what her teachers think of her: Mrs. Whaley's conversational gambit has redefined Ramona for Ramona. Ramona does have to go back to class that afternoon, so she literally faces Mrs. Whaley again almost immediately. For all practical purposes, however, she disappears from Mrs. Whaley's view by radically altering her classroom behavior. As she concentrates on not being a nuisance, "She stopped volunteering answers, and except for the bus ride home and Sustained Silent Reading she dreaded school" (*Age 8,* p. 110). School, always a behavioral challenge for Ramona, becomes terribly "uncomfortable" for the girl determined to fade into the background as a nonentity (p. 110). Ramona the spirited devolves into Ramona the silent as she makes a stringent effort to become a girl whose behavior suits the institution: Girls who stand out as nuisances do not receive approbation. Ramona's reading of the classroom culture combined with her conscious desire to fit into it subsumes the child as she reconstructs herself.

She slips back into the spotlight in the worst possible way when she becomes sick and vomits in class. All Ramona can think of is how right Mrs. Whaley is about her: "Nobody, nobody in the whole world, was a bigger nuisance than someone who threw up in school. . . . She really was a nuisance, a horrible runny-nosed nuisance with nothing to blow her nose on" (*Age 8,* p. 117). At home, Mrs. Quimby tucks Ramona into her own welcoming bed and assures her that Mrs. Whaley understands illness. Nonetheless, Ramona cannot help but think of herself as a "super-nuisance" (*Age 8,* p. 126).

Recovering from her flu allows time for Ramona to make elliptical references to her parents about the nuisance situation. Though she never quite divulges all her concerns to either one of them, as Mackey notes, both her mother and her father let her know that the egg incident and the throwing up were not intentional and are therefore not the nuisance that intentional behavior would have been (1995, p. 23). When her parents agree on this point, Ramona collapses the nuisance persona with the thought that, "Mrs. Whaley could just go jump in a lake" (*Age 8,* p. 151). Ramona resurrects her agency with this declaration, which at first glance seems to restore the child to her former self as a character who faces the world on her own terms.

Then Ramona gets busy on the book report assignment to "sell" *The Left-Behind Cat,* the book Mrs. Whaley sent for her to read. Recovering her physical health as her body recovers and her mental health as she sloughs off the burden of the silent nuisance persona she has assumed for most of the book, the creative child relies on her literacy to help her re-create herself. She emerges from her dependency on her teacher's perception (or, in this case, her perception of her teacher's perception, an echo of when she dropped out of kindergarten when she thought Miss Binney did not love her) for her sense of self-worth. Depending now on her parents and herself, she throws off the final constraints when she determines "to give her book report any way she wanted" (*Age 8,* p. 152). Her way draws from her sick days of watching television, days in which the commercials prove more interesting than the programs, especially the cat food commercials and especially the cat food commercial with the dancing cats that Mrs. Quimby tells her are an effect produced with a camera trick. This produces another sick-day revelation: "The commercials lied. That's what they did. Ramona was cross with cat-food commercials. Cheaters! She was angry with the whole world" (*Age 8,* p. 136). The realization also provides a certain ethical freedom: She does not have to like *The Left-Behind Cat* to sell her classmates on reading it. In a creative rush, the evening before she returns to school she makes three cat masks—one for herself and two for friends—borrows the idiom of the commercial as she writes her report, and phones Sara and Janet to enlist them as a meowing choral background for her report.

Pleased and emboldened by Mrs. Whaley's delighted response to her originality, Ramona seizes the moment after her report while she feels "brave behind her cat mask" to confront her teacher (*Age 8,* p. 158). As the rest of the class leaves for lunch, Ramona protests having been called a show-off and a nuisance. Mrs. Whaley explains, saying, "Oh, Ramona, you

misunderstood. . . . I meant that trying to wash the egg out of your hair was a nuisance for Mrs. Larson. I didn't mean you personally were a nuisance" (p. 160). Cleary lets readers see how much Ramona depends on her cat mask to brace herself for this moment by having Ramona remove it only after Mrs. Whaley helps her understand the miscommunication. It is a very close call for the girl nearly subsumed by the "nuisance" label in her teacher's comment. The nuisance trauma makes clear that the school culture embraces Ramona in the most negative way, so the child very nearly abandons her own sense of herself to earn the approbation of the teacher, whose voice represents the accepted norms of the system. Ramona emerges from this particular conflict stronger in her awareness of herself, but resisting the construction by protesting against a system she feels misnames her, requires great effort. Most telling is that at the age of only eight, Ramona's courage already requires a mask before she can assert herself. Readers who are likely cheering for the success of Ramona's showdown with Mrs. Whaley are not as likely to recognize that this episode reveals one of the best representations of the civilizing process of the hidden curriculum in the Ramona series.

ASSESSMENT

Since reading and writing are issues in each book of the Ramona series—Ramona wants to read and write, is learning to read and write, or is reading and writing—readers see her development toward literacy as an affirmative image of acquiring those language tools. They also see literacy defined in other, social ways as Ramona develops her skills as a reader of books as well as a reader of culture. Not only can she read and write but her years at school have shaped her sense of public and private behaviors. It is no coincidence that Ramona's sense of herself as an individual with some influence on her world depends largely on her having acquired those skills along with her perception of appropriate behavior. Although Cleary emphasizes the humor resulting from the willful child's conflicts with restrictions on her behavior, the books provide a focus on how Ramona (or any subject) is sometimes diminished and sometimes empowered as she moves from one discourse community, from one cultural context to another. The fictional experiences that Zarrillo labels a "case study" of how a child learns to read and write can be shifted slightly to provide the basis for a consideration of literacy as a social construct.

For Ramona, reading and writing, though difficult skills to acquire, are at least a little less confusing and a little more directly empowering than dealing with her new subject position. These skills please Ramona much more than conforming to the strictures imposed by the classroom. She sees the trade-off as worth the compromise of her agency in the school setting when her new literacy allows her a more intellectual and interactive subject position in her family than her great big noisy fusses ever gained her. She becomes empowered in the democratic construct her family represents. When she combines what she has learned about reading discourse communities/ cultures with the language tools she has acquired, Ramona, by almost anyone's definition, becomes a literate person.

The ironies inherent in the power shifts that show Ramona as a less empowered agent when she faces the dominant hegemony of the educational institution but a more empowered agent in her family underscore the complexities of sifting through the ideologies in these texts. Much of the autonomy she relinquishes may be attributed to being socialized into acceptable, civilized behavior. Tantrums tolerated in a preschooler are a good deal less tolerable in an older child; Ramona needs to mature beyond such behavior. But even as she resists the devaluation of her behavior, she is learning that her subject position in the classroom community demands she conform to its rules if she is to succeed within it.

These lessons did not escape one of my student readers who combined her memories of having read the Ramona books as a child with her adult reading of **Ramona Forever.** She pointedly comments,

> When I read the book as an adult, I looked at it in a new light. . . . I analyzed Ramona's personality in public as compared to around her family. In public, Ramona seemed to be somewhat shy and submissive. However, around her family she was seemingly very opinionated and outgoing. Although she was stubborn in both settings, she seemed to verbalize it more in front of her family. This made me think about the ways that society influences girls to be quiet and agreeable, while boys are accepted as being outgoing and even aggressive at times. (Student response)

The student's thoughts, though couched in terms of social influences rather than focusing on the impact of the school experience, tap into Street's claim "that identity and personhood are frequently signified through literacy practices" that too often result from "the notion of a single autonomous literacy" (quoted in Hilton, 1994, p. 12). Certainly Ramona's new maturity appeals to readers who enjoy stories about where they have been or where they are headed, and

certainly Ramona and her readers readily accept her "identity and personhood" as a literate female child who can willfully influence her father's behavior. But the significance of her need for a mask before she feels bold enough to confront Mrs. Whaley cannot be ignored in the context of a culture which, as various social and psychological studies demonstrate time and again, (re)constructs young females into more acquiescent humans through the civilizing processes embedded in the hidden curriculum.

Notes

1. Michael W. Apple, *Teachers and Texts: A Political Economy of Class and Gender Relations in Education,* p. 84

2. Peggy Orenstein, *School Girls: Young Women, Self-Esteem, and the Confidence Gap,* p. 5

3. Beverly Cleary, "The Laughter of Children," p. 564

4. Beverly Cleary, *Ramona the Pest* p. 10

5. Beverly Cleary, *Henry and Beezus*

6. Beverly Cleary, *Henry and the Paper Route*

7. Isabel Beaton, quoted in Isaiah Smithson, "Review: Classrooms, Cultures, and Democracy," p. 580

8. *Pest,* pp. 18-19

9. Pat Pflieger, *Beverly Cleary,* p. 59

10. *Pest,* p. 29

11. Margaret Mackey, "Ramona the Chronotope: The Young Reader and Social Theories of Narrative," p. 99

12. *Pest,* pp. 32-33

13. M. M. Bakhtine and Jerome Bruner, quoted in Mackey, "Chronotope," pp. 97, 98

14. Vivian Gussey Paley, *Boys and Girls: Superheroes in the Doll Corner,* pp. xii, 83, 95-98

15. Beverly Cleary, *Ramona the Brave,* p. 63

16. Brian V. Street, quoted. in Mary Hilton, "The Blowing Dust': Popular Culture and Popular Culture Books for Children," p. 12

17. Paley, pp. 82-83

18. Janet Carey Eldred and Peter Mortensen, "Reading Literacy Narratives," p. 512

19. James Zarrillo, "Beverly Cleary, Ramona Quimby, and the Teaching of Reading," p. 131

20. Beverly Cleary, *Ramona Quimby, Age 8,* pp. 149, 148

21. Lillian Smith, *The Unreluctant Years,* p. 122

22. Joel Chaston's "Reading As If for Life: The Quixotic Reader in the Nineteenth Century" [page 1] provides a study of the artful representation in fiction of the affective power of literature to shape a character's "conception of the world" as characters who read take as exemplars the characters and situations about which they read. In their fiction, writers such as Austen and Dickens demonstrate that "reading literature is connected with the development of the imagination and an empathy for others" 32 (p. 153), a sentiment which lies close to the heart of Cleary's explicit support of reading. Maureen Sanders's "Literacy as 'Passionate Attention'" moves the lens from fiction to the world with a year-long "home study" of her seven-year-old daughter Claire's emerging literacy. [page 20] Sanders's purpose is "to see how [Claire] brought her own meaning to literacy activities" as she moves through the stage of identification with characters to become a reader of the world as well as of fiction. The literature about which Claire becomes passionate is, coincidentally, Cleary's *Ramona* series. Sanders posits that Claire's love of Ramona as a character with whom she identifies leads to other reading and a deeper awareness of her own and other's cultures. Other readers of Cleary's work do not see such an explicit argument for the exemplary power of literacy as Chaston and Sanders posit, though, as I demonstrate, much of it may be deduced on the implicit level.

23. Beverly Cleary, *Beezus and Ramona,* pp. 137-141

24. *Brave,* p. 106

25. Zarrillo, p. 133

26. Beverly Cleary, *Ramona and Her Father,* p. 91

27. *Father,* pp. 156-157

28. Carol Gilligan, Nona P. Lyons, and Trudy J. Hamner, *Making Connections; The Relational World of Adolescent Girls at Emma Willard School*

29. American Association of University Women, *Shortchanging Girls, Shortchanging America: A Call to Action*

30. Mary Pipher, *Reviving Ophelia: Saving the Selves of Adolescent Girls* p.18

31. *Pest,* pp. 142, 143-144

32. *Age 8,* pp. 68-70

References

American Association of University Women, *Shortchanging Girls, Shortchanging America: A Call to Action.* Washington, DC: American Association of University Women, 1991.

Apple, Michael W., *Teachers and Texts: A Political Economy of Class and Gender Relations in Education.* New York: Routledge, 1989.

Bakhtin, M. M., *The Dialogic Imagination,* Caryl Emerson and Michael Holquist (trans.), Michael Holquist (ed.). Austin: University of Texas Press, 1981.

Chaston, Joel, "Reading as if for life: The quixotic reader in the nineteenth-century British novel." Dissertation, University of Utah, 1988.

Cleary, Beverly, *Beezus and Ramona.* New York: Avon, 1955.

Cleary, Beverly, *Henry and Beezus.* New York: Avon, 1952.

Cleary, Beverly, *Henry Huggins.* New York: Dell, 1950.

Cleary, Beverly, *Henry and the Paper Route.* New York: Dell, 1957.

Cleary, Beverly, "The Laughter of Children." *Horn Book Magazine,* 1982, *58,* 55-64.

Cleary, Beverly, *Ramona the Brave.* New York: Dell, 1975.

Cleary, Beverly, *Ramona and Her Father.* New York: Avon, 1975.

Cleary, Beverly, *Ramona the Pest.* New York: Dell, 1968.

Cleary, Beverly, *Ramona Quimby, Age 8.* New York: Avon, 1981.

Eldred, Janet Carey, and Mortensen, Peter, "Reading literacy narratives," *College English,* 1992, *88,* 512-539.

Gilligan, Carol, Lyons, Nona P., and Hamner, Trudy J., eds., *Making Connections: The Relational World of Adolescent Girls at Emma Willard School.* Cambridge: Harvard University Press, 1990.

Hilton, Mary, "'The blowing dust': Popular culture and popular culture books for children," *The Prose and the Passion: Children and Their Reading.* London: Cassell, 1994, pp. 9-19.

Mackey, Margaret, "Looking at Ramona: Reflections on form and limits." *Oregon English Journal,* 1995, *12,* 21-29.

Mackey, Margaret, "Ramona the chronotope: The young reader and social theories of narrative." *Children's Literature in Education.* 1991, *22,* 97-109.

Orenstein, Peggy, *Schoolgirls: Young Women, Self-Esteem, and the Confidence Gap.* New York: Doubleday, 1994.

Paley, Vivian Gussin, *Boys and Girls: Superheroes in the Doll Corner.* Chicago: University of Chicago Press, 1984.

Pflieger, Pat, *Beverly Cleary.* Boston: Twayne, 1991.

Pipher, Mary, *Reviving Ophelia: Saving the Selves of Adolescent Girls.* New York: Ballantine, 1994.

Sanders, Maureen. "Literacy as passionate attention." *Language Arts,* 1987, *64,* 619-633.

Smith, Lillian, *The Unreluctant Years* (1953). Chicago: American Library Association, 1991.

Smithson, Isaiah, "Review: Classrooms, cultures, and democracy." *College English,* 1994, *56, 577 - 584.*

Zarrillo, James, "Beverly Cleary, Ramona Quimby, and the teaching of reading," *Children's Literature Association Quarterly,* 1988, *16,* 131-135.

TITLE COMMENTARY

📖 *THE GROWING-UP FEET* (1987)

Publishers Weekly

SOURCE: A review of *The Growing-Up Feet,* in *Publishers Weekly,* Vol. 232, No. 9, August 28, 1987, p. 76.

Twins Janet and Jimmy are growing up so fast that Mother is sure they are ready for new shoes [in *The Growing-Up Feet*]. But at the shoe store, the twins discover their feet haven't grown up enough to require new shoes. Mr. Markle, the shoe salesman, suggests that they buy pairs of red rubber boots that will grow with their feet. The kids are so excited that they wear the new boots constantly. Father washes the car so the kids will have water to splash in and the mailman, Mr. Lemon, is gratifyingly impressed by the new boots. Cleary has created yet another charming and homey tale—and a fourth felicitous collaboration with DiSalvo-Ryan. Her pastel illustrations, with dabs of bright color (like those boots), underscore Cleary's scenes of domestic harmony.

Janet D. French

SOURCE: A review of *The Growing-Up Feet,* in *School Library Journal,* Vol. 34, No. 21, December, 1987, p. 72.

Preschool twins Janet and Jimmy are disappointed when they go to the shoe store [in *The Growing-Up Feet*] and learn that they haven't outgrown their old shoes yet; they had anticipated new shoes. When an offer of balloons doesn't ease their dismay, Mother buys boots for them instead. The boots are worn through dinner, bedtime, and breakfast. Outside in their boots, the twins are disappointed again, this time to find that there are no puddles to splash in. Now it's Daddy to the rescue; he makes puddles for the children as he washes the car. Alas, alas, the echoes here are not of Ramona, but of Dick and Jane. There is neither tension nor humor to catch a child's interest; the modest problems, if problems they are, get instant resolution from Mother and Daddy. Alas, too, for the endorsement of that common but deplorable American fix: if you're unhappy, I'll buy you something. The illustrations, in watercolors and pastel, are competent and pleasant, but curiously reflect the Dick-and-Jane ambiance of the text—pants for Jimmy, skirts on Janet.

📖 *JANET'S THINGAMAJIGS* (1987)

Publishers Weekly

SOURCE: A review of *Janet's Thingamajigs,* in *Publishers Weekly,* Vol. 231, No. 3, January 23, 1987, p. 68.

In this third picture book about twins Janet and Jimmy [*Janet's Thingamajigs*], Cleary's sure ear for the dialogue of young children is evident. Janet collects small objects which she calls "thingamajigs," (mimicking her mother's expression) and keeps in paper bags in her crib. Jimmy wants badly to touch Janet's things; Janet passionately doesn't want him to do so. Readers, both children and adults, will recognize the true-to-life quality of the twins' bickering and of their mother's exasperation. The problem is resolved as both children voluntarily give up the now babyish thingamajigs when their cribs are replaced by real, "grown-up" beds. [DyAnne] DiSalvo-Ryan's cheery, colorful pencil-and-wash pictures suit the tone of the story exactly.

Susan Helper

SOURCE: A review of *Janet's Thingamajigs*, in *School Library Journal*, Vol. 33, No. 3, March, 1987, p. 142.

The reissue of **Two Dog Biscuits** and **The Real Hole** (both Morrow, 1986) introduced four year olds Janet and Jimmy to a new generation of readers. This new story [*Janet's Thingamajigs*] about the twins portrays sibling squabbles as a part of growing up. Janet likes to collect little treasures and resents Jimmy's handling them. When their mother suggests to Janet that she bag them and put them in a special place, Janet chooses her crib. As the crib fills up and bags begin to spill out of the bars, the day is saved when a surprise—new twin beds—arrives. The bags are forgotten as the twins celebrate a milestone in growing up. DiSalvo-Ryan's full-color pencil-and-watercolor illustrations, large enough to be seen by a group of young listeners, depict the commonplace with warmth. Soft frames are broken occasionally by hands or toys. Two additional strengths are a patient but firm mother and the reassurance of seeing real children, instead of bears or bunnies, dealing with some of the skirmishes of family life.

📖 *A GIRL FROM YAMHILL* (1988)

Mary M. Burns

SOURCE: A review of *A Girl from Yamhill: A Memoir*, in *Horn Book Magazine*, Vol. 64, No. 3, May-June, 1988, pp. 369-70.

Revealing, sensitive, compelling—these are the adjectives which instantly come to mind when reading the remarkable autobiography [*A Girl from Yamhill: A Memoir*]. Yet, in comparison with its unassuming power, they are simply reviewer's clichés. Like Beverly Cleary's tales of childhood, the book speaks directly to the heart with no grandiose style, no pretentious imagery. Candid yet controlled, it demonstrates a kind of courage tempered with grace not often found in today's books, whether for children or adults. It immediately makes one understand why Cleary's books are perennial favorites: they are based on genuine emotion, deeply felt but never exploited. Incidents and details later incorporated into her stories are readily identified: there was a Klickitat Street in Portland, Oregon, where the family moved after farming in Yamhill became economically impossible, and Cleary, then Beverly Bunn, with that creative curiosity so often misunderstood by adults, is the prototype for Ramona. The hardships of the Depression years are eloquently recalled—her father making a razor blade last one year by sharpening it on a glass, the tensions building within the family as jobs become harder to find, the efforts to refurbish used clothing for a growing child. Later these recollections would be transferred to the Quimbys in the Ramona stories, becoming universal experiences, undiminished by time. Most revealing, however, and most painful to encounter, is the author's relationship with her mother. Mabel Atlee Bunn, "a classic figure of the westward emigration movement, the little schoolmarm from the East who stepped off a train in the West to teach school," was also the classic example of a possessive mother who attempted to model her daughter and her daughter's life according to peculiar and difficult standards. She bears little resemblance to Mrs. Quimby, who is much more accessible and understanding. Perhaps, like Louisa May Alcott, who created in Father March a parent she never knew in real life, Cleary formed, from observations of other families, the kind of mother she would like to have had. Certainly, one would never suspect that Ramona or Beezus would have to plead for demonstrations of affection, as did the young Beverly Cleary when, as a fifth-grader, she observed how other children were treated: "I confronted Mother and informed her, 'Some mothers kiss their little girls.' Mother laughed, pulled me to her, and gave me a hug and a kiss—a sweet isolated moment. It was never repeated." In writing the memoir, which traces her life from the early days at Yamhill to her departure for California and college, Cleary is never condemnatory. Rather, the voice is still that of the child and later the young girl who, although bewildered, remained spunky, determined, and alert, who indeed lived up to the spirit of her "pioneer ancestors." A wonderful book.

Judith F. Sheriff

SOURCE: A review of *A Girl from Yamhill: A Memoir,* in *Voice of Youth Advocates,* Vol. 11, No. 2, June, 1988, p. 100.

Generations of young people have read Cleary's books and wondered about the life of the author who created them. Now they have their answer. Cleary's memoir [*A Girl from Yamhill: A Memoir*] is every bit as delightful to read as her stories. We read about her own misapprehensions and fears as a child, about her move from the farm to Portland, about her curious and adventuresome nature as a preschooler and her compliance and anger with parental authority as a teen, about the impact of the Depression on her family's life (especially the toll it takes on her mother's spirit and the corresponding difficulty for Beverly), about school experiences which alternately stifled and encouraged her creativity, and about her parents' very low-key and non-physical love for her, creating comparative security but little warmth.

We also read about her first attempts to put ink on a white surface (handprints on her mother's linen tablecloth), her love of reading and storytelling, her first attempts at creative writing in school, her mother's campaign for a local library with a circulating collection from the Oregon State Library, her insistence until third grade that reading alone was something that was only to be done in school, her belief as a high school senior that writing could not provide her with a living and that she would be doomed to a dull office job, and her frustration at not being able to find funny books about real people to read.

We learn all this and much more, but the memoir ends as Beverly, almost miraculously, is leaving on a bus for junior college. Surely there is a second installment in preparation! What was life like when she finally got away from home? How did she begin writing "for real"? We *must* know more—and the story is best told by Cleary herself. This is a must for library collections serving YAs and adults and is a sure nomination for the Best Books list.

MUGGIE MAGGIE (1990)

Melanie Guile

SOURCE: A review of *Muggie Maggie,* in *Magpies,* Vol. 8, No. 1, March, 1993, p. 28.

Maggie, "a contrary kid", finds her stand against "joined-up writing" getting out of hand as parents, teachers, headmaster and psychologist are consulted

in turn. When she writes her signature with her left hand as an act of defiance and it comes out "Muggie", Maggie knows she is done for. She is "Muggie Maggie" from then on. The cunning device adopted to help her break her own proud deadlock makes entertaining reading. As an added bonus, *Muggie Maggie* could just help young readers master the jump from print to hand writing, since crucial bits of the text are written, not typed, and the plot is a powerful incentive to understand them. This, together with Cleary's usual light, ironic humour and deft dialogue make it a good choice for readers.

Jennifer Taylor

SOURCE: A review of *Muggie Maggie,* in *The School Librarian,* Vol. 40, No. 3, August, 1992, p. 100.

Maggie, who is in the third year [in *Muggie Maggie*], is Clever and Talented: she can read the print in books, and uses the computer at home for writing letters. But she can't see the point of joined up writing, and takes a stand against learning how to do it. Once embarked on her rebellion, she feels she has to stand firm, and spends the time during Mrs Leeper's lessons drawing doodles. When her father convinces her that even printed letters require a signature, she produces a signature of sorts, but her name turns out looking like 'Muggie', which her schoolmates find hilarious. Mrs Leeper is an imaginative teacher and she finds a surefire way of making Maggie want to read and write joined up writing. A simple story, made enjoyable by Maggie's spirited resistance, which will have obvious relevance for reluctant performers; it is well served by Anthony Lewis's line drawings.

STRIDER (1991)

Heide Piehler

SOURCE: A review of *Strider,* in *School Library Journal,* Vol. 37, No. 9, September, 1991, p. 250.

Gr 4-7—Leigh Botts, the protagonist of the Newbery winner *Dear Mr. Henshaw* (Morrow, 1983), is once again recording his thoughts on paper [in *Strider*]. While cleaning his room, he discovers his old diary and is inspired to start writing again. Now 14, he is still dealing with some of the same issues from earlier days—his parents' divorce, concerns about his father's sincerity and financial stability, and insecurities about his own identity and popularity. He also has a few new worries—namely Geneva, a girl, and Strider, a dog. Leigh and his friend Barry find the abandoned pooch on the beach and decide to try "joint custody." It is not the perfect arrangement. Because Leigh's attachment to Strider fills the emotional voids in his life, he becomes reluctant to share him. Eventually, the two boys work through the tensions that threaten their friendship. At the same time, Leigh and his father develop a new understanding. Although the story is centered around Leigh's relationship with Strider, this is more than just "a boy and his dog" book. Cleary's talent for portraying the details of everyday life—both small and significant—is evident here. Her characters are unique individuals and "every children" at the same time. *Strider* lacks the subtle poignancy found in *Dear Mr. Henshaw,* and some readers may find Leigh's interest and responses more appropriate for an 11 or 12 year old than a 14 year old, but Cleary's fans will relate to his challenges and triumphs—whether or not they've read the first title.

Mary M. Burns

SOURCE: A review of *Strider,* in *Horn Book Magazine,* Vol. 67, No. 5, September-October, 1991, pp. 595-96.

Once again, Beverly Cleary proves that she is in complete harmony with the world view of children and adolescents, that she can suggest their diction, articulate their dreams and fears, and create believable, rounded characters without becoming intrusive or manipulative. Leigh Botts, the central character in the Newbery Medal-winning *Dear Mr. Henshaw* is now fourteen. In the opening chapter [of *Strider*], he discovers the diary he kept when he and his mother first moved to Pacific Grove. As he muses over the years which have intervened since he was the new boy in town, the background for the present book is skillfully introduced; therefore, it can be read as an independent entity—a difficult test of any author's storytelling ability. The hurt left by his parents' divorce has not yet fully diminished, nor has his desire for a better home than the landlady's euphemistically described "charming garden cottage." He is also worried about his future. But suddenly these pent-up feelings are subordinated when the abandoned dog he names Strider comes into his life. Commanded to "stay" by its owner, the dog had remained alone on

the beach for two days, refusing to quit its post until befriended by Leigh and his friend Barry. The boys work out a joint custody arrangement designed to thwart objections from the Botts's landlady, but, in his heart, Leigh longs for the dog with an intensity unmatched in recent children's fiction. His feelings are almost palpable, dominating the mood of the story, but never miring it in sentimentality. Indeed, the development of the narrative is vintage Beverly Cleary, an inimitable blend of comic and poignant moments. It is in caring for Strider that Leigh passes from childhood into adolescence: achieving his personal best on the track team, finding a place for himself among his peers, and finally adjusting to his parents' separation. Perhaps the whole wonderful book is best summarized in Leigh's final diary entry: "My dog and I have changed since last summer. . . . I know that I'll just work to beat my own time until I get wherever it is I decide to go. As in track, I'll probably win some and lose some."

PETEY'S BEDTIME STORY (1993)

Publishers Weekly

SOURCE: A review of *Petey's Bedtime Story,* in *Publishers Weekly,* Vol. 240, No. 28, July 12, 1993, p. 80.

Petey is a kid who actually likes bedtime—even if he never quite gets to bed [in *Petey's Bedtime Story*]. The energetic boy splashes wildly in his bath before bounding into the lap of his sleepy mother for a bedtime story. After his yawning father reads him yet another one, the boy induces his patient parents to search under the bed for monsters and to listen to an endless recitation of prayers in which he blesses everyone he knows and says good night to each object in his room. And *then* he demands that they recount the events of the night he was born. When his father suggests that Petey tell the story this time, the child embellishes it with made-up details that young readers will relish—when he was born, he reports, he "was wearing a bow tie and cowboy boots." Because his parents are sound asleep when he finishes his tale, Petey climbs out of bed, heads to the kitchen for a box of cookies and devours them all in his parents' bed, leaving plenty of crumbs. Cleary's text is as buoyant and amiable as its hero, and both his real and fabricated antics are captured cleverly in Small's (*Imogene's Antlers*) stylized pen-and-ink and watercolor pictures, which have an appealing 1950s flavor.

Norine Odland

SOURCE: A review of *Petey's Bedtime Story,* in *The Five Owls,* Vol. 8, No. 3, January-February, 1994, p. 58.

Critics have praised Beverly Cleary as the best writer of dialogue in children's books today, and *Petey's Bedtime Story* is no exception to that observation. Even when reading it for the first time silently, the reader can hear Petey and his parents.

The routine of bedtime will be recognized by children who like to procrastinate. First the bath is finished, but Petey starts to run around the table for one delay. Because it is storytime, Petey does slow down. His mother reads a book about an alligator, and his father reads Petey's favorite book about four baby gophers. By now Petey's parents are tired and yawning, but their son is ready to run and play. He says good night to all his stuffed animals and says his prayers, asking for blessings on everyone he can think of, including the children in his nursery school (except for those who throw sand). Finally, he goes to bed for what he thinks is the best part, the story about the time he was born. Daddy's version of the story is directed by Petey so often that Daddy decides Petey should tell the story. In typical child-like imagination, he tells the story in multiple crises. Petey heard that his mother was taken away in a wheelchair; he thought that was exciting because she would be racing up and down the corridors announcing why she was there. The exaggeration really explodes toward the end of the story when baby Petey arrives wearing a bow tie and cowboy boots.

Parents may not appreciate the final antic, when the parents are asleep in Petey's room and he goes downstairs for a box of cookies and eats them in his parent's bed. The pictures tell the story well; action and humor are present in both pictures and story. There are many clues to the fact that Petey's story comes from his imagination, helping readers understand what's real and what's make-believe. Children from ages two to six are amused and intrigued by the book.

MY OWN TWO FEET (1995)

Kirkus Reviews

SOURCE: A review of *My Own Two Feet: A Memoir,* in *Kirkus Reviews,* Vol. 63, No. 13, July 1, 1995, p. 944.

Continuing her memoirs, begun so successfully in *The Girl From Yamhill* (1988), Cleary here covers [in *My Own Two Feet: A Memoir*] the eventful years that began with her boarding a bus for junior college in California and ended with the publication of her first children's book in 1946. In between she attended the University of California at Berkeley, received a degree in library science, met Clarence Cleary (there is little doubt about the outcome of that romance), worked as a librarian in smalltown Yakima, Washington, in army posts during WW II, and in a book shop for four Christmas rushes in a row. With lively wit, Cleary recounts her many amusing experiences—such as her confusion over being told to count the "little brown things" in the bookstore before the arrival of the Little, Brown sales representative. She never minces words when describing her occasional failures or the strained relations with her parents. In the end, she writes the story of a boy named Henry Huggins; the rest—and we hope it's forthcoming in another installment—is children's book history.

The writer brings the same verve to her own story that has made her fiction classic for nearly 50 years. In her, readers will find a character worthy of even Cleary's imagination.

Bulletin of the Center for Children's Books

SOURCE: A review of *My Own Two Feet,* in *The Bulletin of the Center for Children's Books,* Vol. 49, No. 1, September, 1995, p. 10.

Beverly Bunn leaves home for college in this sequel [*My Own Two Feet: A Memoir*] to the first volume of Cleary's autobiography, *A Girl from Yamhill.* Life in Southern California is a blessed change for Beverly, free—mostly—from her mother's strictures and interference, and as the title says, on her own two feet. With little financial assistance from home, Beverly finds all kinds of jobs, such as babysitting, library work and dress-shortening, to support her tenaciously sought education, which takes her from Chaffey Junior College to Berkeley (where she meets Clarence Cleary) and then to library school at the University of Washington: "Fortunately, memories of the Ontario Public Library reassured me that being a librarian was more interesting than learning to be one." Along with its appeal as a portrait of a beloved author, the book is also a fine example of that thing that used to be called a "college novel," which younger teens would read to look toward the future. There is nothing sentimental about Cleary's memories, but there's plenty of clear-eyed honesty and low-key wit that demonstrate one of this author's greatest gifts—to be able to write for both an adult and juvenile audience without losing the respect or attention of either.

📖 *RAMONA'S WORLD* (1999)

Kirkus Reviews

SOURCE: A review of *Ramona's World,* in *Kirkus Reviews,* Vol. 67, No. 13, July 1, 1999, p. 1052.

Ramona returns [in ***Ramona's World***], and she's as feisty as ever, now nine-going-on-ten (or "zeroteen," as she calls it). Her older sister Beezus is in high school, baby-sitting, getting her ears pierced, and going to her first dance, and now they have a younger baby sister, Roberta. Cleary picks up on all the details of fourth grade, from comparing hand calluses to the distribution of little plastic combs by the school photographer. This year Ramona is trying to improve her spelling, and Cleary is especially deft at limning the emotional nuances as Ramona fails and succeeds, goes from sad to happy, and from hurt to proud. The grand finale is Ramona's birthday party in the park, complete with a cake frosted in whipped cream. Despite a brief mention of nose piercing, Cleary's writing still reflects a secure middle-class family and untroubled school life, untouched by the classroom violence or the broken families of the 1990s. While her book doesn't match what's in the newspapers, it's a timeless, serene alternative for children, especially those with less than happy realities.

Enicia Fisher

SOURCE: A review of *Ramona's World,* in *Christian Science Monitor,* Vol. 91, No. 190, August 26, 1999, p. 21.

Don't kick the summer reading habit: Beverly Cleary has written the perfect accompaniment to back-to-school days.*"Ramona's World"* stars that spunky gal loved by several generations.

Ramona knows that fourth grade is going to be "the best year of her life, so far." She's excited to show off her playground calluses and to share the news of her baby sister.

But while Mrs. Quimby is absorbed in reading*"Moby Dick"* for her book club, Ramona soon embarks on an epic struggle with her own nemesis: spelling.

School isn't only about work, of course. Ramona gets a crush on old friend, Yard Ape, and she experiences the joy of making a new best friend. She and Daisy share the triumph of writing a reprimand to a company that printed "gonna" and "shoulda" in their newspaper ad.

While big sister Beezus, now in high school, learns fancy French words and sneaks off to the mall to get her ears pierced, Ramona is impressed with her own grown-up role as big sister to baby Roberta.

Chaos erupts when Mrs. Quimby entrusts the baby to Ramona's care while she leaves on a quick errand. In a brief 15 minutes, Ramona has to deal with the cat hacking up a hair ball and then rescue baby Roberta, who gets her head stuck in the kitty condo.

New and old friends of Ramona will love to join in her journey as she approaches "zeroteen" and quickly learns more than Ahab ever did about facing challenges.

Fans will hope Cleary and illustrator Alan Tiegreen continue their portraits of Ramona as she enters her teenage years.

Additional coverage of Cleary's life and career is contained in the following sources published by the Gale Group: *Authors and Artists for Young Adults,* Vol. 6; *DISCovering Authors,* Vol. 3; *Dictionary of Literary Biography,* Vol. 52; *Junior DISCovering Authors; Major Authors and Illustrators for Children and Young Adults; Major 20th-Century Writers,* Vols. 1, 2; *Something about the Author,* Vols. 2, 43, 79; *Something about the Author Autobiography Series,* Vol. 20.

Louise Fitzhugh
1928-1974

American author of books for pre-teens.

Major works include *Harriet the Spy* (1964), *The Long Secret* (1965), *Nobody's Family is Going to Change* (1974), *Sport* (1979).

For further information on Fitzhugh's life and works, see *CLR,* Volume 1.

Major work about Fitzhugh: *Louise Fitzhugh* (Virginia L. Wolf, 1991).

INTRODUCTION

Called one of the most original and ground-breaking books of the 1960s, Louise Fitzhugh's *Harriet the Spy* heralded a new genre of novels for children when it was published in 1964. A pioneering book, it marked the true beginning of modern, realistic fiction for children, even though many of the characters (especially the adults) are caricatures. The situations the children are involved in, the conflicting emotions they feel, and the resolutions they grow into—often unromantic and harsh—are experiences and feelings that children encounter in the real world. Fitzhugh's children are portraits of intelligent, imaginative, lonely, urban children living with the emotional anguish of the contemporary American child. *Harriet the Spy* won no awards and caused great controversy among critics, most of whom entirely missed its main point. Children immediately recognized the honesty in *Harriet,* however, and it has become a best seller.

BIOGRAPHICAL INFORMATION

Fitzhugh was born in Memphis, Tennessee, to a wealthy, dysfunctional family. Her parents divorced when she was very young; afterward she lived with her father, who worked in an important position in state government. Her childhood was unhappy, and she was horrified by the racial prejudice she observed around her. She hated the South, and left it as soon as she was able. She attended several schools, studying literature and art, and provided her own illustrations for her books. Her life was peripatetic. She

traveled in Europe, studied painting for a year in Italy, and lived in Washington, D.C., New York, the north shore of New York's Long Island, and Bridgeport, Connecticut.

Fitzhugh's writing career was spotty—she pursued it inconsistently—but her small output was considered by critics to be brilliant. Her first publication, in 1961, was *Suzuki Beane,* for which she was the illustrator. Fitzhugh brought the draft for her first novel, *Harriet the Spy,* to Charlotte Zolotow, senior editor at Harper and Row, and although it was not yet a novel, Zolotow saw the possibilities for something extraordinary. She encouraged Fitzhugh and helped her turn her notes into the finished book that was published in 1964. Ten years later, just eight days before the publication of her third book, *Nobody's Family is Going to Change,* Fitzhugh died of a ruptured aneurysm. She was laid to rest in Bridgeport according to her instructions that she be buried north of the Mason-

Dixon line. Several volumes of her work have been published posthumously, but none have ever achieved either the critical or popular success of *Harriet the Spy.*

MAJOR WORKS

Harriet the Spy is about eleven-year-old aspiring writer Harriet, who, neglected by her busy parents, watches people and writes down what she sees and thinks in the notebook she constantly carries. When her notebook is discovered by her friends and they learn the unpleasant (although honest) things she has written about them, Harriet can no longer be a mere observer, but must take action. As Harriet's world begins to fall apart around her, she finds herself in a moral predicament that requires her to readjust her ideas about herself and her relationship to others. Her faithful companion and nurse, Old Golly, advises her to lie and apologize to get her friends back, providing Harriet with a key to enter the adult world. Because *Harriet the Spy* discussed subjects normally avoided in children's books, many critics disliked it. A child who was "not nice," living among adults and children with all too realistically negative personal traits, was considered a less than perfect heroine for a children's book. Harriet's honesty was too much of a reversal for some critics to understand, and the book was often misinterpreted. Children, however, immediately loved it, and provided testimonials to its having been a pivotal book in many of their lives.

With a theme of "no person ever really knows another," *The Long Secret* is a sequel to *Harriet the Spy,* although it features as its main character one of Harriet's friends, Beth Ellen the Mouse. It is summer, and someone is writing poison-pen letters. When Harriet visits Beth Ellen, they embark on an attempt to try to solve the mystery, and Harriet discovers, to her horror, that Beth Ellen herself is the culprit, bringing Harriet to the conclusion that shy people are angry people. Included in this work is a beautifully written discussion about menstruation, the first mention of the subject ever made in a book for children.

Nobody's Family is Going to Change was published eight days after Fitzhugh's death. In it, she attacks stereotypes, racism, and sexism. Emma Sheriden is black and fat and wants to be a lawyer like her father. Her brother Willie wants to be a dancer. Her conventional parents support neither child and her father is particularly contemptuous of them both. The children are repressed as a means to protect them from preju-

dice as their parents strive to master the values of white middle class society. Eventually, Willie gets his dance lessons and Emma accepts the fact that her father doesn't like her. She realizes that "people are who they are and don't change," but that she has the power to change herself.

Sport, published posthumously, is about another of Harriet's friends. Deserted by his nasty mother when he was small, Sport has inherited money and thereby attracted her attention again. His father has remarried a woman Sport likes and wants to stay with. During the book, Sport shows that he is tough, and that he knows himself and can take care of himself. He survives because of his own resourcefulness, as well as the support of his father and friends.

AWARDS

Fitzhugh was posthumously awarded the Children's Rights Workshop Other Award in 1976.

GENERAL COMMENTARY

Kathy Bird

SOURCE: "The Value of Individualism," in *Elementary English,* Vol. 50, No. 5, May, 1973, pp. 707-14.

Miss Fitzhugh's book, **Harriet the Spy,** tells of impersonal city life and [the] effect this environment has on the individual. The story is about Harriet M. Welsch who wants to be a writer. She constantly carries her spy book around in which she writes important or interesting observations about people and life in general. Through Harriet's observations, Miss Fitzhugh exemplifies to the reader that city life has, to a large degree, rendered the definition of individualism, unviable. Harriet, like many Americans today, feels the self-assuredness of the frontiersman. If she endeavors to do so, she can achieve any goal without hindrance from others. Harriet reveals her self-confidence as she writes, "I will be the best spy there ever was and I will know everything. Everything."[1] Harriet, however, soon finds that she must rely on other people for the attainment of her goals.

Harriet's spy book, full of honest but often derogatory comments about her friends, is found by one of her classmates. For weeks after the incident no one speaks to Harriet. Her father entirely submerged in his business, and her mother preoccupied with social functions, offers her little comfort. Miss Fitzhugh, here, exposes parental neglect and family disorganization as another sad product of city life. The dissolution of the close family unit of the past, she relates to the strong class order demanding unwavering occupational and social loyalty.

Harriet finally finds help because of a letter from her past nurse maid, Ole Golly. Ole Golly advised Harriet to apologize. She writes, "Remember that writing is to put love in the world not to use against your friends. But to yourself you must always be true."[2] Through this bit of wisdom, Miss Fitzhugh excellently describes the place of the individual in today's world. One's individuality must be compromised outwardly to a small degree to accommodate other people, but one must always remain true to oneself. The days of the self-made man surrounded by unlimited opportunities are gone. Although Miss Fitzhugh continues to reinforce the past value of individual worth and creativity, she also emphasizes the important role that other people play in the attainment of an individual's goal in today's world.

Contemporary authors realize the increasing isolation and separation of certain groups within the city, and much of the current literature concerns life in the ghetto. The city has been grouped into blocks of people; membership in these blocks is determined by such criteria as money, education, race, and occupation. Joseph D. Lohman says in a paper given at Southern California Conference on Human Relations Education that "all of us [Americans] are in some measure estranged and alienated from the whole."[3] It is evident, however, that those ranked by members of the community as being inferior feel more estranged and alienated than other accepted groups.

Contemporary authors have seen a change in American living, and its adverse effect on individualism. The problem is man-made, thus the solution must lie with people. All the current books discussed exalt the value of individualism. They agree that it is worth maintaining, but feel it must be redefined in terms of people. The current authors stress the fact that love and security are essential in providing an individual with the will to survive and achieve. Love seems to be the only force powerful enough to fight a highly uniform, impersonal society and to promote the worth of each individual. The literature treated also stressed cooperation and understanding as necessary compo-

nents in dealing with other people. One must get along with people, for they determine to a large degree an individual's success or failure in the realization of his goal.

Throughout the history of American children's literature, individualism has been praised. Individualism has indeed become so real to the American people that it is thought of as a way of life rather than a value guiding lives. The value of individualism up to this day is constantly being reinforced in children's literature. Contemporary works, however, have attempted to redefine individualism so it may be applied more meaningfully to America today.

Notes

1. Louise Fitzhugh, *Harriet the Spy* (New York, 1964), p. 121.

2. Ibid., p. 183.

3. Joseph D. Lohman, "Significant Changes in Our Society: Their Impact on Youth; Their Implications for Education," *Patterns of Power: Social Foundations of Education,* eds. Thomas E. Linton and Jack L. Nelson (New York, 1968), p. 324.

Virginia L. Wolf

SOURCE: "*Harriet the Spy*: Milestone, Masterpiece?" in *Children's Literature,* Vol. 4, 1975, pp. 120-26.

Ten years after the publication of Louise Fitzhugh's **Harriet the Spy,** there remains considerable uneasiness about the novel's status as literature. Ms. Fitzhugh, who was also the author of a sequel, **The Long Secret** (1965), and the co-author with Sandra Scoppettone of **Suzuki Beane** (1961) and **Bang, Bang, You're Dead** (1969), died on November 19, 1974. On the publication of **Harriet,** she was called "one of the brightest talents of 1964."[1] Several short reviews praised the novel for its vigor and originality.[2] On the other hand, in the most extensive review which the book received, Ruth Hill Viguers objected strongly to its "disagreeable people and situations" and questioned its "realism" and its suitability for children.[3]

Today, now that many books are even more overt and harsh in their criticism of contemporary society, such objections are less common.[4] To my knowledge, critics have only briefly and rarely mentioned the novel in recent years. The only prize it has ever received is the Sequoyah Award in 1967, given by the children of Oklahoma. It has been a perennial best-seller for both Harper and Dell. It would seem that the novel survives principally because children are devoted to it. *The Arbuthnot Anthology* does recognize the novel as a milestone of children's literature, praising it as "contemporaneous" and implying that it is a forerunner of those more recent novels valuable for their immediate social relevance.[5] However, since no book ever survives for very long on the basis of its contemporaneousness, such praise is at best a dubious honor.

The novel can be read as social criticism. It is, on one level, an illuminating portrait of contemporary, urban, American life. Harriet's parents are so caught up in their own lives that they do not get to know their own daughter until she is eleven years old. The Robinsons sit in stony silence when alone together and come alive only when they have a chance to display their latest acquisition to a visitor. The Dei Santi family's preoccupation with their store prevents their understanding of one of their sons. The rich divorcee Agatha Plummer retreats to her bed in order to get attention. Harrison Withers lives alone in two rooms with his bird cages and his twenty some cats, trying to outwit the Health Department. The image which arises is one of a fast-paced, materialistic, complex society in which individuals are isolated in their own private worlds.

This isolation results in a failure of communication and consequently in a scarcity of meaningful human relationships. It results in a misunderstanding of unique individuals such as Harrison Withers and Harriet while it encourages conformity. Harriet's world is full of people who have no real understanding of their own special interests or abilities. This is especially evident of her classmates. Pinky Whitehead is a nonentity. Marion Hawthorne and Rachel Hennessey merely ape their mothers. In Harriet's words, "THEY ARE JUST BATS. HALF OF THEM DON'T EVEN HAVE A PROFESSION."[6] Living by means of pretense, the people of Harriet's world are afraid to hear or to seek the truth.

To read the novel as social criticism, however, is to see it in only one dimension. To read it as simply a socially relevant message is to ignore its structure. In its form, the novel is reminiscent of many contemporary adult novels which are constructed on the premise that reality is inevitably a matter of individual perception.[7] In such novels, our experience of

the fictive world is structured by the point of view from which the novel is told. Perceiving, thinking, and feeling as one character does, we learn more about him or her than we do about the world which he or she describes. In other words, limiting us to Harriet's point of view, **Harriet the Spy** is fundamentally a thorough characterization of Harriet.[8] The enveloping point of view is, for the most part, third person, telling us what Harriet feels and thinks but emphasizing what she does, sees, and hears. The notebook entries, which are in the first person, record her actual language and reveal the content and thinking process of her mind. Each point of view enriches the other. The notebook entries reveal the limitations of Harriet's mind as a vehicle for understanding her world, and that which we see over her shoulder, as it were, fleshes out our understanding of the nature and sources of these limitations, allowing us to perceive both her and her world more fully than she does.

The previous description of contemporary society is not Harriet's. We obtain it by synthesizing bits and pieces of what we see by means of Harriet. Furthermore, this portrait of her world allows us insight into Harriet which she only gradually and then only intuitively possesses. We are allowed to see the extent to which this world has shaped and inhibited her. Harriet, too, is virtually isolated from intimacy with other people. This explains her need for window-peeping and writing in her notebooks. Given her environment, these activities are her only opportunities for self-discovery and growth. Imaginatively and ingeniously, she attempts to break out of her isolation, as a spy.

Harriet is, of course, unconscious of this way in which her environment has influenced her. As her notebook entries reveal, she understands herself on a much more superficial level. Ole Golly, her nurse, has given her faith in herself and an enthusiasm for knowing life and for finding her own way:

> OLE GOLLY SAYS THERE IS AS MANY WAYS TO LIVE AS THERE ARE PEOPLE ON THE EARTH AND I SHOULDN'T GO ROUND WITH BLINDERS BUT SHOULD SEE EVERY WAY I CAN. THEN I'LL KNOW WHAT WAY I WANT TO LIVE AND NOT JUST LIVE LIKE MY FAMILY. (p. 32)

With naive self-confidence and extraordinary energy, Harriet attempts to follow this advice. Finding her sources of information limited, she sets up her spy route. So often puzzled by what she observes, she communicates her opinions and questions to a notebook, frequently with a notation such as "THINK ABOUT THAT" (p. 141). Her notebook entries reveal, on the one hand, that she is engaged in self-discovery, learning what she likes and dislikes in the process of honestly stating her responses to what she sees. On the other hand, they are a record of mind unfettered by sympathy and almost totally self-absorbed. Seen through Harriet, the world is no more than a spy-route, no more than a place and an opportunity for amusement and knowledge. Furthermore, in this role, Harriet is no more than a spy. She is an observer rather than a participant. While she is exposed to many different life styles, her experience is only vicarious. She can learn to be honest with herself, but she cannot learn to share. She can learn to evaluate but only to a lesser degree to empathize.

The key to the limitations of Harriet's quest for knowledge occurs very early in the novel with Ole Golly's quotation of a passage from Dostoievsky:

> Love all God's creation, the whole and every grain of sand in it. Love every leaf, every ray of God's light. Love the animals, love the plants, love everything. If you love everything, you will perceive the divine mystery in things. Once you perceive it, you will begin to comprehend it better every day. And you will come at last to love the whole world with an all-embracing love. (pp. 22, 24).

Harriet translates this in terms of her own egocentric experience of the world: "'I want to know everything, everything,' screeched Harriet suddenly, lying back and bouncing up and down on the bed. 'Everything in the world, everything, everything'" (p. 24).

The novel portrays the process whereby Harriet begins to learn to love. Her experience with life for eleven years has been almost totally selfcentered; it has been a process of imbibing rather than of giving. It is not until she loses Ole Golly, her notebook, and finally her friends that she is forced to give a little. Isolated and misunderstood, she is directly confronted with her need for people and by the demand to conform. At first, she meets this demand head on, refusing to give an inch. She forces her parents to find a way of understanding her, and she finally relents only after Ole Golly's letter arrives. By the end of the novel, we must feel that Harriet has moved closer to the human community and that she has done so by accepting that "OLE GOLLY IS RIGHT. SOMETIMES YOU HAVE TO LIE" (p. 297).

Many adults have been horrified by this piece of advice, yet quite simply and straight-forwardly it states a fact of existence with which all children must come

to terms. Negative criticism, especially from a child, usually evokes hostility, and children therefore learn to repress their disagreement and dislike. Unfortunately, in the process of doing so, many, out of fear or guilt, lose touch with these feelings. Having done so, their critical abilities and their trust in their own perceptions are, to varying degrees, lost. They learn to conform, to accept the other person's perception. They become the boring and bored Marion Hawthornes and Robinsons of this world. The beauty of Ole Golly's advice is that it does not question Harriet's truth. It allows her to retain her own individual identity.

Harriet's ability to empathize is still not fully developed at the end of the novel. She is still to some extent locked in her own world. But she has grown. She has learned how to be an onion; she has written a story about Harrison Withers; and in the closing scene of the novel, she is able to imagine what it is like to be Sport and Janie. "She made herself walk in Sport's shoes, feeling the holes in his socks rub against his ankles. She pretended she had an itchy nose when Janie put one abstracted hand up to scratch. She felt what it would feel like to have freckles and yellow hair like Janie, then funny ears and skinny shoulders like Sport" (p. 297).

The novel gives us the experience of Harriet's inner growth. Ultimately, then, it is psychological realism. Realizing this, we should be able to understand why the charge that the novel lacks realism is false or, better, irrelevant.[9] The novel does not attempt to portray reality fully or journalistically. It is rooted in Harriet's experience, and that is a limited experience. If, then, characters seem like caricatures or types, this is justified. We can only experience them when and as Harriet does. The merits of this limited point of view result from the distortion it causes.

In addition to characterizing Harriet, this structural device is the source of the novel's criticism of contemporary urban American society. I do not mean to imply that Harriet is merely Ms. Fitzhugh's mouthpiece. As we have seen, Harriet is often incapable of understanding those whom she observes. Her judgments are simply her emotional reactions to particular individuals. It is not what Harriet says which is the source of our understanding. It is Harriet's quest, her attempt to observe as many ways of life as she can for the sake of finding her own way. Experiencing life with Harriet, we are repeatedly engaged in evaluating a vast range of people in terms of Harriet's likes and dislikes. This process sets up a

ments fall into her. She felt the frustration, the help-lessness, the rage. She wanted to cry, feeling it. She felt like a nothing" (pp. 193-94). She concludes that she loses because it pleases her father, because she wants him to love her and he won't.

I endorse the validity of this perception. We see that Mr. Sheridan must control. His investment in his family is for the sake of proving his strength and rightness. He cannot love either of his children for what they are. They must be what he wants. Emma, unable to be what he wants, overeats, isolates herself, and fantasizes to compensate for her need for approval and to express her anger because she fails to get it. But this anger is turned inward in fear and denial of the rejection which she daily experiences. Such a response to her family is self-destructive. She is a loser. Emma's final realization—"they're not going to change, I have to change" (p. 221)—holds out the only hope.

There is some distortion caused by limiting us to Emma's perspective. Families do change; her parents might be forced to change in response to her change. Furthermore, an adult might be more sympathetic toward the Sheridans, recognizing the source of their present mistakes in their painful childhoods. But if Emma's perception is not whole, it is nevertheless valid.

Louise Fitzhugh's great strength as a novelist is her remarkable insight into the psychodynamics of human relationships and their effects upon children. What Emma learns is what Harriet learns from Ole Golly: a person must find out who she is, be herself, and not just live like her family. Indeed Ms. Fitzhugh's exploration of the necessity for self-love and self-determination is a most fascinating aspect of all her work. She doesn't pull any punches in this novel. Emma's truth is a harsh one, but I am convinced it is the only one worth offering a child in Emma's position, and I believe there are many children similarly enmeshed in hopeless and self-destructive struggles to change their parents.

However, I am not convinced that Emma is capable of perceiving this truth. I am not convinced that the novel establishes that she has sufficient ego strength for doing so. Harriet has Ole Golly's support and guidance over a considerable number of years. I can believe that Harriet can insist upon and verbalize her need for self-discovery and self-determination. For this is what Ole Golly taught her. Ole Golly, like a good parent, gave Harriet permission, gave her lov-

ing approval for her essentially selfish preoccupation with herself. We can believe that Harriet, without guilt or anger, would be able to be honest with herself. There is no Ole Golly in Emma's life and no similar source of approval and support. From where has she gained sufficient faith in herself to be able to love herself in the face of her parents' failure to do so? Her contacts with her peers are new and only tentatively supportive. She, in fact, is more supportive of them than they are of her.

The capacity for psychological insight in this novel is hers and hers alone. Where did she get it? How did she break through her anger and guilt to acceptance and change? She is not only alone; she is also only eleven years old. Coming from homes such as hers, many adults are still unable to achieve her insight without psychiatric help. I can believe that Emma would recognize that her parents do not love her. The incidents of the novel force this recognition. But I cannot believe that she would quit trying to change them and see that the solution for her is to change herself. Harriet faced with total rejection resorts to physical violence. She needs Ole Golly's understanding before she can change.

Emma's insight is valid, but, in my opinion, it is not hers. It is Louise Fitzhugh's. In *Nobody's Family Is Going to Change,* message dominates at the expense of the heroine's credibility. It is an important and worthwhile message, but the novel is flawed. Fascinating and vivid, *Nobody's Family Is Going to Change* is not the literary triumph of *Harriet the Spy.*

Maggie Stern

SOURCE: "A Second Look: *Harriet the Spy,*" in *Horn Book Magazine,* Vol. 56, No. 4, August, 1980, pp. 442-45.

Harriet The Spy was published in 1964. That was the year I read it twelve times. That was the year our school bookstore kept running out of green composition notebooks, and the cafeteria was plagued with requests for tomato sandwiches. A memorable year for many of us.

Now, sixteen years later, I take a closer look at the text as well as a first look at some of the many reviews. Apprehensive about my thirteenth reading (what if I didn't like it anymore!) I tried the reviews first: *Library Journal, The New York Times Book Review, The Junior Bookshelf, Childhood Education,*

The Christian Science Monitor, and a few others. Gloria Vanderbilt in the *Times* told me the plot, essentially; so did *The Junior Bookshelf;* and Ellen Rudin in *Library Journal* raved about the book, saying that "Harriet is one of the meatiest heroines in modern juvenile fiction" and that the novel is a "tour de force" and "bursts with life." So far, so good. I remember the plot vividly and have never doubted or questioned Harriet's realness or life.

Hoping for more than a plot synopsis I turned to *The Horn Book*—to Ruth Hill Viguers's article.

> The arrival of **Harriet the Spy** with fanfare and announcements of approval for its "realism" makes me wonder again why that word is invariably applied to stories about disagreeable people and situations. Are there really no amiable children? No loyal friends? No parents who are fundamentally loving and understanding? I challenge the implication that New York City harbors only people who are abnormal, ill-adjusted, and egocentric. . . . Many adult readers appreciating the sophistication of the book will find it funny and penetrating. Children, however, do not enjoy cynicism. I doubt its appeal to many of them.

None of the reviewers, I thought, closing the book after my next reading, truly looked at what Louise Fitzhugh had so brilliantly done. Louise Fitzhugh was talking about the balance of life. And this balance, and loss of balance, is all seen through Harriet. In a sense Harriet is within us all: that feistiness, fire, honesty, quickness to judge, quickness to be hurt, softness, loudness, and loneliness. Ruth Hill Viguers missed the essence of the book. She missed its humor, richness, and texture.

Time has shown that **Harriet the Spy** is still read, still loved by children. It appears that children have not found Harriet disagreeable, abnormal, ill-adjusted, or egocentric, as Mrs. Viguers suggested. Harriet is a real child, living in a real world. And that is not easy.

Harriet M. Welsch lives in New York City—a city of little order. She is an only child. Her parents, though well-meaning, have little time for her. They also have little understanding of her. Very little. But in contrast to her inept parents there is Ole Golly—the wise, wonderful nurse. It is Ole Golly who understands her, inside and out. It is Ole Golly who loves her as a person in her own right.

Harriet is going to be a famous writer, who knows everything about everything. She has been keeping a notebook since she was eight. Now she is eleven. She spies for practice, in order to write down her observations.

Harriet has found a rhythm in life she can move to. The unconscious rhythm of a child. This is not abnormal: It is basic, fundamental for every human being. For years Harriet's routine has been the same—her reading in bed with a flashlight until Ole Golly takes it away, her daily tomato sandwiches, her spying, her writing. These activities are her very breath of life.

In the first half of the novel everything goes according to plan for Harriet. She rides with the tide. She spies and writes and eats tomato sandwiches. There are no conflicts. She writes exactly what she sees, without censoring anything:

> MISS WHITEHEAD'S FEET LOOK LARGER THIS YEAR. MISS WHITEHEAD HAS BUCK TEETH.

> TODAY A NEW BOY ARRIVED. HE IS SO DULL NO ONE CAN REMEMBER HIS NAME.

And without her knowing it, or even thinking about it, some of her perceptions are brilliant. The inherent brilliance of a child.

> I THINK THAT LOOKING AT MRS. GOLLY MUST MAKE OLE GOLLY SAD. MY MOTHER ISN'T AS SMART AS OLE GOLLY BUT SHE'S NOT AS DUMB AS MRS. GOLLY. I WOULDN'T LIKE TO HAVE A DUMB MOTHER. IT MUST MAKE YOU FEEL VERY UNPOPULAR.

Feel is the important word here. It doesn't make you unpopular; it makes you *feel* unpopular. These flickers of brilliance come naturally to Harriet.

The first major shift in her pattern comes when Ole Golly leaves. The break is difficult for Harriet, but not unbearable, and she compensates by writing more. Ole Golly says, "'Life is a struggle, and a good spy gets in there and fights.'" Harriet does. Her ability to feel more deeply is reflected in her writing.

> I WILL NEVER FORGET THAT FACE AS LONG AS I LIVE. [She is writing of Harrison Withers, a regular member of her spy route.] DOES EVERYBODY LOOK THAT WAY WHEN THEY HAVE LOST SOMETHING? I DON'T MEAN LIKE LOSING A FLASHLIGHT. I MEAN DO PEOPLE LOOK LIKE THAT WHEN THEY HAVE LOST?

With Ole Golly gone, everything feels more intensified, but life is endurable, and Harriet is able to maintain some kind of order. Some kind of balance.

But when her friends steal her notebook, invade it, and turn against her, she loses her balance completely. The tide changes, and Harriet is caught in the current. It is now that she becomes obsessed and that her writing becomes obsessive. "I THINK I WILL WRITE DOWN EVERYTHING, EVERY SINGLE THING THAT HAPPENS TO ME." She is in a state of panic. Proportion is distorted: Focus is lost. All she has is her writing. It becomes a means of getting back at the world, of alleviating her anger. Now writing has taken on a new dimension. It is something she is conscious of, something to be thought about. Her whole world has been shaken up, turned upside down, and rattled like a snow-scene paperweight. Everything is whirling chaotically.

In school all she can do is write. She neither listens in class nor does her homework. And when she is forbidden to take her composition book to school, she goes numb. Freezes. Her world becomes void of all meaning. Void of all order. "Everything bored her. She found that when she didn't have a notebook it was hard for her to think. The thoughts came slowly, as though they had to squeeze through a tiny door to get to her, whereas when she wrote, they flowed out faster than she could put them down."

> I DON'T FEEL LIKE ME AT ALL. I DON'T EVER LAUGH OR THINK ANYTHING FUNNY. I JUST FEEL MEAN ALL OVER. I WOULD LIKE TO HURT EACH ONE OF THEM IN A SPECIAL WAY.

And she does, too. Robbed of her very breath, she becomes that someone else. For the first time she is deliberately mean. Caught in the struggle, she doesn't know what to do. But Ole Golly comes through. In a letter she tells Harriet that she must do two things: Apologize and lie. *"Little lies that make people feel better are not bad."*

By listening to Ole Golly, by reflecting upon the situation herself, and ultimately by lying, Harriet moves from innocence to experience. In accepting this adult logic and in making it her own, she becomes more adult. There is order in her life again, a new balance. "NOW THAT THINGS ARE BACK TO NORMAL I CAN GET SOME REAL WORK DONE." In the struggle, Harriet has changed. One knows her writing, also, will change. It will be realized, deeper, and more reflective. "She made herself walk in Sport's shoes, feeling the holes in his socks rub against his ankles. She pretended she had an itchy nose when Janie put one abstracted hand up to scratch." She has gone beyond Harriet M. Welsch and into the "shoes" of others, a major step in becoming an adult. A major step in becoming a writer.

Through Harriet one sees the process of life, the human struggle. From unawareness to awareness—from order to chaos to new order. Louise Fitzhugh wrote a remarkable book.

Hamida Bosmajian

SOURCE: "Louise Fitzhugh's *Harriet the Spy*: Nonsense and Sense," in *Touchstones: Reflections on the Best in Children's Literature,* Vol. 1, edited by Perry Nodelman, Children's Literature Association, 1985, pp. 71-83.

> "The time has come," the Walrus said,
> "To talk of many things:
> Of shoes—and ships—and sealing wax—
> Of cabbages—and—kings—
> And why the sea is boiling hot—
> And whether pigs have wings."

This mock profundity is uttered by the Walrus of Lewis Carroll's "The Walrus and the Carpenter" just before he and the Carpenter proceed to devour the eager little oysters who had been foolish enough to accept his invitation for "a pleasant walk, a pleasant talk along the briny beach." The nonsense in Carroll's poem seems at first merely casual, but grows into a non-sense vision that is hypocritical, aggressive and cruel, especially towards ignorantly innocent child-like beings. The diverting surface of Carroll's poem reflects and confirms the nature of things in what we call the real world.

Louise Fitzhugh reminds us of the poem, and the relationship between pain and nonsense, at the moment of Harriet's first crisis in **Harriet the Spy.** Harriet overhears that her beloved nurse Ole Golly has not only been fired, but even decided herself that "the time has come" to part from Harriet. Harriet is shocked and yet feels "a tiny threat of excitement . . . that Ole Golly *must* mean that she, Harriet, was able to take care of herself" (128). Ole Golly notices that Harriet has been listening, and covers her commonsensical decision by starting to quote the stanza from Carroll's poem. Harriet gleefully takes her turn reciting the lines, thereby retarding the moment of what will be a very painful separation. Children and adults can read **Harriet the Spy** with similar glee, and divert themselves from the alienation, anxiousness and pain that pervade much of the novel. But under the comic nonsense on the surface, as Anita Moss points out, "Fitzhugh's novel resonates with social consciousness and with just indignation," and her grotesque characterizations "attempt to shock readers into awareness that middle-class urban children may be lost in the wilderness" (292-3). The whimsical or nonsensical characters Harriet observes during her spy route by peeping into windows do indeed appear to have come from some kind of alien looking-glass world.

"Nonsense" means more than comic silliness or senselessness; it also has metaphysical meanings referring to what transcends physical and sensical perceptions as well as rational comprehension. What is beyond sense is *non*-sense, and non-sense is also relevant to *Harriet the Spy.* We are told that Harriet remembers only two fragments from the Bible: "The sins of the fathers" and the sentence "Jesus wept" (189). When she is completely alienated from her classmates, she recalls only the first, as she compulsively tries to orient herself through quoting and writing. Though Harriet is not conscious of it, "the sins of the fathers" as visited upon the children points up the problem of neurotic repetitions or reactions from one generation to another, as well as obsessive compulsiveness in one's daily life. The narrator reminds us that Harriet also knows "Jesus wept" (John, 11:35), a sentence that occurs in the Bible when Jesus learns that Lazarus has already been buried. Both quotations express Harriet's central movement from alienation and loss in grief to renewal. Harriet enters her "dark night of the soul" and writes "When I wake up in the morning I wish I were dead" (200), but she is also able to write "I love myself" (210).

A third kind of nonsense is a feeling, especially the feeling of an ontological emptiness, a condition Harriet observes in many people and experiences herself after Ole Golly leaves: "I feel all the same things when I do things alone as when Ole Golly was here. The bath feels hot, the bed feels soft, but I feel there's a funny little hole in me that wasn't there before, like a splinter in your finger, but this is somewhere above my stomach" (132). It is the emptiness of alienation, of disconnectedness, and Fitzhugh even brings it out in her illustrations, which show eccentrically isolated individuals against a blank page; there is no ground for these figures. In the final analysis, Harriet's problems are not *caused* by Ole Golly's departure; they exist all along and are symptomatic of a certain way of life. Yet, from the beginning she is offered signs that will lead out of alienation: "Ole Golly says there is as many ways to live as there are people on the earth and I shouldn't go round with binders but should see every way I can. Then I'll know what way I want to live and not just live like my family" (32).

The three parts of the novel show the stages in Harriet's quest, a limited quest, for as an eleven year old she is in her "latency period," though discomforting references to "dancing school" or "turning into young women any day now" as well as her own interest in the courtship behavior of others foreshadow the changes that lie ahead. But for now she is still a neat, compulsive, upper middle class urban child who loves to play "Town," go on her spy route, and write in her notebook. Part one can be called "The End of an Illusory Routine Life" since from the first chapter on Fitzhugh undermines Harriet's obsession with routine, and ends the first part with Ole Golly's departure into a new life of her own.

Part Two interrelates breakdown and breakthrough. The day Harriet feels her inner emptiness is also the day she is assigned the seemingly nonsensical role of an onion in the Christmas play, a role through which she will communicate much to her parents. Her breakdown is accelerated when her classmates discover what she has written about them in her notebook. They victimize her by staining her with ink, but Harriet refuses to be defined as victim and becomes increasingly aggressive, until she finally creates chaos in the classroom by placing a frog in one of the desks. Her destructive behavior motivates her parents to seek the help of a therapist and of school officials, who channel her aggressions and creativity constructively by appointing her editor of the sixth grade page. In part three Harriet achieves integration—social integration with all its ambiguity and, more important, integration within herself. She will not be able to transform the world, but for a moment she and her two best friends walk free and open along the river. It is the typical ending of ironic comedy as Northrop Frye outlines it, and reminiscent of *Huckleberry Finn.*

Harriet the Spy meshes two modes of fiction—satire and psychological realism—through which the sense and nonsense of the story are revealed. Both modes are ironic, but satire often employs irony through nonsensical and comic aggression, whereas psychological realism seriously examines the nonsense of human life. Adult readers tend to be more accepting of children's literature that meshes the modes of romance and psychological realism as, for instance, in Lucy Boston's *The Children of Green Knowe.* Yet children are appreciative readers of satire, because of its aggression and its violation of taboos. The popularity of Roald Dahl's *Charlie and the Chocolate Factory,* that sickly sweet satire against a consumer society, proves Northrop Frye's point that "invective is one of the most readable forms of literature" (224). *Harriet the Spy* has the taboo-breaking aggressiveness of satire, but also channels the energies of satire towards Harriet's growth and development.

Frye argues that "the satirist has to select his absurdities, and the act of selection is a moral act." Satire's militant irony attacks human self-deceptions, particularly the illusions of perfection, but as Edward W. Rosenheim suggests, it undercuts the pleasure of militancy with a direct advocacy of truths or norms. At the deepest level of significant satire is the militant ironist as disappointed idealist who finds that people do not want to be reformed, much less redeemed. It is here that *Harriet the Spy* reveals its darker side, for as Harriet discovers her own resilience—a resilience that many children discover in children's literature—there comes with it the unuttered resignation that the world will remain as it is.

The satiric fantasy or fiction of *Harriet the Spy* is shaped by both the narrator and by Harriet's entries into her notebook. Much of the humor of the novel comes from the distance the intelligent mind puts between itself and what it perceives. Bergson's "momentary anesthesia of the heart" is operative here as persons and events are perceived with a certain rigidity, as possessing a "mechanical inelasticity" (62-4). Sometimes Harriet and the narrator agree in their perceptions, but at other times Harriet, especially in her insistence that her routines are perfect, becomes the satiric target. All the characters have at least a degree of inelasticity about them, and perceive others with a momentary anesthesia of the heart. Psychological realism is the corrective that probes the *motivations* for inelasticity and anesthesia.

The satiric truths or norms begin that probing. Harriet herself utters two truths, albeit preconsciously. When she rehearses her onion dance and her mother comments derogatorily on both the assignment and Harriet's performance, Harriet says: "Miss Berry assigned the onion part, *I'm* making up the *Dance*" (166). She asserts that the world may define her, but that she has a choice about how to work with that definition. She utters her second truth when she advises her therapist, who just lost to her in Monopoly, "I'll bet if you didn't take so many notes, you'd play better" (255). She learns that writing is a powerful means of coping and organizing but that it cannot replace experiencing life.

It is to be expected that Ole Golly as the "wise woman" in Harriet's life would project truths and values; she does in her own strange and nonsensical

way. If Harriet is obesssed with writing, Ole Golly is obsessed with quoting from her vast store of reading. However, she offers her quotations as rigid absolutes, quite out of context, and is unable to interpret them for Harriet. She cites Dostoevski on the importance of developing an empathetic relation to life: "Love all creation . . . If you love everything, you will perceive the divine mystery of things. Once you perceive it, you will comprehend it better every day. And you will at last come to love the whole world with an all embracing love" (23-24). Though the quotation is crucial for the novel's values, Harriet does not understand it, and Ole Golly cannot explain it to her. Preferring knowledge to love, Harriet rejects the quotation and screeches in a state of ego inflation: "I want to know everything . . . everything in the world . . . I will be a spy and know everything." By the end of the novel Ole Golly's ideas about love are less an impossible dream. In her letter she advises Harriet that we have to lie to make people feel better, and that we need to "remember that writing is to put love in the world, not to use against your friends. But to yourself you must always tell the truth." She also tells her former ward, "I guard my memories and love them but I don't get in them and lie down. You can even make stories from yours, but remember *they don't come back*. Just think how awful it would be if they did. You don't need me now. You are eleven years old which is old enough to get busy at growing up to be the person you want to be." She signs off with "no more nonsense" (276-77) and Harriet is ready to accept her advice of sensible love.

The incident that offers an example of the satiric truth is the visit of Ole Golly's boyfriend Mr. George Waldenstein to Harriet's house. He is a whimsical middle aged delivery boy on a bicycle who is also the stereotypical suitor, as he presents himself with a bunch of roses, "his mustache glistening in the light and his shirt front so white it was almost blinding" (111). He has known "another life" as a jeweler who had money, a family, an ulcer, and a life that was "so much dust in my hands." "We all make choices," he says as he tells how he left everything in order to find life again. Now, while he is not against moderate ambition, he knows that life will "'never be dust again . . . because I have—I have myself now. I know the value . . . the value of things.' He tried desparately to express himself" (115). Waldenstein is the only character in the novel who undergoes an adult process of maturation from deadness of heart, to awareness of alienation, to choice and change, to the rediscovery of joy in life, and who remains at the same time open to a future with others, as his marriage to Ole Golly demonstrates. His comical eccentricities are readily accepted, for this reasonable and kind man is at home with himself and communicates most closely the values that Fitzhugh admires. He is in more than one sense a delivery man! By showing that Waldenstein went through a major crisis and matured, the author also universalizes Harriet's crisis and communicates subliminally to the child reader that these cross-road moments are recurrent in the human quest.

While Harriet, too, is the target of satire, her inelasticities are viewed with gentle ridicule because she is still a child and because she is capable of self criticisms: "Blah, Blah, Blah, I always do carry on a lot. Once Ole Golly said to me, 'I could never lose you in a crowd, I'd just follow the sound of your voice.'" (36) As Virginia Wolf points out, *Harriet the Spy* is fundamentally a thorough characterization of Harriet who is unconscious of the way in which her environment has influenced her. Wolf sees psychological realism manifesting itself through Harriet's inner growth and not through the description of the "reality" of her environment (121). The unreality of satiric exaggerations can actually be seen as an attempt to stave off as negative pedagogy those images that would hinder her growth.

The psychological realism of this novel cannot be reduced to a simple matter of cause and effect. We cannot say that Harriet's upwardly mobile parents have failed as parents and have simply transferred their responsibilities to Ole Golly, for Harriet does not perceive her parents as having failed her and she is not aware that she is suffering neglect. From an objective definition of parenting Harriet's parents do fail, but the reader who blames them must overlook several moments in the novel where Harriet and her parents have good communication and take pleasure in each other's company. Nor do all children break down when their nurse departs. To some extent Harriet's problem can be seen as her blessing. Perhaps because of her intelligence and sensibility, she is at an early age acutely aware of the problem of disconnectedness in people's lives, a problem that affects her also. In spite of her writing ability, she is not yet intellectually and emotionally able to cope with the problem of alienation by placing a symbolic system between herself and reality; she experiences pain with that special pathos of the child—uncomprehendingly and preanalytically.

If the child in early infancy experiences wholeness in a cosmically centered ego to whose needs and wishes the world seems to cater, and learns only slowly that

the world and the ego are not co-extensive, then Harriet has made some interesting adjustments which explain why many readers perceive her as younger than she is. She is not the center of her parents' life nor of the world around her and she copes with her isolation by connecting herself mechanically through routines, through playing "Town," through spying, and through writing. But even as she tries to control the world through her notebook, she records fragmented images and reflections that emphasize her lack of connectedness. Only at the very end does she begin to shape a story, does she combine fragments into a meaningful structure. Fitzhugh, however, does not tell us what the story is about.

Routine gives Harriet a tenuous connectedness. She always has tomato sandwiches for lunch, cake and milk after school, bedtime at nine-thirty, milk after her mother says "drink your milk" and feels reassured with each recurrence or reminder. Her routines have created a stimulus-response scenario and, as the world responds to her, she gets the illusion of connectedness. In accordance with Piaget's conceptions of ritual and routine, her routines become symbols of success that the desired thing will happen. (156-7). One part of her wants to be the sole definer of her world and she is unaware of how dependent she is on what she defines. She feels her disconnectedness only after Ole Golly has left, and she then breaks many of her routines, primarily so as not to be reminded of her aloneness.

Her need to define and manipulate is clearly revealed in the opening chapter of the book, when she plays "Town." With a strong sense of *logos* she tells her friend Sport that first one has to *name* the town and the people, of which there should be no more than twenty-five (clearly a small town fantasy!). As a writer she makes up worlds: "When I say that's a mountain, that's a mountain." But once she has defined the town, she finds her greatest "fun" in imagining how everyone is having different experiences" at this very minute." She recognizes the importance of autonomy, and intuits that people have their private selves which can be observed but must not be intruded upon. The first chapter establishes this when Ole Golly takes Harriet and Sport along on her weekly visit to her simple mother, an infantile and aggressive solipsist in whose presence Ole Golly says to Harriet, "Behold . . . a woman who never had any interest in anyone else, nor in any book, nor in any school, nor in any way of life, but has lived her whole life in this room, eating and sleeping and waiting to die" (18). Harriet is shocked at Ole Golly's directness, yet Harriet makes similarly brutal statements about others in her notebook. Ole Golly's mother also functions as an object lesson for the negative life of a person who exists totally through routine.

On her spy route Harriet hovers on the threshold of possibilities. She appropriates the word *spy* to her own needs, almost as if aware of the arbitrariness of names. Her fantasies about her future "profession" include an office like that of a lawyer or dentist: "on the door it can say 'Harriet the Spy' in gold letters, and then it can have office hours like the dentist's door has and underneath it can say *Any Spy Work Undertaken*" (78). She really knows nothing about espionage, its lying and betrayal, but incarnates the word *spy* when she dons her "spy clothes" through which she slips into the persona of a quiet and secretive observer in an alienated world, a persona quite different from her noisy braggart self. Unlike "real spies," who are always in the service of a greater power, Harriet spies for herself alone, and confides for the sake of memory by recording in her notebook all that she observes and feels. Her apparently unusual activity covers the fact that the adult world is always observed by children in mute silence and often with much anxiousness. The child takes in the world as if she were God's spy. Ole Golly reminds her of the godlikeness of spying when she encourages her to study the Greeks and Romans because "those gods spied on everybody all the time" (38).

The people on Harriet's spy route are literally framed by the apertures through which she observes them and thus become concentrated sets for problems that reflect her life. Subsconsciously she *chooses* her objects of espionage. The Dei Santi grocery-story-family reveals to her that a large family does not necessarily share intimacy. They are stereotypical, and unreflective as they collide and reconcile, yet remain in their isolated eccentric patterns. She decides that she would not want to be part of them. The person she identifies with most is Harrison Withers, a recluse whose name aligns him with Harriet. He lives with twenty-six cats and makes wicker cages, but has no human contact. Harriet would "wither" if she were to imitate him. During the time that Harriet mourns her loss of Ole Golly, Withers is forced to relinquish his cats and goes into a deep depression, but, as Harriet is beginning to recover herself, he smuggles a tiny arrogant kitten into his apartment and once more absorbs himself blissfully in making his cages and caring for his pet. While Harriet likes him because he loves what he does (72), he is also an objective cor-

relative for her tensions between freedom (cats) and confinement through routines (cages).

Another object lesson is the rich lady Amanda Plummer who, like Harriet, takes to her bed in order to escape the problems of being alive, but finally decides to engage herself in a whirl of social activities. The most negative image on her route is the Robinsons, a childless couple in love with things that they show off to their acquaintances. This solipsistic twosome purchase a large statue of a wooden baby, as an image of perfection of the child that is seen but never heard. Pathetic as they are, the Robinsons conclude that it is just perfect that they do not have any children (68).

Harriet refuses to be a wooden baby in her parents' life, though the reader gets the impression that they would not have been displeased had she been a pleasant object to be paraded on appropriate occasions. Both parents are very extroverted and image-conscious—he is in show business, she is his ornament for his many social occasions. In their house Harriet is less the secretive spy than the braggart tomboy and, in spite of her neat and tidy little room and her routines, she becomes the upsetter of their order as she forces them to become more involved parents. She is, however, unable to change them in any fundamental way, for, as is typical of this milieu, the parents do not become engaged in a growth process as parents but enlist "support systems"—Ole Golly, the psychiatrist, the school official—all of which are in a monetary relation to them.

At first glance Ole Golly seems the ideal nanny. Harriet is surprised when she learns that her name is Catherine, a formal name, whereas "Ole Golly" has comforting, humorous and nonsensical connotations. Yet Ole Golly is neither old nor is she a kind of "gee golly" person in her speech or actions. Her name signals her all-encompassing importance in Harriet's life, for "golly" is a diminutive substitute for God in oaths and exclamations. Though she always remains in the realistic mode, she has some of the mythic dimensions that adhere to the great nanny figures in children's literature, such as Mary Poppins. There are intimations of the "great mother" as she brings nurturance and order into Harriet's life, but she is also deeply troubled in her relation to her mentally deficient mother, as Harriet herself notices (19-20). That relation exemplifies the severe realization that we are often powerless to change people who are intimately related to us, and that the only things we can do then is change the direction of our lives. This Ole Golly does when she marries George Waldenstein.

Harriet's parents appreciate Ole Golly because she is "pure magic" as she manages Harriet; and Harriet loves to be thus managed, and does not realize that the continued presence of the nurse would thwart her development through infantilization, be it through the reinforcement of routines or through condescension to Harriet's level of operating. Harriet seems to know subconsciously that the great mother can become demonic if not devouring, for, as she is deep into her crisis over having lost Ole Golly, she has two nightmares. After a bad day during which she was teased by her classmates, particularly Sport who told her that she did not look like an onion in her dance, Harriet dreams that "Ole Golly was rolling around on the floor and cawing like a crow. She kept coming at Harriet, and Harriet would run. Ole Golly's eyes were red rimmed and shining blue. Her face had black feathers suddenly and a big yellow beak with teeth. Harriet screamed in her dream" (177). The second nightmare begins as a wish-fulfillment as "Ole Golly, seated in a rocker and wearing a warm yellow flannel bathrobe, rocked Harriet on her lap as she held her very close" (262). We are not told how this dream becomes a nightmare, but Harriet screams Ole Golly's name in panic as the positive image turns into a nightmare so strong that the memory of it is repressed.

Thus Harriet does dreamwork to free herself from her dependence on Ole Golly, who now, instead of quoting literature, caws like an evil omen. Her sharp features metamorphose into an old crow rolling aggressively and inappropriately on the floor, an acceleration of what Harriet does in her onion dance. While yellow was Ole Golly's favorite color and her yellow room the epitome of coziness, the color of beak and bathrobe threatens now to devour and envelop. The nonsense of dream images makes much sense in Harriet's development. It is also significant that, as she cries out in each dream, her mother comes and holds her. The first time she accepts her mother's comforting, but the second time she turns to the wall and pretends to sleep. She needs to see herself through independently.

A symbol that becomes crucial in Harriet's growth is the onion, a role assigned to her rather haphazardly, but Fitzhugh's choice of an onion is not accidental. An onion is a bulb beneath the ground; it is nourishing potential, not a fruit. As a symbol for the self it suggests something quite different from another symbol of the self: the kernel in the nut (the fruit of a tree). Both are compact, round, self-contained, but the latter signifies centered essence while the former

projects the self as many-faceted, very much in keeping with the existential implications of becoming. The nut is much more the symbol of being the mature self. In her onion self Harriet can be regressive, as she rolls around the room in a fetal position bumping aggressively into things, all under the guise of "I am doing my homework." But her part also furthers her education in empathy as she learns to feel herself into something that is quite unlike her.

The onion dance rehearsal also makes her parents realize that they don't know their child well enough. As both are in her room—for the first time in the novel they are in Harriet's space—and watch her efforts, Mr. Welsch recommends the Stanislavsky method for empathetic acting. He, too, tries to be an onion. On a humorous level father and child begin to communicate well until Harriet suddenly jumps up and starts to write in her notebook about what Ole Golly would think about her being an onion. Harriet has had a good time with her parents in the intimate space of her room and her sudden break from them suggests that she feels she is betraying Ole Golly. She overhears her parents agree outside her door that they must get to know her better and she writes: "Why don't they say what they feel? Ole Golly said 'Always say exactly what you feel. People are hurt more by misunderstanding than anything else.' Am I hurt? I don't feel hurt. I just feel funny all over" (171). Her parents have actually perceived quite a bit of what Harriet feels and Harriet herself does not *say* what she feels. Finally, the end of the novel expresses a deep communication between Harriet and her two friends about anyone *saying* anything. Ole Golly's dictum will need to be qualified by experience.

Ultimately, *Harriet the Spy* reveals the resilience of children as they grow through each other. The onion part aligns her with a group effort of her class, but the class also brings about the crisis through which she can release all her feelings. While chasing around in the park, the children pick up her notebook and read all the aggressive comments she has recorded about them. She is ostracized not only by those students whom she despises, but also by her friends Janie and Sport. Janie wants to be a scientist who invents explosives, a fantasy through which she deals with her negative feelings towards her mother, and she is struck deep when she reads: "Who does Janie Gibbs think she's kidding? Does she really think she could ever be a scientist?" (184) Her fantasy is, of course, no more outrageous than Harriet's. Sport is hurt even more deeply; he cries after Janie reads to him, "Sometimes I can't stand Sport. With his worrying all the time and fussing over his father, sometimes he is like a little old woman" (182). Sport, who is growing up motherless and who does all the housework for his writer-father, has dreams of order in his very confused life and always manages to be kind. He is the most sensitive of all the children in the book, perhaps because he has more responsibilities than anyone else.

Harriet, then, commits hubris, and her braggart self will need to be punished without breaking the comic narrative patterns. She becomes the class's scapegoat when they spill ink over her. She rushes home and immerses her stained little body into her own private warm and womb-like bathtub, crying silently all the time. But her classmates are also blocking characters who, with the exception of her friends, deserve to be deflated. Therefore, when Harriet creates havoc in the class by placing a frog in one of the desks, her aggressive behavior is not tolerated by her environment, but the reader is on her side, especially since she expresses her resurgence of her indomitable spirit that refuses to turn destructively against her self.

At the end she prints a retraction about what she has said about her peers, lying a bit as Ole Golly advised in her letter. On the day the paper comes out she stays home and works hard on a story. Satisfied with her work, she goes for a walk by the river in the park: "There was a cold wind off the water, but the day was one of those bright, brilliant shiny days that made her feel the world was beautiful, would always be, would always sing, would hold no disappointments" (295). She writes a bit, but mainly "she sat there thinking, feeling very calm, happy and immensely pleased with her own mind." When Ole Golly had quoted Wordsworth's "That inward eye which is the bliss of solitude" (106), Harriet had not understood; but now, though Fitzhugh puts her in a windy park and not into an Eden, Harriet experiences her moment of all-oneness in which she loves and accepts herself.

"She looked up and down the walk. No one was in sight. She looked out over the water to the neon sign whose pink greed spoiled the view at night." Fitzhugh has Harriet move subtly from the inner contentment of self-realization back into the fallen world where the beckoning light is one of greed and not of hope. The images of alienation will remain part of life. Then, she sees Sport and Janie coming towards her looking like "dolls from the distance" and making "her think of the way she imagined the people when she played Town. Somehow this way she could see

them better than she ever had before." At first her perception is that of subject to object, but then she views them more and more subjectively as she tries to imagine what it would feel like to be them.

The two children stand wordlessly before her in the cold wind: "Harriet looked at their feet. They looked at her feet. Then they looked at their own feet." Now Harriet tests them if they are willing to accept her. She opens her notebook, "watching their eyes as she did. They watched back. She wrote: Ole Golly is right, sometimes you have to lie. She looked at Sport and Janie. They didn't look angry." After the embarrassed looking at each other's feet, they make eye contact and Harriet concludes that she can get some real work done now that things have gone back to normal. But they are not back to normal, things have changed for the better. There is a genuine and chastened acceptance of each other, as all three "turned and walked along the river." Feelings are so strongly shared that nothing needs to be said. Harriet will not bring back Ole Golly, she neither can nor wants to perfect her parents, she will continue to have to put up with hypocritical classmates, but she will be able to integrate herself and have a strong and meaningful friendship with Janie and Sport. The three little oysters walking by the river's shore will not be swallowed by a greedy Walrus and Carpenter!

Through its artistry the end of *Harriet the Spy* reveals once more that this book is literature for children. Its honesty and complexity do not perpetuate myths of innocence or the hope that all problems can be resolved in happiness if we just love one another. Rather, the book affirms that the difficulties and pains of growing up are more than likely rehearsals for life's continuing crises and changes, unless one chooses to numb one's feelings and vulnerabilities. The open-ended closure of the novel is a moment of integration between three children who experience at that point neither inelasticity nor anesthesia of the heart. Louise Fitzhugh and Harriet M. Welsch relate the nonsense and sense of human life through their fictions and prepare the young reader in a literate way not only for life, but also for the nonsense and sense of literature such as *King Lear*, where a "very foolish fond old man" promises his daughter that he and she will sing like birds in the cage "and take upon's the mystery of things, as if we were God's spies."

References

Bergson, Henri. "Laughter." *Comedy*. Ed. Wylie Sypher. New York: Doubleday, 1956.

Fitzhugh, Louise. *Harriet the Spy.* New York: Dell, 1964; rpr. 1978.

Frye, Northrop. *Anatomy of Criticism.* Princeton, NJ: Princeton U Press, 1957.

Moss, Anita. "Louise Fitzhugh." *Twentieth Century Children's Writers.* Ed. D. L. Kirkpatrick. New York: St. Martin's Press. 1978. 292-3.

Piaget, Jean. *The Child's Conception of the World.* Totowa, NJ: Littlefield, Adams, and Co., 1975.

Rosenheim, Edward W. *Swift and the Satirist's Art.* Chicago: U of Chicago Press, 1963.

Wolf, Virginia L. *"Harriet the Spy:* Milestone, Masterpiece?" *Children's Literature* 4 (1976).

Lissa Paul

SOURCE: "The Feminist Writer as Heroine in *Harriet the Spy,*" in *The Lion and the Unicorn,* Vol. 13, No. 1, June, 1989, pp. 67-73.

1989 marks the twenty-fifth anniversary of **Harriet the Spy.** That would make Harriet thirty-six. Never mind. In the story she is forever eleven. The astonishing thing is that the book shows few signs of becoming dated. Although Harriet's parents don't exactly look like "baby boomers," Harriet herself still looks very much a "yuppie puppy." In my undergraduate children's literature classes, students are often surprised to find that the story is older than they are. But the book is always a winner, and 25 years on, it has achieved the status of an American classic along with *Charlotte's Web* and *Where the Wild Things Are.* So there is good reason to keep trying to account for its continuing success.

Reviews and articles that deal with **Harriet the Spy** are uninspiring. Many critics (see, for example, Stern; Molson; "Another Look"; Wolf; Egoff) desire to give it the equivalent of the Good Housekeeping Seal of Approval, to sanctify it in spite of its questionable morality. What none of the critics recognize in **Harriet the Spy** is that very rare species, a successful female *künstlerroman.* A double feminist trick is in play. Fitzhugh tricks critics into a 'doublethink' where, in order to sanction the book, they have to make lying and gossip look like appropriate ways of getting along in society. And Harriet tricks her audience into accepting her notebook gossip (which made her a social outcast) as fiction (which makes her popular).

Many of the marks of the feminist writer are visible in Harriet: she prefers a small-scale form of writing (the private notebook); she juggles her role in society (her popularity with her classmates) with her role as a writer (which demands selfishness); she is concerned with being truthful, but ultimately discovers that that necessitates lying; and she finds that domestic gossip constitutes a valid form of fiction.

Harriet's success as a feminist writer is particularly remarkable because she knows no literary foremothers. Ole Golly is a reader, not a writer. She reads mostly nineteenth-century fiction by male writers, and it is clear even to Harriet that Ole Golly usually doesn't quite understand what she reads. She quotes a lot, but can't explain the quotations. The only real writer in the book, Sport's father, is the antithesis of Harriet. Where Harriet is methodical and orderly, a creature of habit, Sport's father is disorderly (there is a gym sock lying in his bedroom, Harriet notices). Harriet likes her meals on time, Sport's father does not care what he eats, or when, and he often writes all night. Even though we never know what kinds of books Sport's father writes, we know about his domestic habits, and how they define his life as a writer.

Some of the differences between Harriet and Sport's father are characteristics of differences between male and female writers. In *A New Mythos: The Novel of the Artist as Heroine 1877-1977,* Grace Stewart points out that women embody "domesticity, selflessness, and the status quo" (12), and so are fundamentally at odds with the male myth of the artist who is essentially selfish and concerned with everything but domestic order and creature comforts. Harriet is, in fact, quite unlike what she imagines a writer to be. Even in the game of Town she makes up at the beginning of the book, the writer she creates is a man— one who spends his time in a bar.

That Harriet assigns the role of writer to a man is just a small example of the patriarchal conventions that inform her concept of what writing is. The holdup, the chase scenes and the jolly, booming doctor delivering a baby, all belong to the genre of popular adventure. Her Town, at this stage, is sterile, like the garden of hibiscus blossoms Mary tries to "grow" at the beginning of *The Secret Garden.* Harriet, like Mary, doesn't yet understand the nature of her art—or the art of her nature. Only at the end of the book does Harriet begin to play Town using something close to the Stanislavsky method. She moves away from "male-order" adventure stories and tries to feel what it would be like to be Sport or Janie (Molson, "Portrait").

In some ways, Harriet reminds me of another famous notebook keeper of roughly the same vintage—Anna Wulf in Doris Lessing's 1962 novel *The Golden Notebook*. Both Anna and Harriet care passionately about being taken seriously as writers. They both accurately observe and record the details of ordinary life, and they try to understand what love is and how family dynamics work. I'm not suggesting that ***Harriet the Spy*** is modeled on *The Golden Notebook* (Anna is politically conscious in a way that Harriet is not—and has a range of experience unavailable to an 11-year-old), but both are apprenticeship novels about women writers, and both date from a time when women were beginning to reclaim their heritage as writers and to name the territory about which they write.

Both novels share common concerns: truth in fiction is a critical one. Anna and Harriet worry about being truthful. Anna talks about "problems of being truthful in writing, (which is being truthful about oneself)" (336). But Anna has trouble telling the truth in her notebooks. She keeps trying, but she keeps writing different versions of truth, that is, she writes fictions. Ole Golly, in her letter, assures Harriet that she must "put down the truth" (275) in her notebook. Yet one of the major factors in the success of ***Harriet the Spy*** is the way Harriet subversively turns truth into fiction and so makes lying look like a socially desirable thing.

Like many women writers, Harriet and Anna are acutely conscious of the need to keep their notebooks away from prying eyes. They see writing as fundamentally private, not a public occupation. But when the privacy of their notebooks is disturbed, the consequences demonstrate a critical difference in the endings of their respective novels. Anna, in Doris Lessing's novel, loses as a writer in order to re-integrate herself as a participant in society. The last entry in "The Golden Notebook" section is a description of a short novel written in the hand of her lover, Saul Green. Anna loses her own female story about family relationships in favor of a "male-order" story about war. And she loses her necessarily selfish, isolated existence as a writer in order to take on her traditionally female role as nurturer and comforter. She gets a job as a marriage counsellor, joins the Labour party and teaches delinquent children two evenings a

week. Anna is caught in a trap Linda Huf recognizes. In *A Portrait of the Artist as a Young Woman*, Huf says that the female artist is "torn not only between life and art but, more specifically, between her role as a woman, demanding selfless devotion to others, and her aspirations as an artist, requiring exclusive commitment to work" (5). Harriet, unlike Anna, is not torn.

Harriet wins, both as a writer and as a participant in society. She turns the disaster of the discovery of her notebook into a triumph. At her lowest point, with her notebook confiscated, Harriet has no comfort from either her writing or her friends. But in the end, she gets everything. She turns her private notebook gossip into a public gossip column for the school newspaper—and is praised for her efforts by her teacher, parents and peers. And she gets her friends back.

The difference between the two novels is characteristic of the difference that often shows up between children's literature and women's literature—of that period, anyway: children win, women don't. In the end, Harriet is able to function both as a writer, and as a member of her school community. Anna, on the other hand, gives up writing in order to be a participant in the community.

It is the fact that Harriet wins in the end that makes the book such an unusual female *künstlerroman*. Both Grace Stewart's *A New Mythos* and Linda Huf's *A Portrait of the Artist as a Young Woman* show that apprenticeship novels by women novelists are often about failure: Jo March loses in Louisa May Alcott's *Little Women*, Anna Wulf loses in Doris Lessing's *The Golden Notebook*, and Esther Greenwood loses in Sylvia Plath's *The Bell Jar*. Male artists, unlike female artists, are indulged in their selfishness.

Grace Stewart says that a female writer working within a patriarchal tradition is "handicapped" because "she must consciously or unconsciously reject the image of woman as passive, weak, selfless, and unthinking or accept her unwomanliness if she actively and selfishly seeks experience, knowledge, and pleasure" (14). Harriet manages both. It is only very recently that there has been a trend towards recognizing that women are not always doomed to confined lives and to silence, that there are, as Nina Auerbach says in *Woman and the Demon*, "gestures towards reconstruction" (228). Harriet belongs in Auerbach's camp.

My sense of how just how successful—and subversive—a heroine Harriet is comes, in large degree, from my experience of teaching the book in undergraduate classes. Students often begin with comments to the effect that it is "cute"—a term they quickly learn to expunge from their vocabularies. Then they try to find a moral message and cite good advice Ole Golly gives Harriet in her letter. When pressed about what that advice is, students balk. It usually takes several direct requests to get them to say that Ole Golly tells Harriet she has to lie.

While it is true that professional critics have been disturbed by Ole Golly's advice for some time, my students' reluctance to acknowledge it indicates how deeply it shakes their conviction that stories for children must have morals that conform to the overt rules of society. Fitzhugh gets away with making lying look like solid, moral advice. But lying, of course, is part of the arsenal of weapons that the successful trickster heroine uses to survive. Penelope, for example, lies to save herself from lecherous suitors; and Charlotte in *Charlotte's Web* lies, or exaggerates, to save Wilbur. The trickster heroine must appear conforming and obedient, while at the same time remaining true to herself, her life, and her art. Emily Dickinson's prophetic lines, which almost look like advice to the aspiring female writer, come to mind in this context: "Tell all the Truth but tell it slant—/ Success in Circuit lies" (506).

If lying is a survival tactic for the feminist writer, gossip is the preferred subject matter: "gossip, like novels is a way of turning life into story" (7), says Rachel Brownstein in *Becoming a Heroine*. It is not until Harriet learns to exploit her natural inclination towards gossip that her writing career takes off. Grotesques, freaks, lonely and disconnected people are the true subjects of her fiction. The ride on the subway (where Harriet notes a "WOMAN WITH ONE CROSS-EYE AND A LONG NOSE"), and the visit to Ole Golly's mother (Harriet thinks about writing a story about "MRS. GOLLY GETTING RUN OVER BY A TRUCK"), constitute our first glimpses of Harriet's real interests. What Harriet sees is a kind of peep show of a variety of freaks and misfits: the Robinsons with their silent obsession for "perfection," Mrs. Plummer and her self-indulgent indolence. As I've written elsewhere (see "Enigma Variations"), women tend to write about inside stories, and about the gossip that occurs in the enclosed spaces that occupy so much of their lives.

Harriet turns her voyeuristic activity of spying on Harrison Withers—and the gossip about him she confides to her notebook—into fiction. She even ends up looking like a moralist. Although we aren't actually

given the story that Harriet tells about Harrison Withers, we are told it is a story with a moral: "IT WAS HARD MAKING UP HIM FINDING THE CAT BUT I THINK I MADE UP A GOOD MORAL—THAT IS THAT SOME PEOPLE ARE ONE WAY AND SOME PEOPLE ARE ANOTHER AND THAT'S THAT." The curious thing about the moral is that it isn't a moral at all, at least not in the sense that a moral distinguishes between right and wrong conduct. For Harriet, a moral can be simply an acknowledgement of difference—an appropriate feminist moral in the light of post-structuralist discussions about difference as the way to defer meaning and to accord value to non-patriarchal traditions. As Rachel Blau du Plessis says in "For the Etruscans," it is "always the meaning, the reading of difference that matters, and meaning is culturally engendered and sustained. . . . And as such, these differing experiences do surely produce (some) different consciousnesses, different cultural expressions, different relations to realms of symbols and symbol users" (260). There is a difference today, for example, in our current attitude towards gossip. It is no longer necessarily devalued as a female pastime.

In *Gossip,* Patricia Meyer Spacks exonerates gossip from its tarnished reputation. Originally gossip meant "god-related," a kind of god-parent of either sex (25). As the term came to mean a person who stayed with a woman while she was in labour, it became associated with women's talk at a lying-in, and was devalued (men, of course, don't gossip). Spacks also argues that suppressed groups use gossip to gain verbal control over their superiors. That is what makes it such an appropriate form for women and children.

This theoretical introduction to gossip usually cuts little ice with the students. They don't understand what gossip has to do with **Harriet the Spy.** So last year I decided to run a practical demonstration. We had a gossip session in class, Harriet style. It showed more dramatically than any theoretical discussion just how subversive a book **Harriet the Spy** is.

The tension was palpable that day. The students, predictably, brought in gossip items about faculty members, about their superiors. The items covered exactly the range of gossip in Harriet's notebooks, in Anna Wulf's notebooks, and in the theoretical account that Spacks gives of gossip: concerns about smells and personal, especially drinking, habits; speculation about socially unacceptable relationships (in this case between faculty members, and between faculty members and students); and speculation about a faculty move to get an unpopular professor removed from his position. As Harriet says about the items in her notebook, there were nice things too. But those were not the items of interest.

Although the exercise did raise the class consciousness as to the power of gossip, I'll not run another session. It made my ears burn, and I was personally uncomfortable on behalf of my colleagues. If anything, it made me realize the way gossip, in order to be intimate, has to be shared by people in a common condition. As a professor, I'm now forever excluded from gossip among students about professors. Harriet finds that out too. The gossip she shares in her column is designed to engage all readers in common secrets. She doesn't learn anything as noble as being nice to other people. Harriet simply learns that public gossip is sanctioned, though private gossip is condemned.

What I like about **Harriet the Spy,** and what I know that children like (when I share the book with them) is the way Harriet gets away with lying, gossiping, and with being generally rude. In the tradition of tricksters from Anansi to Tom Thumb, she says all the things that all of us want to say but don't dare. Like another famous trickster writer, Charlotte, in *Charlotte's Web,* Harriet is both "a true friend and a good writer."

As a feminist writer, Harriet learns to reconstruct herself, to adapt. She resolves the splits—between life and art, between truth and lying, and between gossip and fiction—that destroy many women writers. The success of **Harriet the Spy** lies in the reader's subversive identification with Harriet's apparent conformity and her real subversion. That's why the book maintains its status as a classic of contemporary children's literature.

Works Cited

Auerbach, Nina. *Woman and the Demon: The Life of a Victorian Myth,* Cambridge: Harvard UP, 1982.

Brownstein, Rachel M. *Becoming a Heroine: Reading about Women in Novels.* Harmondsworth: Penguin, 1984.

Emily Dickinson, *The Complete Poems of Emily Dickinson.* Ed. Thomas H. Johnson. Boston: Little Brown, 1960.

Egoff, Sheila. *Thursday's Child: Trends and Patterns in Contemporary Children's Literature.* Chicago: American Library Association, 1981.

Fitzhugh, Louise. *Harriet the Spy.* New York: Dell Yearling, 1964.

Huf, Linda. *A Portrait of the Artist as a Young Woman: The Writer as Heroine in American Literature.* New York: Frederick Unger, 1983.

Lessing, Doris. *The Golden Notebook.* London: Granada Panther, 1973.

Molson, Francis. "Another Look at *Harriet the Spy.*" *Elementary English* 51 (1974): 963-70.

———. "Portrait of the Young Writer in Children's Fiction." *Lion and the Unicorn* 1.2 (1977): 77-90.

Paul, Lissa. "Enigma Variations: What Feminist Theory Knows About Children's Literature." *Signal* 54 (1987): 186-202.

Plessis, Rachel Blau du. "For the Etruscans." *Debating Texts: Readings in 20th Century Literary Theory and Method.* Ed. Rich Rylance. Toronto: U of Toronto P, 1987.

Spacks, Patricia Meyer. *Gossip.* Chicago: U of Chicago P, 1986.

Stern, Maggie. "A Second Look: *Harriet the Spy.*" *Horn Book* 56 (1980): 442-45.

Stewart, Grace. *A New Mythos; The Novel of the Artist as Heroine 1877-1977.* Monographs in Women's Studies. St. Alban's: Eden Press, 1979.

Townsend, John Rowe. *Written for Children: An Outline of English Language Children's Literature.* 3rd ed. Harmondsworth: Penguin, 1987.

White, E. B. *Charlotte's Web,* New York: Harper and Row, 1980.

Wolf, Virginia L. "*Harriet the Spy:* Milestone Masterpiece?" *Children's Literature* 4 (1975): 120-26.

George Shannon

SOURCE: "The Work of Keeping Writing Play: A View through Children's Literature," in *Children's Literature in Education,* Vol. 21, No. 1, 1990, pp. 37-43.

When Harriet M. Welsch, the best known spy and child writer in children's literature, clutches her green composition book marked "Private" and screams,

"I'm not *playing*. Who says I'm *playing*. I'm WORK-ING!"[1] she is echoing the weary, defensive voice of endless writers. She is also, as they are, wrong. Her writing *is* play—the pastoral play described by minds as diverse as Elizabeth Bowen[2] and Sigmund Freud[3] and experienced by all artists who feel most fully alive when creating.

Regardless of the semantic conundrum surrounding the words *work* and *play,* stories about young writers such as Harriet are dominated by pastoral metaphors, affirming their authors' vision of writing as play. This is not to say writing is free of risk or inner tension, but that it is pastoral *because* of them. The essence and endurance of play, as explored as Huizinga[4] in *Homo Ludens,* requires the tensions and antitheses that are also the essence of the pastoral, including impulse and order, insecurity and confidence.[5] Both play *and* the pastoral create order within chaos, or, in the case of the writer, literature within life.[6]

Harriet's work, indeed every writer's work, is creating and maintaining the pastoral field or garden of play she needs *in order* to write. It is the work that dominates the adult *Kunstlerroman* and its characters struggling to play just as thoroughly as the play itself dominates those published for children, including, three of the best: *Cherries and Cherry Pits* by Vera Williams,[7] **Harriet the Spy** by Louise Fitzhugh, and *A Sound of Chariots* by Mollie Hunter.[8]

To a degree all juvenile *Kunstlerroman* are an echo of the pastoral legends of great artists like Cimabue discovering the shepherd boy Giotto, who was so filled with talent he spent his days drawing pictures on stones. Harriet and Bridie, respectively, of **Harriet the Spy** and *A Sound of Chariots,* are both nurtured by pastoral adults, but Bidemmi and the narrator of *Cherries and Cherry Pits* are direct descendents of these legends.

Young Bidemmi draws and tells stories as readily as she breathes. "Before you can even ask Bidemmi any questions," the narrator tells us, "about [one] story, such as how come the names of all the man's children start with D, she has another piece of paper ready and is drawing."[9] The narrator fosters Bidemmi's garden by literally opening her door and offering fresh play things. "I'm often standing there with a marker of some kind or color she doesn't have yet."(4).

The characters in Bidemmi's stories vary greatly, yet all share a love of eating cherries and spitting out the pits. Her final story is about herself. In it she care-

fully plants all the pits from *her* cherries and tells them to grow. Within this autobiographical story Bidemmi works to protect her garden in progress, chasing away all who might do it harm. Her work pays off. She ends up with cherries to share with everyone which allows more people to eat cherries and spit out the pits and "all the cherry pits start to grow," explains Bidemmi, "until there is a whole forest of cherry trees right on our block." Williams's final illustration depicts Bidemmi having completed a drawing of her own images holding a miniature cherry tree amidst the garden forest she has grown.

Like Bidemmi, Harriet, and Bridie each have a classic pastoral co-singing friend and nurturer. Harriet and Ole Golly, with her sunny yellow room, vase of flowers, and big flowered quilt on which Harriet loves to bounce, are forever reciting quotes and lines of poetry to one another. One of their most poignant scenes occurs right after Ole Golly has been fired. Calling from the bottom to the top of the stairs, Ole Golly and Harriet recite alternating lines from Lewis Carroll's nonsense poem "The Walrus and the Carpenter." Their antithetical personalities (i.e., impulse and order) are equally pastoral. So complete is the garden world they share that when Ole Golly leaves, Harriet's emotional world is destroyed and her writing is thrown open to literal attack.

Bridie shares a similar garden of poetry and song with her father before he dies:

> They always met half-way on the stretch of road
> it was his job to patrol, at the edge of the wood
> where the grass was short and thick on the road-
> verge and they could sit and look at the waves of
> the Firth . . . after the picnic-tea, her father taught
> her songs and they sang them together."[10]

Bridie's mother is also a wonderful storyteller. Mr. Gladsmuir, the minister, and Mr. Miller, a friend of her late father, are additional pastoral companions. Mr. Gladsmuir didn't mind her "noticing the pleasure he took in the singing sound of the words when he quoted a bit of the Bible himself." (184). Mr. Miller lets her borrow any books she wants and discusses them with her as an equal. It is Mr. Miller who recognizes the pastoral essence in Bridie's own writing and reads her the lines from Marvell's poem that are the source of the novel's title: "But at my back I always hear, / Times wing d chariot hurrying near" (194).[11]

Bridie's final pastoral companion of childhood is Dr. McIntyre, her English teacher, "with his deep, rolling voice and a delight as keen as her own in the everlastingly beautiful complex structure of language" (217). His pastoral definition of writing as "absorbing things into the fabric of experience and putting them forth again in a finer form" (236) becomes, for Bridie, an epiphany.

Harriet and Bridie also experience books—as the Eastern proverb states—as gardens carried in the pocket. Harriet reads at breakfast, at school, at night under the covers, and any other times not spent spying or writing. "How I love to read," she thinks to herself. "The whole world gets bigger just the way Ole Golly said it was when Mr. Waldenstein proposed."[12] Bridie reads everything from Bible stories to so many secular stories on the Sabbath she is sure her chances for heaven are slim. For Bridie reading is connected with another experience of pastoral union. She quickly learns the "value of her mother's description of her as being 'deaf as a post when she has her nose in a book,'" as it lets her listen (like Harriet at the luncheonette) to adults visit and slip "through all the cracks she had discovered in the solid wall of the grown-up world" (182).[13]

Even more intense than their pastoral joy of reading is Harriet and Bridie's delight in re-creating the experience through their own writing. *Harriet the Spy* opens with Harriet writing in the form of playing Town beneath a courtyard tree. Through her edicts to Sport we learn that the "fun," the play, is in reordering reality. Bridie begins telling stories to eager listeners during lunch recess at school and enjoys adding more and more imaginary detail and "building an entire new tale of her own devising out of the original one" (188). She often spins "the story out, as much for her own pleasure in telling it as for the thrill of holding an audience with it" (188). Bridie's writing on paper is described in terms of the theater, another form of ordered play within a larger chaos: "She was hidden like a prompter and her people were acting out a story [but] when she was stuck for a word, they prompted her" (84). The pleasure both Harriet and Bridie feel when writing almost anything is summed up by Fitzhugh when Harriet's green notebook, which she usually has always with her, is returned to her after punishment: "She grabbed up the pen and felt the mercy of her thoughts coming quickly, zooming through her head out the pen onto the paper. . . . She wrote a lot about what she felt, relishing the joy of her fingers gliding across the page, the sheer relief of communication."[14]

Both Harriet and Bridie, like Bidemmi, lose track of the temporal world while writing. Harriet becomes so absorbed in writing that she often forgets others are in the room. When Bridie begins to write on her new story, sparked by her parent's love letters, everything around her goes dead: "The clock on the kitchen mantelpiece had stopped ticking. The voices of William and the Others scrabbling over some game on the floor had vanished along with the furnishings of the room. She was alone in a new, strange world."[15]

While Harriet and Bridie are, at times, able to dismiss mentally their physical surroundings, they also search out secluded locations where they can be free of others who do not understand their need for pastoral time. Bridie creates her special candle-lit place barricaded behind trunks in the box-room at the top of the stairs. Harriet likes to write in the park, especially after Ole Golly is gone. This need for felicitous space—so often amusing to nonartists—is vital to pastoral play. It helps create a sphere outside of necessity, utility, time, and external control, thereby enhancing the play mood of "rapture and enthusiasm."[16]

As Harriet and Bridie mature, leaving the child's creative world to enter that of the adult, they find their pastoral garden under increasing attack. They can no longer ignore the fact that few understand their passion and that many find it superfluous and unredeeming. Through their reading and schooling they also become aware of literary conventions and expectations, and of the response of an audience.

Both girls are mocked for their love of words and writing. Bridie finds she must struggle to protect her vision in the face of weak teachers who berate her for her unique writing style and insist she change her words, which would change the heart or "feel" of her writing. Harriet is at first hurt and baffled, then angered by her friends' rejection of her after they read her private spy notes. Later, when her writing is printed in the school paper, the reality of an audience makes the usually bold Harriet horribly nervous: "Suppose, she thought on her way to school, I stink? . . . Suppose . . . Suppose . . . She was trembling by the time she got to class" (283).

To survive as an artist and maintain one's pastoral garden, the artist must "be willing to live with uncertainty, to risk failure and opprobrium, to return time and again to his project until he satisfies his own exacting standards, while speaking with potency to others."[17] Harriet and Bridie triumph, and we know they will continue to do so because they are determined and self-assured. Possessing these traits, however, does not mean an easy time. They are only emotional muscles that must be worked full force as Harriet and Bridie stubbornly do. At times the work of keeping writing play only stops when the writer is writing.

Fitzhugh and Hunter further convey the work Harriet and Bridie will encounter by including contrapuntal characters from adult *Kunstlerroman*. Their presence not only informs the young writers of more work ahead but enhances their sense of pastoral play by showing the adult's sense of pastoral-lost.

Harriet has an immediate source of comparison in Sport's father. She knows he often writes all night (*his* felicitous space?), is always worried about money, and needs Sport to keep his life in order. Sport calmly tells her that writers don't care what they eat, have bad dreams, and "only care what you think of them" (49). When playing Town, Harriet puts Mr. Fishbein, the writer, in the bar.

Bridie's father was a passionate orator and was often tossed out into the street for what he said. She knows no published writers, but at the same time that Mr. Miller celebrates her desire to write poetry he adds that it is the least lucrative of the arts.

Such references to the cold economics of writing forecast yet another attack on Harriet's and Bridie's gardens as they become adults: the gulf between writing as a gift created to share and writing as a commodity to sell. If they are to keep their pastoral gardens green, they must maintain a "protected giftsphere," states Hyde, and personal "rituals for both keeping [these opposing realities] apart and bringing them together" at the appropriate times (276).[18] Still more work to keep their beloved writing play.

Harriet and Bridie's greatest strength and the essence of the juvenile *Kunstlerroman* is that they remain focused on re-creating the pastoral experience of literature rather than the related work. They are inspired by the play—their fusion with literature and that of passionate fellow readers, *not* writers. It is also the focus they need for the final and most internal steps toward completing their garden.

Slowly but surely, they begin to experience Keats's "negative capabilities"—"capable of being in uncertainties, Mysteries, doubt, without any irritable reaching after fact and reasons."[19] Through talking with Dr. McIntyre, Bridie begins to accept that as a writer she will always be surrounded by mysteries and feel a certain loneliness, and that her writing rather than answers will be her comfort. Near the end of *Harriet*

the Spy Harriet begins to relinquish her need to judge and categorize. She concludes her first story on paper with what she considers a "GOOD MORAL—THAT IS THAT SOME PEOPLE ARE ONE WAY AND SOME PEOPLE ARE ANOTHER AND THAT'S THAT."[20] She has begun to absorb Ole Golly's beloved pastoral quote from Dostoevsky: "If you love everything, you will perceive the divine mystery in things. Once you perceive it, you will begin to comprehend it better every day. And you will come at last to love the whole world with an all-embracing love" (24).

Ole Golly's quote of Dostoevsky's, however, goes beyond accepting mysteries and uncertainties to genuine perception or empathy. This, as Margulies explores, is the next vital step in a writer's maturity. And while empathy is a gift, the artist must still work to develop it.[21]

Harriet and Bridie have long been filled with curiosities about others and what goes on in their heads, but it is not until the conclusions of their respective novels that they experience full empathy. For Bridie the experience occurs with her mother. Throughout much of her story Bridie has angrily distanced herself from her mother and has even been ashamed of her widow's grief. When Bridie is finally able to feel herself into her mother's experiences, she not only becomes proud of her but is able to feel and express her love again.

Harriet's transitional experience of empathy is the culminating scene of *Harriet the Spy* and appropriately takes place in the park. She begins to "play" herself into the lives of two friends who had rejected her because of the nonempathetic honesty of her spy notes. Sport and Janie

> "were so far away they . . . made her think of the way she imagined the people when she played Town. Somehow this way she could see them better than she ever had before. . . . She made herself walk in Sport's shoes, feeling the holes in his socks rub against his ankles. She pretended she had an itchy nose when Janie put one abstracted hand up to scratch. She felt what it would feel like to have freckles and yellow hair like Janie, then funny ears and skinny shoulders like Sport." (297)

It is a vital pastoral experience for Harriet in another way as well. Sport and Janie acknowledge Harriet's need to write, even, Fitzhugh says with irony, if what she is secretly writing is "SOMETIMES YOU HAVE TO LIE" (297). Her two friends wait silently for her to finish, then join her in a walk along the river.

At this point the stories of Harriet and Bridie appropriately end. They are in the pastoral garden of union and play they have worked to re-create, and we are convinced of their abilities in keeping it green (making both their sequels listless and anticlimatic). Fully at play, they are as oblivious of us as Bidemmi is of her observer in *Cherries and Cherry Pits*. If we are to share their pastoral garden again it will be as their equals "in play"—as readers of the gifts they write.

Notes

1. Louise Fitzhugh, *Harriet the Spy,* p. 233

2. Elizabeth Bowen, quoted in Victoria Glendinning, *Elizabeth Bowen,* p. 36

3. Sigmund Freud, "Creative Writers and Daydreaming"

4. Johan Huizinga, *Homo Ludens,* p. 10

5. Lore Metzger, *One Foot in Eden,* p. xii

6. Huizinga, p. 10

7. Vera Williams, *Cherries and Cherry Pits*

8. Mollie Hunter, *A Sound of Chariots*

9. *Cherries and Cherry Pits,* p. 13

10. *A Sound of Chariots,* p. 50

11. Andrew Marvell, "To his Coy Mistress"

12. *Harriet the Spy,* p. 136

13. *A Sound of Chariots,* p. 16

14. *Harriet the Spy,* p. 240

15. *A Sound of Chariots,* p. 80

16. Huizinga, p. 132

17. Howard Gardner, *Art, Mind, and Brain,* p. 90

18. Lewis Hyde, *The Gift,* p. 275

19. *The Letters of John Keats,* p. 193

20. *Harriet the Spy,* p. 277

21. Alfred Margulies, "Toward Empathy," p. 1031

References

Fitzhugh, Louise. *Harriet the Spy.* New York: Harper & Row, 1964.

Freud, Sigmund. "Creative Writers and Daydreaming. (1908). *Standard Edition,* Vol. 9, pp. 142-153.

Gardner, Howard. *Art, Mind and Brain: A Cognitive Approach to Creativity.* New York: Basic Books, 1982.

Giedion-Welcker, Carola. *Constantin Brancusi,* trans. by Maria Jolas and Anne Leroy. New York: Braziller, 1959.

Glendinning, Victoria. *Elizabeth Bowen.* New York: Knopf, 1978.

Huizinga, Johan. *Homo Ludens: A Study of the Play-Element in Culture.* Boston: Beacon Press, 1950.

Hunter, Mollie. *A Sound of Chariots.* New York: Harper & Row, 1972.

Hyde, Lewis. *The Gift: Imagination and the Erotic Life of Property.* New York: Viking, 1979.

Keats, John. *The Letters of John Keats, 1814-1821,* Vol. 1, ed. by Hyder Edward Rollins. Cambridge: Harvard University Press, 1958.

Margulies, Alfred. "Toward Empathy: The Uses of Wonder," *The American Journal of Psychiatry,* 1984, *141,* 1025-1033.

Metzger, Lore. *One Foot in Eden: Modes of Pastoral in Romantic Poetry.* Chapel Hill: University of North Carolina Press, 1986.

Williams, Vera. *Cherries and Cherry Pits.* New York: Greenwillow, 1986.

J. D. Stahl

SOURCE: "Satire and the Evolution of Perspective in Children's Literature: Mark Twain, E. B. White, and Louise Fitzhugh," in *Children's Literature Association Quarterly,* Vol. 15, No. 3, Fall, 1990, pp. 119-22.

Georges Poulet, in "Phenomenology of Reading," argues that books are not merely objects among others, but that our experience of reading a book is an experience of entering into a consciousness which in turn invades our consciousness as readers. In other words, reading is a complex mutual inter-penetration of the reader's and the author's consciousness. Poulet writes: "The extraordinary fact in the case of a book is the falling away of the barriers between you and it. You are inside it; it is inside you; there is no longer either outside or inside" (351). Poulet's reflections on the nature of reading have particular value for the critic of children's literature, for the *author* and the presumed *reader* of literature for children differ in age, perspective, and the nature of their consciousness perhaps as much as any reader and writer communicating in the same language can be assumed to do. To state the obvious, adults write books for children, and, in the main, children read them.

What does this mean? Must we assume that the adult author constructs a simplified version of the world as adults experience it, more or less accessible to the child? Or should we believe, along the lines of Maurice Sendak's sense of a vital, mysterious connection to his child consciousness, that the most gifted adult authors of children's literature maintain a form of childhood within themselves, through *which* they are able to replicate an almost mystical connection with the mythic truths and obsessions of childhood? An examination of the nature of the satiric voice in children's literature can perhaps offer some insights into this possibly too artificial polarity. Satire is, after all, a conscious mode of alienation—a technique of alienating the reader from familiar methods of seeing and thus inducing a sense of the absurd, or moral insights, or simply a heightened if estranged sense of reality. If we can determine how various authors of children's books use satiric techniques of alienation, often through the appropriation of adult forms of literacy by children, perhaps we can determine how the seeming contradictions of adult and child perspectives in the text can be reconciled, if at all. My assumptions about what childhood is are subjective and debatable, but then any definition of childhood—or for that matter, adulthood—will be.

I should like to offer, as a starting point, a partial definition of adulthood, in Western culture, as an awareness of the objective network of causality operating in the world. Of course such an awareness is a matter of degree, and operates in a variety of possible realms, but mastery of the principles and details of cause and effect in the realms of human activity might be thought of as one measure of adulthood. This is of course a rationalist bias, but it need not exclude receptivity to transcendent or irrational forces operating in the world; in fact, any comprehensive

accounting of cause and effect will include a form of the "indeterminacy principle" with all that that implies about the subjectivity of the perceiver.

It is probably much more difficult to define what the essence of a childhood perspective is, and one might debate whether, like consciousness itself, it can be defined at all. But a useful, partial definition of childhood perception might be that subjectivity in which the child naturally sees itself as the center of a mythopoetic universe. The adventure of self-discovery for the child in the middle range of ages (approximately six to twelve) is still largely the exploration of the external world, which is perceived as numinous and infinitely signifying. The social world is a given of the universe—its relativity and conditionality still hidden. On the other hand, the realm of fantasy is still real or much closer to real than it is for adults. The contrast between the absoluteness of social realities and the plausibility of fantasy is essential to a consideration of what satire can mean to children.

Given these assumptions as starting points, we can examine works of Mark Twain, E. B. White and Louise Fitzhugh as a testing-ground for a theory of the distinctive nature of satire in children's literature. Twain, White, and Fitzhugh all use forms of writing that are simultaneously subjective and objective. In all three writers' works, naive and sophisticated perceptions and means of expression fuse or intermingle just as the reader's and the writer's consciousness intermingle. Whereas Mark Twain presents us with a narrator who is a naive reporter, observing adult culture with limited comprehension, E. B. White shows us a "child" who infuses adult forms of expression with ironic, grown-up meaning as well as child-like feeling, and Louise Fitzhugh creates a child who appropriates adult forms of literacy and transforms them to suit her own purposes. Thus we can see Mark Twain, E. B. White and Louise Fitzhugh as representative of an historical evolution in the satiric voice in children's literature.

The freedom—or limitation—of the reader is selectivity. Huck Finn, the boy, models this selectivity as he "reads" his culture and society. His "reading" of his culture's signifiers about race is notoriously naive, as for example when he expresses dismay at the fact that Tom Sawyer is willing to help free a slave, or in his famous response to Aunt Sally Phelps's question about whether anyone was hurt in the steamboat explosion. Will children understand the satiric point? The answer, of course, depends on the individual child, but not on the child in isolation—rather, on the child's knowledge and attitudes about slavery, about race, and about morality as much as on the child's temperament and intellect.

Mark Twain, in any case, presents us with a sympathetic, largely reliable child narrator whose naive limitations themselves serve, by a kind of forceful indirection, to satirize social conditions and their unconscious internalization. Huck's innocent admiration of the social superiority of the Grangerfords or of Tom Sawyer is the satiric foil to these characters' failings. Instead of having Huck *judge* the evils of Southern society for us, Twain allows us to see Huck's inner contradictions. Huck is compassionate towards the Duke and the Dauphin, his oppressors, in the famous moment when they are ridden out of town on a rail. He is cruel to Jim, his friend and protector, in the practical jokes of the rattlesnake and of the episode in the fog. Yet these contradictions are overshadowed by the hypocrisies and inconsistencies of the society Huck innocently and admiringly observes. Huck's uncritical reporting about the sham elegance and civilization of the Grangerfords and Shepherdsons, for example, becomes a satirical tool of alienation, like Swift's use of diminished or magnified size.

It is probable that most children respond to the texture of the reporting—the vividness of Huck's observations—rather than to their satiric implications. This is not quite true of E. B. White's satiric stance, which is generally so gentle and urbane that it is more accurately designated as ironic. Yet the adults in *Charlotte's Web* are no less absurd and potentially dangerous than in *Huckleberry Finn:* Mr. Avery for example threatens the central character with an ax, an act no less life-endangering than the intimate terror of Pap in delirium tremens. More significantly, adults' values and perceptions are shown to be skewed: as Charlotte observes, people will believe anything they see in print, and with human beings it's always "rush, rush, rush" to get to the other side of whatever it may be—the Queensborough Bridge, for example—without the necessary reflection on the meaning and purpose of life.

These satiric half-truths form part of White's comic attack on adult values in *Charlotte's Web*. But the major use of satire in that novel achieves something quite ironically different: the empowerment of the child through the satiric use of adult poses and voices. The sophistication of White's use of satire lies in the fact that he allows the child figure to express child-like emotions and perceptions through adult forms of speech. So, for example, when the lamb rudely tells Wilbur that pigs mean less than nothing to him, we hear an adult voice—skillful in its comic leaps between the philosophical and the vernacular—argue with inexorable reasoning when Wilbur replies:

> What do you mean, *less* than nothing? I don't think there is any such thing as *less* than nothing. Nothing is absolutely the limit of nothingness. It's the lowest you can go. It's the end of the line. How can something be less than nothing? If there were something that was less than nothing, then nothing would not be nothing, it would be something—even though it's just a very little bit of something. But if nothing is *nothing,* then nothing has nothing that is less than *it* is. (28)

Because the child can identify with the emotion of Wilbur's speech if not with its form, George Poulet's observation about reading in general is appropriate to the child's consciousness of what is happening in this passage: "I am a consciousness astonished by an existence which is not mine, but which I experience as though it were mine" (355).

Is Wilbur's logic-chopping speech implausible for a seven to nine year old (to set Wilbur's psychological age rather high)? Yes, in terms of skill and reasoning. But it is not at all implausible as a statement of *emotion*—the feeling of having been slighted and insulted, the resentment that causes one to wish to demolish one's opponent's logic. Similarly, when Wilbur seeks to identify his as yet unknown friend who spoke to him, unseen, in the barnyard, he uses a public voice, a formal adult voice, such as a child might hear over a school public address system. "Attention, please! Will the party who addressed me at bedtime last night kindly make himself or herself known by giving an appropriate sign or signal!" (34).

In a sense what is mocked here is the pretentious adult voice. Yet, again, ironically, the *feeling* is authentic: Wilber is vulnerable, exposed, presenting an intimate plea in a public arena. The established if somewhat ridiculous voice of the P.A. system announcer empowers him to state his plea for companionship, his cry of the lonely heart, with a minimum of shame. The child reader is free to see in Wilbur's manner of speaking either an exposure of the absurdity of adult ways of speaking or a legitimation of the child's way of feeling—or both.

White's writing for children is permeated by an acceptance of subjectivity and relativity. Though adults behave foolishly—as when they claim to have discovered a miraculous pig, immune to the fact that a *spider* has been writing in the web—they are not excoriated for their stupidity. Similarly, Wilbur's excessive politeness when he offers his cooperation to Charlotte in her efforts to save his life is not shown as sycophancy, merely as understandable eagerness to survive. Even Templeton's rapacious self-interest is tolerantly satirized in the images that symbolize his acquisitiveness: the rotten egg and its stench, and the barrel shape Templeton himself assumes. His defense of pleasure over abstinence—a short, enjoyable life is better than a long, miserable one—is a classic of self-justification, and is treated with wry grace and humor. Templeton's self-obsession is not so much condemned as revealed for what it is. Adult and child motives are allowed to mingle and to illuminate each other in tolerant ways in *Charlotte's Web*.

The satiric humor in Louise Fitzhugh's **Harriet the Spy** is of a much more blunt and sometimes brutal sort. Essentially, the satiric perspective of Fitzhugh's novel is a caustic attack on adults. Like Twain and White, Fitzhugh approximates the perspective of a child—in this case, a sophisticated, complex, precocious child—but her satire is much more radically grounded in the assumption of the child's interests. Harriet appropriates adult purposes through her use of grown-ups' forms of literacy, such as the diary, the gossip column, and the editorial. Adults are seen foreshortened, authentically distorted by the child's legitimate but limited point of view. Mrs. Plumber finds the true meaning of life in lying in bed all day long, until the doctor tells her she must lie in bed, when she changes to wishing to do anything but stay in bed. The Dei Santis act out their melodramatic but superficial emotions on a grand scale. And finally, the Robinsons satirically enact the absurdity—the infantilism—of obsession with material wealth, perfectly symbolized by the huge wooden doll baby holding a tiny adult woman in her palm. This art object satirizes the immaturity of such aesthetes, completely self-absorbed and vacuous. Whereas Twain attacks the contradictions of adult consciousness and White plays with the limitations of unimaginative adult realism, Fitzhugh combines and transforms these techniques of satire into something considerably more complex. She drastically forces her work towards the exclusion of the adult perspective through a variety of methods. She employs not only ridicule but also extrapolation, reversals, comic symmetries, and ultimately the subsumption of the adult's reality by the child.

Ridicule is obvious in the portrayal of the dance teacher who, writhing and flopping about on the floor,

talks rapturously about the farmer preparing the field for plowing in a recital with obvious sexual double entrendres. Sexuality and romance are represented as realms of experience that are not merely incomprehensible to Harriet but ridiculous, even grotesque. (Cf. Harriet's statement that Ole Golly's romance with Mr. Waldenstein has something to do with liking wurst, or Harriet's mother's absurd attempt to explain what falling in love was like by talking about Mr. Welsch throwing up at her feet.) It is clearly accurate to talk about the book as a form of social satire, as critics since Virginia L. Wolf have done.

By extrapolation, the dullness of adult conformity to upper-middle class behavior is criticized through the behavior of Marion Hawthorne, the "lady Hitler," and her friends, who play bridge and have tea parties just like their elders. Even in her painful isolation, Harriet is glad that she is not like those members of the spy-catchers' club. She knows she has individuality and a sense of purpose in life. Her "professions" of spying and writing are expressions of her adventuresome sense of discovery. They are also her heuristic means of self-discovery: of measuring by adult roles (mostly negative) what she could, but does not want to become, and, in the case of her notebooks, of keeping in touch with her perceptions and emotions. As Lissa Paul has argued, and as is shown by her rebellion against the conformities expected of her, such as dancing lessons (leading to debutante balls, acting properly with boys, etc.), Harriet is indeed a feminist writer.

Harriet's life is authentically hard. She experiences the existential crises of Ole Golly's leaving and of being ostracized by her peers after they read her notebook. But, hard as her life is, it is always real. Adults, on the other hand, are shown satirically to live unreal, inauthentic lives, lives of bad faith, to use Sartre's phrase. It is true that there are sympathetically portrayed adults, such as Ole Golly and Mr. Waldenstein, but even they have touches of inauthenticity: Ole Golly's tedious sententiousness, for example, and Mr. Waldenstein's fake compliments to Harriet. Adult rationality is shown to be absurd, while Harriet's myth-making is represented as truthful and meaningful. The adult who has the least falseness, Harrison Withers, is an alienated artist, very much like Harriet, and a kind of double reflecting Harriet's interests and identity.

Harriet, by choice, lives in a world of adults and of adult-like children, from her game of Town to her choice of friends who have professions such as chemistry or accounting, to her aspiration to publish in *The New Yorker*. But her point of view is adamantly a child's and Fitzhugh's narrator not only approximates but extrapolates her consciousness into the artistry of the adult creator by imitating Harriet's blunt descriptive style in the third-person narration. Thus, in Fitzhugh's work, the adult reality is subsumed by the child's. Poulet's notion of interpenetration applies here: only the balance of forces can shift, as it does here, to allow the child, paradoxically, dominance over the adult.

The satiric strains in the works of Twain, White, and Fitzhugh may be regarded as exemplifying different solutions offered by authors of children's literature to the inherent contradictions of adult writers attempting to recreate and address childhood consciousness. Twain uses Huck's naive voice to allow us to see satirically the contradictions of adult moral and social hypocrisy. White ironically foreshortens or flattens his adult characters, and empowers his child characters and readers through an adept appropriation of adult language. But Fitzhugh combines these strategies: adults are seen reduced and foreshortened, from a child's perspective, but not with an indulgent sense of irony. Instead, they are scathingly exposed and attacked, in a conflict in which Harriet, the authentic child, sees, knows, and says how wrong adults are. The method of this exposure is the process in which Harriet's language remains child-like, but the literary forms she appropriates are adult (the journal, the newspaper, and ultimately the short story). Adult forms are expropriated to express child-like vision.

Once, didactic literature for children defined children as adults wished to see them. In the nineteenth century, writers like Twain and Carroll reacted against the dominant, hypocritical moralism by exposing the absurdities of adult morality. But in the late twentieth century, children's literature is arriving at a new and different synthesis of adult and child perspectives. The targets of satire also shift in this historical progression. In Twain's work, evil characters are exposed as evil, while in White's book characters are not so much evil as short-sighted and deceived by outward forms, and in Fitzhugh's novel individuals are self-centered and blinded by self-obsession. As the example of Fitzhugh demonstrates, contemporary children's literature has immersed itself in the ethical subjectivity of the child. Or, to put it somewhat differently, writer and reader are collaborating to define adults as children tend to see them. Satire in children's literature has become a subversive tool, not merely to attack specific adult failings, but to rethink the world through children's eyes, with adults' verbal art. The process of this rethinking is achieved through a satiric disjunction between the forms of language in children's literature and the uses to which those forms are put.

Works Cited

Fitzhugh, Louise. *Harriet the Spy*. New York: Harper & Row, 1964.

Paul, Lissa. "The Feminist Writer as Heroine in *Harriet the Spy*." *The Lion and the Unicorn* 13.1 (1989): 67-73.

Poulet, Georges. "Phenomenology of Reading." *Contemporary Literary Criticism; Modernism Through Post-structuralism*. Ed. Robert Con Davis. New York and London: Longman, 1986.

Twain, Mark. *Adventures of Huckleberry Finn*. Ed. Walter Blair and Victor Fischer. Berkeley: U of California P, 1985.

White, E. B. *Charlotte's Web*. New York: Harper & Row, 1952.

Wolf, Virginia L. "*Harriet the Spy:* Milestone, Masterpiece?" *Children's Literature* 4 (1975): 120-126.

Virginia L. Wolf

SOURCE: "Portrait of the Artist as a Girl: *Harriet the Spy*," in *Louise Fitzhugh,* Twayne Publishers, 1991, pp. 49-73.

The genius of **Harriet the Spy** is that it explores the experiences of an outsider content to be one. It both celebrates and critiques Harriet's personality and the environment that produced her. Fitzhugh portrays Harriet as a thoroughgoing eccentric. In light of her inevitable career as an artist, Harriet's self-absorption and her fascination with her own mind take on additional meaning. Fitzhugh sets the stage for a complex and moving exploration of the artist as necessarily both selfish and lonely, of the outsider as potentially both a threat to and a benefactor of society, of the nontraditional female as displaying more self-esteem but less empathy than the traditional female, of the child nurtured intellectually but not emotionally, and of much more. **Harriet the Spy** is a book rich in emotional and intellectual power. And all of its power arises from Fitzhugh's discovery and understanding of Harriet M. Welsch, the outsider *par excellence*.

THE CRITICS

To evaluate the significance of **Harriet the Spy,** one must, therefore, understand and appreciate its heroine, as all too often readers have failed to do. Its first reviewers were, unfortunately, often off the mark, which accounts for the book's never having won an award given by adults. The *Book Week* review calls Harriet "precocious, intense, egocentric and mean," the one in the *Christian Science Monitor* speaks of "rather a pathetic figure—too pathetic, one hopes, for young people to admire," and Ruth Hill Viguers in *Horn Book* settles for "disagreeable" as a description for all the book's characters.[1] Even 10 years later, the review in the *Times Literary Supplement,* although essentially favorable, judges Harriet's suffering in the middle of the book as evidence that her spying "has got out of hand,"[2] and Francis Molson in "Another Look at **Harriet the Spy**" sees her not as self-absorbed and egocentric, but rather as "groping towards self-acceptance and respect."[3]

The most recent studies of the book also make errors in their judgment of Harriet. Perry Nodelman describes her as an arrogant observer who lacks respect for other people (Nodelman, 136-37); Hamida Bosmajian sees her as coping "with her isolation by connecting herself mechanically through routines" and as trying "to control the world through her notebook";[4] and Lissa Paul calls her a feminist writer.[5]

To be fair, these lengthy studies of the novel have all increased understanding of Harriet. But each in its special focus has illuminated only one portion of her personality. Molson's interest is in the development of the writer, which he sees as requiring enormous self-esteem. I contend that Harriet already loves herself before the novel begins and that what she learns is not self-acceptance but empathy or increased understanding and, therefore, acceptance of others.[6] But what Molson says about Harriet's using her writing to understand the world is correct and explains what reviewers have seldom understood. She is not "mean"; she does not intend that anyone see her notebook. She writes for herself.

Nodelman's and Bosmajian's analyses of the novel are giant leaps forward. Still Nodelman's perception of Harriet as arrogant and lacking respect requires qualification. Harriet does not know she is either. The degree to which Harriet is innocent, that is, ignorant of how others might perceive her, especially as she reveals herself in her notebook comments, has too often been missed by her critics. She is merely being honest about what she sees and thinks and would be startled to learn she is judged "arrogant." Bosmajian's insightful psychological and philosophical reading of the novel goes beyond Nodelman's breakthrough identification of **Harriet the Spy** as satire to show that the novel "meshes two modes of fiction—satire and psychological realism" (Bosmajian, 73). Bosmajian comes closer than any other critic to seeing truly that Harriet is a heroine, recognizing "her indomitable spirit that refuses to turn destructively against her self" (Bosmajian, 81). But rather than stress Harriet's strengths, Bosmajian focuses on the difficulties life poses for Harriet—the disconnectedness (the nonsense) that characterizes Harriet's life on the psychological, social, and metaphysical levels.

Her analysis stresses the struggling, troubled Harriet and not the intensely alive and vibrant Harriet, who is also there in Fitzhugh's novel. It is true that Harriet's routines grant her the psychological security that her environment does not provide and that she writes in her notebook in order to possess what she sees, that is, to remember, analyze, and understand the life she observes. Routines and notebooks are techniques used by many creative people to impose discipline and order on fertile imaginations and intense sensibilities that might otherwise prove confusing and overwhelming. As such, they are a means of survival and psychological health. They create the space and distance—the control—necessary for creativity. It is only when they become the end rather than the means that such techniques are psychologically destructive—only when they are an attempt to control life rather than a means of self-expression.

Lissa Paul's "The Feminist Writer as Heroine in **Harriet the Spy**" celebrates Harriet as a trickster figure, both successful and subversive. In Paul's words, such a heroine appears "conforming and obedient, while at the same time remaining true to herself, her life, and her art" (Paul, 70). She thus "gets away with lying, gossiping, and with generally being rude" (Paul, 72). This reading of **Harriet** is certainly correct, but again, partial—denying the price Harriet pays for being herself, attributing motivation to her that she never consciously realizes, and needing the corrective of Bosmajian's reading. Breaking free of stereotypes about women and girls and revealing the dangers of individualism, Fitzhugh is a feminist writer. Harriet is at best only beginning to become one.

HARRIET'S PERSONALITY

Incorrect, partial, or insufficiently qualified as these analyses of Harriet may be, they establish the depth and fullness of Fitzhugh's characterization. For readers of *Harriet the Spy,* its heroine exists as if she were a real person, as in a way she was. She was perhaps based on several people, including Louise Fitzhugh.

In *Me Me Me Me Me,* M. E. Kerr's autobiographical account of adolescence, there is a chapter called "Marijane the Spy."[7] Marijane Meaker is M. E. Kerr's real name. "Marijane the Spy" is the story of 11-year-old Marijane's spying on and persecution of Millicent, a young girl who came to live in Marijane's hometown to be near her father, a convict at the local prison. Before she gets into the story proper, Kerr tells us of her window peeping as a child, of her brother's hanging a sign saying "Marijane the Spy" on her door, and of her listening to everything her mother—a great gossip—said on the phone. There are obvious parallels in Fitzhugh's novel: the name on the sign, window peeping, and listening to her mother's gossip (Harriet, of course, listens to everyone's). The story and novel are also similar in their concerns with innocence, arrogance, and insensitivity. Kerr tells us what she learned: "I think the experience with Millicent started me focusing in a little on the underdog. I think I felt my first real shame at how I'd treated someone, and I know that [in my writing for young adults,] I . . . try to point out that prejudice of any kind is wrong, that winning and losing in life isn't everything" (Kerr, 58).

Relating that she had told her friend, Louise Fitzhugh, about her childhood experience, Kerr also establishes an explicit connection between *Harriet the Spy* and "Marijane the Spy": "We used to swap stories and discuss ideas, and when she wrote her first book for young people, called *Harriet the Spy,* I said, "Hey, wait a minute! That's my story! I told you I was Marijane the Spy, and you stole that idea from me!' Louise said all kids are spies when they're little. She was and I was . . . and she just beat me to the punch and told the story first" (Kerr, 58).

Although Fitzhugh may have taken from Meaker the idea of spying and something of her character at 11, Alixe Gordin points out that she also took ideas for Harriet from other sources. For example, Harriet's spy outfit is exactly the favorite play clothes worn as a child by another friend, Betty Beard, a California writer and actress. Fitzhugh undoubtedly used a variety of sources, including her own childhood. The result was that she complexly explored and universalized the idea of a child's spying.

Unlike Marijane, Harriet never experiences shame, but then her motive for spying is not to gain power over or to torment others, but to gain knowledge of how others live so that she will "know what way I want to live and not just live like my family" (*Harriet,* 32). Following Ole Golly's advice to "see every way I can" (*Harriet,* 32), she becomes a spy, for how else is a child, especially in our disconnected society, to learn about the lives of many adults except by listening in on their conversations and by watching them secretly at every opportunity that presents itself. As Harriet knows very well, Ole Golly does not approve of window peeping and listening at corners. She has taught Harriet the importance of privacy. She doesn't let Harriet invade hers, and she respects Harriet's. At one point in the novel, she prevents Harriet's listening to her father's explosive response to a high-stress day. Clearly, she would not approve of Harriet's spy route, as Harriet certainly knows. But inventive and curious as Harriet is, she comes up with spying as a way of getting the information she requires.

Marijane Meaker and Louise Fitzhugh as girls undoubtedly shared the intelligence, imagination, curiosity, creativity, and vitality that characterize Harriet. To a large extent, we can believe that these traits are a child's genetic inheritance—a matter of inclination and temperament. They are, furthermore, those necessary for a writer, and it is as such that Fitzhugh celebrates them in Harriet. To become a writer, a child needs to see, contemplate, understand, and remember many people engaged in many events in many different places. To observe life and to record it in a notebook are the fundamental processes involved. What's more, what one records must be what one honestly thinks and not what is nice or what one should say. The more unfettered the mind, the more likely original and honest perceptions are. Thus, even as Fitzhugh uses Harriet's notebook to reveal her limitations, she relishes Harriet's honest, critical, totally egocentric observations of others and often uses them as apt judgments of characters.

SATIRIZED CHARACTERS

In her honest and earnest—if innocent—attempt to find out about life and herself, Harriet is a fairly adequate measure for all of the other characters, many of whom have settled for meaningless and disconnected lives. All of her classmates but her friends, Janie and Sport, and shy Beth Ellen Hanson, whom Harriet can't figure out, are, in Harriet's opinion, boring conformists and followers. Rather than seek and nourish their potential as individuals, Marion Hawthorne, Rachel Hennessey, Carrie Andrews, and Laura Peters will grow up to live just like their mothers; Pinky Whitehead and the boy with the purple socks, just like their fathers. Along her spy route, Harriet observes other examples of limited or failed lives. Again out of fear and/or ignorance, adults settle for the safe and sure rather than risk love and loss. The Dei Santis don't understand why Fabio needs the truck or in any way must differ from his older brother Bruno, who, like Mama and Papa, lives his whole life for the store. Rich Mrs. Agatha Plumber takes to her bed and thereby avoids life. The Robinsons reduce life to buying and displaying possessions; their "perfect lives" allow for total control and—consequently—complete sterility. They have walled out the possibility of intimacy with or genuine caring for another human being. They never even talk when alone.

FAVORED CHARACTERS

The one person on her route toward whom Harriet feels mostly positive is Harrison Withers, their shared initials revealing their connection. Harrison is an artist, who loves his work and his cats. He and Fabio are the only people Harriet spies on who have and pursue an individual passion in life, and Harrison is the only one with whom she identifies. But his seemingly total isolation from all human contact troubles her, introducing what all students of the *Künstlerroman* see as a major conflict for all artists—that between living and creating, between relationships and art (Beebe, 21-64 and Huf, 5-14). Perceptively, Bosmajian identifies Harrison as "an objective correlative for her [Harriet's] tensions," noting that "Harriet would 'wither' if she were to imitate him" (Bosmajian, 78). Linda Huf emphasizes this conflict as looming especially large in lives of female artists because their conditioning leads them to value others over themselves, and relationships over work (Huf, 5-14). In any case, Harriet is aware that she differs from Harrison in as many ways as she resembles him, even while she worries about his (her) being alone.

Clearly, Harriet also admires Sport and Janie and by the end of the novel, to some extent, Beth Ellen. Ole Golly and her boyfriend, Mr. Waldenstein, and Dr. Wagner, the psychiatrist Harriet's parents take her to visit at the end of the novel, are role models, as to some extent is her father (based on Alixe Gordin, who was also in the television business and is temperamentally very similar). It is not, in other words, that Harriet is unloving or uncaring, but rather that at a remarkably early age, she knows whom she values and why. Always these are people who, like her, are unique individuals—eccentrics. They are all to some extent loners and outsiders, both because they enjoy

and require time for understanding, expressing, and developing themselves as individuals and because there are few people like them. Finally, they are, like Harriet, intelligent. They rely heavily on the mind rather than the emotions. Putting distance between them and the world, intelligence largely defines each of them.

Surely such understanding of Harriet and those she cares for came from Fitzhugh's understanding of herself and her many artist friends—and perhaps her "out" gay friends. Outrageously eccentric herself, she enjoyed flamboyant and creative self-expression, but was also angered by the way others less enamored of themselves feared and disliked such display. The key to much of her work is her distress, which most often is expressed as biting satire of conformity, with such responses to the unusual. But in *Harriet the Spy,* she also celebrates what she cherished in people—their capacity to be unique, surprising, and fascinating, and—at their best—their capacity for self-knowledge and self-expression that deepens and widens our understanding of the human condition.

OLE GOLLY

The source of Harriet's desire to discover and be herself is Ole Golly. As Harriet tells us, "OLE GOLLY SAYS THERE IS AS MANY WAYS TO LIVE AS THERE ARE PEOPLE ON THE EARTH AND I SHOULDN'T GO AROUND WITH BLINDERS BUT SHOULD SEE EVERY WAY I CAN. THEN I'LL KNOW WHAT WAY I WANT TO LIVE AND NOT JUST LIVE LIKE MY FAMILY" (*Harriet,* 32).

It is, of course, not merely Ole Golly's advice, but rather their relationship that nurtures Harriet's eccentric individualism. Ole Golly is Harriet's spiritual and emotional mother. She is also the mother Ole Golly herself (and Louise Fitzhugh) never had but desperately needed. The visit to Ole Golly's mother early in the book is not gratuitous satire of fat, uninvolved people, as some readers have suggested. It rather provides the background information necessary to our understanding Ole Golly and her role as Harriet's surrogate mother. As a parent, Ole Golly encourages awareness of life's variety and possibilities. She teaches Harriet to choose what she likes best rather than blindly to accept whatever happens to come along. She teaches her to avoid a life of pure routine. And she teaches her to believe that such choice is possible by providing her with an example of someone who made exactly such a choice—herself.

In other words, knowing full well the despair of not being understood and of not having one's potential nourished, she gives Harriet exactly the opposite of what her mother gave her as a child. She demonstrates that one need not grow up to be like one's family. She loves and understands Harriet for who she is, not requiring that Harriet be like her, and Harriet responds as would any child to such a mother. She listens to and respects Ole Golly, and she tries to live as Ole Golly suggests. She attempts to find out who she is and how she wants to live.

Ole Golly, writes Marijane Meaker, "sounds very much like my old friend [Fitzhugh]." Psychologically, seeing Ole Golly as the adult Louise Fitzhugh, now capable of nurturing the child Louise, makes a great deal of sense. But I also suspect that Ursula Nordstrom, Fitzhugh's editor for her first two novels, may have been a source for Ole Golly. As Charlotte Zolotow remembers, *Harriet the Spy* came to her desk at Harper & Row as an account of Harriet's comments on her spy route. She recognized the genius of the work and recommended that the writer be worked with to expand and develop what she had submitted. As Ursula Nordstrom notes in her interview with Roni Natov and Geraldine DeLuca for *Lion and the Unicorn,* she took Ms. Zolotow's advice and became Fitzhugh's mentor in the creation of the novel.[8] As Nordstrom notes of Fitzhugh, "she wasn't so sure of herself with *Harriet*" (Natov and DeLuca, 125). But Nordstrom's identification of honesty as the essential feature of Fitzhugh's work and of all great writers and illustrators for children (Natov and DeLuca, 124) is what's crucial in her discussion of her editorial relationship with Fitzhugh, since honesty about one's feelings and desires is what Ole Golly teaches Harriet. Surely, we may suspect that Nordstrom functioned as an Ole Golly for Fitzhugh.

In any case, Ole Golly teaches Harriet to trust and believe in herself. She gives her a healthy ego. Egocentricity, in other words, is not such a bad thing if it reflects a healthy love of self. If innocent, as it always is in a child, it is never simply arrogance, but rather the child's true expression of self, limited as she is in her capacity for empathy by incomplete cognitive development. It is also her only defense against those who would force her to deny her true being. Finally, it is the self-absorption required for self-understanding and for creative expression.

HARRIET'S DEVELOPMENT

The child or artist who never learns what she has in common with all other people, even those whom she perceives as severely flawed, is, however, a crippled creature, and thus Fitzhugh shows us the process whereby Harriet begins to learn to empathize with those who are quite different from her. The central point of Bosmajian's analysis of Fitzhugh's novel is that it unmasks the disconnectedness that characterizes Harriet's (and our) world. Deep and abiding love for that which is outside one's self is, of course, the only means of connection—love of others, love of nature, love of work, love of a supreme being or power or spirit that infuses life with meaning.

Harriet is by far more connected than most of those upon whom she spies. Nevertheless, she feels little connection with those less fortunate than she has been. Her notebook comments are judgments rarely qualified by compassion. She does not understand that people, including her, are always the product of their environments, inhibited and damaged to the extent that they are insufficiently and inappropriately nurtured. She has been lucky enough to have money, comfort, education, and care. She has suffered very little.

It is not until Ole Golly leaves that Harriet learns how dependent she is on others for happiness. Only after she has experienced the pain of isolation and rejection does she begin to understand that love and understanding are essential needs. With Ole Golly gone, Harriet reaches out to her parents and her friends in an attempt to fill the gap. A series of efforts fail. Her parents are hurt when she turns away from their attempts to help her develop her onion part for the Thanksgiving dance. They do not understand her need to write in her notebook and see it as rejection, and she does not understand their reaction. Playing tag, when she does not like the game but needs to avoid an empty house, she forgets about and loses her notebook, which is found and read by her classmates. In response to all the unpleasant comments Harriet wrote about them, her friends then exclude and harass her.

She considers changing, for example, not taking a tomato sandwich for lunch, but Ole Golly has taught her well. Most children would conform to end the alienation that Harriet experiences, but Harriet is too sure and fond of herself to do so. At one point she analyzes her friends' behavior in her notebook, speculating about how Ole Golly would see it: "THEY'RE TRYING TO CONTROL ME AND MAKE ME GIVE UP THIS NOTEBOOK, AND SHE [Ole Golly] ALWAYS SAID THAT PEOPLE WHO TRY TO CONTROL PEOPLE AND CHANGE PEOPLE'S HABITS ARE THE ONES THAT MAKE ALL THE TROUBLE. IF YOU DON'T LIKE

SOMEBODY, WALK AWAY, SHE SAID, BUT DON'T TRY AND MAKE THEM LIKE YOU. I THINK SHE WOULD HATE THIS WHOLE THING" (*Harriet,* 226).

Clearly, Harriet here reveals that by writing in her notebook she is trying to control herself—her understanding of the world—and not the world. When her classmates try to control her, rather than conform or retaliate, Harriet turns to what she still has to love—her notebook and writing. She does not try to control other people.

When her mother takes her notebook away, however, Harriet has no safe and trusted outlet for her feelings and thoughts, and she does change. She feels and acts mean, throwing pencils at her classmates, planting a frog in one of their desks, and looking hateful at all of them, even her former friends. Everything that matters to her is gone—Ole Golly, her notebook, her friends, and her schoolwork. Rather than being her allies, her parents side with those who want to control and change Harriet. She is completely alone. Not to fight back at this point would be to surrender her selfhood. Fortunately, even though her parents have never really troubled themselves enough to get to know her, they recognize her aggression as a change in behavior, and they care enough to seek understanding when they need it. They do not attempt, as many parents surely would, merely to reform or discipline Harriet. Had they done so, we must suspect the novel would have ended tragically. Once again, however, Harriet is the fortunate child. If not able or willing to seek understanding on their own, her parents are enlightened and wealthy enough to seek psychiatric help, and Dr. Wagner provides the key to the resolution of Harriet's trouble.

We never know exactly what he tells the Welsches, but what they do afterward allows us to infer what it must have been. They write Ole Golly, who then tells Harriet in a special delivery letter what to do to regain her friends and not deny the truth written in her notebook, how to deal with missing someone who has moved away, and why writing stories is better than taking notes. They visit Harriet's teacher, who then makes Harriet and Beth Ellen coeditors of the class newspaper, and they begin to talk about their lives whenever Harriet is around.

Nothing here criticizes Harriet. What all of these changes strongly imply is rather that her world has failed Harriet. Always it must be remembered that Harriet is 11 years old. She is, furthermore, a young

11 because she has never been required to take much responsibility for others. Ole Golly has cared for her and taught her to care for herself, but no one else has paid much attention. No one else understands Harriet or attempts to explain the world to her. She is, therefore, enormously dependent on Ole Golly, so much so that she cannot deal with her loss or with her friends' rejection alone.

The point is that we are all dependent, which Harriet must learn if she is ever to be able truly to care for herself and others. It is one thing to love oneself and not to fear rejection and harassment—not to let others control one. But it is quite another to live without the love of others—to experience total abandonment. No one can and survive. Babies die. Fear of abandonment leads children to distort who they are and to conform in order to maintain some semblance of connection. Adults, if they continue their deceptions and deny their true feelings, are more dead than alive. Harriet's world is full of such children and adults, and only Ole Golly has stood between her and them. But without Ole Golly, Harriet is lost because she does not know how to get what she needs.

Ole Golly never requires that Harriet understand and love her; indeed, she does not reveal much of herself to Harriet, perhaps because her past causes her great pain. In any case, her relationship with Harriet is much more intellectual than emotional, suggesting that her own need for self-control conflicts with her need for love. Harriet's parents, teachers, and friends are similarly reticent. Thus, Harriet's egocentricity has been allowed mostly to go unchallenged. She has had only to care for herself. She has never been required to see from another's point of view. She has never been required to see how much she, like everyone, needs love, and she must if she is ever to understand and love others—if she is ever to be a writer. Indeed, Harriet has never been required or allowed to do much of anything; she has been rather thoroughly taken care of—by a nurse, a cook, a private school. Thus, she takes and seldom gives.

So she needs Ole Golly's advice that she apologize and lie to her friends. She needs a way to give that does not compromise her and that, nevertheless, respects their feelings. To lie about her notes is the way to regain her friendships. She maintains her sense of the notes as expressions of her honest feelings and thoughts, but she honors her friend's pain upon hearing the notes read aloud to their classmates. She had never intended that anyone read her notebooks. She is not responsible for their pain. She does not really think they should have been hurt. But she can lie and apologize and thereby acknowledge their feelings at no price to her or to them. Harriet also needs Ole Golly's advice that she get busy writing stories, and she needs her job as editor. Writing is another form of giving. At its best, as Ole Golly notes, "writing is to put love into the world, not to use against your friends" (*Harriet,* 278). Finally, Harriet needs her parents. She needs to know what they think and feel and do. She needs them present and interested in her life.

Everyone in Harriet's world, in other words, is isolated—the nonconformist from others and the conformist from her or his true self. Ole Golly provides insight into the only possible way out of this isolation. The only bridge between people is love such as Ole Golly shows her mother, Harriet, and Mr. Waldenstein, such as she describes in her quotation of a passage from Dostoyevsky. The passage advises, "Love all God's creation" (*Harriet,* 22), and promises that "if you love everything, you will perceive the divine mystery of things. Once you perceive it, you will begin to comprehend it better every day. And you will come at last to love the whole world with an all-embracing love" (*Harriet,* 24).

At this early point in the novel, Harriet reveals her selfishness by her misunderstanding of the quotation. Her response is "I want to know everything, everything" (*Harriet,* 24). She fails to hear Ole Golly's caution: "It won't do you a bit of good to know everything if you don't do anything with it" (*Harriet,* 24).

As the story unfolds, so does our awareness of the irony and complexity of the human condition, chiefly as it is reflected in Fitzhugh's characterization of Harriet. She is both the product of her world and its greatest critic, both its victim and its heroine. In other words, Harriet is fully implicated in the world she inhabits, as we all are in our own. Humility is necessary. No one is better than anyone else. One's truth is only one's truth—important, even vital, to one's life, but not unchanging or universal.

By the end of the novel, Harriet has begun to understand human interdependence and to empathize with others. She has tried to be "AN ONION . . . A BENCH IN THE PARK, AN OLD SWEATER, A CAT, AND MY MUG IN THE BATHROOM" (*Harriet,* 295). She has "made herself walk in Sport's shoes, feeling the holes in his socks rub against his ankles. She pretended she had an itchy nose when

Janie put up one abstracted hand to scratch. She felt what it would feel like to have freckles and yellow hair like Janie, then funny ears and skinny shoulders like Sport" (*Harriet,* 297). She concludes, "OLE GOLLY IS RIGHT. SOMETIMES YOU HAVE TO LIE" (297). She and her friends are back together, each accepting the other for who she or he is. Janie and Sport wait in silence until she finishes writing in her notebook. Then "all three of them turned and walked along the river" (298).

Given her environment, Harriet has come a long way. Certainly, her last response to Marion Hawthorne and the three other girls playing bridge suggests that Harriet has acquired at least some empathy even for those whom she does not admire: "I'm glad my life is different. I bet they'll be doing that the rest of their lives—and she felt rather sorry for them for a moment. But only for a moment. As she walked along the street, she thought, I have a nice life. With or without Ole Golly, I have a nice life" (*Harriet,* 293). I have even argued (Wolf, 125) that Harriet has begun to learn the meaning of the Dostoyevsky passage, as proven by her restatement of it in her own words: "SOME PEOPLE ARE ONE WAY AND SOME PEOPLE ARE ANOTHER AND THAT'S THAT" (*Harriet,* 277).

Harriet is no saint; she does not at the end "love the whole world with an all-embracing love." Human beings rarely—if ever—get to that state. But Harriet has begun to see "the divine mystery in things" (*Harriet,* 24). She sees "THAT'S THAT." She has a glimmer of the wisdom that informs Fitzhugh's novel.

THEMES

Harriet the Spy shows us that to be human is to be both uniquely oneself and the product of an environment. It is to love oneself and others in accordance with one's needs and circumstances at the moment. It is, to use existential terminology, both to be and to become—to perceive and experience the ideal and then by some shift of perception or experience to move on to disorder and confusion, to arrive at another experience of perfect being, and to repeat the whole process over and over again. Moving between being and becoming, between vision and action, between self and others, between independence and dependence, humans strive for perfection and are always imperfect—caught between contradictory needs and impulses and demands. Always in process, always changing, such creatures can never fully understand themselves and can never be fully understood. Each human being is "the divine mystery" incarnate. This is both the glory and the challenge of humanity. We can know, and we can never know. We can see enough to realize how much we don't see. To assert one's intellect in the face of such mystery is only to deny reality. The only meaningful posture is humility and compassion—or love.

This is the wisdom that Harriet begins to learn. Bosmajian points to how *Harriet the Spy* resembles "*King Lear,* where a 'very foolish fond old man' promises his daughter that he and she will sing like birds in the cage 'and take upon's the mystery of things, as if we were God's spies'" (*Bosmajian,* 82). Nodelman is the first to see Harriet as assuming a godlike stance. He notes her posture when she plays town and her interest in the Greek gods as a result of Ole Golly's characterization of them as spies. He is, of course, concerned to establish her arrogance. Bosmajian goes beyond recognizing Harriet's arrogance to explore her glory as one of "god's spies." In her words, "the child takes in the world as if she were God's spy" (*Bosmajian,* 77). Without minimizing Ole Golly's humanness, Bosmajian also explores her mythical role as the wise woman or fairy godmother or god. Especially interesting is her pointing out that "'golly' is the diminutive substitute for God in oaths and exclamations" (*Bosmajian,* 78). Paul enriches Bosmajian's observations by nothing that Harriet's writing is essentially gossip, which Patricia Meyer Spacks in *Gossip* exonerates as originally meaning "god-related" (Paul, 71).

God's spy is, of course, an apt metaphor for how we have often thought of children since the time of Wordsworth and the romantics.[9] Innocent, trusting, and uncorrupted, they—we sometimes are able to believe—are in contact with the divine in a way that conscious, frightened, and flawed adults find impossible. Fitzhugh incorporates this use of the metaphor in her characterization of Harriet, but without ignoring the arrogance, cruelty, and selfishness of the egocentric child. The essence of Fitzhugh's presentation of Harriet as a heroine is as God's spy, much like Carroll's of Alice, Twain's of Huckleberry Finn, and Salinger's of Holden Caulfield.[10] All of these children are innocent, vital outsiders eager to figure out what the world is all about. All are better than the world they seek to find a place in—mostly because their hearts are alive and responsive and they are innocent of their own fallibility. We see Harriet's vitality in her fascination with the world, in her bottomless appetite for information about people, in her insatiable curiosity. We see her innocence in her

belief that she can know everything. We see that spying is clearly her lifeline in a world characterized by disconnectedness.

HARRIET AS A WRITER

But as long as Harriet spies for herself alone, she runs the risk of mistaking herself for God. Until she confronts her own vulnerability, she lacks empathy, and as long as she fails to feel others' need for love and acceptance, she excludes herself from "the divine mystery." She also has no need to share her understanding of life. She remains a taker (of notes, primarily), an observer, an outsider, a child. Only after her own experience of vulnerability fosters compassion for others, does she truly begin her career as God's spy, beginning to share her gossip with others.

"God's spy" has been a metaphor for the artist as long as it has been for the child.[11] The romantics saw the artist as a unique individual who possesses a stronger connection with the divine (due to an intense sensibility) than the average person and who consequently preserves this connection into adulthood when others may lose it. Certainly, this description of the artist fits Harriet (and Fitzhugh).

But until Harriet understands that "SOME PEOPLE ARE ONE WAY AND SOME PEOPLE ARE ANOTHER AND THAT'S THAT," she has no reason to communicate with others. She does not reach this understanding until she has experienced her own need for and right to acceptance for who she is. Isolated and misunderstood, she at last recognizes others' need for acceptance even when she does not understand and could not stand to be like them. In other words, by nature, she is compelled to investigate how and why people live as they do, but before she is ready to write, she must learn that the reasons for an individual's choices and behavior (including her own), although worthy of attention, exploration, and appreciation, are ultimately beyond her understanding. She must learn to love and to perceive "the divine mystery," for then she "will comprehend it better every day . . . [and] come at last to love the whole world with an all-embracing love" (*Harriet,* 24).

Harriet the Spy, as I have noted throughout, is as much a *Künstlerroman* as a *Bildungsroman*. During the same year that Beebe published his study of the *Künstlerroman* and long before Huf's *Portrait of the Artist as a Young Woman* or any of the other recent feminist studies of the female artist,[12] Fitzhugh gave us this insightful portrait of the artist as a girl. Indeed, this aspect of *Harriet the Spy* is an incredible accomplishment and, therefore, worthy of special attention.

The only critics to focus on Harriet as a budding writer are Francis Molson and Lissa Paul. Molson's main contribution to our understanding of Harriet as a writer is his analysis of the importance of her notebook. He recognizes it as the means whereby she practices writing—not merely as the selection and organization of words, but also as a thinking tool—as a way of organizing and understanding herself, what she observes, and the relationship between the two. He comments on her shuttling between description and analysis and on her growing ability with the latter as she acquires self-understanding. He speaks to the role of the imagination in her acquiring that understanding. He also sees that "spying, with its virtually exclusive concern for the quickly observable, was too restrictive, and her imagination suffered. Like a cartoonist, she saw only one or two physical features or actions and forced these to represent the whole person" (Molson, 970). As a spy, Harriet is, therefore, a remarkable tool for Fitzhugh's witty and sharp satire. But, as Molson points out, by increasing her capacity for empathy, Harriet develops her imagination and, I might add, allows Fitzhugh to deepen the novel's significance. What Molson fails to consider is the role of Harriet's egocentricity. Paul focuses sharply on this feature, noting that Harriet "says all the things that all of us want to say but don't dare" (Paul, 72).

Beebe and Huf, like many others (Meyer Abrams, Milton C. Nahm, and Dorothy L. Sayers, for example, cited in note 11) who have studied individual writers or the characteristics of writers in general, emphasize that writers often display what can seem like monstrous egotism, and readers have traditionally been willing to forgive any display of ego (at least in male writers) for the sake of the story. Perhaps it takes abundant self-love to believe one has something worth saying to others. Surely it does to spend the long hours alone, exploring one's own mind. Such a person must be an introvert, and psychologists tell us that one's orientation inward or outward is probably inborn.[13] So the extent of one's self-involvement may very well be genetically determined—or at least indicated and then determined by the influence of environment on this inborn tendency. But self-involvement is not necessarily egotism. Since the time of romantics, there has been a tendency to see artists as godlike (Byronic) as well as the tendency to see them as god's spies (Wordsworthian). Both tendencies require artists to see themselves as special and gifted. Both require pride, but the latter is grounded in humility and service. Fitzhugh's view is the latter. What's more,

she rejects the former as a real possibility. She shows that the more thoroughgoing the egocentricity, the less likely any writing will be done, for the writer feels no need to reach out to others.

But if Fitzhugh shows that Harriet needs to move beyond self-love to love of others, she does not condemn her for her egocentricity, nor does she in any way criticize genuine self-love. Quite to the contrary, she celebrates Harriet's love of self as essential to her worth as a person, to her capacity to love others, and to her ever becoming a writer. Harriet is not perfect. Fitzhugh and Harriet are well aware of Harriet's flaws, most of which result from her abundant energy. But she loves herself. She loves her mind, her gift for words, the pursuit of information and understanding, and the joy of communication. She loves her life, and she is proud to be different—to be a loner and an eccentric. Surely, she was born to become much of who she now is. She would not, however, be as content with herself as she is from the beginning of the book had it not been for her fortunate circumstances, especially Ole Golly, who has given her unconditional love, that is, permission to be herself.

That Fitzhugh recognized the need for a woman as role model and mother in the life of a girl born to be an artist is remarkable. Given her own absent mother and her lifelong grief over her absence, perhaps she created what she knew she had missed and always needed. In any case, her insight and creation is amazing in light of the usual absence of strong, nurturing adult women in *Künstlerromane* by women. Huf points out that female artists generally portray themselves as self-created, lamenting the absence of role models (Huf, 153-55). What's more, the largest obstacle to women's achieving careers as writers is the lack of permission in their environments for them to be what they feel they were born to be. In other words, brought up to think of others and condemnation of one's acts and can cause great distress for young children and other highly sensitive individuals. It conditions a person to think of others, but it can also result in excessive self-denial, as it has in many women, inhibiting the development of many female artists and surely preventing the development of some. Finally, we must question the value of behavior motivated by shame rather than love, no matter how much we may wish to foster altruism.

There is nothing in *Harriet the Spy* that questions or criticizes Harriet's self-love, even when she is selfish and unsympathetic. The novel is an unqualified celebration of self-love as necessary in a developing writer. Indeed, as I have already discussed, the novel shows that love of others, as psychologists these days are always saying, is firmly rooted in self-love.[14] What must be transcended by a writer (and any child who is to mature) is not self-love or even selfishness, but egocentricity, that is, the inability to see from others' points of view. But the novel does not criticize the child for this inability. It rather seems to accept as a given that to be human is essentially to be egocentric and that to be empathetic is difficult for most of us and impossible when our environment is not supportive, especially when we are cognitively and emotionally unready, as we must be during childhood. Thus, Fitzhugh emphasizes that self-love is essential in a writer's childhood and that empathy, although ultimately necessary to the writer, is secondary in her development.

Another amazing feature of Fitzhugh's novel is Harriet's lack of shame when her friends read the unflattering things that she has written about them. Earlier, when I noted the parallels between Marijane the Spy and Harriet the Spy, I mentioned that they differ in regard to shame. Marijane assumes responsibility for her hurtful treatment of Millicent, even though she had not been intentionally or consciously malicious. She recognizes Millicent's pain and identifies her own behavior as its source. She undergoes a "fortunate fall"—that is, she falls from innocence into consciousness of her capacity to hurt others. Having done so, she experiences intense guilt, or shame, which leads her to accept responsibility for the effects she has on others and to change herself to prevent any recurrence of such an experience.

Opinions vary about the value of shame. The traditional view, still that of many contemporary theologians, is that it is the source of conscience, social responsibility, maturity, and often religious conviction. In other words, it is the means to the fortunate fall.[15] But the last 25 years have produced many case studies in which shame emerges as a psychological block that prevents or at least inhibits individuals' realization of their potential (Bradshaw, 243-45). In light of these contradictory views of shame, Fitzhugh's portrait of Harriet as refusing to judge writing in her notebook as wrong is extremely interesting, as is Ole Golly's advice that Harriet must lie about what she wrote to regain her friendships.

Harriet does not take responsibility for her friends' pain. She feels no shame. Rather depression and then rage are her very healthy responses to her classmates'

harassment. The only adult she fully respects does not suggest that she should feel guilty about what she has done. Yet Harriet matures as a result of the experience. She takes responsibility for the situation, without blaming or denying herself, by telling her friends that her comments about them were lies. The experience of isolation teaches her something about herself, and it is her increased self-knowledge that results in her increased empathy. Made aware of her own vulnerability, she begins to perceive how vulnerable others are.

To a large extent, the process Harriet undergoes could be described as normal cognitive development. If developmental psychologists are correct, children are really incapable of altruism resulting from empathy with those very unlike themselves until they acquire the ability to do formal operations, which involves a cognitive shift that may occur around 11 years of age.[16] In other words, Harriet's experience of rejection comes at a time when she is ready to learn from it.

The central point is that shame requires some rejection of self, some sense that one's own desires and truth not only conflict with those of others, but also cause them pain. It requires judgment and condemnation of one's acts and can cause great distress for young children and other highly sensitive individuals. It conditions a person to think of others, but it can also result in excessive self-denial, as it has in many women, inhibiting the development of many female artists and surely preventing the development of some. Finally, we must question the value of behavior motivated by shame rather than love, no matter how much we may wish to foster altruism.

In any case, Fitzhugh and Ole Golly do not require Harriet to be shamed, and the novel implies that unqualified self-love is necessary to her development as a writer, as has already been discussed. Also important, however, is the writer's connection with the world. This connection makes self-exploration meaningful, providing the means whereby the writer comes to see herself in others and to see others in herself and to be intrigued by what she does not and perhaps never will understand. In addition, self-love makes the solitude required by writing enjoyable. Loving herself, the writer can be alone and not be lonely, suggesting the resolution of a major conflict in many writer's lives.[17]

But were self-love the entire solution, *Harriet the Spy* would never have been written, and Harriet would not be as preoccupied with Harrison Withers's isolation as she is. Her response to him in Book 1, in fact, sets up a major concern of the novel, that is, the deadening effects of emotional isolation. Book 2 explores its effects on Harriet, and Book 3 indicates the solution—being loved by others. Harriet correctly identifies the greatest obstacle to her becoming a writer—her fear of loneliness.

This fear suggests that she knows unconsciously that she is trapped in her own ego and does not know how to break out, and, indeed, Book 2 reveals that this is the case. First, Ole Golly having left, she confronts her dependence, that is, her need for love and understanding. Second, she shows that she does not know how to take emotional responsibility for herself. She merely expects others to understand and love her, never realizing that she might let them know her ideas and feelings or find out what theirs are. With the help of Dr. Wagner, her parents, Ole Golly, and her teachers, Harriet finally begins to take emotional responsibility for herself. She begins to communicate with others. But first she had to experience her vulnerability, her need for others, her insufficiency. She had to experience the isolation she had instinctively feared when spying on Harrison Withers and to discover the limits of her considerable self-love. Having done so, she is ready to try to explain herself to others and to try to understand and explain others to herself. "SOME PEOPLE ARE ONE WAY AND SOME ARE ANOTHER WAY AND THAT'S THAT" (*Harriet,* 277).

CONCLUSION

Loneliness is the principal emotional illness in Harriet's world, and quite obviously love is its antidote. In a fairy tale, people come to love each other and live happily ever after, as would we all if love were so easy to come by and keep. In the realistic *Harriet the Spy,* we see why it is not. We see the necessity for self-love and the obstacles to it. We see the essential vulnerability of every individual and the fear it engenders, especially in children, who must depend on others for the satisfaction of their needs for love and understanding. We see that even those who truly love themselves must communicate to bridge the gap between themselves and others, but that egocentricity often prevents or inhibits communication. Finally, we see that only those who love themselves and accept their essential dependence will attempt communication.

But what Harriet learns does not assure that she will live happily ever after—far from it. She has changed so little that Perry Nodelman could say that she "does not change" (Nodelman, 136). By the end of the novel, she has confronted her need for others, she has demonstrated empathy, and she has exhibited some humility. Her situation has changed, and in response, so has she—but only a little. I don't mean to minimize the shift in cognition she experiences and, thereby, to contradict what I have said about it throughout this chapter. Learning to see from others' points of view is a major step in human development. But it is not accomplished over night. As Harriet's newspaper stories reveal, although she is often empathetic, she continues to judge people harshly: "MRS. AGATHA K. PLUMBER IS . . . A VERY STUPID LADY" (*Harriet,* 284) and "FRANCA DEI SANTI HAS ONE OF THE DUMBEST FACES YOU COULD EVER HOPE TO SEE" (*Harriet,* 285).

That she does so for other's consideration not only indicates her willingness to reach out for their understanding and appreciation, it also makes her vulnerable, as Harriet realizes all too well. Her horror and joy as she reads her own words reveal her awareness that she risks rejection. Fortunately, only those whom she does not respect (Marion Hawthorne and Rachel Hennessey) express disapproval. But we know that if she ever becomes a published writer, her blunt honesty will meet with great opposition. We need only remember the critical reception of *Harriet the Spy.*

The point is that no matter how much Harriet has changed, the human condition is what it is. As the novel closes, her friends, parents, and teachers understand her a bit better than they had. For the moment, life is not only better, but also joyful. Harriet can be herself and also be loved. But this momentary balance will not last, even though, with luck, Harriet will repeatedly experience it in her life. The conflict between self-love and her need for others will arise again and again as she ages and changes. Like everyone, she remains essentially confined to her ego and yet dependent on others.

She like everyone, will get caught up in her life, understanding of the other may prove impossible, and she will experience rejection. Eventually, she may achieve understanding, communication may mend the breach, and she may reestablish connection. But understanding of others requires similar experience, self-understanding, and emotional distance. It requires great intelligence, sensitivity, and self-love. It is, therefore, often impossible.

Communication is equally difficult, requiring not only love for and understanding of oneself and others but also an inclination for and skill with some medium—

words, paint, or music, for example. Fitzhugh suggests that the artist is driven not only to understand life, but also to express that understanding in a certain medium. She further suggests that the decision to share arises from a desire for understanding from others, and that the achievement of understanding depends, in part, on the other half of communication: the audience. She shows that the audience's willingness to receive the artist's expression depends on their possession of many of the same qualities characteristic of the artist.

We need only to remember Harriet's bluntness and the people who inhabit her world to understand that her future suffering is inevitable. She has much to learn about successful communication, given this audience. Indeed, many of the people of Harriet's world are so controlled by fear that it is not at all likely that they will ever understand her. They conform to avoid the risk of rejection. A thoroughgoing eccentric at 11 years of age, she risks rejection nearly every time she puts pen to paper. To be sure, her comments about her classmates in the newspaper are much softer than those in her notebook. She has learned. But softness and sympathy are not her gifts. Vitality, curiosity, honesty, and self-love are. Like Fitzhugh, she will, therfore, continue to offend and threaten readers.

Finally, we cannot know whether or not she will always be able to regain a satisfying balance between her need to be herself and her need for love. There are too many unknowns, and the book remains open-ended. What we can know is that she has enormous potential as a writer. As an outsider who loves herself, she has a great deal to say to society about the importance of being oneself and about the dangers of conformity and of other responses to fear of rejection, but only if she learns how to write out of love for her readers and they do not respond with painful and abundant rejection. Truly, Harriet represents both the wonder and the danger of self-love.

Notes

1. Reviews of *Harriet the Spy*: *Book Week,* 10 January 1965, 18; *Christian Science Monitor,* 25 February 1965, 7; and *Horn Book* 41 (February 1965), 74-76.

2. Review of *Harriet the Spy, Times Literary Supplement,* 5 July 1974, 715.

3. Francis Molson, "Another Look at *Harriet the Spy,*" *Elementary English* 51 (October 1974): 967; hereafter cited in the text as Molson.

4. Hamida Bosmajian, "Louise Fitzhugh's *Harriet the Spy*: Nonsense and Sense," in *Touchstones: Reflections on the Best in Children's Literature,* ed. Perry Nodelman (West Lafayette, Ind.: Children's Literature Association Publications, 1985), 76; hereafter cited in the text as Bosmajian.

5. Lissa Paul, "The Feminist Writer as Heroine in *Harriet the Spy,*" *Lion and the Unicorn* 13 (June 1989): 67-73; hereafter cited in the text as Paul.

6. Virginia Wolf, "*Harriet the Spy:* Milestone/ Masterpiece?" *Children's Literature* 4 (1975): 120-26; hereafter cited in the text as Wolf.

7. M. E. Kerr, *Me Me Me Me Me* (New York: Harper & Row, 1983); hereafter cited in the text as Kerr.

8. Roni Natov and Geraldine DeLuca, "Discovering Contemporary Classics: An Interview with Ursula Nordstrom," *Lion and the Unicorn* 3 (Spring 1979): 124-25; hereafter cited in the text as Natov and DeLuca. Here Nordstrom describes her mentoring of Fitzhugh.

9. See the following for a discussion of the romantic view of the child: Peter Coveney, *Poor Monkey: The Child in Literature* (London: Rockliff, 1957), especially chap. 1, "The 'Cult of Sensibility' and the 'Romantic Child,'" 1-14; Hoxie Neale Fairchild, *The Noble Savage: A Study in Romantic Naturalism* (New York: Russell & Russell, 1961), especially chap. 10, "The Child of Nature and the Noble Savage," 365-85; and Robert Pattison, *The Child Figure in English Literature* (Athens: University of Georgia Press, 1978), especially chap. 3, "The Sentimental Aspects of the Child Figure: Wordsworth as Heretic," 47-75.

10. See Ihab Hassan's *Radical Innocence: Studies in the Contemporary Novel* (Princeton, N.J.: Princeton University Press, 1961) for a discussion of how the tradition of the innocent as God's spy continues to function in more recent novels.

11. This is the essential subject of Beebe's book—thus the title *Ivory Towers and Sacred Founts.* See also Meyer Abrams, *The Mirror and the Lamp: Romantic Theory and the Critical Tradition* (New York: Oxford University Press, 1953); Paul Cantor, *Creature and Creator: Mythmaking and English Romanticism* (Cambridge: Cambridge University Press, 1984); Milton C. Nahm, *The Artist as Creator: An Essay on Human Freedom* (Baltimore: Johns Hopkins University Press, 1956); and Dorothy L. Sayers, *The Mind of the Maker* (New York: Harcourt, Brace, 1941).

12. For example, Gilbert and Gubar, Hatterer, Hedges and Wendt, and Hiatt. Also Judy Chicago, *Through the Flower: My Struggle as a Woman Artist* (Garden City, N.Y.: Doubleday, 1977), and Carol Pearson and Katherine Pope, *The Female Hero in American and British Literature* (New York: R. R. Bowker, 1981).

13. See Alexander Thomas and Stella Chess, *Temperament and Development* (New York: Brunner/Mazel, 1977), 21-24 and 257-58. The propensity for introversion is measured in the child's instinctive withdrawal from, not approach to, new people, places, or things. See also A. H. Buss and R. Plomin, *A Temperament Theory of Personality Development* (New York: John Wiley & Sons, 1975), and Jerome Kagan and H. Moss, *Birth to Maturity* (New York: John Wiley & Sons, 1962).

14. See Rollo May's *Man's Search for Himself* (New York: W. W. Norton, 1953) and Erich Fromm's *The Art of Loving* (New York: Harper & Row, 1957) for discussion of self-love as the basis of love of others.

15. Two excellent studies that acknowledge both the positive and the negative results of shame are John Bradshaw, *Healing the Shame That Binds You,* (Deerfield Beach, Fla.: Health Communications, 1988), hereafter cited in the text as Bradshaw; and Carl D. Schneider, *Shame, Exposure, and Privacy* (Boston: Beacon Press, 1977).

16. See William Damon, *The Moral Child: Nurturing Children's Natural Moral Growth* (New York: Free Press, 1988), especially 10-17, but also chap. 2, "Empathy, Shame, and Guilt," 13-29.

17. This is the thesis of Anthony Storr's *Solitude*.

Additional coverage of Fitzhugh's life and career is contained in the following sources published by the Gale Group: *Authors and Artists for Young Adults,* **Vol. 18;** *Dictionary of Literary Biography,* **Vol. 52;** *Junior DISCovering Authors; Major Authors and Illustrators for Children and Young Adults; Something about the Author,* **Vols. 1, 24, 45.**

Lois Lowry
1937-

American author of fiction and nonfiction for children and young adults.

Major works include the "Anastasia" series (1979), *Autumn Street* (1980), *Number the Stars* (1989), *The Giver* (1993), *Looking Back: A Book of Memories* (1998).

For further information on Lowry's life and works, see *CLR,* Volumes 6 and 46.

INTRODUCTION

Lois Lowry has gained a loyal following among young readers and critics for her sensitive, humorous, and realistic portrayals of modern preadolescents and teenagers and the dilemmas and choices they face. Probably best known for her lighthearted and imaginatively plotted "Anastasia" books for middle-grade readers, Lowry has also explored in other books—such as her two Newbery Medal-winners *Number the Stars* and *The Giver*—the darker issues that fascinate so many children as they attempt to understand the complex, morally challenging, and sometimes sinister adult world they are poised to enter. Both styles of writing have garnered universal praise for Lowry as a creator of lively, tight-knit plots, witty dialogue, and intelligent and likable protagonists with whom readers can easily identify. Her books convey her fascination with "the general continuity of life, the beginnings and ends, transitions, people's adjustments to change"—themes that she explores in a wide range of settings. Sometimes poignantly, sometimes hilariously, she shows her young readers that knowing when to laugh, especially at themselves, is a powerful way to prevail over whatever problems they encounter. Adults in her fictional worlds may have acquired some wisdom and compassion, but none of them pretend to have all the answers. Indeed, Lowry measures the success of each of her books by how well it helps her readers "answer their own questions about life, identity, and human relationships."

BIOGRAPHICAL INFORMATION

Born the daughter of an army dentist stationed at Pearl Harbor, Hawaii, Lowry moved at the outbreak of World War II to Pennsylvania where she enjoyed a

secure childhood at her maternal grandparents' home. Recalling the influences of her early years, Lowry recounts, "[It] was from the hallowed ground of a half-remembered childhood that fiction would eventually find its way to the surface." Having learned to read by the age of three, Lowry skipped from first to third grade and remained a voracious reader. At age eleven, Lowry and her family moved to Japan, where her father was stationed for two years. Upon returning to the States, she attended boarding school and graduated from high school at sixteen. She then attended Pembroke College, the women's branch of Brown University, and began to study writing. However, in 1956 at age nineteen, as was common for young women in the fifties, she left college after only two years to be married. Her husband, Donald Grey Lowry, attended Harvard Law School while she worked part-time. Soon her husband was an attorney and she had four children all under the age of five and had put aside her writing aspirations. As her children grew older, she returned to college to complete her degree. She also began to pursue an interest in photography. By the time her youngest child was in high school, she was finally writing professionally—two textbooks and magazine articles and stories—and had also become a photographer. She wrote her first novel after a Houghton Mifflin editor noticed one of her stories and asked whether she had ever thought of writing for children. *A Summer to Die,* inspired by her own experience with the death of her sister Helen from cancer in her twenties, was published in 1977—the same year she was divorced, after twenty-one years of marriage. Since then, Lowry has written numerous books for middle-grade readers and others, all of them shaped by her own memories of childhood and experiences raising two sons and two daughters.

MAJOR WORKS

Anastasia Krupnick is Lowry's most popular creation. Over the course of a series that began in 1979 with the publication of *Anastasia Krupnick,* this intelligent and high-spirited girl reaches a new level of maturity with each volume in the series. In the first book, ten-year-old Anastasia is naturally anxious about the arrival of her first sibling. Her sympathetic parents give her the honor of naming the baby, and after considering various horrible possibilities over the course of the book, she finally chooses "Sam," also the name of her grandfather. In *Anastasia Again!* (1981) the family moves to a suburb of Boston. While Anastasia is reluctant to leave her beloved Cambridge neighborhood, she soon makes new friends, including the recurring character Gertrude Stein, her elderly neighbor. This book illustrates the often conflicting needs of a twelve-year-old child's desire to be independent on the one hand yet still intimately involved in family decisions on the other. Consistently praised by critics, books in the "Anastasia" series are noted for Lowry's engaging portrayal of a supportive yet comic family, as well as the cleverly drawn characters and genuine dialogue. At the core of each of the books is Lowry's honest exploration of understanding adolescence. Summarizing the central theme of the "Anastasia" novels, critic Carrie Carmichael notes, "Lois Lowry addresses every teenager's fear: being weird." Taking on the point of view of Anastasia's precocious little brother Sam, Lowry began another series in 1988. Appealing to a younger audience, the series of Sam books chronicles the adventures of young Sam, highlighting the humor in the innocent misunderstandings of childhood.

In addition to her comic fiction, Lowry has written novels with more serious themes. *Autumn Street,* based upon Lowry's experiences during the 1940s, provides a much darker vision of childhood. Depicting the theme of coming of age amidst violent and tragic events, the novel appeals to both adult and juvenile audiences. In *Rabble Starkey* (1987) Lowry explores the relationships of twelve-year-old Rabble with her mother, who had been fourteen when Rabble was born, and the Bigelow family for whom Rabble's mother serves as housekeeper and babysitter. A warm and poignant tale, *Rabble Starkey* addresses the complexities of "broken" families and resonates with children coping with less than ideal circumstances in their own lives.

Number the Stars, an historical account of Nazi-occupied Denmark during World War II, garnered the prestigious Newbery Medal in 1990. Inspired by the recollections of a close Danish friend of Lowry's, the novel centers on the Johansen family, who shelter a Jewish friend of ten-year-old Annemarie when the occupying German army tries to round up Danish Jews. Eventually the Johansens smuggle the entire family out of the country and to safety in Sweden. Written for a young audience, *Number the Stars* avoids explicit description of the horrors of war, yet manages to convey without oversimplification the sorrow felt by so many people who were forced to flee their homeland. Newbery Committee chair Caroline Ward remarked, "Lowry creates suspense and tension without wavering from the viewpoint of Annemarie, a child who shows the true meaning of courage."

The Giver, Lowry's second work to receive the Newbery Medal award, is in many ways her most ambitious novel to date—and her most successful in the view of many critics. The novel is set in a future society in which all choice and conflict have been eliminated in favor of the reigning value of Sameness and placid comfort. When twelve-year-old Jonas is selected to receive from the Giver the burden of all the community's memories, he begins to learn the very high price that has been paid for living "without color, pain, or past." As Ilene Cooper pointed out in *Booklist, The Giver* "makes an especially good introduction to the genre [of anti-Utopian novels] because it doesn't load the dice by presenting the idea of a community structured around safety as totally negative. There's a distinctly appealing comfort in sameness that kids—especially junior high kids—will recognize." Praised for its multiple levels of meaning, the novel is especially noted for its ambiguous ending in which Jonas and his foster brother escape the community, leading critics and readers to ponder several different possible outcomes to the book. Described as a companion piece rather than a sequel to *The Giver* is Lowry's *Gathering Blue* (2000), another novel concerning a futuristic society. Unlike the community in *The Giver* that is replete with living comforts and security, the world of *Gathering Blue* is harsh, primitive, and near anarchy. In this work, the protagonist, Kira, an orphaned and disabled girl, is fortuitously saved from death in a society that routinely gets rid of its weaker members. Having learned embroidery from her mother, Kira is given the important task to weave the elaborate tapestry robe of the Singer, a character whose task is to present the history of society as told through song. Critics laud the richly drawn characterizations in *Gathering Blue* and commend Lowry's ability to imagine a world in which its young protagonist struggles intelligently against hardship and the disillusioning forces that pervade.

Inspired in part by her readers' queries as to where she gets her ideas for stories, Lowry wrote *Looking Back: A Book of Memories*. In this unconventional autobiography that mimics the fragmented form of memory, she combines family photographs with anecdotal narrative and quotes from her books to present a collage of significant life events that form the genesis of her fiction. Less an informative resource than a glimpse into the events that shaped Lowry as a writer, the book presents a selective view of important people (and dogs) in Lowry's life. Imbued with a conversational, often humorous tone, Lowry also addresses such sorrowful events as her sister's death as well as her son's sudden death in a military plane crash. In this autobiography, the photographs often take precedence over the text; in some cases, the words describing a photo are conveyed in a succinct paragraph. The work is described by Peter D. Sieruta in *The Horn Book Magazine* as a "snapshot autobiography—a loosely constructed series of memories frozen in time, and it is left to the reader to fill in the gaps." Critics praise the natural blend of humor and poignancy that characterize *Looking Back* and note that reading Lowry's autobiography, one has the sense of flipping through a family album, gaining a sense of the author's personal insights that underlie her works.

AWARDS

Lowry is the recipient of numerous awards, including the International Reading Association award in 1978 for *A Summer to Die*; Children's Book of the Year

and American Library Association (ALA) Notable Book citation in 1979 for *Anastasia Krupnik*; ALA Notable Book citation in 1980 for *Autumn Street*; American Book Award nomination in 1983 for *Anastasia Again!*; ALA Notable Book citation in 1983 for *The One Hundredth Thing about Caroline*; the Children's Book of the Year in 1986 for *Us and Uncle Fraud*; the Golden Kite Award, Child Study Award, and *Boston Globe/Horn Book* Award all in 1987 for *Rabble Starkey*; several awards, including the Newbery Medal and National Jewish Book Award in 1990 for *Number the Stars*; and the Newbery Medal in 1994 for *The Giver*.

AUTHOR COMMENTARY

Lois Lowry

SOURCE: "How Do You Do: An Introduction," in *Looking Back: A Book of Memories,* Houghton Mifflin Company, 1998, unpaged.

When I was a child—very shy, very self-conscious—I was sometimes taken by my mother to events at which I would be introduced to adults who swooped at me with toothy smiles and unanswerable questions. I had a tendency to look at the ground, scrunch the hem of my dress in my hand, chew on a strand of my own hair, and scuff one shoe against the other during those painful moments.

"Look up!" my mother used to tell me. "Hold your shoulders straight! Look people in the eye! Hold out your hand! Say, 'fine, thank you, how are you?'"

I tried, but it was excruciating. I wasn't fine at all, holding out my nail-bitten hand for a stranger to shake. I was paralyzed, mute, and hoping for a trap door to open beneath me so that I could disappear with a whoosh into some dark cavern where I could curl up with a book until the grownups stopped their socializing.

I still don't like introductions very much. Have you met my nephew, who once scored the winning touchdown for a college in the Midwest? I'd like you to meet Aunt Emma, who is visiting from Seattle, where she raises hybrid peonies. May I present Ogden Weatherbee, who invented the gyrating oscilloscope? I know you will enjoy making the acquaintance of Miss Smirkling, who does wonderful charcoal portraits of miniature poodles as a hobby. And here is Cousin Florence, with her triplets!

Trap-door time!

But I am all grown up now, so I have learned to stand up straight and hold out my hand. Here I am, looking you right in the eye. I would like to introduce you to this book. It has no plot. It is about moments, memories, fragments, falsehoods, and fantasies. It is about things that happened, which caused other things to happen, so that eventually stories emerged.

At Boston's Logan Airport, in Terminal C, there is a kinetic sculpture: a sculpture that moves. Even though Terminal C has a food court, a seafood restaurant, a bookstore, and even a beauty parlor, it is the always-in-motion, pinging, dinging sculpture that commands the attention of everyone: travelers, toddlers, and trash collectors.

A ball sets off from the top (*ding!*) and makes its way through tubes, across intersections, down lifts and stairs and slides; along the way it bumps into another ball (*chime!*) and sets that one rolling around corners and along passages, and eventually it, too, collides (*ping!*) with another and sends it on its way.

Everything that happens causes something else to happen. Just like life.

A dog bites a mailman and the mailman drops his bag and scatters some letters on a lawn. One disappears under a bush and is lost. Maybe it was a love letter. Maybe the woman who failed to receive the letter decided the heck with it and went to law school—or to Australia—or to a therapist; and because of that, the man who sent the letter (but received no reply) decided to buy a dog to keep him company; and then he took the dog to obedience classes, where it met a dog who had bitten a mailman, and . . .

Well, you get the idea.

Stories don't just appear out of nowhere. They need a ball that starts to roll.

Kids ask me all the time: "How do you get ideas?"

When I try to answer, in a general way, they zero right in. "Yes," they say, "but how did you get the idea for—"

Here, in this book, I have tried to answer some of the questions. I looked back, in order to do so, through snapshots of my own past. Here are some of the balls—*ping!*—at the moment when they start their trip down that complicated passageway that is called life but that also, magically, becomes fiction along the way.

I have given them titles. Strange, evocative titles, some of them, like "Looming Huge" and "Opening a Trunk." They may make *you* look back and recapture memories of your own. From the memories may come stories. Tell them to your friends. To your family. Tell them to me, won't you? Now that we've been properly introduced?

How do you do!

Lois Lowry

SOURCE: "Impossible Promises: Adapted from the 1999 Anne Carroll Moore Lecture," in *School Library Journal*, Vol. 46, No. 4, April, 2000, p. 56.

> . . . there are times—times of anguish—when an impossible promise to someone you love is as sweet as a cinnamon-smudged fingertip, as nourishing and necessary as the sunlight that comes, still, to consecrate Autumn Street in summer.—from *Autumn Street* (Houghton, 1980)

Autumn Street, though its actual name is different, was a real place. It was the place of my childhood years, the time in my life when everything in the present seemed immutable and everything in the future seemed so filled with promise. The trees that bordered it grew from ancient roots that pushed the sidewalk bricks up into irregular wedges. Roller-skating, I knew the dangerous topography of those sidewalks as well as I knew the contour of my own scraped and scabbed knees.

I wrote in that concluding passage of *Autumn Street* that sunlight consecrated the street. I knew that rather overwhelming verb when I was just a child, because Lincoln had used it when he stood at a place not very far away from my childhood home; Gettysburg was just down the road, and we were all brought up on battlefield history. " . . .we cannot consecrate—we cannot hallow—this ground," Lincoln had said. "The brave men, living and dead, who struggled here, have consecrated it. . . ."

My *American Heritage Dictionary* tells me that to consecrate means to set apart as sacred. And for me, it is true: the street was blessed. Every bit of earth in which a child has dug with a bent shovel, each root-chunked sidewalk where a child has skated and fallen and skinned her knees—they are all battlefields, the places of our past—they are all consecrated by childhood and by memory. Each of us, in our own personal history, has some hallowed acreage of the heart, where struggles took place. Where promises were made.

The first place that became part of the vital landscape of my childhood was my grandfather's house. The war had begun. Four years old, aware but uncomprehending, I felt my parents' anguish and the tension in our New York apartment. Then, in what seemed no time at all, my father, a major in the army, was gone. My mother took us to Pennsylvania, to the home where she had grown up.

Everything was in order there, and brightly lit; the prisms of the crystal chandelier reflected the silver and the light with such intensity that there were not even shadows in the corners. For a moment I felt very safe.

Everything in order, and not even shadows in the corners. At Grandfather's there was a cook in the kitchen, always stirring, it seemed to me, pots of wonderful things—I remember chicken-corn soup, a Pennsylvania favorite. In the laundry room behind the kitchen, a laundress—she was actually called that—perpetually ironed; the sheets smelled of sunshine and starch. There was a porch, with a hammock and a swing: two of the most comforting pieces of furniture there can be, both of them probably recalling the back-and-forth bedtime motion of a mother's lap.

A tall clock stood on the staircase landing and I could hear it from my bedroom; its ticks and chimes marked the cadence of my childhood.

Safe.

Safe.

My sister slept in the bed next to mine. We whispered to each other, planning our futures: we would go to Hollywood and meet June Allyson and Van Johnson. We would marry brothers, and live next door to one another. We would have swimming pools and children and dogs. The war would end. Sometimes we held hands across the space between our beds. We listened to the voice of the clock together.

Promise.

Promise.

In my first book for young people, *A Summer to Die* (Houghton, 1977), there is a scene in the book where the parents and the younger daughter—confronting together the fact that the other daughter, hospitalized, is not going to live—dance together in the warm kitchen as old music plays on the radio.

> I held my arms tight around the two of them as we moved around in a kind of rhythm that kept us close, in an enclosure made of ourselves that kept the rest of the world away. . . .

But if the dwellings of our childhood offered us the kind of embracing enclosure that our memory wants us to believe they did—they were not the only promise of our early landscapes. The second one came from the schools we attended. The promise of knowledge—there it was, in those books!—and the teachers who were there every morning to greet me, and to lean over me at my desk, arm across my shoulders, speaking softly, acknowledging my work, correcting me gently and with infinite patience.

The elementary school I entered in Pennsylvania was the same one that my mother had attended as a child. She had gone into that same first-floor first grade classroom, had perhaps sat with folded hands at the same desk. Maybe some of the scuff marks on that old wooden floor had come from her little shoes many years before mine. She had learned the multiplication tales in the same third grade where I would.

And down the street, in a different direction from my school, was the third sanctuary of my childhood. In that safe little town, I walked alone from the time I was six or seven to the public library, and up what seemed to me then a lengthy flight of marble steps. When I went back for a visit, I found only a short flight of granite. But they felt like marble, then. They felt magic.

And inside was magic, too. Vast, and hushed, like a cathedral. I chose my books, stood on tiptoe to put them on the librarian's high counter and waited while she stamped them with her mysterious tool. Thump. Thump. When I was small, I never understood what the thumping was, never connected it to the stamped date in the back of the book. It seemed completely logical to me that the librarian had the power to thump my books twice with her hand, and it made them mine for a few days.

Going home, there were all the connections, like a follow-the-dots: a line from one to the next: home to library; next a short visit with Mr. Barnhart, a gray-haired Norman Rockwell of a grocer, who sometimes gave me a penny candy; and then a peek into the baby carriage halfway up Pomfret Street, to see the Yeagers' baby boy, Leonard, as he napped on their front porch. Finally, up the back steps into the kitchen at Grandmother's house, where the cook would be waiting with a cookie; and then into the room called the parlor—or onto the side porch if it were summer—and Mother would be waiting there, knitting or writing a letter, eager to see what books I had brought. The encompassing line would have come full circle and surrounded me—an enclosure made of ourselves—and I was home, embraced, tantalized with the smells from the kitchen, and my sister would practice her piano lesson, playing "Country Gardens" again and again in the room we called the library, where the piano and the books all lived. And the tall clock would tick and chime.

Safe.

Safe.

Promise.

Promise.

I left that town when I was 11 years old. I moved halfway around the world—and then to other places, other towns—and into the world of adults. But it was from the hallowed ground of a half-remembered childhood that fiction would eventually find its way to the surface.

A few years ago, when I was invited to speak at a Penn State conference, my brother went with me. After the conference, we drove down to the little town of our childhood and walked through the quiet streets. Jon and I stood for a moment, on that trip, in front of a funeral home. The last time we had stood there together was when our sister's body lay inside. We were young, and sad, and uncertain, then; and I think we were probably both frightened by the sudden awareness of how tenuous everything was: how easily it could slip away. The immutability, the permanence of everything, seemed to dissipate on the day our sister died. It was as if the raised bricks in the sidewalk, the places we had learned to roller-skate over, had suddenly shifted and heaved again, without warning; and now we had to look at what had been thrust upward and dislodged, had to learn how to find our footing again.

Later we described the trip to our mother. She was by then in the final year of her life, blind and bedridden. But she liked to reminisce. Perhaps she

had told me many of the same stories from her childhood when I was young—but then, eager to grow up, bored with family lore, I had only half-listened. Now I paid attention as she described those same consecrated streets.

"My best friend was [she named the child]. My brother and I played with her and her brother every day. They lived next door," she told me. "Their father was a professor at the college. Math, I think. Maybe chemistry." I nodded, listening to her, enjoying her nostalgia, marveling at her memory that was going back now probably 80 years.

"But he beat them," she said suddenly.

"Excuse me?" I asked.

"He would come home and go out in the yard and cut a switch from a tree," she said. "And then he would whip the children with it. We could hear them yelling. My mother would close the windows on that side of the house.

"Isn't that odd?" she said. "That we never said anything? I suppose today it would be called child abuse."

I agreed with her that it was odd, and sad, and startling. Privately I was thinking: that quiet street. Those large, lovely houses. All of those closed windows. All of those shadows in the corners.

I can tell from the letters that I receive that dwellings no longer hold the security that mine once did for me. Kids write to me and describe their own lives: how they move from house to house, to a trailer, to an apartment, to a grandmother's; and their tangled family trees, crowded with step-siblings, jailed uncles, cousins gone to foster care, pregnant teenage sisters, dead-beat dads.

One child wrote that her parents were defrosted. Just a slip of the pen, surely. She must have meant divorced. But for a moment, reading her sweet letter—in which she asked if we could be friends—I pictured them melting, actually, their bodies sliding out of the stalwart, solid posture of parenthood into an oozing, useless puddle on the floor.

The letters that I get from children come often from classrooms. Schools are still there, passionate teachers are still there, and the promise is still there, for kids, that knowledge is there for them, and learning can change their lives.

But teachers, I am told, are not allowed to hug their students anymore; and so no child of today will remember, as I have all my life, the feeling of my first grade teacher's arm around my shoulders.

A friend who is a child psychologist says this: "There is only one thing worse than feeling hopeless, helpless, and worthless. And that is feeling hopeless, helpless, worthless, and alone."

My mother's little friend, whipped each night by her father, went out each morning and was greeted by neighbors who—including my own grandmother—had closed their windows against the sound. How alone that child must have felt. How helpless.

She would have had books in her home, certainly. The same father who whipped her was also, after all, a college professor. But what would her books have been? *Elsie Dinsmore*? *The Five Little Peppers*? There would have been no resource or comfort in that fiction.

Some years back, a relative sent me a lengthy family tree from my father's side of the family. I discovered, to my surprise, that my father had once had a brother who died as a child. "Yes," he acknowledged, when I asked him. "He died of meningitis.

"But that must have been terrible for you! You've never mentioned it."

"Well," he said, "people didn't talk about things like that. You just tried to put it out of your mind."

I pictured my father as a little boy in a stern, silent Wisconsin household, instructed to put out of his mind the fact that his brother was dead. How helpless he must have felt. How alone.

He had books, Horatio Alger tales. He had told me that he read those, as a child. Small help, there, for a child's grief.

The little girl whose parents are defrosted? She wrote to me and asked me to be her friend, and I said yes— but among her other friends, close at hand, are countless other friends in books, friends whose parents have melted away as well. Picture today's children feeling hopeless, worthless, helpless, and alone who have needed, and found, Gilly Hopkins, or Maniac Magee.

When my son Grey was an air force pilot in Germany, he met and married a lovely young German woman named Margret. Their little girl, Beanie, was born four years later, and when the Bean was almost two—much too young to understand—her father kissed her good-bye one spring morning and went off on what should have been a routine flight. But the plane had a mechanical problem and my son's life ended that morning.

The following April, Beanie and her mother came to visit me for two weeks. By now she was two and a half. By now she could talk. German was her first language, of course; but she was learning English, too, and though she called me Oma in the manner of German toddlers, she knew the word Grandma as well, and what it meant.

During the second week, my daughter-in-law, Margret, was invited out to dinner by friends who had come to see her during her visit to the states. She was concerned because she had not left Beanie with a sitter since that day the previous spring, when Bean's papa had gone off with a smile and a wave and never returned. But I assured her that we would do just fine, the Bean and I.

So she slipped away while my granddaughter and I were playing a game. Only later, when the sun had set and the game had become boring, Beanie realized that her mother was gone. I can only guess the painful fragments of memories that must have flooded back to her then. Terrified, she ran to the closed front door, collapsed on a heap there on the floor, crying desperately and calling in German words that I couldn't understand.

Finally, shuddering with sobs, she took my hand when I suggested books, and went with me to the stack of her favorites. She knew exactly which one she wanted: *Owl Babies*.

Then she curled up on my lap, still whimpering, and watched the pages intently while I read the story of the owl babies who wake up in the night and realize that their mother is gone.

"I want my mother," the smallest owl baby says again and again. I could feel Beanie tense in my arms, sharing his plea.

Finally, of course, Owl Mother—who has simply been out hunting for food for her babies—swoops home, and her great wings enfold the three little ones. Bean touched that page with her small hand, tracing with her finger the outline of those wings. "Read it again," she whispered, her cheeks still wet with tears.

My granddaughter and I read *Owl Babies* over and over that night. When Beanie's mom, just like Owl Mother, came home at last, her child was groggy with exhaustion and grief. But she had survived an evening which must have seemed to her, at first, unsurvivable. How helpless she must have felt. How alone.

But how brave and wise she was, to know what we all have come to know: that a book is the one promise, which is not impossible to keep.

TITLE COMMENTARY

STAY!: KEEPER'S STORY (1997)

Eva Mitnick

SOURCE: A review of *Stay!: Keeper's Story,* in *School Library Journal,* Vol. 43, No. 10, October, 1997, p. 134.

Gr 5-8—A puppyhood spent in a trash-strewn alley behind a French restaurant may not seem like the most auspicious of beginnings [to *Stay!: Keeper's Story*], but luckily Keeper was born with three great assets—a glorious tail, a way with words, and a healthy ego. His natural charisma leads him to relationships with several humans, from a homeless man to a photographer who turns the pup into a model famous for his sneer, but it is only after he meets little Emily that he finds his true home and his true name. Keeper tells his own story, sprinkling it with many keen observations about the natures of dogs, cats, and humans. He has a particular fondness for rhymed couplets, as in the gem (composed to pacify a couple of fierce felines): "Fur so fine! Eyes agleam!/You rival me in self-esteem!" Keeper's slight tendency toward pomposity will amuse readers, especially when they can come up with a rhyme that eludes him, and though a final rendezvous with his lifelong enemy does damage to one of his assets, he retains enough of the other two to make this story a "glorious tale." This book will find an audience, but it is more sophisticated in voice, tone, and vocabulary than Lowry's other titles for young readers, and the references to the fashion world, French foods, and *Gourmet* and *Vanity Fair* magazines may elude children. Kelley's pen-and-ink illustrations portray a dog whose rather ragtag appearance is amusingly at odds with Keeper's own vision of himself.

Kirkus Reviews

SOURCE: A review of *Stay!: Keeper's Story,* in *Kirkus Reviews,* Vol. 65, October 15, 1997, p. 1584.

Through a delightfully funny and distinctive first-person narration, Lowry (*See You Around, Sam!,* 1996, etc.) introduces a lovable new canine, given cuddly characterization in Kelley's black-and-white illustrations. Keeper tells his own story [in *Stay!: Keeper's Story*], from his "sordid" beginnings as a puppy begging for scraps behind a French restaurant, to his turn as a homeless man's companion, to his rise as a sneering fashion model, to his current role as a child's pet. Keeper is an intelligent, observant narrator, full of hilarious commentary on human behavior and with a penchant for poetry. Lowry's hero and his picaresque story are laugh-out-loud funny, and occasionally heartbreaking. Readers will be relieved to know, however, that this dog's life has a happy ending.

Ellen Mandel

SOURCE: A review of *Stay! Keeper's Story,* in *Booklist,* Vol. 94, No. 5, November 1, 1997, p. 472.

Gr. 5-8. His sophisticated speech and well-bred manners belie his wretched, back-alley origins. Keeper, as the narrator [of *Stay!: Keeper's Story*] comes to be called, was one of four puppies born to an elegant dog, who taught her young to rely on their senses, avoid cars and other dangers, and relish the French cuisine she procured from cooks and dishwashers in a neighborhood restaurant. These same restaurateurs found Keeper's siblings while he hid nearby, and when his mother soon departed, the plucky pup began composing rhyming couplets as a distraction and motivation to get on with life. Keeper allied himself, first, with a homeless beggar; next, with a professional photographer; and, finally, with a little girl and her mother. All three relationships proved mutually nurturing and beneficial to a point, and through Keeper's accounts of them, readers learn all there is to know about dog care—from Keeper's point of view, that is. The loquacious pup's humor, sensitivities, and positive attitude also teach much about loyalty, love, loss, and perseverance. An enchanting tale—one not to be missed by dog lovers and Lowry fans alike.

Janice Del Negro

SOURCE: A review of *Stay!: Keeper's Story,* in *Bulletin of the Center for Children's Books,* Vol. 51, No. 5, January, 1998, p. 165.

The canine narrator [of *Stay!: Keeper's Story*] is a mongrel with class, a poetically inclined, refined animal of good up bringing if not bloodlines. He leaves the relative safety of his first home (an alley outside a French restaurant) for the perils of the wide world in search of a human friend, and he finds one in the guise of Jack, a homeless alcoholic who lives under a bridge and is happy to use Lucky, as he calls the dog, to attract loose change from passersby. After Jack dies of unexplained causes, Lucky finds himself a new friend, a photographer who uses Pal's (Lucky's new name) natural talent for sneering on command to make himself rich. Pal runs away from this unsatisfactory arrangement and finds a home with a girl and her mother, who name him Keeper. He is ecstatically happy; then he sees another dog who looks remarkably like him on TV, recognizes it as his long-lost sister, and engineers a tearful reunion. Keeper speaks directly to the reader, à la Victorian heroes and heroines, and he sees himself in a heroic and literary light. The narration is tonally uneven, however, the style is mannered rather than involving, and Keeper's periodic essays into poetry distract from the story. That's too bad, because the lost-dog plot has a lot of kid appeal, and Lowry can be very amusing about aspects of canine life. Black-and-white illustrations are generously scattered throughout, and they lend an air of rakishness to the proceedings undelivered by the actual text.

Roger Sutton

SOURCE: A review of *Stay!: Keeper's Story,* in *Horn Book Magazine,* Vol. 74, No. 1, January/February, 1998, pp. 76-77.

The versatile Lowry proves a dab hand at the animal saga [in *Stay!: Keeper's Story*], here chronicling the up-from-the-gutter story of Keeper, formerly and variously known as Lucky, Pal, and The Dog. As Lucky, he befriended Jack, a homeless man, and the author here dares invest the comedy with darkness, as Lucky sadly but philosophically watches Jack die. Lucky becomes Pal when he is taken up by a photographer, who makes Pal, with his trademark sneer, a TV star; Pal gets fed up when the burdens of celebrity close in, and he hears himself called one too many times, "The Dog." So he runs away and finds the home of Emily and her mother (and the cats Bert and Ernie), gets the name Keeper, and finds his past catching up with him in the most dramatic, and ultimately pleasant, ways. As narrator, Keeper is a writer of some courtly style, and his occasional doggerel

("Fur so fine! Eyes agleam! / You rival me in self-esteem!") enlivens both the elegant tone and the slapstick action. This one practically sits up and begs to be read aloud.

LOOKING BACK: A BOOK OF MEMORIES (1998)

Publishers Weekly

SOURCE: A review of *Looking Back: A Book of Memories,* in *Publishers Weekly,* Vol. 245, No. 34, August 24, 1998, p. 58.

Lowry (*The Giver, Number the Stars*) deftly dances between humorous and heartbreaking with this ingenious memoir [*Looking Back: A Book of Memories*]. Unlike most autobiographies, this one forgoes a linear chronology in favor of a more inventive thematic organization.

Lowry introduces each section with an excerpt from one of her novels, followed by one or more anecdotes—each inspired by a photograph of herself or her family. "Reaching Across," for example, features a photo of Lowry and her older sister, Helen, and offers insight into their closely knit relationship; the pair are the models for the exuberant younger and practical elder sisters who appear again and again in Lowry's fiction. Three chapters ("Dogs," "More Dogs" plus "And Dogs One More Time") explain why canines repeatedly show up in her books.

In addition to recurring themes, Lowry cites examples of a single, powerful image that becomes a central idea in a novel. In "Bonds," for instance, a quote from *The Giver* introduces an idyllic picture of Lowry's daughter lying on the back of a horse in the Maine summer sun reading a book. Lowry, the daughter of an itinerant army major, then describes her wish to give her children the things she never had, "a house that was always ours, books that were always there to be read again and again, and pets that followed you home and were allowed to stay." Lowry tenderly relates the recent death of her eldest son Grey in "Sadness" alongside photographs of him with his wife and little girl, and demonstrates how families in fiction and in fact keep their loved ones alive by telling their stories.

The unorthodox structure allows Lowry to take creative license to great effect: at critical junctures, she pairs pictures of her mother and herself at the same age and imagines what they might have said to each other at that stage of life. In one such vignette, Lowry recalls that she lost Grey within two years of the age at which her mother lost her daughter Helen (Lowry was 58, her mother was 56) and imagines a conversation between them, and how they might have comforted each other.

Lowry unfolds her history in a glorious arc, invisibly threading its parts into a unified whole. Her connection of the everyday details of the everyday details of her life to the larger scope of her work adds a new dimension to her novels and may well encourage readers to speak and write honestly about their own experiences. A compelling and inspirational portrait of the author emerges from these vivid snapshots of life's joyful, sad and surprising moments. All ages.

Barbara Scotto

SOURCE: A review of *Looking Back: A Book of Memories,* in *School Library Journal,* Vol. 44, No. 9, September, 1998, p. 221.

Grade 5-Up. Imagine sitting on a sofa with a friend and listening with fascination while she tells you about the pictures in her photo album. That is the feeling one has when browsing through this book [*Looking Back: A Book of Memories*] of Lowry's family snapshots and reading her lively commentary on them. Readers will chuckle as they hear the tale of the frozen rat she attempted to revive by heating it in the oven and will smile knowingly at the unhappy look on her face when she was forced to wear lederhosen her mother brought home from Europe. The author's voice comes through strongly as she shares both her happiest and saddest times. Though the organization is somewhat chronological, many photos are loosely grouped by topic—"War," "Adolescence," "Opening a Trunk" and so forth—which allows her to make connections between people and events. She introduces each photo, or group, with a quotation from one of her books, making a connection between an event in her life and its fictional counterpart. In *The Giver* (Houghton, 1993), Lowry writes about the importance of memory, and here, she shows her readers the important role it plays in her own life—how she has used her memories in her work, how they have helped her get through difficult times, and how they enrich and connect us. Much more intimate and personal than many traditional memoirs, this work makes readers feel that Lowry is an old friend.

Kirkus Reviews

SOURCE: A review of *Looking Back: A Book of Memories,* in *Kirkus Reviews,* Vol. 66, October 15, 1998, p. 1534.

A unique format for a memoir—Lowry (*Stay!,* 1997, etc.) offers up quotes from her books, dates, black-and-white photographs, and recollections of each shot, as well as the other memories surrounding it [in *Looking Back: A Book of Memories*]. The technique is charming and often absorbing; readers meet Lowry's grandparents, parents, siblings, children, and grandchildren in a manner that suggests thumbing through a photo album with her. The tone is friendly, intimate, and melancholy, because living comes with sorrow: her sister died of cancer at age 28, and Lowry's son, a pilot, died when his plane crashed. Her overall message is taken from the last words that son, Grey, radioed: "You're on your own." The format of this volume is accessible and it reflects the way events are remembered—one idea leading to another, one memory jostling another; unlike conventional autobiographies, however, it will leave readers with unanswered questions: Who was her first husband—and father of her children? Why are her surviving children hardly mentioned? Why does it end—but for one entry—in 1995? It's still an original presentation, one to be appreciated on its own merits.

Carolyn Phelan

SOURCE: A review of *Looking Back: A Book of Memories,* in *Booklist,* Vol. 95, No. 5, November 1, 1998, p. 490.

Gr. 4-8. This unusual book [*Looking Back: A Book of Memories*] contains photographs from Lowry's past and her reflections on them. In the introduction, she suggests that the book will answer readers who ask, "How do you get ideas?" Toward that end, every section begins with a quotation from one of Lowry's books that relates in some way to the subject of the photo. Think of yourself sitting down with Lowry and looking through her albums while she stops and points at pictures of herself as a child and a teenager, photos of her parents and siblings and, then, more recent pictures of her children and grandchildren. Each picture evokes a memory that is a paragraph to a couple of pages long. Readers who remember the deftly portrayed family relationships in Lowry's novels will be fascinated by pictures of Lowry, her older sister, and her younger brother, as well as the often amusing tales of their youth. The mood is not always light, though, and few will be unmoved by Lowry's reflections on her son Grey's death in 1995. The only downside to the book is the thought of hundreds of other writers poring over their photo albums in hopes of a similar publication. Only a writer with Lowry's blend of humor, detachment, and storytelling ability could make the form work. And perhaps it will work only for readers who love her novels. Even so, that means a large potential audience.

Janice Del Negro

SOURCE: A review of *Looking Back: A Book of Memories,* in *Bulletin of the Center for Children's Books,* Vol. 52, No. 5, January, 1999, p. 174.

Lowry's autobiography [*Looking Back: A Book of Memories*] is more like a conversation over an old photo album than it is a chronology of her life's events, and as such it is very satisfactory. The text is written around photographs—of Lowry as a child, of her siblings, her parents, her children, her grandchildren—and while talking about the events they depict, Lowry gives her thoughts about their meaning to both her life and her art. Chapters (each two pages or less) open with quotes from Lowry's books; each has a kernel of humor or emotion that will carry readers through till the open-ended conclusion. If readers are looking for the usual birthdate, major accomplishments, future plans school report information they won't find it here, but Lowry's candid, friendly revelations will give readers intimate insight into a favorite writer's history.

Peter D. Sieruta

SOURCE: A review of *Looking Back: A Book of Memories,* in *Horn Book Magazine,* Vol. 75, No. 1, January, 1999, p. 87.

[*Looking Back: A Book of Memories* provides a broad] perspective on an author's life, tracing Lowry's entire lifespan to date and, in fact, going further back in time to provide a look at her mother's early life at the turn of the century. Each of Lowry's memories is highlighted by a clear black-and-white photograph, captioned by date, that reveals much about the author, her feelings, and the people she loves. Perhaps working under the assumption that "a picture is worth a thousand words," Lowry lets the photographs do much of the talking, and her own text is succinct, thoughtful, and very much to the point. The written commentary that accompanies each picture is sometimes as brief as a single paragraph.

"Stories don't just appear out of nowhere," Lowry states in the book's introduction. They are made from "memories, fragments, falsehood, and fantasies . . . things that happened, which caused other things to happen, so that eventually stories emerged." Leap-frogging through time, Lowry links not-so-disparate moments in short chapters that are introduced with pointedly appropriate or subtly apt quotations from her own published works. The chapter named "Wet Ones" begins with a quote from Anastasia Krupnik stating her grudging willingness to change her brother's diapers—"Only wet ones, though. Nothing else"—and is followed by six-year-old Lois's joyful reaction to having a baby brother in 1943, and a memory of her daughter Alix's jealousy of her own baby brother in 1962.

Lowry has written what is essentially a snapshot autobiography—a loosely constructed series of memories frozen in time, and it is left to the reader to fill in the gaps. Lowry's early, warm recollections of her protective older sister Helen are later followed by an attractive photograph of the teenaged Helen on the beach and the stark statement that "ten years after that, at twenty-eight, she will die of cancer." There is little further commentary. But many readers will realize that Lowry has already explored the grief of a sister's death elsewhere—in her first published novel, *A Summer to Die.* Other memories are shared more fully. The author is quite forthcoming in describing "the saddest day of my life" when her Air-Force-pilot son is killed in a plane crash. The memories of his funeral and the family's recovery are poignantly recalled.

. . . [T]here are moments when Lowry seems to be writing for an adult audience. Young readers will empathize with the bookish, animal-loving young Lois, especially as she dramatizes scenes from a favorite childhood book, *The Yearling,* unhappily wears lederhosen and a feathered cap that her mother bought in Switzerland, and, as a teenager tired of her "stodgy, dull" name, creates a new moniker ("Cynthia Randolph") when making an appointment at the beauty parlor. But her discussion of finding a new love after divorce needs more adult commiseration, and children may not connect with the scenes in which Lowry engages in fantasy conversations with her mother. Despite these inclusions, Lowry's autobiography is consistently readable. . . . *Looking Back* has a subtle power that remains long after the last page of the memory album is closed.

Kathleen Beck

SOURCE: A review of *Looking Back: A Book of Memories,* in *YOYA,* Vol. 22, No. 1, April, 1999, p. 76.

Reading Lowry's latest [*Looking Back: A Book of Memories*] is a lot like sitting down with a favorite aunt to leaf through the family photo album. As the subtitle indicates, this is "a book of memories." Photographs of the author, her children, her mother as a child, her pets, houses, and so forth accompany quotations from her books and brief musings about people and experiences in her life. Some of the incidents are funny, some poignant, but all offer insight into the author and her work. As a professional resource, this title has limited usefulness. Though it is a very attractive and appealing volume, it is not at all systematic and leaves out sizable chunks of the subject's life. Readers who want a true autobiography will have to wait, but fans will enjoy the warmth and informality of the presentation and be intrigued by glimpses of the inspiration for some of her popular novels. They may even be inspired to sit down with an older relative and hear some of their own family stories, because, as the author states, "Looking back together, telling our stories to one another, we learn how to be on our own."

ZOOMAN SAM (1999)

Stephanie Zvirin

SOURCE: A review of *Zooman Sam,* in *Booklist,* Vol. 95, No. 21, July 1, 1999, p. 1947.

Gr. 3-5, younger for reading aloud. In the third book in Lowry's series about Anastasia's spunky little brother [*Zooman Sam*], Sam Krupnick really comes into his own: his dream of becoming someone special (Chief of Wonderfulness) comes true when he learns how to read. His nursery-school classroom is the setting for much of the story, and Lowry has preschool dynamics down beautifully—from the patient and loving but harried teachers to the energetic kids, in tears one moment, giggling delightedly the next. Her setup is fresh and funny as well: the baseball caps Sam wears as "zooman" (there wasn't enough room to put "zookeeper" on his Future Job Day costume) do more than promote sports teams and identify the animals zookeepers care for; they reinforce Sam's blossoming reading skills. Lowry gets

everything about Sam just right. Joyous, grumpy, sad, surprisingly delightful by turns, he's hard to resist; and he knows his loving, warmly drawn family is behind him all the way. The ease with which Sam confronts some fairly complicated language at the close is a bit of a stretch, but his surprise and pride at being able to read will strike a chord among readers, and his wholly childlike trials and tribulations will make wonderful read-alouds.

Kirkus Reviews

SOURCE: A review of *Zooman Sam,* in *Kirkus Reviews,* Vol. 67, July 15, 1999, p. 1135.

For "Future Job Day" at Sam Krupnik's nursery school [in *Zooman Sam*], the four-year-olds have been instructed to dress up as representatives of their desired profession. Sam doesn't want to be a fireman, as do all the other boys in his class. Instead he wants to be "somebody important, somebody interesting, somebody more than ordinary," a secret concept he privately and quite marvelously dubs "the Chief of Wonderfulness." With the assistance of his impossibly even-tempered mother and ever-helpful sister, Anastasia, Sam dresses up in a spiffy homemade zookeeper's costume. Sam's teacher allows Sam to tell his class about a different zoo animal every day, a privilege that he finds both thrilling and challenging. The plotting is leisurely, the story is slender, and a subplot about the training of the family dog barely registers. This cast of familiar characters isn't as vibrant as usual, and the material runs out of steam before the novel ends. Fans of the Sam books may find satisfaction in the nicely foreshadowed but still unanticipated punch line.

Janice Del Negro

SOURCE: A review of *Zooman Sam,* in *Bulletin of the Center for Children's Books,* Vol. 53, No. 1, p. 21.

Sam decides to dress up as a zookeeper for "Future Job Day" at nursery school [*Zooman Sam*]. With the help of his mother and sister, he contrives a costume that's just right, and he is unique among the many firemen in his class. Sam's search for the perfect costume parallels his search for meaning in those collections of letters called words. By the end of this book, Zooman Sam has turned into Bookman Sam, and he feels that "Chief of Wonderfulness" feeling because he has become a proud reader. Lowry has the dynamics of nursery-school participants down pat, and listeners are bound to recognize themselves and their friends in Sam's classmates as they interact, interrupt and interfere in daily lessons. (Sam's nursery school teacher, Mrs. Bennett, is a saint.) Sam's internal thought processes are winningly depicted, and his anxieties and accomplishments are both realistic and funny. Subplots involving training the family dog, Sleuth, and Anastasia's romantic interest in friend Steve are duly commented on by the point-blank-frank Sam, whose reflections provide a close-up view of the congenial Krupnik family. There is an ease to Lowry's prose that makes this a surefire read aloud, and older readers-alone may enjoy looking back (with an independent reader's sense of indulgence) and remembering when they were little. Black-and-white line drawings head each chapter, with full-page illustrations making an amiable addition to an amiable text.

Roger Sutton

SOURCE: A review of *Zooman Sam,* in *The Horn Book Magazine,* Vol. 75, No. 5, September, 1999, p. 613.

It's Future Job Day at Sam's nursery school [***Zooman Sam***], and not only has his mom made him a "Zooman Sam" jumpsuit, his sister Anastasia has acquired for him a whole mess of sports caps with such fitting logos as Tigers and Cubs. In a class filled with future firefighters, Sam's zookeeping aspirations really stand out, and he's especially thrilled when his teacher tells him he can wear a different cap each day and tell the other children about each animal: "For six weeks he could stand in front of the circle and feel that feeling of being the most interesting person in the room." This is a slender thread on which to hang an entire novel, but Lowry spins interesting variations on her theme, and the book ends with a swell (and well-prepared) surprise. Sam remains every middle-grader's little brother; parents, too, will be amused.

📖 *GATHERING BLUE* (2000)

Ilene Cooper

SOURCE: A review of *Gathering Blue,* in *Booklist,* June 1, 2000, p. 1896.

Gr. 5-8. In what might be described as a companion to ***The Giver*** (1993), Lowry once again brings readers to an alternative civilization [in *Gathering Blue*] and introduces a young person who will be entrusted to pass on its history. This time, though, she will have the opportunity to plot its future, too. Kira is lame and a recent orphan, so she is not surprised when she is brought before the Council of Guardians to justify her existence. Unexpectedly, she finds a champion who brings her to live in the Council Edifice, where her talent for embroidery and her intuitiveness make her the choice for an important job—repairing the robe of the Singer, who each year sings the history of the world, with the events meticulously embroidered on the robe he wears. At first Kira cannot believe her luck. She makes a friend, Thomas, who carves the Singer's wooden staff, and learns the delicate art of dyeing her threads from a crone who lives outside the village. She is even able to maintain her friendship with the sassy, loyal urchin Matt. Slowly, however, Kira begins to see that all is not right in her world. Lowry is a master at creating worlds, both real and imagined, and this incarnation of our civilization sometime in the. future is one of her strongest creations. The coarseness and brutality of the people, the abundance of the land's natural resources, and the intricacies of the society make this setting as rich as Kira's most glorious colors. There is richness in the characters, too, all of whom are detailed with fine, invisible stitches. Only the final bit of plotting falters: too much is disclosed too quickly, and answers to questions about how Kira will achieve her objective—to create a kinder future as reflected by her stitching on the robe—are left as hints (perhaps this bodes well for a sequel). Lowry has clearly addressed the issue of what happens when a young person becomes disillusioned with society; it would be equally interesting to know how she thinks worlds evolve into better places.

Publishers Weekly

SOURCE: A review of *Gathering Blue,* in *Publishers Weekly,* Vol. 247, No. 31, July 31, 2000, p. 96.

After conjuring the pitfalls of a technologically advanced society in ***The Giver***, Lowry looks toward a different type of future to create [*Gathering Blue*, a] dark, prophetic tale with a strong medieval flavor. Having suffered numerous unnamed disasters (a.k.a., the Ruin), civilization has regressed to a primitive, technology-free state; an opening author's note describes a society in which "disorder, savagery, and self-interest" rule. Kira, a crippled young weaver, has been raised and taught her craft by her mother, after her father was allegedly killed by "beasts." When her mother dies, Kira fears that she will be cast out of the village. Instead, the society's Council of Guardians installs her as caretaker of the Singer's robe, a precious ceremonial garment depicting the history of the world and used at the annual Gathering. She moves to the Council Edifice, a gothic-style structure, one of the few to survive the Ruin. The edifice and other settings, such as the Fen—the village ghetto—and the small plot where Annabella (an elder weaver who mentors Kira after her mother's death) lives are especially well drawn, and the characterizations of Kira and the other artists who cohabit the stone residence are the novel's greatest strength. But the narrative hammers at the theme of the imprisoned artist. And readers may well predict where several important plot threads are headed (e.g., the role of Kira's Guardian, Jamison; her father's disappearance), while larger issues, such as the society's downfall, are left to readers' imaginations. Ages 10-up.

Ellen Fader

SOURCE: A review of *Gathering Blue*, in *School Library Journal,* Vol. 46, No. 8, August, 2000, p. 186.

Gr. 5-9—In Kira's community [in **Gathering Blue**], people's cotts, or homes, are burned after an illness. After her mother dies suddenly, homeless Kira finds her former neighbors coveting the land where her cott once stood. They also resent that Kira, who was born with a deformed leg, wasn't abandoned at birth, in accordance with the society's rules. The Council of Guardians recognizes her skill at embroidery and lets her live in the Council Edifice, the one large old building left after the Ruin. Her job is to repair and restore the robe that the Singer wears during the annual Gathering that recounts the history of her community and to complete a blank section, which is to depict the future. When her young friend Matt journeys "yonder" and returns with the plants Kira needs to create blue dye and knowledge of a wider world, she pieces together the truth. The power-hungry Guardians have lied and manipulated the villagers in order to maintain their status. Kira is united with her father, whom she had believed was dead, but decides to stay at the Edifice until she embroiders a peaceful future on the robe. As in Lowry's **The Giver** (Houghton, 1993), the young protagonist is chosen by powerful adults to carry out an important task;

through the exploration of this responsibility, knowledge grows, and a life-altering choice must be made. Lowry has once again created a fully realized world full of drama, suspense, and even humor. Readers won't forget these memorable characters or their struggles in an inhospitable world.

Roger Sutton

SOURCE: A review of *Gathering Blue*, in *The Horn Book Magazine,* Vol. 76, No. 5, September, 2000, p. 573.

Long rumored to be a sequel to the author's Newbery medal-winning **The Giver** (rev. 7/93), Lois Lowry's new novel [**Gathering Blue**], save for a teasing hint near its end, is instead more of a parallel speculation on the nature of the future of human society. Life in Kira's community is nasty, brutish, and, for the ill or disabled, short: those unable to make their own way are taken to the Field of Leaving to die. For some reason Kira is an exception. Born with a twisted leg, she has always thought her survival was allowed by the fierce protection of her mother, whose death begins the novel, and by the honored position of her late father, killed by beasts during a hunt. But when Kira survives an attempt by the other women to drive her out of the village and instead is given a comfortable position—and an important task—in the Hall of Guardians, readers gradually become aware of the secrets poised at the heart of the community, ones that hide a truth far darker than even the grim surface. Lowry's dispassionate style is all the more telling for its understatement, and the even pace of the narrative provides an effective counterpoint to the seemingly anarchic nature of Kira's world. While the book shares the thematic concerns of **The Giver**—most prominently, the importance of memory—it adds a layer of questions about the importance of art in creating and, more ominously, controlling community. Kira is a gifted weaver who has been given the task of restoring and extending the tapestry-story told on the ceremonial robe worn by the Singer during the annual presentation of the Song, a ritual enactment of human history from creation through its cycles of prosperity and famine, peace and devastation. In the course of her work she meets Thomas, a young man who has been given the work of restoring and carving anew the staff the Singer holds to guide him through his long performance, and Jo, a little girl being taught the Song in order to follow the elderly Singer in his (as Kira discovers, to her horror) chained footsteps. The thematic threads are not always woven as securely as they might be into the fabric of the story; in particular, Lowry seems not to have completely worked out to what dark purposes the Guardians intend to put Kira (and Thomas). We know they want her to weave their version of history into the robe, but to what end? Still, the novel contains a number of good questions that will reward contemplation, and if the perhaps-sighting of *The Giver*'s Jonas—or Gabriel?—in the end seems gratuitous, the book succeeds quite well in providing a satisfying story, richly imagined.

Additional coverage of Lowry's life and career is contained in the following sources published by the Gale Group: *Authors and Artists for Young Adults,* Vols. 5, 32; *Dictionary of Literary Biography,* Vol. 52; *Junior DISCovering Authors; Major Authors and Illustrators for Children and Young Adults; Major 20th-Century Writers,* Vol. 2; *Something about the Author,* Vols. 23, 70, 111; *Something about the Author Autobiography Series,* Vol. 3.

How to Use This Index

The main reference

> **Baum, L(yman) Frank**
> 1856-1919 .... **15**

lists all author entries in this and previous volumes of *Children's Literature Review.*

The cross-references

> See also CA 103; 108; DLB 22; JRDA;
> MAICYA; MTCW; SATA 18; TCLC 7

list all author entries in the following Gale biographical and literary sources:

AAYA = *Authors & Artists for Young Adults*
AITN = *Authors in the News*
BLC = *Black Literature Criticism*
BLCS = *Black Literature Criticism Supplement*
BW = *Black Writers*
CA = *Contemporary Authors*
CAAS = *Contemporary Authors Autobiography Series*
CABS = *Contemporary Authors Bibliographical Series*
CANR = *Contemporary Authors New Revision Series*
CAP = *Contemporary Authors Permanent Series*
CDALB = *Concise Dictionary of American Literary Biography*
CDBLB = *Concise Dictionary of British Literary Biography*
CLC = *Contemporary Literary Criticism*
CMLC = *Classical and Medieval Literature Criticism*
DA = *DISCovering Authors*
DAB = *DISCovering Authors: British*
DAC = *DISCovering Authors: Canadian*
DAM = *DISCovering Authors: Modules*
      DRAM: *Dramatists Module;* *MST:* *Most-Studied Authors Module;*
      MULT: *Multicultural Authors Module;* *NOV:* *Novelists Module;*
      POET: *Poets Module;* *POP:* *Popular Fiction and Genre Authors Module*
DC = *Drama Criticism*
DLB = *Dictionary of Literary Biography*
DLBD = *Dictionary of Literary Biography Documentary Series*
DLBY = *Dictionary of Literary Biography Yearbook*
HLC = *Hispanic Literature Criticism*
HLCS = *Hispanic Literature Criticism Supplement*
HW = *Hispanic Writers*
JRDA = *Junior DISCovering Authors*
LC = *Literature Criticism from 1400 to 1800*
MAICYA = *Major Authors and Illustrators for Children and Young Adults*
MTCW = *Major 20th-Century Writers*
NCLC = *Nineteenth-Century Literature Criticism*
NNAL = *Native North American Literature*
PC = *Poetry Criticism*
SAAS = *Something about the Author Autobiography Series*
SATA = *Something about the Author*
SSC = *Short Story Criticism*
TCLC = *Twentieth-Century Literary Criticism*
WLC = *World Literature Criticism, 1500 to the Present*
WLCS = *World Literature Criticism Supplement*
YABC = *Yesterday's Authors of Books for Children*

Author Index

CLR Cumulative Nationality Index

AMERICAN

Aardema, Verna **17**
Aaseng, Nathan **54**
Adkins, Jan **7**
Adler, Irving **27**
Adoff, Arnold **7**
Alcott, Louisa May **1, 38**
Aldrich, Bess Streeter **70**
Alexander, Lloyd (Chudley) **1, 5, 48**
Aliki **9, 71**
Anderson, Poul (William) **58**
Angelou, Maya **53**
Anglund, Joan Walsh **1**
Armstrong, Jennifer **66**
Armstrong, William H(oward) **1**
Arnold, Caroline **61**
Arnosky, James Edward **15**
Aruego, Jose (Espiritu) **5**
Ashabranner, Brent (Kenneth) **28**
Asimov, Isaac **12**
Atwater, Florence (Hasseltine Carroll) **19**
Atwater, Richard (Tupper) **19**
Avi **24, 68**
Aylesworth, Thomas G(ibbons) **6**
Babbitt, Natalie (Zane Moore) **2, 53**
Bacon, Martha Sherman **3**
Ballard, Robert D(uane) **60**
Bang, Molly Garrett **8**
Baum, L(yman) Frank **15**
Baylor, Byrd **3**
Bellairs, John (A.) **37**
Bemelmans, Ludwig **6**
Benary-Isbert, Margot **12**
Bendick, Jeanne **5**
Berenstain, Jan(ice) **19**
Berenstain, Stan(ley) **19**
Berger, Melvin H. **32**
Bess, Clayton **39**
Bethancourt, T. Ernesto **3**
Block, Francesca Lia **33**
Blos, Joan W(insor) **18**
Blumberg, Rhoda **21**
Blume, Judy (Sussman) **2, 15, 69**
Bogart, Jo Ellen **59**
Bond, Nancy (Barbara) **11**
Bontemps, Arna(ud Wendell) **6**
Bova, Ben(jamin William) **3**
Boyd, Candy Dawson **50**
Brancato, Robin F(idler) **32**
Branley, Franklyn M(ansfield) **13**
Brett, Jan (Churchill) **27**
Bridgers, Sue Ellen **18**
Brink, Carol Ryrie **30**
Brooks, Bruce **25**
Brooks, Gwendolyn (Elizabeth) **27**
Brown, Marcia **12**
Brown, Marc (Tolon) **29**
Brown, Margaret Wise **10**
Bruchac, Joseph III **46**
Bryan, Ashley F. **18, 66**
Bunting, Eve **28, 56**
Burch, Robert J(oseph) **63**

Burnett, Frances (Eliza) Hodgson **24**
Burton, Virginia Lee **11**
Butler, Octavia E(stelle) **65**
Byars, Betsy (Cromer) **1, 16, 72**
Caines, Jeannette (Franklin) **24**
Calhoun, Mary **42**
Cameron, Eleanor (Frances) **1, 72**
Carle, Eric **10, 72**
Carter, Alden R(ichardson) **22**
Cassedy, Sylvia **26**
Catalanotto, Peter **68**
Charlip, Remy **8**
Childress, Alice **14**
Choi, Sook Nyul **53**
Christopher, Matt(hew Frederick) **33**
Ciardi, John (Anthony) **19**
Clark, Ann Nolan **16**
Cleary, Beverly (Atlee Bunn) **2, 8, 72**
Cleaver, Bill **6**
Cleaver, Vera (Allen) **6**
Clifton, (Thelma) Lucille **5**
Climo, Shirley **69**
Coatsworth, Elizabeth (Jane) **2**
Cobb, Vicki **2**
Cohen, Daniel (E.) **3, 43**
Cole, Brock **18**
Cole, Joanna **5, 40**
Collier, James L(incoln) **3**
Colum, Padraic **36**
Conford, Ellen **10, 71**
Conrad, Pam **18**
Cooney, Barbara **23**
Cooper, Floyd **60**
Corbett, Scott **1**
Corcoran, Barbara **50**
Cormier, Robert (Edmund) **12, 55**
Cox, Palmer **24**
Creech, Sharon **42**
Crews, Donald **7**
Crutcher, Chris(topher C.) **28**
Cummings, Pat (Marie) **48**
Curry, Jane L(ouise) **31**
Curtis, Christopher Paul **68**
Cushman, Karen **55**
Dalgliesh, Alice **62**
Danziger, Paula **20**
d'Aulaire, Edgar Parin **21**
d'Aulaire, Ingri (Mortenson Parin) **21**
Davis, Ossie **56**
Day, Alexandra **22**
de Angeli, Marguerite (Lofft) **1**
DeClements, Barthe **23**
DeJong, Meindert **1**
Denslow, W(illiam) W(allace) **15**
dePaola, Tomie **4, 24**
Diaz, David **65**
Dillon, Diane (Claire) **44**
Dillon, Leo **44**
Disch, Thomas M(ichael) **18**
Dixon, Franklin W. **61**
Dodge, Mary (Elizabeth) Mapes **62**
Domanska, Janina **40**
Donovan, John **3**

Dorris, Michael (Anthony) **58**
Dorros, Arthur (M.) **42**
Draper, Sharon M(ills) **57**
Dr. Seuss **1, 9, 53**
Duke, Kate **51**
Duncan, Lois **29**
Duvoisin, Roger Antoine **23**
Eager, Edward McMaken **43**
Ehlert, Lois (Jane) **28**
Emberley, Barbara A(nne) **5**
Emberley, Ed(ward Randolph) **5**
Engdahl, Sylvia Louise **2**
L'Engle, Madeleine (Camp Franklin) **1, 14, 57**
Enright, Elizabeth **4**
Epstein, Beryl (M. Williams) **26**
Epstein, Samuel **26**
Estes, Eleanor (Ruth) **2, 70**
Ets, Marie Hall **33**
Feelings, Muriel (Grey) **5**
Feelings, Tom **5, 58**
Ferry, Charles **34**
Field, Rachel (Lyman) **21**
Fisher, Aileen (Lucia) **49**
Fisher, Dorothy (Frances) Canfield **71,**
Fisher, Leonard Everett **18**
Fitzgerald, John D(ennis) **1**
Fitzhugh, Louise **1, 72**
Flack, Marjorie **28**
Fleischman, (Albert) Sid(ney) **1, 15**
Fleischman, Paul **20, 66**
Forbes, Esther **27**
Foster, Genevieve Stump **7**
Fox, Paula **1, 44**
Freedman, Russell (Bruce) **20, 71**
Freeman, Don **30**
Fritz, Jean (Guttery) **2, 14**
Frost, Robert (Lee) **67**
Fujikawa, Gyo **25**
Gaberman, Judie Angell **33**
Gag, Wanda (Hazel) **4**
Gaines, Ernest J(ames) **62**
Galdone, Paul **16**
Gallant, Roy A(rthur) **30**
Gantos, Jack **18**
Garden, Nancy **51**
Gauch, Patricia Lee **56**
Geisel, Theodor Seuss **53**
George, Jean Craighead **1**
Gibbons, Gail **8**
Giblin, James Cross **29**
Giovanni, Nikki **6**
Glenn, Mel **51**
Glubok, Shirley (Astor) **1**
Goble, Paul **21**
Goffstein, (Marilyn) Brooke **3**
Gordon, Sheila **27**
Gorey, Edward (St. John) **36**
Graham, Lorenz (Bell) **10**
Gramatky, Hardie **22**
Greene, Bette **2**
Greene, Constance C(larke) **62**
Greenfield, Eloise **4, 38**

Nationality Index

CLR Cumulative Title Index

Title Index

Title Index

Title Index

Title Index

Title Index

Title Index

Title Index

Title Index